PRAISE FOR
THE MULTIPLIER EFFECT OF INCLUSION

At Target, we see incredible power in a single three-letter word: and. We talk about the "power of and" and the value created when we make space for each other—diversity and inclusion. As Tony draws on his personal history and decades-long career advising the leadership of some of the world's largest companies, he rightly concludes that diversity alone is simply not enough given the ever-evolving demographic shifts taking place in today's environment. Inclusivity must be an equal component of an organization's culture. *The Multiplier Effect of Inclusion* is a must-read for any manager who understands that building more diverse and inclusive teams results in better business outcomes and greater innovation.

—Brian Cornell
Chief Executive Officer
Target Corporation

Diversity and inclusion is not new as a concept. Many organizations give it lip service but very few truly embrace it as a competitive advantage. Superficial hiring and employee network groups are not enough to truly move organizations and our society forward. Dr. Byers convincingly points out that we must embrace inclusion as a way of life within organizations to see the true benefits. He demonstrates that the best organizations in the world leverage "social diversity" of thinking to ensure that the best ideas win in order to elevate organizational performance.

Dr. Byers and I worked together at Starbucks where he was the Chief Diversity Officer. I was thrilled when he decided to expand his impact through his consulting practice and writing. My hope is that every organization captures the key lessons found within *The Multiplier Effect of Inclusion* and puts them into practice. When this happens, we win as a society.

—Martin Tracey
Chief People Officer
Enjoy Technology, Inc.

I have known Dr. Tony Byers for over a decade. We met while working for Cargill in Minneapolis—Tony in Diversity and Inclusion (D&I) and myself in Strategy and Business Development. We bonded around a passion for the work of D&I, and Tony has remained a close friend and mentor.

I'm excited about Tony's new book and the opportunity it presents to add another thoughtful voice to the discussion of D&I. In *The Multiplier Effect of Inclusion*, we are reminded that when effectively practiced, the work of D&I presents organizations with an opportunity to grow, innovate, and create value for shareholders. I have found when the subject becomes too much about the politics of D&I rather than the well-researched and undeniable truth that it is good for business, its importance as a creator of value for organizations and society gets "lost in translation." Tony brings us back to the immutable truth that D&I creates value, and the work specifically on Inclusion, multiplies our efforts across organizations.

—Willard L. McCloud III
Global Lead—Diversity, Inclusion & Culture
Pfizer
New York, New York

The tools and insights Tony shares in his book have been instrumental in elevating my diversity and inclusion leadership space—*The Multiplier Effect of Inclusion* gives you the "how" for achieving business results. Any

City 'Different' Alphabet: SANTA FE

The image is part of a series of city alphabets by Lehmann and is used courtesy of the artist.

City Different Alphabet: Santa Fe Key

A: Aspens, Artist brushes, Saint Francis of Assisi, Acoma pots, Santo Tomás de Abiquiú Church, Adobe, Arroyos, Acequia Madre

B: Basket, Bird pattern (Pueblo motif), Blanket/Boots, Bison/Buffalo, Cathedral Basilica of St. Francis of Assisi, Basketry, Santa Fe Baldy, Beaded Bag, Burro (loaded with wood)

C: Sand Hill Cranes, La Conquistadora (Our Lady of Peace), Concho belt, Chair (traditional design), Carved Column, Conquistador, Chile ristra, Church of San Miguel, Canales, Coiled basket, sacred Circle, Coyote, Coyote fence, Carved Corbel, Carreta

D: Cathedral Doors, Datura, Dancers, Day of the Dead (figure), Drum, Dream catcher, Door (Santa Fe style)

E: Earth Mother, Elk, Extraterrestrial, Eagle, El Rancho de las Golondrinas (mill)

F: Feathers, Flamenco, Farolitos, skeleton Fandango, Flag, 505 (area code), New Mexico Museum of Art (previously Museum of Fine Art)

G: Rio Grande, Grasshopper, Georgia's poppy, Golondrina, Grasses, Gecko, Palace of the Governors, Guitarrón

H: Hollyhocks, Horned toad, Hacienda, Hopi pottery, Hat, Horse, Hornos

I: Indian paintbrush, Indian pinto pony, Indian pottery

J: Juniper, Jackalope, Jingle dancer, Jemez Mountains, Jewelry

K: Kokopelli, Kiva, Katsinas

L: Ladder (Pueblo style), Leaping deer, La Llorona (the Weeping Woman), Lavender, D. H. Lawrence (chair), Labyrinth, Archbishop Jean-Baptiste Lamy, Loretto Chapel (staircase)

M: Matachine palmas, Milky Way, Mariposa, Matachine dance steps, Mantilla comb, Margaritas, Maize, Mariachi Musicians, Manta

N: Navajo blanket and Necklace, NSEW (cardinal directions)

O: O'Keeffe (cow skull), Obelisk (Plaza monument), Opera House, Owl, Olla

P: Petroglyphs, Portal, Piñon cone, Pueblo Pottery, Prickly Pear cactus, Pickup truck, Prairie dog

Q: Quarterhorse, Quadricentennial (400 Years!), Quesadilla

R: Rosary, Route 66, Road Runner, Canyon Road, Ramada, Rail Runner Trail, Raven, Rabbit brush, Retablo

S: Squash blossom necklace, Story-teller dolls, Stink bug, Sunflowers, Skull, Sangre de Cristo Mountains, Santa Fe River, Santa Fe Chief train, Sun rays

T: Two Grey Hills rug, Tumbleweed, Santa Fe Trail, Tin work, Torreón, Tools

U: Utensils, Burnt Umber, UFO

V: Virgin de Guadalupe, Vigas, Virga, don Diego de Vargas

W: Wide-brimmed Spanish hat, Weaving, Windmills, Window on Canyon Road

X: eXtreme Sports (snowboarding and mountain biking), "X" form in pottery decoration

Y: Yucca, Yavapei baskets, Yei (Holy Spirits)

Z: Zia symbol, Zaguán, Zozobra, Zodiac (stars and sky)

Wen Hi Wo Nin Tu Kon Nin, Ha Toe Wibo Un Chani
—Tewa

Con buenos libros no estás solo.
—Spanish

With good books you are not alone.
—English

Three Compadres. Linoleum block cut by Harold E. West, c. 1930s.

Contents

Preface

With its long and unusual history, its ever-evolving cultural identity, its unique architectural style, and its lauded position as a locus of the arts, Santa Fe has been the subject of many books, from scholarly studies to sleek coffee-table productions. This is a different kind of book about the City Different. Touching on topics from the epic and the extraordinary to the idiosyncratic and the commonplace, the book covers a broad swath of history, but by no means does it present a comprehensive picture of Santa Fe. It strives to be accurate, but undoubtedly much of it will be challenged—and should be.

More than four hundred years old, the old and new city of Santa Fe is still, as always, an eccentric center of exchange. The decision to commemorate the 1610 establishment of *la villa real de Santa Fé* with a year-plus acknowledgment of its 400-year history led to city-wide events, symposia, books, and discussions. Working with the Santa Fe 400th Commemoration Committee's History Task Force, the *Santa Fe New Mexican* published a question about the city every day for 400 days. The answer appeared in the paper the next day, along with that day's new question. Initially introduced as "trivia about Santa Fe," these tidbits were meant to be fun as well as informative; they did not appear in chronological order, and they touched on disparate themes and topics.

This book developed from the newspaper series. It includes 400 questions relating to Santa Fe, each immediately followed by an answer and, in all but a few instances, a reference or references for further information. While many of the original questions have been revised or replaced and most of the answers and references have been expanded, the book preserves the apparently random organization of the questions and the spirit of play that comes from this approach. The History Task Force subcommittee, which helped put this book together, included Adrian Bustamante, the late Gerald T. E. González, Rick Hendricks, Michael King, Joseph P. Sánchez, and Cordelia Thomas Snow. More about them and others who have helped with this project may be found in the acknowledgments.

In addition to the questions, answers, and references, the book contains an extensive bibliography, several study guides that may be helpful to teachers and students, and plentiful illustrations scattered throughout. Most of the images have captions, but some are unidentified, with the words "What Is It?" above them. Some of these images may be recognizable to readers right away, while others may be harder to place. Use your imagination, and if you want to know for sure, a key to these images appears after the questions, toward the end of the book.

How does one "use" this book? However you like. Dip into it at random, or read it from cover to cover. Whatever approach you take, we expect that it will stimulate lively discussion and debate about what makes history, including your own, and may perhaps lead you to more discoveries about our remarkable city.

—Elizabeth West, Santa Fe, 2012

What Is It?
(See Answer Key #1)

Introduction

Santa Fe is unique among cities in the United States because it has gone through four eras of sovereignty in the four centuries since its founding. The questions in this book address historical and recent events, personalities (famous, infamous, and obscure), ghosts, trends in the city's appearance, and myriad other facts and legends across the span of Santa Fe's long history. Arranged nonchronologically, the questions loosely follow the order in which they appeared in the local newspaper, the *Santa Fe New Mexican*, during the yearlong commemoration of the founding of Santa Fe in 1610. Among other advantages, this nonchronological approach to the city's history and cultures creates surprises that come as the reader turns the pages. The questions and answers mine material from archives and published works as well as information sent in to the newspaper by citizens, some of whose families have been here for generations and others of whom are relatively recent arrivals. This introduction briefly describes the eras of Santa Fe's history to give a framework for the questions, while trying not to give away any of the answers.

The Native Americans

Millennia before the Spanish arrived, Paleo-Indians were in the valley in which Santa Fe would eventually be founded. Archaeologists have found nuanced evidence of the presence of hunters and gatherers in the area dating from at least thirty-five hundred years ago. At that time the climate was wetter, and these nomads made seasonal forays into the area. Evidence of pit houses built by their descendents has been found in the Fort Marcy area. Around eight hundred years ago, as the people adapted to agriculture, small surface dwellings began to appear, forming small pueblos. Between four and six centuries ago, during what is called the Coalition Period, large pueblos were being built in the area. By the time the Spanish explorers arrived, in 1540, the large pueblos had been abandoned for over a hundred years; the valley of the Santa Fe River was used for hunting and gathering and, more significantly, for religious purposes by the Pueblo people.

Today the people from the surrounding pueblos contribute significantly to the multicultural fabric of Santa Fe, with strong presences in the arts, commerce, and tourism. Perhaps more than in most other North American communities, Native Americans' historical and ongoing involvement in Santa Fe has played a vital and defining role in the city's cultural identity.

The Spanish Colonists

The Spanish arrived in 1598 to settle the area. They chose the valley of the Santa Fe River to build their capital in 1610. No documentary evidence exists regarding this choice, but it is plausible that the river and hillside springs made the area well-suited for agriculture. Also, perhaps the Franciscan missionaries wanted the colonists away from the Pueblos so the Pueblos wouldn't be influenced by the bad example of some of the colonists, which might make it more difficult to convert them. Whatever the reasons for choosing the site, the Spanish government had regulations for establishing Santa Fe as a *villa*. Given the frontier conditions of the province, the founding governor and his staff could follow these regulations only to the degree that circumstances allowed. Detailed information regarding the founding of *la villa de Santa Fé* may be found in the answers to some of the questions and will not be discussed here.

By 1638 the population of the *villa* consisted of about fifty families and numbered some two hundred *españoles* and *mestizos*. This number very probably included the *indios mexicanos* and other *indios* who lived in the Barrio de Analco. Many of those who came with Juan de Oñate in 1598 were second-generation *criollos*—born in the New World into well-to-do Spanish families who were not used to laboring in the fields. They had expected another rich empire such as the one their ancestors had found in Mexico. Most of the original families did not remain in New Mexico after Oñate was removed from office in 1607 since there were no riches to be found in the area. As a result, Santa Fe almost did not get founded because the Spanish crown was not convinced the colony was worth the effort of maintaining it. The friars insisted that it was; they claimed to have converted thousands of natives to Christianity and were afraid they would revert to "paganism" if the colonists left. Though the friars grossly over-counted their converts, the king's advisers believed them, and Philip III relented, allowing the colony to continue as a missionary colony at the crown's expense. A new governor was sent to New Mexico and instructed to found a *villa* to be the capital of the province. A recolonization effort was mounted since few of the original families remained. These and earlier families included Crypto-Jews, whose scions would contribute significantly to the history of the *villa*.

Most of the colonists coming to the New World from Spain were men, and many of them married Mexican Indian women. By the time the second wave of settlers arrived in the area, the majority had been born in Mexico and were of mixed ethnic ancestry, primarily *mestizos* and some *mulatos*. These new settlers brought with them both Spanish and Mexican customs that in time would take on a distinctly New Mexican character.

Of necessity the new *villa* was primarily a subsistence-farming community. As in every society, however, an upper class consisting of governmental officials and other elites made the decisions. Some elites were given *encomiendas*, grants of Pueblo communities on whom they could levy taxes in return for protecting and acculturating the natives. This system had evolved in Spain as a way of governing new territory during the eight hundred years of reconquering the peninsula from the Muslims. For the *encomenderos*, however, the levying of taxes in the form of labor and foodstuffs took priority over the acculturation of the natives. The Franciscan friars who were assiduously working to convert the Pueblos to Christianity resented the interference of the *encomenderos*, who were taking the Indians from their daily work and religious duties. As a result Santa Fe became the stage for a bitter conflict between church and state, which led the natives to realize how divided the Spanish colony's society was.

By 1680 the Pueblos had had enough of both the *encomenderos'* exploitation and the missionaries' aggressive attempts to convert them. They revolted, and the colonists fled to El Paso del Norte—present-day Juárez, Mexico. During this period the recently founded *villa* of Santa Fe underwent its first transformation: it became a two-story pueblo inhabited by Tano Indians from the Galisteo Basin. When the colonists did return, under Governor Vargas, twelve years later, the Tanos were asked to vacate the pueblo; they refused and the colonists had to fight their way into Santa Fe. The Tanos were expelled and moved to the Santa Cruz area, north of Santa Fe. The *villa* gradually evolved back into a mixed European and native town. Land was allotted to the returnees as well as to newcomers, who began to build homesteads near the Plaza and up and down the Santa Fe River. The Barrio de Analco was reoccupied, as was Agua Fría and the Barrio del Torreón. For the natives important changes resulted from the Reconquista: the *encomienda* system was eliminated, and the friars stopped forcing conversion on them.

To increase the population in New Mexico, families were recruited from the interior of Mexico. These plebeian newcomers were more *amestizados* (having mestizo features) than the former colonists because *peninsulares* (colonists born in mainland Spain) and *criollos* were by then even more in the minority in the New World. Culturally the group was now a New World people, having adopted Mexican traits and tastes, including foods such as chile and pinto beans as staples, clothing, and a vocabulary incorporating Mexican and Pueblo words. The world view of these plebeians had changed in Mexico over the previous 180 years, since their European ancestors' arrival. Communication was too slow for the colonists to continually reaffirm their European-only cultural origins. Essentially, as happens in all colonial societies, they developed a sense of place, identity, and lifestyle from the land—they had become a New World people even though they were still Spanish subjects.

Santa Fe's population increased slowly over the eighteenth century. The 1790 census counted some 2,637 *vecinos* (tax-paying citizens). Of these *vecinos*, 66 percent were classified as *españoles*, even though most were of mixed ethnic origin. *Español* was the preferred social status, and many in the upper echelons of society took on that identification, whether they were descendants of the original colonists or had simply become successful farmers, ranchers, or government officials. Captured Native American children sold to the colonists by nomadic tribes entered the society as servants and after reaching maturity were freed and became *vecinos*. Intermarriage with the Pueblo peoples was sparse because the Pueblos practiced endogamy.

Like most agricultural subsistence societies, Santa Fe and the rest of the colony hung on by a thread economically. New Mexico's lifeline was trade on the Camino Real, which extended into the interior of Mexico as far as Mexico City. Upper-class Santa Fe traders exported sheep, woven woolen goods, piñon, and buffalo hides, among other items. In return the traders brought back iron utensils, tools, clothing imported from Spain and its other colonies, religious items, chocolate, and other goods. But an imbalance of trade existed because the peso used in New Mexico (*peso de la tierra*) was worth only 75 percent of the Mexican silver peso.

The Mexican Period

In 1821, after an eleven-year war, Mexico achieved independence from Spain. New Mexico fell under the sovereignty of the new Republic of Mexico. Eager for trade with other nations, Mexico included among its first acts the repeal of Spain's restrictive trade laws with other countries. Hearing of this, William Becknell, an enterprising Missourian, came to Santa Fe to trade later that year. These events led to the opening of the Santa Fe Trail, which brought better manufactured goods at lower prices. New Mexicans now looked to the United States for their trade and commerce. The trail was soon connected with the Camino Real for trade with the Mexican interior, and Santa Fe became the nexus for both trails. As a result a few U.S. citizens began to establish residence in Santa Fe.

Politically, however, Mexico's centrist policies were hurting New Mexico. In 1835 Albino Pérez, from Mexico, was appointed governor and was charged with enforcing the law requiring the province to pay taxes to Mexico City. The lower-class population resented this law and killed the governor during the Revolt of 1837. Fearing this unrest would disrupt the Santa Fe trade, the elites, by then called the Ricos, helped the government squelch the rebellion. The plebian rebel leaders were executed on the Santa Fe Plaza.

By 1846 another, more serious problem confronted Mexico. The United States forced Mexico into a war over its northern provinces. In August of 1846, U.S. troops marched into Santa Fe and claimed the province for the United States. The lower-class population revolted but to no avail. Since the conquest suited their economic interests, many of the Ricos sided with the conquerors. The insurrection lasted only from December 1846 through July 1847. Some Santa Feans who had earlier plotted a conspiracy against the United States were jailed and so did not participate in the battles. After the conquest, a U.S. military presence was kept in Santa Fe until 1904, which added to the economy of the area. New Mexicans were now under U.S. sovereignty, and Santa Fe would begin to experience more change than it had in its more than two centuries of existence.

The Era of the United States

When Mexico opened the Santa Fe Trail, a few outsiders, including U.S. citizens, settled in Santa Fe; after the conquest by the United States, more began to arrive. At first there was little to attract these emigrants, but then some realized that besides trading, the way to wealth lay in the possession of land. It wasn't excellent agricultural land, as it was in the Midwest. Rather, it was land that had timber, livestock grazing potential, and possibly undiscovered mines. The Spanish/Mexican land-grant system of land tenure, which was different from that of the United States, attracted the emigrants because the grants were issued to communities, including large common areas for grazing and timber. Santa Fe was not one of these land grants per se—it was a town grant, a governmental center where these grants were registered once a way was found to defraud the grantees of their land. Members of the most notorious group included lawyers and politicians; this group was dubbed the Santa Fe Ring.

Under the United States, Santa Fe was no longer referred to as *la villa* but as a town or a city. The population was still mostly "Mexican," but the economic power had passed to the "Anglos" from the United States. The town's appearance, which some easterners described as a collection of scattered bricks, had not changed in centuries. The displeased newcomers sought changes they hoped would enhance the attractiveness of the town by giving it an eastern U.S. look. During the last quarter of the nineteenth century, a progressive movement began to shape Santa Fe into a more modern city that would attract eastern emigrants and investors. The city fathers saw the railroad as a key to development and made efforts to attract one. These progressives began to advocate for Victorian architecture to replace rustic-looking adobe buildings. In the 1890s the first three-story building was built on the Plaza. In 1891 the city was incorporated, with eight thousand citizens included in its boundaries. Gambling and prostitution were outlawed (these vices went underground), and saloons had to be licensed. As a result of tension between Hispanics and Anglos, two mayors were elected, one Hispanic and one Anglo. (It soon became a one-mayor system.) A city water system was created, and Hispanic farmers were angered by the loss of their irrigation water when a dam was built in Santa Fe canyon. The farmers demonstrated, but they were defeated by the progressives. Electric street lights were erected and sidewalks constructed. Traditional portals were removed from the exteriors of many buildings in order to give them a less Mexican look. Postcards were printed depicting Santa Fe as a beautiful city that rivaled those in the East. Of course, this was extreme promotional exaggeration, but it got the word out about Santa Fe.

When the hoped-for railroad bypassed the city, the merchants were despondent, and so the city issued $150,000 in bonds to entice the Atchison, Topeka & Santa Fe Railroad Company to construct an eighteen-mile spur from Lamy to Santa Fe. A few years later, the Denver & Rio Grande Western Railroad came in from Colorado. The railroads brought travelers who saw the city and the area in a different light from that of earlier emigrants. Many of these travelers were antiquarians fed up with the over-industrialization of the East; they were delighted by what they found in the Southwest and in Santa Fe, in particular. Here they found two cultures with a slower-paced lifestyle, coupled with clean air and bright light, which brought out the colors of the landscape. They soon began to convince the city fathers that the area's cultures not only were valuable in and of themselves and needed to be preserved but also were an asset that could be tapped by the development of tourism. As buildings were remodeled, architecture returned to a revived Spanish/Pueblo style, now called Santa Fe style, and the portals, so characteristic of this style, reappeared. Artists, archaeologists, and writers extolled the cultural qualities of the area, and tourism and art became major industries. Since then Santa Fe has been careful to preserve and protect its cultural heritage.

Native Americans, Hispanics, and all of the city's other inhabitants (a mixture of people of different ethnicities, often referred to collectively as "Anglos") have created a multicultural city that allows for harmony as each group offers unique contributions to Santa Fe's way of life. The questions in this book reflect upon the long and interesting history of our town. They are presented from the perspective of its citizens, who submitted the questions generated from their sense of place and their love for their city. It is our hope that you, the reader, will gain a similar perspective and appreciation of Santa Fe, the City Different.

—Adrian Bustamante, Santa Fe, 2012

The oldest known photograph of the Santa Fe Plaza, October 1861, showing the Elsberg-Amberg wagon train. Courtesy of Palace of the Governors Photo Archives (NMHM/DCA), #011254.

Questions

1. What does "Santa Fe" mean?

"Santa Fe" means "Holy Faith."

Read: "Santa Fe: City of Holy Faith," by Pedro Ribera Ortega, *La Herencia*, Fall 2001.

Linoleum block cut by Harold E. West, c. 1930s.

2. At least four flags have flown over Santa Fe—what are they?

Flags that have flown over Santa Fe include those of Spain, from 1610 to 1821; Mexico, from 1821 to 1846; the Confederacy, for a few weeks in the spring of 1862; and the United States, from 1846 to 1912 as a territory and from 1912 to the present as a state. Today flags for the City of Santa Fe and the State of New Mexico join the U.S. flag in the City Different.

In 2001 the North American Vexillological Association (NAVA), which is devoted to the study of flags, determined that New Mexico has the best-designed flag of any state in the United States.

3. When was Santa Fe first called "the City Different" and by whom?

In 1920 the Chamber of Commerce officially used this nickname in a brochure; the following year Santa Fe author Oliver La Farge and others popularized it as well.

The concept of promoting Santa Fe and its unique heritage had first been suggested by Edgar Lee Hewett and Sylvanus Morley, of the School of American Archaeology, shortly after New Mexico had achieved statehood, in 1912. In the early 1900s, the *Santa Fe New Mexican* quoted Hewett as saying: "In no other state of this Union is the trend of life so clearly shaped by art as in New Mexico. Art has rescued this state from the commonplace and made it conscious of its own fine character. The arts have kept Santa Fe from becoming an 'up-to-date' burg and made it unique and beautiful. Artists and writers constitute only a small percentage of the population, but their influence is wherever you look."

In 2010, four hundred years after the official founding, *Travel and Leisure* magazine voted Santa Fe the United States' number-one cultural getaway.

Read: "The City Different," Santa Fe Chamber of Commerce, 1920, available in the Southwest Collections of the New Mexico State Library; *The Man with the Calabash Pipe: Some Observations*, by Oliver La Farge, Sunstone Press, 2011 (first published 1966); and *The Art of New Mexico: How the West Was One*, by Joseph Traugott, Museum of New Mexico Press, 2007.

4. What Pueblo name for Santa Fe and the surrounding area refers to where ancestors of the modern Pueblo people lived and traded long before the arrival of the Spaniards in the sixteenth century?

Oga Po Ge, Ogapogeh, and *O'gha Po'oge* are all spellings for the most commonly used Pueblo name for the Santa Fe area; the name was given by the Northern Tewa and Southern Tewa and Tano Pueblo peoples. *Kua-P'o-Ge* and *Po'o-Ge* are two variations. "White Shell Water Place" is one translation: *Oga* = shell, *Po* = water, *Ge* = place of, and *Kua* = shell beads. The beads were made from the shells of inland fresh-water snails, or from *olivellae* (sea snails) traded from the Pacific Ocean or the Gulf of Mexico. Beads and shells were used in trade, both as commodities, such as ornaments, and as currency.

Read: "A Pueblo Perspective of the History of Santa Fe," by Gregory A. Cajete, in *White Shell Water Place*, Sunstone Press, 2010; "The Ethnogeography of the Tewa Indians," by John Peabody Harrington, *29th Annual Report of the Bureau of American Ethnology*, Smithsonian Institution, 1907–08; and *Snails, Shellfish, and Other Mollusks*, by Daniel Gilpin, Compass Point Books, 2006.

Olivellae Shells. Drawing by Anita H. Lehmann, 2011. These exotic sea snails (*olivellae*) and the beads made from them came in trade from the south (the Gulf of Mexico) and the west (the Pacific Ocean, off the California coast). They were one of many kinds of shells used in trade by Native Americans.
Image courtesy of the artist.

5. In 1609, who was appointed to establish a new *villa* (chartered town) that was to become the capital of the Province of New Mexico, in northern New Spain?

Don Pedro de Peralta was appointed by Viceroy don Luís de Velasco, who represented King Philip III of Spain in Mexico City, the capital of New Spain, to formally establish Santa Fe as a *villa* and the capital of the Província de Nuevo México, in northern New Spain. The *villa* was established in about March of 1610 and was referred to as *la villa de Santa Fé*.

New Spain, established in 1521 after Spain's conquest of the Aztec Empire, was formally called the Viceroyalty of New Spain (Virreinato de Nueva España); it included the Spanish East Indies and the Spanish West Indies. New Castile, with its capital in Lima, Peru, was the other viceroyalty at the time; later divisions led to the Viceroyalty of New Granada, formed in 1610, with its capital in Cartagena, and the Viceroyalty of Río de la Plata, in 1776, the capital of which was Buenos Aires.

Read: "Origins of City Different Not So Simple," by Marc Simmons, foreword in *All Trails Lead to Santa Fe,* Sunstone Press, 2010; and *New Mexico: Past and Future*, by Thomas E. Chávez, University of New Mexico Press, 2006. The official Peralta documents are in the Archivo General de Indias, in Seville, Spain. A copy may be found at the Palace of the Governors.

Don Pedro de Peralta points something out to an unidentified settler in *The Founding of Santa Fe*, a monumental bronze sculpture by Dave McGary, 1992. The monument is located in Peralta Park, west of the post office, at the corner of Grant Avenue and Paseo de Peralta. Photograph by E. West, used with permission of Dave McGary.

6. What is the earliest known map of *la villa de Santa Fé*?

The Urrutia map, the earliest known map of Santa Fe, was drawn in 1766 by Lieutenant don José de Urrutia and shows residential houses scattered up and down the Santa Fe River.

Read: *Jamestown, Quebec, Santa Fe: Three North American Beginnings*, by James C. Kelly and Barbara Clark Smith, Smithsonian Books, 2007.

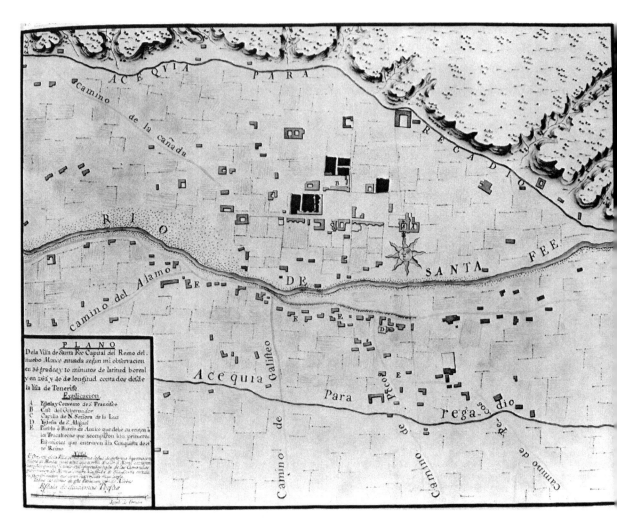

Map of Santa Fe drawn by Lieutenant José de Urrutia in 1766. Explanation:
A—Church and Convent of Saint Francis (Parroquia);
B—Casa Real/Government House (Palace of the Governors); C—Chapel of Our Lady of Light;
D—Church of Saint Michael (San Miguel); E—Pueblo and Barrio de Analco (on the other side of the river).
A copy of the Urrutia map is in the Palace of the Governors, at the New Mexico History Museum.

7. Where is the original Urrutia map held today?

The original map is in the British Museum, in London.

Read: "Fact-Finding Mission Led to an Early Map of Santa Fe," by Marc Simmons, *Santa Fe New Mexican*, October 18, 2008.

8. Did Route 66 ever go through Santa Fe?

Yes. The original route, first laid out in 1926, followed College Street—now Old Santa Fe Trail—toward the Plaza to the back (or south end) of La Fonda hotel, then along Water Street to Galisteo Street to join Cerrillos Road.

See signs in Santa Fe that point out the old Route 66. Also, read *Route 66 across New Mexico: A Wanderer's Guide*, by Jill Schneider, University of New Mexico Press, 1991; *American Route 66: Home on the Road*, by Jane Bernard and Polly Brown, Museum of New Mexico Press, 2003; and *Molly's Route 66 Adventure*, by Dottie Raymer, Pleasant Company, 2002.

What Is It?
(See Answer Key #2)

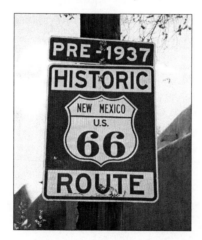

9. Which American colony is older, Plymouth Colony or Santa Fe?

Santa Fe, by at least ten years.

Read: *Plymouth Colony: Its History and People, 1620–1691*, by Eugene Aubrey Stratton, Ancestry, 1986; *Cultures Collide: Native Americans and Europeans, 1492–1700*, by Ann Rossi, National Geographic Children's Books, 2004; and *Making Haste from Babylon: The Mayflower Pilgrims and Their World, A New History*, by Nick Bunker, Knopf, 2010.

10. Where are the oldest rocks in the Santa Fe area?

The Sangre de Cristo Mountains, the southernmost part of the Rocky Mountains, are made of igneous and metamorphic rocks, pre-Cambrian (pre-fossil) rock more than 1 billion years old.

The name Sangre de Cristo means "blood of Christ" and dates from the early 1800s, although where it came from is not known. Early Spanish documents refer to the mountain range as La Sierra Madre (the mother range) or La Sierra Nevada (the snowy range), and the first English-speaking trappers referred to the mountains as "the Snowies."

Various sources may have been the inspiration for the current name: apocryphal legends involving the mountains' supposedly blood-like pink glow at sunset, references to similarly named locations further north, and possibly the influence of a religious confraternity called La Fraternidad Piadosa de Nuestro Padre Jesús Nazareno, active from the late eighteenth century into the twentieth century and popularly called Los Hermanos Penitentes (the Penitent Brothers), a sect with a focus on the passion and death of Christ.

The Santa Fe Plaza is 7,000 feet (2,134 meters) above sea level and at approximately latitude 35° north and longitude 105° west.

Read: *The Geology of Northern New Mexico's Parks, Monuments, and Public Lands*, edited by Greer Price, New Mexico Bureau of Geology and Mineral Resources, 2010; *The Place Names of New Mexico*, by Robert Julyan, University of New Mexico Press, 1998; and *The Penitentes of New Mexico: Hermanos de la Luz = Brothers of the Light*, by Ray John de Aragon, Sunstone Press, 2006.

11. What book helps define New Mexico's early Hispanic families?

Origins of New Mexico Families: A Genealogy of the Spanish Colonial Period, by Fray Angélico Chávez, Museum of New Mexico Press, 1992 (first published 1954).

What Is It?
(See Answer Key #3)

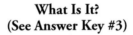

12. When did the Carmelite Order come to Santa Fe?

The Carmelite Order, a Catholic contemplative religious order, found a home in Santa Fe in 1945 with the arrival of six of their sisters, who desired a quiet place for their work. In 1946 they settled at their current property, which had been the Santa Fe Inn and which was later deeded to Archbishop Edwin V. Byrne and the Catholic Church. In the early 1900s the property, on Camino del Monte Sol, was used as the location for Sunmount Sanatorium (a place for the treatment of tuberculosis).

The Carmelite Order was founded as the Order of the Brothers of Our Lady of Mount Carmel in the twelfth century, perhaps on Mount Carmel. The first order is the friars, the second order is the nuns, and the third order is laymen. Santa Fe's Carmelite Order consists of the second order, nuns, who are cloistered.

Read: "The Carmelite Order," by Benedict Zimmerman, in *The Catholic Encyclopedia*, 1908; "Season of Solemn Simplicity," by Craig Smith, *Santa Fe New Mexican*, December 24, 1994; and "Sun Mountain, A Place for Healing," by Peter N. Ives, *Santa Fe New Mexican*, August 8, 2009.

13. Which Santa Fe newspaper's first edition consisted of one page in Spanish and three pages in English?

The *Santa Fe New Mexican*, first published on November 24, 1849, as a weekly newspaper, was originally a bilingual publication. Recently the paper has published a weekly section in Spanish. During 2010 the paper published a twelve-part series as part of the commemoration of the 400th anniversary of the founding of Santa Fe in 1610 by Spain.

Read: *Santa Fe, Its 400th Year: Exploring the Past, Defining the Future*, edited by Rob Dean, Sunstone Press, 2010; "*Santa Fe New Mexican*: 150 Years, 1849–1999," *Santa Fe New Mexican* special supplement, July 11, 1999; and "City Changes; Families Remain: Deep Cultural Roots Provide Stability amid Cultural Transformation," by Phaedra Haywood, *Santa Fe New Mexican*, December 5, 2010.

The editorial staff of the *Santa Fe New Mexican* shares the warmth around a stove in the newspaper's office, early 1900s. Courtesy of Palace of the Governors Photo Archives (NMHM/DCA), #15275.

🐏

14. What was in the bottle that the World War II warship the USS *Santa Fe* was christened with?

Water from the Santa Fe River. Caroline Chávez, niece of U.S. senator Dennis Chávez, did the honors. The water had been blessed by the archbishop of Santa Fe. Some folks were needlessly worried that not using the traditional champagne might cause bad luck. The ship, a light cruiser, was commissioned on November 24, 1942. The naval manual stressed the importance of teamwork and obedience; it was said that "good men on poor ships are better than poor men on good ships."

Read: *Lucky Lady: The World War II Heroics of the USS* Santa Fe *and* Franklin, by Steve Jackson, Carroll & Graf, 2003.

🐏

15. What is the architectural significance of the Roundhouse?

One of the more distinctive state capitol buildings in the United States, the New Mexico state capitol, also known as the Roundhouse, was designed by architect W. C. Kruger and dedicated on December 8, 1966. Its shape is inspired by the Zia sun-symbol, from Zia Pueblo, whose people consider four a sacred number, representing the four directions: North, East, South, West.

The Roundhouse is the fourth building housing the seat of government for the area that includes what is now the State of New Mexico. The first, whose foundations were laid in 1610, is the Palace of the Governors, the oldest public building in continuous use in the United States. The Spaniards called it La Casa Real (the Royal House, or the Government House); its packed-earth floors and thick adobe walls housed the royal governor along with his family and various administrative offices. Fifty-nine governors used the Palace under Spanish rule. Fourteen governors used it under Mexican rule. After the United States' conquest of Santa Fe and the northern part of Mexico in 1846, territorial governors used the Palace. In 1880 Governor Lew Wallace requested money for a renovation of the building, but the U.S. Congress refused, and therefore a bond issue was passed by New Mexicans in 1885 to construct a new capitol.

Completed in 1886, Santa Fe's second capitol building was considered "the pride of citizens from Las Cruces to Taos." It burned down on May 12, 1892. Citizens and government officials tried to save as much as possible, including the Spanish and Mexican archives. The next day Governor L. Bradford Prince wired the U.S. secretary of the interior for a congressional appropriation to replace it. Again Washington denied the request, so the territorial legislature authorized a bond issue for another new capitol on the same spot.

The third capitol was completed in 1900. The dedication day featured a large parade, including Governor Miguel Otero and Archbishop Peter Bourgade, who rode together in a carriage. Fifty years later a major capitol makeover replaced the neoclassical design with territorial-style brown stucco, and the building was renamed the Bataan Memorial Building, in honor of the New Mexicans on the Bataan Death March of World War II. That building still exists, but the fourth and newest capitol building was constructed across the street to the east, on Don Gaspar Avenue.

(By the way, a "capitol"—with an "o"—is the *building* where a legislature holds its sessions; "capital"—with an "a"—means several different things: the top of an architectural column, accumulated wealth, a letter larger than the ordinary small letter of an alphabet, the definition of a crime punishable by death, acknowledgment of something most serious, and the capital *city* and seat of government of a state or a country.)

Read: "Zia Symbol Inspires Plan," *Santa Fe New Mexican*, December 8, 1966; *State Capitals*, by Thomas G. Aylesworth, Gallery Books, 1990; *The New Mexico State Capitol, 1963–1980: A Twenty Year Development Plan*, privately printed by Architects Associated, 1963; *New Mexico's Palace of the Governors: History of an American Treasure*, by Emily Abbink, Museum of New Mexico Press, 2007; and *Ghost Soldiers: The Forgotten Epic Account of World War II's Most Dramatic Mission*, by Hampton Sides, Doubleday, 2001.

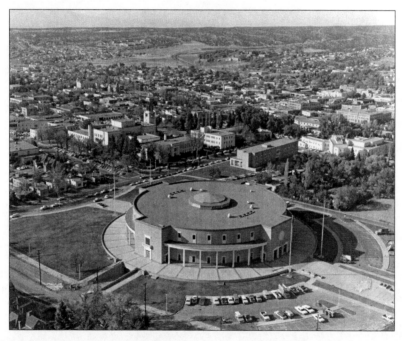

The New Mexico State Capitol, the Roundhouse. The 1967 aerial photo shows the truncated Zia symbol design of the building. The rays of the Zia sun symbol extend from the east, south, west, and north of the building by the walkways and driveways. Photograph by Dick Kent. Courtesy of Palace of the Governors Photo Archives (NMHM/DCA), #91176.

16. Who was don Bernardo de Miera y Pacheco?

A Spaniard from the mountains of the province of Santander, Miera y Pacheco was born in 1713 in the region called Cantabria. He came to Santa Fe in the entourage of Governor Francisco Antonio Marín del Valle in 1756. A talented santero, sculptor, painter, cartographer, linguist, soldier, military tactician, architect, astronomer, geologist, engineer, farmer, and mathematician, don Bernardo de Miera y Pacheco has been called a "polymath" by scholars since he had knowledge and expertise as well as skill in so many areas. He was also an adventurer who is credited with drawing the first map of New Mexico, from actual on-the-ground observation, detailing Native American pueblos and Spanish villages. Miera y Pacheco's map was submitted to the viceroy of New Spain by the governor in 1758.

Read: "The Versatile Bernard Miera y Pacheco," by Marc Simmons, *Santa Fe New Mexican*, September 7, 2002; and "Santa Bárbara Comes Home: A Lost Retablo by a Founder of the Santero Tradition Returns to the Palace of the Governors," by Josef Díaz, *El Palacio*, Spring 2011.

Map of New Mexico, c. 1758. Oil on canvas by don Bernardo de Miera y Pacheco.
Miera y Pacheco toured the province to collect the necessary data for the map.
Courtesy of Palace of the Governors Photo Archives (NMHM/DCA), #135340.

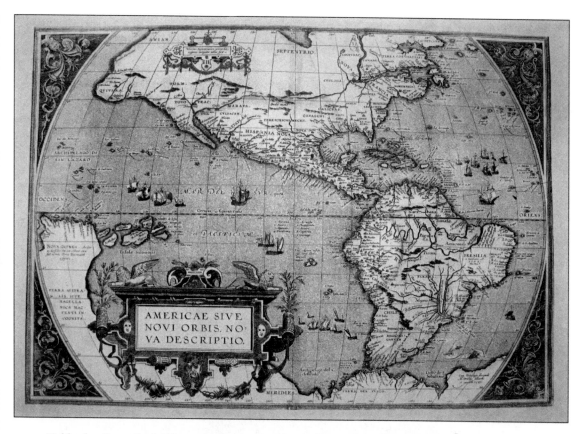

Unlike don Bernardo de Miera y Pacheco's map, the map put together by Abraham Ortelius in Antwerp, the Netherlands, in 1564 was a compilation and was not based on any firsthand experience of the map's area. Ortelius relied on other maps, and he was influenced by Jacques Cartier's discoveries for France as well as by information about Spain in the New World. Compared to other contemporary maps, Ortelius's map shows more detail, and his work was one of the first outside Spain to use the place-names used by the Spanish. The name of this map is *Americae sive Novi Orbi, Nova Descriptio*. It was presented in a collection of maps called *Theatrum Orbis Terraum*, published in Antwerp in 1570. Reproduced courtesy of Dumont Maps & Books of the West, Santa Fe.

17. What surprising information came to light around 1995 about Miera y Pacheco?

It was determined that don Bernardo de Miera y Pacheco was the primary artist/carver of the altar screen (*retablo*) that is now at Cristo Rey Church, on Canyon Road. Measuring eighteen feet wide by fourteen feet high, it was carved in very high relief out of white stone, quarried from an outcrop between San Ildefonso Pueblo and Española, and then delicately colored. The screen was originally commissioned in 1760 and paid for by Governor Francisco Antonio Marín del Valle and his wife, Ignacia Martínez de Ugarte, for La Capilla Castrense, the military chapel, officially called Nuestra Señora de la Luz (Our Lady of Light). One of the finest of eighteenth-century New Mexican churches, La Castrense was situated on the south side of the Santa Fe Plaza from 1760 until 1859, when it was sold and converted to a house and later to a store. The *retablo* was dismantled and moved to St. Francis Cathedral, where it was reassembled in the sanctuary behind the main building and stored for safe-keeping. In 1939 it was moved to Cristo Rey Church, which was built by the archdiocese expressly to house it.

The Miera y Pacheco *retablo* is one of the most beautiful and valuable pieces of colonial art in the Americas.

Read: *Historic New Mexico Churches*, by Annie Lux, with photographs by Daniel Nadelbach, Gibbs Smith, 2007; *Transforming Images: New Mexican Santos In-Between Worlds*, edited by Claire Farango and Donna Pierce, Pennsylvania State University Press, 2006; "La Castrense on the Santa Fe Plaza," by Gregg Gonzales, *La Herencia*, Winter 2007; and "New Mexico's Indo-Hispano Altar Screens," by Robin Farwell Gavin, *El Palacio*, Winter 2011. Also, visit Cristo Rey Church, at the base of Upper Canyon Road, to see the altarpiece.

The *retablo* (altar screen) by don Bernardo de Miera y Pacheco, in the old Parroquia section of the cathedral, where it was stored for sixty years. Photograph by Charles Lummis, c. 1890. Courtesy of Palace of the Governors Photo Archives (NMHM/DCA), #010023.

The Miera y Pacheco *retablo* behind the altar at Cristo Rey Church, its permanent home, on Canyon Road.
Photograph by Tyler Dingee, c. 1960.
Courtesy of Palace of the Governors Photo Archives (NMHM/DCA), #073786.

18. How were *caminos* (roads or paths) in Santa Fe historically named?

According to their destinations. Some examples include Agua Fria Street, Old Pecos Trail, Cerrillos Road, Old Taos Highway, and, more recently, Airport Road.

These days streets and roads are named for almost anything, including people, animals, colors, and places: St. Francis Drive, San Isidro Crossing, Camino and Avenida Juliana, Richards Avenue, Siringo Road, Buckman Road (named for the destination lumber camp of logger Henry Buckman, who made a fortune cutting timber on Spanish land grants in the early 1900s), Washington Avenue, Herradura Road, Charley Bentley Drive, Camino de la Familia, Artist Road, Flagman Way, Montezuma Avenue, Camino Carlos Rey, Bishop's Lodge Road, Lois Lane, Zafarano Drive, Governor Miles Road, Zepol Road (the opposite of Lopez), Gooney Bird Way, Quail Run Drive, Camino de Leon, Paseo del Coyote, Viaje Pavo Real, Jaguar Drive, Baca Street, Burro Alley, Plaza Azul, Camino Blanca, Cerros Colorados, Mesa Verde Street, Camino Rojo, Pen Road (named for the old state penitentiary), Chicoma Vista, Santa Clara Drive, Cochiti Street, Hopi Road, Tesuque Drive, Nambe Street, San Juan Drive, San Felipe Avenue, San Ildefonso Road, Navajo Drive, Santo Domingo Street, Zuni Street, Sol y Luz Loop, Camino del Monte Sol (once called Telegraph Hill since some of the first telegraph lines were placed along its route), Camino de las Animas, Cielo Court, Valentine Way, Kiva Road, Shoofly Street, Rio Grande Avenue (named for the railroad, not the river), Calle Primavera, Rodeo Road, etcetera.

Read: "Caminos de Santa Fe," by Aaron Martínez, *La Herencia*, Winter 2006; and *Street Maps: Santa Fe County, Los Alamos, Española, Taos*, Horton Family Maps, 2011.

What Is It?
(See Answer Key #4)

19. When was the Santa Fe Indian School (SFIS) founded?

The school was founded in 1890 as a boarding school for middle- and high-school Native American children from the state's pueblos. It is located on Cerrillos Road. The All Indian Pueblo Council gained sovereign status in ownership of the land and the school about a hundred years after it was founded.

The Santa Fe Indian School Spoken Word program was started in 2007; it strives to continue the ancient Native American tradition of storytelling through the modern format of performance poetry.

Read: *One House, One Voice, One Heart: Native American Education at the Santa Fe Indian School*, by Sally Hyer, with an introduction by Joseph Abeyta and an essay by Margaret Connell Szasz, Museum of New Mexico Press, 1990; *Pueblos of the Rio Grande: A Visitor's Guide*, by Daniel Gibson, Rio Nuevo Publishers, 2001; *Ready-to-Use Activities and Materials on Desert Indians: A Complete Sourcebook for Teachers K-8*, by Dana Newmann, Center for Applied Research in Education, 1995. Also, listen to *Moccasins and Microphones*, by the Santa Fe Indian School Word Team, with Timothy P. McLaughlin, coach (recorded at Stepbridge Studios, 2010).

The Santa Fe Indian School track team, 1954. Photograph by Harold Hanson.
Courtesy of Palace of the Governors Photo Archives (NMHM/DCA), #HP.2009.09.37.

20. Where did Charles Lindbergh land his airplane when he visited Santa Fe, in 1927?

On a landing strip near Cerrillos Road, across from the Santa Fe Indian School.

Read: *Lindbergh*, by A. Scott Berg, Putnam, 1998.

Amelia Earhart's backup plane, at the Santa Fe County Municipal Airport.
Photograph by Paul Reinwald, 2011. Courtesy of the photographer.

21. What local liberal arts college was initially established as a high school by the Bureau of Indian Affairs during the administration of President John F. Kennedy?

The Institute of American Indian Arts (IAIA) originally opened its doors on the campus of the Santa Fe Indian School in 1962. It has relocated twice, moving to its permanent, 140-acre campus in the Rancho Viejo subdivision, south of town, in the summer of 2000.

Read: *History of Indian Arts Education in Santa Fe: The Institute of American Indian Arts with Historical Background, 1890 to 1962*, by Winona Garmhausen, Sunstone Press, 1988.

An Institute of American Indian Arts (IAIA) art department faculty gathering, in 1966. Front row: Terence Shubert, Seymour Tubis, James McGrath. Second row: Lloyd K. New, Fritz Scholder, Otellie Loloma, Josephine Wapp. Third row: Kay Wiest, Allan Houser, Terry Allen, Roland Meinholz. Back row: Neil Parsons, Leo Bushman, Ralph Pardington, Louis Ballard. Courtesy of IAIA Photo Archives.

22. A buffalo has moved from Cerrillos Road to the Rancho Viejo area southeast of town. What buffalo is it?

The life-sized metal sculpture of a buffalo was made by students working with Professor Allan Houser in the 1960s; it is now at the Institute of American Indian Arts (IAIA).

See the buffalo at the center of the IAIA campus, on Avan Nu Po Road. (*Avan Nu Po* means "water serpent" in the Tewa language.)

23. Who was the only Hispanic governor to serve during the territorial period, and who also purchased the "first state automobile" in Santa Fe?

Miguel Antonio Otero served as governor from 1897 to 1906. He paid for the first governor's car in 1904; it was a Ford.

More than fifty years later, the Japanese artist Chuzo Tamatzu, who lived and worked at his studio on the corner of Garcia Street and Canyon Road with his wife, Louise, was often seen driving around Santa Fe in his Model T Ford.

Read: *My Nine Years As Governor of the Territory of New Mexico, 1897–1906*, by Miguel Antonio Otero, Sunstone Press, 2007 (first published 1940); and "First 'State Car' Gave Governor Otero Some Headaches," by Marc Simmons, *Santa Fe New Mexican*, September 10, 2005.

Governor Miguel Antonio Otero. Photograph taken in the Prince Studio, 1906. Courtesy of Palace of the Governors Photo Archives (NMHM/DCA), #050609.

Nina Otero-Warren, niece of Governor Miguel Otero, drove an electric car in the early 1900s. Courtesy of the New Mexico State Records Center and Archives, Bergere Family Photograph Collection, #21252.

24. Who was the poet who arrived in 1920 to give a talk about Chinese poetry, got the flu, fell in love with the town and its people, and became a "premier host of Santa Fe" for nearly fifty years? He entertained Frieda and D. H. Lawrence, Igor Stravinsky, Aldous Huxley, Clara Bow, Martha Graham, Stephen Spender, Manuel Chávez (later called Fray Angélico Chávez), Vachel Lindsay, Mary Austin, W. H. Auden, Alice Corbin and William Penhallow Henderson, John Collier, Etna West Wiswall, Errol Flynn, Rita Hayworth, Mark Twain, Paul Horgan, Edna St. Vincent Millay, Carl Van Vechten, Robert Oppenheimer, Consuelo Baca and Oliver La Farge, Robert Frost, and Ansel Adams, among many others.

Witter Bynner. As well as being one of the most outstanding hosts in Santa Fe, he was well respected for *The Jade Mountain*, his translation of Chinese poetry. His portrait was drawn by Khalil Gibran. He said he dated Mark Twain's daughter, and he and Edna St. Vincent Millay talked about getting married. (He and his friends were drawn to her because of her poem "Renascence.") Willard "Spud" Johnson was an early love of his, and Robert Hunt was his companion of more than thirty years at the end of his life. Witter Bynner died in 1968.

The photographer Ansel Adams referred to the riotous parties Bynner and Hunt gave as "Bynner's bashes." Adams's son, Michael, tells the story that on November 1, 1941, while out photographing the northern New Mexico landscape, Adams realized that it was getting late in the day and he needed to hurry back to Santa Fe for a party at Witter Bynner's place. But he noticed a beautiful scene unfolding as the moon rose, so he stopped his car and made time to take the shot. The resulting image became one of Adams's most famous: *Moonrise, Hernandez*. Adams often played the piano into the early morning hours at Bynner's parties.

The Inn of the Turquoise Bear, a bed-and-breakfast, is located on Buena Vista Street on the Bynner property. (The portrait by Gibran is owned by the inn.)

Read: *Who Is Witter Bynner? A Biography*, by James Kraft, University of New Mexico Press, 1995; *Light Verse and Satires*, by Witter Bynner, edited by James Kraft and William Jay Smith, Farrar, Straus and Giroux, 1978; *Collected Poems*, by Edna St. Vincent Millay, Harper Perennial, 1981; and *Ansel Adams at 100*, by John Szarkowski, Little, Brown, 2001.

**Robert Oppenheimer, 1962.
Private collection.**

Consuelo Otile Baca La Farge, Oliver La Farge's wife.
Watercolor by Olive Rush, c. 1940s.
Courtesy of John Pen La Farge.

Self-portrait by Witter Bynner, 1945.
Courtesy of the New Mexico State
Records Center and Archives,
Betty Farrar Photograph Collection,
#36633.

What Is It?
(See Answer Key #5)

25. What disease created a booming healthcare industry in New Mexico in the 1890s?

Tuberculosis. Many sanatoriums were built around the United States to help people who were ill with the infectious disease, and one of the most famous was Sunmount Sanatorium, on Camino del Monte Sol, in Santa Fe. Sunmount's popularity was partly attributable to the town's culture, as well as its dry climate. Bronson Cutting was one of many easterners who came out for the cure; he stayed to become an editor of the *Santa Fe New Mexican* and also a U.S. senator during the 1930s. Senator Cutting died in an airplane crash in 1935 and was replaced by Dennis Chávez. The economic boom created by the disease ended with the introduction of antibiotics, in the 1940s.

The preferred spelling of the word for the facility or resort that takes care of people with illnesses such as tuberculosis is "sanatorium." It derives from the Latin verb *sanare*, "to cure" or "to heal." An alternate spelling of sanatorium, "sanitarium," is usually associated with a psychiatric hospital.

Read: "When Doctors and Hospitals Were Scarce," by Marc Simmons, *Santa Fe New Mexican*, August 9, 2003; "The Cure at the End of the Trail: Seeking Health While Transforming a Town," by Nancy Owen Lewis, in *All Trails Lead to Santa Fe*, Sunstone Press, 2010; and *Bronson M. Cutting: Progressive Politician*, by Richard Lowitt, University of New Mexico Press, 1992.

Sunmount Sanatorium, c. 1907. John Gaw Meen Photograph Collection.
Courtesy of Palace of the Governors Photo Archives (NMHM/DCA), #23504.

What Is It?
(See Answer Key #6)

26. When did Carl Sandburg visit Santa Fe, and what are the titles of two poems he wrote about it?

Sandburg visited Santa Fe in the 1920s and along with Witter Bynner and other writers gave readings at the Sunmount Sanatorium. "Santa Fe Sketches" and "Alice Corbin Is Gone" are two poems Sandburg wrote about Santa Fe.

Santa Feans are readers and writers, and the town has been home to various small book publishers and presses since the 1800s. Some of the following Santa Fe book publishers are no longer printing and others are still thriving: Ancient City Press, Arzo Press, Aurora Press, Clark's Studio, Clear Light, Coyote Junction Press, Fisher Press, John Muir Publications, Laboratory of Anthropology, Lumen Incorporated, Morris Press, Ocean Tree Books, Open Heart Publishing, Pennywhistle Press, Red Crane Books, Red Mountain Press, Rydel Press, School for Advanced Research Press, Sherman Asher Publishing, Stagecoach Press, Sunstone Press, Synergetic Press, and Western Edge Press.

The first printing press to operate in New Mexico was brought up from Mexico to Santa Fe in 1834 by Ramón Abréu. The first book to be printed in New Mexico was a school text, printed in Santa Fe in early 1835, titled *Cuaderno de Ortografía*. Within a year of the press's arrival in Santa Fe, it was sold to Padre Antonio José Martínez and soon moved to Taos. (The press operator, Jesús María Baca, also moved to Taos, to serve as pressman.)

The Press of the Palace of the Governors, officially established in 1972 as the Print Shop and Bindery and often called the Palace Print Shop, is still producing books and prints in approximately the same place where a printing office was located as early as 1844. Today the print shop, part of the New Mexico History Museum, has various old presses on display, along with a historically accurate version of part of Gustave Baumann's studio and press, in rooms off the yard behind the Palace of the Governors. Visitors can get a glimpse of the important role printing and printing presses have played in Santa Fe history.

It has been said that there are more writers per capita in Santa Fe than anywhere else in the United States. No wonder, then, there are so many fine presses, publishers, editors, local book stores, libraries, and readers in the City Different!

Read: *Santa Fe and Taos: The Writer's Era, 1916–1941*, by Marta Weigle and Kyle Fiore, Sunstone Press, 2008; "Modernist Writers Shared Passion for New Mexico," by Lynn Cline, *Santa Fe New Mexican*, October 1, 1999; *Passions in Print: Private Press Artistry in New Mexico, 1834–Present*, by Pamela S. Smith and Richard Polese, Museum of New Mexico Press, 2006; and *But Time and Chance: The Story of Padre Martínez of Taos, 1793–1867*, by Fray Angélico Chávez, Sunstone Press, 1981.

Alice Corbin Henderson and William Penhallow Henderson duded up. Courtesy of Palace of the Governors Photo Archives (NMHM/DCA), #059757.

27. Which ranch, about twenty miles south of Santa Fe, became a living-history museum?

El Rancho de las Golondrinas. The museum opened in 1972 on property owned by Santa Feans Leonora Frances Curtin Paloheimo and her husband, Yrjö Alfred Paloheimo. Leonora Frances Curtin and her mother, Leonora Muse Curtin, originally purchased the property in 1932. (The elder Leonora was the daughter of Eva Scott Muse Fényes.) The two Leonoras improved the buildings of the ranch for their own use. Later the younger Leonora married Y. A. Paloheimo, whose vision, along with the encouragement of their friend John Gaw Meem, helped recreate a traditional Spanish colonial, northern New Mexico *rancho*. In 1986 the Paloheimos set up a trust to administer the museum. Mr. Paloheimo died later that year; his wife died in 1999. Today El Rancho de las Golondrinas is a popular nonprofit living-history museum, open from Wednesday through Sunday, June through September. *El Rancho de las Golondrinas* means the Ranch of the Swallows.

Read: *El Rancho de las Golondrinas: Living History in New Mexico's La Ciénega Valley*, by Carmella Padilla, Museum of New Mexico Press, 2009; *El Rancho de las Golondrinas: Spanish Colonial Life in New Mexico*, by Louann Jordan, Santa Fe: Colonial New Mexico Historical Foundation, 1977; "The Three Wise Women," by Virginia Scharff and Carolyn Brucken, *Chronicles of the Trail* (quarterly journal of El Camino Real de Tierra Adentro Trail Association), Winter 2011; and *Spanish Pioneers of the Southwest*, by Joan Anderson, E. P. Dutton, 1989.

Las Golondrinas. The photograph, by George Ancona, shows part of a reenactment at the gate entrance to a family household. One can imagine the polite greetings being exchanged.

28. What are Santa Fe's two oldest neighborhoods?

One is the Barrio de Analco, south of the Plaza and the Santa Fe River, in the area that includes the San Miguel Mission. *Analco* means "the other side of the river" in Nahuatl (the language of the Aztecs, or Mexica). The barrio was also called the Barrio de San Miguel. The other barrio, on the north side of the Santa Fe River, around the cathedral and the Plaza, was known as the Barrio de San Francisco. These barrios were in use in the early 1600s.

The word *barrio* comes from the Spanish word meaning a "ward of a Spanish or Spanish-speaking city" and is derived from the Arabic *barriya*, meaning "open country," which in turn derives from *barri*, meaning "outside" (of the city) and possibly referring to where wild animals live or to the less civilized parts of a city.

Read: "Barrio de Analco: Its Roots in Mexico and Role in Early Colonial Santa Fe, 1610–1780," by William Wroth, in *All Trails Lead to Santa Fe*, Sunstone Press, 2010; *Jamestown, Quebec, Santa Fe: Three North American Beginnings*, by James C. Kelly and Barbara Clark Smith, Smithsonian Books, 2007; and *Nahuatl As Written: Lessons in Older Written Nahuatl, with Copious Examples and Texts*, by James Lockhart, Stanford University Press, 2001.

Ortiz Street. Photograph by T. Harmon Parkhurst, c. 1915.
Courtesy of Palace of the Governors Photo Archives (NMHM/DCA), #144777.

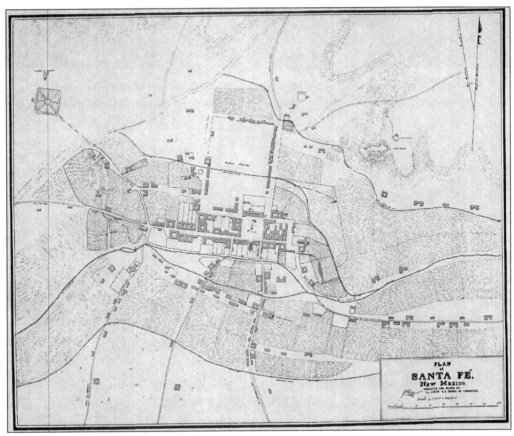

The map shows cultivated land around the edges of town. Barrio de Analco and San Miguel Church are in the lower center of the map, south of the Plaza. Plan of Santa Fe by 1st Lieut. U.S. Corps of Engineers Jeremy Francis Gilmer, 1846. Courtesy of Fray Angélico Chávez History Library.

View of Santa Fe, c. 1875, looking north across the river from the roof of Saint Michael's College on College Street. The houses and fields of Bario de Analco are in the foreground, the Santa Fe River bridge is in the middle, farther is the Loretto Chapel, and beyond that the Plaza. Photograph by George C. Bennett. Courtesy of Palace of the Governors Photo Archives (NMHM/DCA), #010135.

View of Santa Fe, 1881, looking south across the river at San Miguel Church and Saint Michael's College. Photograph by Ben Wittick. Courtesy of Palace of the Governors Photo Archives (NMHM/DCA), #015852.

29. Through what federal government program did Santa Fe artists and writers get the opportunity to work and to preserve New Mexico's culture and history?

The Works Progress Administration, later the Works Project Administration (WPA), was an independent agency funded directly by Congress; it put people to work in the 1930s as artists and writers, as well as architects, ethnographers, and musicians. It often coordinated work with the Civilian Conservation Corps, another popular part of President Roosevelt's New Deal.

Read: *American-Made: The Enduring Legacy of the WPA; When FDR Put the Nation to Work*, by Nick Taylor, Bantam Books, 2008; and *Treasures on the New Mexico Trails: Discover New Deal Art and Architecture*, compiled and edited by Kathryn Flynn, Sunstone Press, 1995.

30. In 1926 Sheriff Isias Alarid swore in the first female deputy sheriff in Santa Fe. What was her name?

Albina Lucero. She was also a *partera* (midwife), a *curandera* (healer), a rancher, a poet, a hunter, and a gold miner, as well as a mother of four children.

Other female firsts in Santa Fe include Debbie Jaramillo, mayor in 1994; Lily Gonzales, career police officer with the Santa Fe Police Department in 1964; Beverly K. Lennen, police chief in 2003; Joanna Callaway, volunteer fire fighter in 1986; Wendy Wagner, fire fighter with the Santa Fe Fire Department in 1987; Barbara Salas, fire chief in 2009; Fran Gallegos, municipal judge in 1996; Dora Battle, city councilor, in 1976; and, in 2011, New Mexico's first female governor, Susana Martinez, from Las Cruces, who became a part-time Santa Fean.

Read: "Albina Lucero: A Woman of Conviction," by Lydia Rivera, *La Herencia*, Summer 1994; "Reflecting All the Right Choices," by Gussie Fauntleroy, *Santa Fe New Mexican*, December 27, 1998; *Santa Fe Originals: Women of Distinction*, by Athi-Mara Magadi, Museum of New Mexico Press, 2003; and *A Tribute to the Women of Santa Fe*, by William Constandse, Utama Publications, 1983.

**Albina Lucero. Photographer unknown.
Courtesy of Ana Pacheco, *La Herencia*.**

31. When did Bishop Jean Baptiste Lamy first arrive in Santa Fe?

August 9, 1851. Lamy chose to leave his native France in 1840 to answer the call for Catholic missionaries in Ohio. He was appointed to the newly created vicariate of New Mexico in 1850. As an active progressive, he built churches, including Santa Fe's cathedral (which became a cathedral basilica in 2005) and the Loretto Chapel, and created new parishes, schools, and St. Vincent's Hospital and Orphanage. He planted many fruit trees and plants that reminded him of his native France. He encouraged priests and others from France to come to Santa Fe—by the late nineteenth-century 80 percent of the city's priests were French. Lamy often disagreed with Padre Antonio José Martínez, of Taos, about policy; he excommunicated Martínez in 1858. Lamy became Santa Fe's first archbishop when the diocese was elevated to an archdiocese in 1875. He died of pneumonia in 1888.

Read: *Archbishop Lamy: In His Own Words*, edited and translated by Thomas J. Steele, LPD Press, 2000; and compare with *Death Comes for the Archbishop*, by Willa Cather (Vintage Classics, 1990), a well-written but inaccurate novel supposedly based on Lamy. Also read *But Time and Chance: The Story of Padre Martínez of Taos, 1793–1867*, by Fray Angélico Chávez, Sunstone Press, 1981.

The drawing on the card shows what St. Francis Cathedral would have looked like if the building had been completed the way Bishop Lamy had planned. A sketch of him is in the cameo, upper left. Courtesy of Palace of the Governors Photo Archives (NMHM/DCA), #010005.

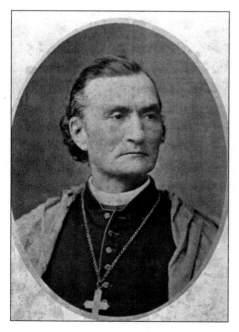

Bishop Jean Baptiste Lamy, c. 1870. Courtesy of Palace of the Governors Photo Archives (NMHM/DCA), #009970.

32. Where is a giant *olla* located in Santa Fe?

Look for the eight-foot hanging art piece, up high, in front of the Southside Public Library. It is a woven *olla*, created by Randy Walker, made of steel and acrylic braid. An *olla* is a large, rounded, wide-mouthed earthenware jar or pot used for storing water. This large art object is one of the City of Santa Fe Arts Commission pieces, many of which are part of the Art in Public Places Collection.

Santa Fe's other commissioned public art pieces include *San Francisco de Assis* (in front of City Hall); *Homage to the Burro* (at Burro Alley); and several interesting bus/transit shelters, including one at the Railyard Park, near the corner of Cerrillos Road and Guadalupe Street, and another in the shape of a silhouetted tree, on Airport Road, west of Sweeney Elementary School. Several stelae bus-stop markers along Cerrillos Road honor the trails and roads of Santa Fe. Works of art are scattered around town, and many of the pieces are found in or near public parks.

Santa Fe has many parks. Frenchy's Field is the name of the seventeen-acre meadow purchased by Bernard Parachou, a French Basque dairy farmer who worked for Slade's Dairy in the early 1900s and then ran the Sunshine Dairy from 1933 until 1983. One of Santa Fe's community gardens is now located in Frenchy's Field; the park also has a walking track and a labyrinth. Another popular park is the Cornell Rose Garden, on Galisteo Parkway, between Alta Vista Street and Cordova Road; named for Harvey Hiram Cornell, a landscape architect who died in 1962, it is a peaceful place where people enjoy quiet pastimes such as reading, meditation, tai chi, and perhaps a friendly game of croquet.

Other city parks include Patrick Smith Park, between East Alameda and Canyon Road, where many Frisbee games are played; Pueblos del Sol Park, on Nizhoni Drive at Governor Miles Road; Las Acequias Park, on Calle Atajo, off Airport Road; Cathedral Park, at East Palace Avenue, next to the St. Francis Cathedral Basilica; Bicentennial Park, between Alto Street and West Alameda; Fort Marcy Park and Magers Field, off Biship's Lodge Road; the Cross of the Martyrs, on a hill north of downtown with 360-degree views, can be accessed from Paseo de Peralta via a steep walkway with plaques highlighting the city's history; De Vargas Park, a skateboard park at the corner of Guadalupe Street and West Alameda; one of the smallest parks in the city, Entrada Park, at the intersection of Don Diego, Guadalupe, and Cerrillos; and the Frank S. Ortiz Park, a large park off Camino de las Crucitas where dogs can run free. Most Santa Fe city parks are open from 8 a.m. to 10 p.m.

Read: *Spanish Dishes from the Old Clay Pot = Olla Podrida*, by Elinor Burt, Ross Books, 1977; and *Dogs That Know When Their Owners Are Coming Home, and Other Unexplained Powers of Animals*, by Rupert Sheldrake, Three Rivers Press, 2011.

What Is It?
(See Answer Key #7)

33. Who created the first archive of Spanish Colonial documents, a primary source of New Mexico's colonial history?

During the 1880s, the territorial librarian Samuel Ellison was the first to arrange the documents and books under specific headings.

Ralph Emerson Twitchell was one of several people, including librarian Facundo Pino, who rescued the Spanish Archives from a fire in May of 1892 that destroyed the territorial capitol building. After leaving Missouri, Twitchell, at age twenty-six, joined the law office of Henry L. Waldo, for the Atchison, Topeka, and Santa Fe Railway, where he worked for the rest of his life. But his first interest was New Mexico history, and in 1911 and 1912 he published *Leading Facts in New Mexico History*, a comprehensive, multivolume history intended to be accessible to all readers. He angered many Hispanos and others with his history of the Mexican War and his English-only stance. He also angered many Pueblo people and others with his support of the Bursum Bill.

Read: *The Spanish Archives of New Mexico*, by Ralph Emerson Twitchell, with foreword by Estevan Rael-Galvez, Sunstone Press, 2008 (first published 1914); and *New Mexico's Spanish and Mexican Archives: A History*, by Robert J. Tórrez, Center for Land Grant Studies, 1994.

34. Who led 1,600 men from Fort Leavenworth, Kansas, to Santa Fe—one of the longest marches in military history—in order to take possession of a foreign capital for the United States, the first time such an act had occurred?

Brigadier General Stephen Watts Kearny led his men into Santa Fe in 1846. He used diplomacy, as well as the show of force, and drew on his cultural sensitivity and civil intelligence to communicate with the people of Santa Fe. Although he was in the city for only six weeks, during that time he regularly attended Sunday Mass at the cathedral to show respect. After the conquest and before traveling on to California, Kearny appointed Colonel

Alexander William Doniphan to write a new code of civil laws, which became known as "the Kearny Code," in both English and Spanish. It was a quickly assembled collection of U.S. and Mexican laws, and it is still the basis of New Mexico's Bill of Rights and legal code. Doniphan was left in charge while Kearny was gone.

"Manifest Destiny" was the influential slogan used in the 1800s to invoke the idea of divine sanction for the territorial expansion of the United States. (A New York newspaper editor coined the phrase "Manifest Destiny" in 1845.)

Read: *Winning the West: General Stephen Watts Kearny's Letter Book, 1846–1847*, by Hans von Sachsen-Altenburg and Laura Gabiger, Pekitancui, 1998; *Turmoil in New Mexico, 1846–1868*, by William A. Keleher, Sunstone Press, 2007 (first published 1952); *The Little Lion of the Southwest: A Life of Manuel Antonio Chaves*, by Marc Simmons, Sage Books, 1973; and *Manifest Destinies: The Making of the Mexican American Race*, by Laura E. Gómez, New York University Press, 2007.

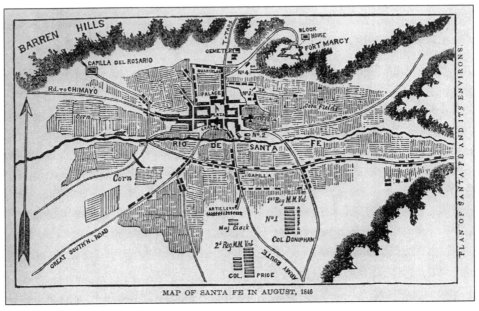

MAP OF SANTA FE IN AUGUST, 1846

Colonel Alexander William Doniphan, who was left in charge after Kearny departed for California, used this 1846 map of Santa Fe. It shows "Barren Hills" and Fort Marcy at the top, the Palace and the Plaza in the center, the Rio de Santa Fe across the middle, and cornfields around town.

35. What was the reaction of Santa Feans in 1846 to their city's sudden transformation from a Mexican town to a possession of the United States?

For most there was fear—of bodily harm and of loss of their familiar way of life. Eventually, there was grudging acceptance, and for some there was hopeful enthusiasm. Years later José Leandro Perea, who had become a leading rancher, remembered the events of 1846, saying, "I knew it would ultimately result in making our people freer and more independent than they ever could be under their former government."

Read: *New Mexico: An Interpretive History*, by Marc Simmons, University of New Mexico Press, 1988; "The United States' Occupation of Santa Fe: My Government Will Correct All This," by John P. Wilson, in *Santa Fe: History of an Ancient City*, edited by David Grant Noble, School for Advanced Research Press, 2008.

General Stephen Watts Kearny. Unattributed image.
Courtesy of Palace of the Governors
Photo Archives (NMHM/DCA), #009940.

36. From what and where did General Kearny die?

He contracted yellow fever in 1847 in Veracruz, Mexico, and returning to Saint Louis, Missouri, died in 1848.

Read: *Stephen Watts Kearny: Soldier of the West*, by Dwight L. Clarke, University of Oklahoma Press, 1961.

37. When did a bank on the Plaza begin the annual public display of working model trains in its lobby during the winter holidays?

Since 1954 the First National Bank of Santa Fe has invited the public to see and hear their lobby display in December.

Another model train display is often set up among the trees at the end of Plaza Fatima during the Christmas Eve farolito walk near Acequia Madre.

Read: *Christmas in Santa Fe*, by Susan Topp Weber, Gibbs Smith, 2010.

38. What winter event is observed and honored by the Pueblo peoples and others in the vicinity of Santa Fe?

The winter solstice. *Solstice* is a Latin term meaning "the sun is standing still." The event is usually celebrated with dances.

Read: "Pueblo Dances Share the Shifting of Cycles," by Stephen Powell, *Santa Fe New Mexican*, December 20, 1996; and *Dance Ceremonies of the Northern Rio Grande Pueblos*, High Desert Field Guides, 2005.

Kiva at San Ildefonso Pueblo. Photograph by T. Harmon Parkhurst, c. 1925–1945.
Courtesy of Palace of the Governors Photo Archives (NMHM/DCA), #003693.

39. When and where was the first public celebration of Kwanzaa in Santa Fe?

In December of 1997, at the College of Santa Fe, now the Santa Fe University of Art and Design.

Read: "Kwanzaa Celebration Salutes African American Ancestry," by Jodi Garber, *Santa Fe New Mexican*, December 26, 1997.

40. When was Hanukkah first celebrated on the Santa Fe Plaza?

In 1997 the Jewish organization Chabad celebrated the Festival of Lights by lighting a giant menorah on the Plaza.

Read: *The Family Treasury of Jewish Holidays*, by Malka Drucker, Little, Brown, 1994; and *Hanukkah: Eight Nights, Eight Lights*, by Malka Drucker, Holiday House, 1980.

41. What winter-holiday morality play and procession is a blend of Spanish and Aztec ancestral traditions?

Las Posadas, which features a reenactment of Mary and Joseph's seeking a place for Mary to deliver her baby. Santa Fe locals and visitors alike celebrate the event on the Santa Fe Plaza during the Christmas holidays.

Read: *Las Posadas: An Hispanic Christmas Celebration*, by Diane Hoyt-Goldsmith, Holiday House, 1999; "History of Las Posadas," by Maurilio Vigil, *La Herencia*, Winter 2002; and *The Night of Las Posadas*, by Tomie de Paola, C. P. Putnam's Sons, 1999.

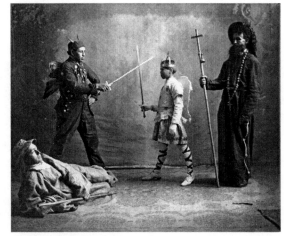

42. What annual Spanish and Mexican drama is reenacted in Santa Fe at Christmas?

Los Pastores, the medieval religious drama about the shepherds and the introduction of the Christ child to the Three Kings. It has been presented by La Sociedad Folklórica de Santa Fe in the Santuario de Guadalupe.

Read: *Santa Fe Christmas*, by Christine Mather, Museum of New Mexico Press, 1993; "Celebrating Old-Fashioned Christmas in New Mexico," by Marc Simmons, *Santa Fe New Mexican*, December 25, 2004; and *Los Pastores: A Mexican Play of the Nativity*, by M. R. Cole, Houghton Mifflin, 1907.

A Los Pastores performance in Santa Fe, c. 1915. Photograph by Aaron B. Craycraft. Courtesy of Palace of the Governors Photo Archives (NMHM/DCA), #013695.

43. What Christmas tradition did children celebrate in Santa Fe and northern New Mexico prior to World War II?

Los Oremos, during which children would go door to door, recite a special prayer, and receive a gift of candy or fruit from the people of the neighborhood.

Read: "Los Oremos: A Christmas Story," by Maurillio E. Vigil, *La Herencia*, Winter 1995.

Holiday Party in Winter. Linoleum block cut by Harold E. West, c. 1930s.

44. How is Christmas Eve traditionally referred to in Santa Fe?

La Noche Buena, the good night, meaning the best of all nights.

Read: *Noche Buena: Hispanic American Christmas Stories*, edited by Nicolás Kanellos, Oxford University Press, 2000; "La Noche Buena y Nuestros Antepasados," by R. J. Miera, *La Herencia*, Winter 1996; and *La Noche Buena: A Christmas Story*, by Antonia Sacre, Abrams Books for Young People, 2010.

45. How was Christmas morning celebrated in Santa Fe in the late 1890s?

In the old Spanish and Mexican way, after church services, hundreds of colorfully dressed people crowded into the Plaza to wish each other Feliz Navidad (Merry Christmas).

Read: *Christmas in Old Santa Fe*, by Pedro Ribera Ortega, Sunstone Press, 1997.

Wood vender's wagon on Palace Avenue, at the Plaza, December 1918. The Museum of Fine Arts (now the New Mexico Museum of Art) is in the background. Photograph by Wesley Bradford. Courtesy of Palace of the Governors Photo Archives (NMHM/DCA), #012986.

Vigas and shadows at the New Mexico Museum of Art.

46. The Spanish colonizer and governor don Diego de Vargas reported that his advisors had pressed him to attack the Pueblo people on Christmas Eve, but he held out for the siege and forceful reconquest of Santa Fe until when?

December 29, 1693. Perhaps Vargas had hoped for an agreement at Christmastime with the Pueblo people who had control of Santa Fe. His second entry into Santa Fe and reconquest of New Mexico was not a bloodless event, as the first ritual repossession of Santa Fe in around July of 1692 had been. By bringing colonists, friars, and soldiers back with him from El Paso, Vargas showed that the Spaniards were coming to stay and take control, which some of the Pueblos bitterly resisted.

After a long, arduous trek, late in 1693, the colonizing expedition that had made the journey with Vargas camped northwest of the Plaza in the freezing weather, near where the Rosario Chapel is now; there they waited through frustrating attempts at negotiations with the Pueblo people who had control of the old governor's palace building, which they had built into a stronghold that could hold more than a thousand people. But negotiations broke down; there was disagreement among the Pueblo groups, and everyone was hungry, cold, and tired. The Battle of Santa Fe, four days after Christmas, was fierce, and because the Pueblo people were split and forty fighting men from Pecos joined the colonists, the Spaniards won. Vargas ordered seventy of the men who refused to surrender executed. The remaining four hundred others were allotted to the soldiers and colonists for ten years of servitude.

Vargas spent most of his first term as governor fighting the Pueblo peoples. He was also resented by many Spaniards because of his arrogance and alleged bad governance. Separated from his family, in a town he didn't particularly like, Vargas was often sick. There were food shortages during the winter of 1695 and 1696, an epidemic of plague, and speculation that the Pueblos were considering another uprising, which did occur, in the spring of 1696. During this last battle, Vargas and his soldiers were aided by five Pueblo groups, and the resistance to Spanish domination ended. By 1697, however, the difficulties of colonization probably contributed to the willingness of some of the colonists to testify supporting a suit brought by the six-member *cabildo* (town council) against Vargas. He was jailed in the Palace of the Governors on October 2 by the replacement governor, don Pedro Rodríguez Cubero.

After more than a year and half of imprisonment, Vargas was let go. He left for Mexico City, where it took almost two years of legal wrangling for him to clear his name of all charges. He was reappointed to the governorship of New Mexico and returned in November of 1703, but he died the following spring, probably from dysentery, while campaigning against the Apaches. He was buried under the church in Santa Fe at that time; where his remains are located now is uncertain, since his bones were moved in about 1716 to (it is assumed) the parish church that later became the site for the cathedral.

Read: "Diego de Vargas: Reconqueror, Governor," by Rick Hendricks, *Telling New Mexico: A New History*, edited by Marta Weigle, with Frances Levine and Louise Stiver, Museum of

New Mexico Press, 2009; *Remote Beyond Compare: Letters of Don Diego de Vargas to His Family from New Spain and New Mexico*, edited by John L. Kessell, University of New Mexico Press, 1989; and "By Force of Arms: Vargas and the Spanish Restoration of Santa Fe," by John Kessell, in *Santa Fe: History of an Ancient City*, edited by David Grant Noble, School for Advanced Research Press, 2008.

This is an almost life-sized portrait of don Diego de Vargas, oil on canvas by Julio Barrera, date unknown. A reproduction of the painting hangs in the Palace of the Governors. Vargas's full name at the end of his life was don Diego de Vargas Zapata y Luján Ponce de León y Contreras y Salinas, Marqués de Villanueva de la Sagra y de la Nava de Braciñas. Courtesy of Palace of the Governors Photo Archives (NMHM/DCA), #011409.

47. Who is La Conquistadora?

La Conquistadora (Our Lady of the Conquest), also known as Our Lady of Peace, is the oldest recognized Marian figure, or carved depiction of Mary, still venerated in the United States. She is a wooden statue about thirty-six inches tall. She was brought north from Mexico by fray Alonso de Benavides, who came to Santa Fe to become the *custos* (custodian, or head) of the Franciscans in New Mexico. The historian Fray Angélico Chávez believed that the statue was carved in Los Palacios, a small town near Seville, Spain, and that she was brought to Mexico by Cortez.

Saved from destruction during the Pueblo Revolt in August of 1680, La Conquistadora was returned to New Mexico in 1693, during the successful reconquest by don Diego de Vargas, who vowed to build a chapel for her in thanks. She resides at St. Francis Cathedral Basilica, in the Conquistadora Chapel. Once a year she stays at the chapel built for her by Vargas, Rosario Chapel, which is on the site near where he camped for about a week during the reconquest.

La Conquistadora, in her Conquistadora Chapel, in the cathedral basilica, is on the National Register of Historic Places.

Read: *La Conquistadora: The Autobiography of an Ancient Statue*, by Fray Angélico Chávez, Sunstone Press, 1983 (first published in 1954); "Our Lady of Conquest," by Pedro Ribera Ortega, *La Herencia*, Summer 1994; and *Our Lady of Conquest*, by Fray Angélico Chávez, Sunstone Press, 2010 (first published in 1948).

La Conquistadora in St. Francis Cathedral. Photograph by Tyler Dingee, 1951.
Courtesy of Palace of the Governors Photo Archives (NMHM/DCA), #073832.

48. Who was the man believed to have saved La Conquistadora from a fire during the Pueblo Revolt in 1680, and what happened to him?

Francisco Gómez Robledo is thought by some to have rescued the wooden figurine, an image of the Virgin Mary, during the Pueblo Revolt.

In 1662 Robledo had been arrested and tried at an Inquisition tribunal in Mexico City on charges of secretly practicing Judaism. He was absolved of the charges and returned to New Mexico, where his mother, Ana Robledo, was in charge of dressing La Conquistadora.

Read: *To the End of the Earth: A History of the Crypto-Jews of New Mexico*, by Stanley M. Hordes, Columbia University Press, 2005; "New Mexico's Sephardim: Uncovering Jewish Roots," by Emma Moya, *La Herencia*, Winter 1996; and "Culture and Memory: A Sephardic Photo Journey," by Cary Herz, *La Herencia*, Winter 2003.

What Is It?
(See Answer Key #8)

49. What other buildings have occupied the site where the St. Francis Cathedral Basilica is today?

A succession of *parroquías*, or parish churches, has been on this site, since adobe architecture requires constant upkeep. The first was a small parish church, built by the Spanish after Santa Fe became a *villa* in 1610. At that time the church fronted the Plaza, which was larger than it is today. In 1630 a second, slightly larger church replaced the original one. In 1692, when the Spanish regained control after the Pueblo Revolt, a more substantial adobe church was built; called La Parroquia, it was completed in 1714 and honored Saint Francis. It served the community for almost a hundred and fifty years.

In 1869 Bishop Lamy organized the building of a new, stone cathedral around and over the old church. The stone was quarried at Cerro Colorado, south of the *villa*, near what is now Lamy, New Mexico. French architects and Italian stonemasons were brought to Santa Fe. By 1884 the main part of the new cathedral was finished, and the old church was torn down from underneath it and removed through the front door. The cathedral was not complete when funds ran low—the two spires remained unfinished.

Read: *Bishop Lamy's Santa Fe Cathedral, with Records of the Old Spanish Church (Parroquia) and Convent Formerly on the Site*, by Bruce T. Ellis, University of New Mexico Press, 1985.

The parish church, or Parroquia, in 1867. Photograph by Nicholas Brown. Courtesy of Palace of the Governors Photo Archives (NMHM/DCA), #010059.

This image of "The New Cathedral" appeared in *Harper's New Monthly Magazine* in 1880. Courtesy of Palace of the Governors Photo Archives (NMHM/DCA), #074486.

50. Who was doña María Gertrudis Barceló, and what popular novel tells a version of her story?

Prior to the United States' occupation of Nuevo México, doña María Gertrudis Barceló (often called Doña Tules) was widely known as an astute Santa Fe businesswoman. She ran a very successful saloon and gambling house frequented by a cross-section of society including politicians, New Mexican and American traders, soldiers, and locals. She was a talented monte dealer, renowned for her skill, precision, and savvy timing in the popular game of chance. When the U.S. Army couldn't meet the troop payroll after it had entered and taken Santa Fe in 1846, she lent the money for that purpose.

The Wind Leaves No Shadow is the title of a 1950s novel about her.

Read: "Doña Tules, Una Gran Dama de Santa Fe," by Ana Consuelo Matiella, *La Herencia*, Fall 1994; "A True Picture of Doña Tules," by Barbara Harrelson, *Santa Fe New Mexican*, October 21, 2007; "Gambling Queen: Revisiting Santa Fe's Ever-Controversial Doña Tules," by Richard McCord, *Santa Fean*, May 2005; *Doña Tules: Santa Fe's Courtesan and Gambler*, by Mary J. Straw Cook, University of New Mexico Press, 2007; and *The Wind Leaves No Shadow*, by Ruth Laughlin, Caxton, 1951.

"Try Your Luck with Doña Tules." At a costume *baile* (ball) for the closing of the Magoffin House, in about 1949, Nina Otero-Warren is dressed as doña María Gertrudis Barceló, informally known as Doña Tules. Will Shuster, in the hat, and others gather around hoping to win at a game of chance. Most likely they will not be lucky since Doña Tules was very practiced at the monte table. Photographer unknown. Courtesy of the New Mexico State Records Center and Archives, Bergere Family Photograph Collection, #24617.

"Welcome to the Capital" arch at the southwest corner of the Plaza. Photograph by Jesse Nusbaum, 1912. Courtesy of Palace of the Governors Photo Archives (NMHM/DCA), #016725.

51. What documents contribute to the debate regarding the founding date (and the founder) of Santa Fe?

The Juan Martínez de Montoya papers. A translation is available to scholars at the Fray Angélico Chávez History Library, next door to the Palace of the Governors and the New Mexico History Museum. The papers were purchased from a London dealer in antiquities by the State of New Mexico in 1994.

Captain Juan Martínez de Montoya arrived in the province of New Mexico in 1600, as part of the relief expedition sent in support of Oñate. The papers refer to apparent accomplishments achieved by Martínez de Montoya, and some historians have suggested they may offer clues to the establishment of a settlement at what became Santa Fe, prior to the official founding of the *villa* in 1610. The matter of interpreting the documents requires more study, research, and debate. Oñate, Martínez de Montoya, and Peralta are names some historians associate with settlements in northern New Spain and with the founding of Santa Fe. The uncertainties in the Martínez de Montoya papers are absent in the Peralta documents, which contain explicit instructions from the viceroy of New Spain about founding a *villa*.

Read: "Juan Martínez de Montoya, Settler and Conquistador of New Mexico," by France V. Scholes, *New Mexico Historical Review*, 1944; the introduction, by Joseph P. Sánchez, in *All Trails Lead to Santa Fe*, Sunstone Press, 2010; "Thirty-eight Adobe Houses: The Villa de Santa Fe in the Seventeenth Century, 1608–1610," by José Antonio Esquibel, in *All Trails Lead to Santa Fe*, Sunstone Press, 2010; the Juan Martínez de Montoya Papers, Fray Angélico Chávez History Library, Santa Fe, New Mexico; *The Last Conquistador: Juan de Oñate and the Settling of the Far Southwest*, by Marc Simmons, University of Oklahoma Press, 1991; *A Narrative History of Colonial New Mexico, Arizona, Texas, and California*, by John Kessell, University of Oklahoma Press, 2002; *The Spanish Frontier in North America*, by David Weber, Yale University Press, 1992; and *New Mexico: Past and Future*, by Thomas E. Chávez, University of New Mexico Press, 2006.

52. When a child was born on New Year's Day, what name would traditionally be given to her or him in Hispano families?

Manuela or Manuel, coming from "Immanuel," meaning "God is with us."

Read: "El Día de Los Manueles," *La Herencia*, Winter 2001.

53. On New Year's Day of what year was it reported on the front page of the *Santa Fe New Mexican* that Santa Fe had been "discovered," that it was attracting the affluent, and that a period of unprecedented development had begun?

On New Year's Day of 1982, the *Santa Fe New Mexican* proclaimed that 1982 would be another year for the discovery of Santa Fe, one of the most frequently rediscovered cities in the world. The previous year *Esquire* magazine called Santa Fe "the right place to live" in a cover article.

Read: *The Myth of Santa Fe: Creating a Modern Regional Tradition*, by Chris Wilson, University of New Mexico Press, 1997; and "The Right Place," by Lee Eisenberg, *Esquire*, May 1981.

54. Who was Archbishop Lamy's "adopted" Native American son?

The story of Lamy's adopted son is speculative, but Miguel Lamy probably lived with Bishop Lamy in the late 1860s and was probably born in June of 1861. He may have been a Navajo child who was a survivor of the 1864 forced relocation of nearly eight thousand Navajo men, women, and children from Arizona to Fort Sumner, New Mexico, on what was referred to as the Long Walk. Kit Carson, under orders from General James Carlton, was in charge of this forced relocation, and destitute orphans were sometimes sold off by their extended families to New Mexicans along the march. These orphans were treated as servants or slaves. An arrangement for the Lamy adoption may have occurred when Kit Carson, who was a friend of Lamy's, was in Santa Fe. It is recorded that a Miguel Lamy married Mercedes Ramírez in 1898. There is a story about Miguel fighting off a bear attack and damaging his left arm in the process. He was known to be skilled at making *gamuza* (buckskin). He had several children and listed his occupation at varying times as hunter, wood seller, and herder. He died on August 29, 1938. The legend about his relationship to the archbishop is most likely true.

Read: *Archbishop Lamy: An Epoch Maker*, by Louis H. Warner, Santa Fe New Mexican Publishing Company, 1936; and "The Legend of Miguel Lamy," by Delfina Rodriguez de Foley, *La Herencia*, Spring 2006.

In the bishop's garden, c. 1880. Jean Baptiste Lamy is second from the left, and J. P. Machebeuf is third from the left. Second from the right, in the background, may be the Native American boy Miguel. Courtesy of Palace of the Governors Photo Archives (NMHM/DCA), #049017.

55. Who was considered Santa Fe's first Jewish "mayor"?

Willi Spiegelberg was named probate judge in 1880, a post that included the ceremonial duties of mayor. Spiegelberg and his brothers ran a very successful mercantile business, carrying a variety of goods, from "a pin to a piano," imported from the east and from Europe. They used some of the profits to improve their buildings, which they considered part of their civic duty. By 1872 the Spiegelberg brothers had one of the largest wholesale operations in the West; they eventually expanded their commercial business to include a charter for the Second National Bank of Santa Fe, mail route contracts, mining projects, land speculation, construction, and supplying military posts and Native American agencies.

Willi Spiegelberg was the most politically active of the brothers, and his educated, energetic, and cultured wife, Flora Langerman Spiegelberg, was a great asset to him in his career. They had met and married in Germany, when he was visiting his parents in Nuremberg, where she was being educated. She was seventeen and he was thirty. After a year-long honeymoon through the European cities of Vienna, Munich, Paris, and London, he returned to Santa Fe and his business interests. The couple traveled across the country by steam railway car and then stage coach, arriving in Santa Fe late on a moonlit night in 1875. The popular Willi and his new bride were met by an enthusiastic crowd of Willi's brothers and friends in buggies, on horseback, and even on burros. This group and a band of Mexican musicians accompanied them to Willi's brother's house, where General Devens, commander of the territory, welcomed them with his military band playing "Lohengrin's Wedding March."

Flora Langerman was a dynamic, well-educated young woman at age sixteen, when she became engaged to Willi Spiegelberg in Nuremberg, Germany, in 1873. Originally from New York City but raised in Germany, she was fluent in English, German, and French and had studied Latin and history as well as the piano. Her husband spoke German, Spanish, and English as well as four Native American dialects. He was the youngest of six brothers, all of whom worked in the family mercantile business. Photograph courtesy of Felix and Susan (Spiegelberg) Warburg, San Francisco, California.

Flora Spiegelberg eventually became a pillar of Santa Fe society and an outstanding first lady of Santa Fe. She later said of her arrival in Santa Fe: "At the time I was the eighth [Anglo] woman in Santa Fe. There were about fifty American men, officers and merchants, and a Mexican population of two thousand. Amid clean and happy surroundings, I soon forgot all the privations I had endured and I became a satisfied member of the community."

Flora started the first nonsectectarian children's school, on property she purchased, where she had a three-room schoolhouse built. She created special children's gardens where she taught nature study lessons. She also conducted two religious schools herself; one was a Sabbath school, on Saturdays, for Jewish children, and the other was a Sunday school for Catholic children. (One of her young students was Arthur Seligman, who became governor of New Mexico in 1930.) She and Willi had two daughters, Betty and Rose. She later also wrote children's books and a memoir.

Flora developed passions for the piano, the French language, and gardening, interests she shared with Bishop Lamy, with whom she developed a close friendship. Lamy planted two willow trees with his own hands in the front yard of the Spiegelberg house on Palace Avenue (at the corner of Paseo de Peralta, where a gallery is now) and sent gifts of fruit, wines, and flowers to the Spiegelbergs and other Jewish families on Rosh Hashanah, the Jewish New Year. Lamy also had the four consonants of the Hebrew name for God (the tetragrammaton) inscribed above the entrance to St. Francis Cathedral in gratitude to the Jewish community for its financial support for the cathedral's construction and to honor his friendships within the community.

The official position of mayor was established later, when Santa Fe was incorporated. William T. Thornton was elected the first official mayor of Santa Fe in 1891. For a time a member of the powerful political group called the Santa Fe Ring, Thornton is particularly remembered for trying, unsuccessfully, to have the capital moved from Santa Fe to Albuquerque.

Read: "Alcaldes and Mayors of Santa Fe, 1613–2008," by Albert J. Gallegos and José Antonio Esquibel, in *All Trails Lead to Santa Fe*, Sunstone Press, 2010; *The Far Southwest, 1846–1912*, by Howard R. Lamar, Yale University Press, 1966; "Flora Spiegelberg: Grand Lady of the Southwest Frontier," *Southwest Jewish History*, Winter 1992; *Jewish Pioneers of New Mexico*, compiled and edited by Tomas Jaehn, Museum of New Mexico Press, 2003. Also, see the "Spiegelberg Family Collection, 1871–1880," in the Fray Angélico Chávez History Library. Thornton's papers are in the State Records Center and Archives, in Santa Fe.

The Spiegelberg brothers, left to right: Willi, Emmanuel, Solomon Jacob, Levi, and Lehman, c. 1865–1870. Elias, the sixth brother, had died before the photograph was taken. The Spiegelberg firm was one of the largest in Santa Fe in the late-nineteenth century. Photograph by Sarony. Courtesy of Palace of the Governors Photo Archives (NMHM/DCA), #011025.

The Spiegelberg Brothers storefront, on the south side of the Santa Fe Plaza, c. 1885. Courtesy of Palace of the Governors Photo Archives (NMHM/DCA), #150156.

56. Which Fiesta Queen lived to be more than a hundred years old?

Amelia Sena Sánchez was the Santa Fe Fiesta Queen in 1927. She died in 2003, at the age of 109.

Read: "Confessions of a Fiesta Queen," by Kathryn M. Córdova, *La Herencia*, Fall 2002; and *Turn Left at the Sleeping Dog: Scripting the Santa Fe Legend, 1920–1955*, by John Pen La Farge, University of New Mexico Press, 2001.

A Fiesta Queen and her attendants float during the Historical Parade, Fiesta, 1952.
The queen that year was Maria Rosina Casados. Photograph by Natt N. Dodge.
Courtesy of Palace of the Governors Photo Archives (NMHM/DCA), #106557.

57. What was the name of the well-known and popular bar in the 1950s and 1960s where gay men and lesbians were openly welcomed?

Claude's Bar, on Canyon Road. It was run by Claude James. Later there was the Senate Lounge, downtown.

Read: "Claude's Bar and Other Legends," by Soledad Santiago, *Santa Fe New Mexican*, September 29, 2006.

58. Who was the original founder of the Pink Adobe restaurant, and where was she from?

Rosalea Stevens Murphy, a successful artist from New Orleans, came to Santa Fe in the 1940s. She opened the restaurant in 1944, and it has been in the Murphy family for three generations. Another Santa Fe restaurant that has been owned by one family for three generations is The Shed—its sister restaurant's name, La Choza, means "the shed" in Spanish.

Read: "50 Years in the Pink," by John Villani, *Santa Fe New Mexican*, July 8, 1994. For a current list of Santa Fe restaurants, visit the website urbanspoon.com.

59. Who attended the Governor's Ball, at the Palace of the Governors, in 1839?

Everyone. "All the beauty and fashion attended and all the rabble, for, true to their republican principles, none can be refused admission," commented a visiting U.S. citizen who attended Governor Manuel Armijo's ball. The stratifications of early nineteenth-century Santa Fe society were blurred in social situations; this version of a democratic society grew out of the necessity of having to help each other by sharing resources in order to survive.

Read: "When Santa Fe Was a Mexican Town: 1821 to 1846," by Janet LeCompte and Joseph P. Sánchez, in *Santa Fe: History of an Ancient City*, edited by David Grant Noble, School for Advanced Research Press, 2008.

Baile. Pen and ink drawing by Harold E. West, c. 1930s.

60. How did Santa Fe's state-of-the-art, nonprofit performing arts center, the Lensic, get its name?

In the 1930s, a Mrs. P. I. Smithwick received twenty-five dollars for her winning-entry response to an open call from the owner, Nathan Salmon, for the theater's name. "Lensic" uses the initials of Salmon's grandchildren (Salmons and Greers): Lila, Elias (John) Jr., Nathan, Sara, (Mary) Irene, and Charles.

Read: "Anchor for the Arts," by Devon Jackson, *Santa Fean*, February/March 2011.

61. What street in Santa Fe was on the verge of becoming a hangout for artists beginning in the 1950s, and how much did an average apartment there cost to rent?

Canyon Road, $25 to $30 a month.

Read: "On the Road Again: Old Friends, Traditions on View, Celebrating Canyon Road's Impressionists," by Emeliana Sandoval, *Santa Fe New Mexican*, October 7, 1994.

Early 1900s along Canyon Road. El Zaguán is on the right.
Courtesy of Palace of the Governors Photo Archives (NMHM/DCA), #031821.

62. Where were some of the first garages and dealerships for motor cars in Santa Fe? And who is the patron saint of the kitchen?

In the early 1900s, near the southwest corner of Sandoval and West San Francisco Streets, O. W. Anderson had a dealership that had a garage where he also did repairs. The first Ford motor cars became available in 1903. Earl Mays was a Ford dealer who had his office at 102 East Palace Avenue. On the northeast corner of Don Gaspar Avenue and Water Street was a repair garage with gas pumps. By 1930 this garage property became a restaurant called the K. C. Waffle House, owned by Gus Mitchell. It was later replaced by the Mayflower Café. In the 1970s it became the Golden Temple Conscious Cookery and then, briefly, Pogo's Eatery. In 1978 it became and has remained Café Pasqual, named for the patron saint of the kitchen, San Pascual Bailon. If a cook is having trouble in the kitchen, as when the biscuits don't rise or the chile burns, he or she may remember San Pasqual and proceed more carefully, more mindfully, and the saint may help. Other saints who may help in the kitchen are Elizabeth, Marta, and Michael.

Read: *Santa Fe: A Pictorial History*, by John Sherman, Donning Company, 1996; *How to Live Well without Owning a Car*, by Chris Balish, Ten Speed Press, 2006; and *Saints and Seasons: A Guide to New Mexico's Most Popular Saints*, by Ana Pacheco, Gran Via, 2005.

Interior of the K. C. Waffle House, at Don Gaspar Avenue and Water Street. Photograph by T. Harmon Parkhurst, c. 1925–1945. Courtesy of Palace of the Governors Photo Archives (NMHM/DCA), #050968.

63. What was the name for the system used by the early Spanish colonists to receive tribute payments and labor from the Pueblo peoples?

In early colonial times the *encomienda* system permitted the governor to give grants to individuals to collect tribute from the Native Americans. These *encomenderos* received the tribute in return for providing protection and education. If the tribute could not be collected in kind, then the amount due was converted to a value of time that could be paid in labor, under the *repartimiento* system. This system was intended to benefit all involved. According to the Laws of the Indies, all native labor was paid. However, this did not always occur.

Read: "Indian Slavery and the Birth of Genizaros," by Ramón A Gutiérrez, in *White Shell Water Place*, Sunstone Press, 2010; "Indian Slavery: The Genízaros of New Mexico," by Jason Silverman, *Native Peoples*, July/August 2011; *Captives and Cousins: Slavery, Kinship, and Community in the Southwest Borderlands*, by James F. Brooks, University of North Carolina Press, 2002; "The Vargas Encomienda," by Lansing B. Bloom, *New Mexico Historical Review*, October 1939; and "The Vargas Encomienda," in *That Disturbances Cease: The Journals of Don Diego de Vargas, New Mexico*, edited by John L. Kessell, Rick Hendricks, and Meredith D. Dodge, University of New Mexico Press, 2000.

64. What local performer popularized flamenco music in Santa Fe in the 1960s?

Vicente Romero. His brother was the guitarist Ruben Romero. María Benítez and her dance troupe have continued and expanded Romero's legacy, and Santa Fe is host to various other troupes and flamenco artists as well.

Read: *¡Olé! Flamenco*, by George Ancona, Lee & Low Books, 2010.

65. What city park was named the Martin Luther King Jr. Park and when?

Located at Calle Serena (*serena* means "peaceful"), near Rodeo Road and Camino Carlos Rey, the park was dedicated on August 28, 2007. Martin Luther King Jr. was a visionary thinker who influenced millions of people to find ways to do the right thing, especially in relation to multiracial understanding among differing groups. As a minister, an activist, and a leader in the African-American Civil Rights movement of the 1960s, he stood for peaceful solutions to complex problems. His most famous speech, "I Have a Dream," given in Washington, D.C., on August 28, 1963, called for racial equality and an end to discrimination. He said, "Injustice anywhere is a threat to justice everywhere."

Read: "New City Park Will Be Named for MLK," by Julie Ann Grimm, *Santa Fe New Mexican*, July 26, 2007; *El Día de Martin Luther King, Jr.*, by Mir Tamim Ansary, Heinemann Library, 2003; and *I May Not Get There With You: The True Martin Luther King, Jr.*, by Michael Eric Dyson, Free Press, 2000.

66. Who said, "Every calculation based on experience elsewhere fails in New Mexico"?

General, diplomat, attorney, artist, author, Chautauqua lecturer, and New Mexico territorial governor Lew Wallace is credited with this admiring complaint. Wallace wrote the classic novel *Ben Hur*, published in 1880, while he resided in the Palace of the Governors. The book has never been out of print, and years later it was made into a successful Broadway play and a popular movie. His wife, Susan Elston Wallace, wrote *Land of the Pueblos*.

Ben Hur was the second-most popular work of fiction during the nineteenth century. The most popular was *Uncle Tom's Cabin, or Life among the Lowly*, the anti-slavery novel by Harriet Beecher Stowe. Her novel originally appeared as a forty-week serial, beginning in June of 1851, in *National Era*, an abolitionist periodical; it was published in book form by John Jewett in 1852. The first widely read political novel in the United States, the book and its impact were criticized by slavery supporters but praised by abolitionists. Two later protest-literature books said to have been influenced by *Uncle Tom's Cabin* are *The Jungle*, by Upton Sinclair, and *Silent Spring*, by Rachel Carson.

Read: *The Sword and the Pen: A Life of Lew Wallace*, by Ray Boomhower, Indian Historical Society, 2005; "N.M. Supplied Lew and Susan Wallace with Plenty of Stories to Record," by Marc Simmons, *Santa Fe New Mexican*, May 25, 2002; *Ben Hur: A Tale of the Christ*, by Lew Wallace, Modern Library, 2002; *The Land of the Pueblos*, by Susan E. Wallace, Sunstone Press, 2006; *Uncle Tom's Cabin*, by Harriet Beecher Stowe, Barnes & Noble Classics, 2003; and "Truth or Legend? In Santa Fe, Sometimes It's Hard to Know the Difference," by Barbara Harrelson, *Santa Fe New Mexican*, May 15, 2011.

67. What happened to the old post office building after the post office moved to its current location on Federal Place?

In 1990 the Institute of American Indian Arts opened their Museum of Contemporary Native Arts (MoCNA) in the building, which was updated to accommodate the museum while preserving its Pueblo-style architecture. The building is located downtown, opposite the Cathedral Basilica of Saint Francis, east of the Plaza.

Read: *Creativity Is Our Tradition: Three Decades of Contemporary Indian Art at the Institute of America Indian Arts*, by Rick Hill, Nancy Marie Mitchell, and Lloyd New, R. R. Donnelley & Sons, 1992.

U.S. Post Office and Federal Building, Cathedral Place, c. 1934.
Courtesy of Palace of the Governors Photo Archives (NMHM/DCA), #056431.

68. Who boasted that Santa Fe, which he referred to as a "City Beautiful," was the first city in the New Mexico Territory to have paved streets; proudly noted the "civic usefulness of women" because the Women's Board of Trade was supporting the public library and caring for the Plaza, the only decent park in town at the time; and suggested that a municipal bathhouse would be beneficial to civic life?

Mayor Arthur Seligman wrote the *First Annual Report of the Mayor of Santa Fe* in 1911. The report also contains a request for a complete sewerage system by the Sewer Committee. The chairman, Roman L. Baca, and committee members Canuto Alarid and Charles A. Wheelon mentioned that several territorial buildings, including the capitol and the executive mansion, were discharging their sewage into the Santa Fe River, which was deemed not only illegal but unhealthy for the community.

Read: *First Annual Report of the Mayor of Santa Fe, April 1st, 1910 to March 31st, 1911*, by Mayor Arthur Seligman, New Mexican Printing Company, 1911.

What Is It?
(See Answer Key #9)

Left (top) and right (bottom) halves of a panoramic view of Santa Fe, looking northeast from the state capitol, 1916. Courtesy of Palace of the Governors Photo Archives (NMHM/DCA), #010144 and #010148.

69. Why did the photographer Tyler Dingee airbrush one of his photographs of the Palace of the Governors in the spring of 1960?

Dingee airbrushed a photograph of the Palace of the Governors to remove unattractive nonhistoric paraphernalia, including telephone lines, in order to present to the U.S. Post Office a photograph that they could use for a stamp to commemorate the 350th anniversary of the founding of Santa Fe. The first day covers were issued in Santa Fe on June 17, 1960.

Other stamps honoring Santa Fe artists include pottery images painted by Ford Ruthling and, more recently, the "Willie and Joe" characters created by Bill Mauldin. As part of the post office's American Treasures series, four New Mexican Rio Grande rugs were featured in 2004.

A commenorative stamp honoring New Mexico's centennial of statehood was issued in Santa Fe on January 6, 2012, featuring a landscape painting by Doug West titled *Sanctuary*.

Read: *Santa Fe: A Pictorial History*, by John Sherman, Donning Company, 1996.

70. Which street in downtown Santa Fe starts as a one-way street heading west at its eastern end, then briefly becomes a two-way street, then a one-way street heading east in the middle, and then becomes a two-way street at its western end?

Water Street.

See for yourself.

71. Santa Fe used to be an oasis, with plentiful water from the Santa Fe River, as well as marshes, springs, and ponds. Water Street was named for what waterway?

The Río Chiquito, which was fed by springs, joined the Santa Fe River and ran near where Water Street is today. Another water-related street name, Cienega Street, is three blocks east of the Plaza. *Ciénega* means "swamp." The higher water table in this area has been a challenge to builders of large downtown projects.

Read: *The Return of the River: Writers, Scholars, and Citizens Speak on Behalf of the Santa Fe River*, edited by A. Kyce Bello, Sunstone Press, 2011; *The Santa Fe Acequia Systems: Summary Report on Their History and Present Status*, by David H. Snow, City of Santa Fe Planning Department, 1988; and "Water Problem Demands Thought, Cooperation," by Consuelo Bokum and Edward Archuleta, *Santa Fe New Mexican*, October 25, 2000.

72. What are the names of the Santa Fe River reservoirs that supply the City of Santa Fe with some of its water?

Nichols Reservoir and McClure Reservoir are located in the Santa Fe Canyon watershed. A third reservoir was drained because of a crack in the dam wall. Called "Two Mile Dam," it had been made of earth tamped down by goats. The Canyon Road water treatment plant treats water from the Santa Fe River reservoirs. Other places from which Santa Feans get their water include private wells; the Santa Fe city well field, southwest of the downtown area; the Buckman well field, near the Rio Grande; and the Buckman Direct Diversion Project, one of the largest, most complex, and most expensive non-federal infrastructure projects ever built in Santa Fe County, co-owned by the City of Santa Fe and Santa Fe County.

Into the twentieth century, one could drink water from the Rio Grande without concern. This is no longer the case. Amigos Bravos, Friends of the Wild Rivers is a New Mexico nonprofit organization dedicated to restoring and preserving the Rio Grande and other New Mexico rivers and watersheds.

See the City of Santa Fe website. Also read *Water: The Epic Struggle for Wealth, Power, and Civilization*, by Steven Solomon, Harper, 2010.

What Is It?
(See Answer Key #10)

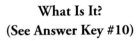

73. Whose 1704 will reveals a bequest to the deceased's friends and family of more than one hundred pounds of chocolate and sugar, a sign of wealth at the time?

Don Diego de Vargas was born in Spain and died at age sixty, during his second term as governor of the Província de Nuevo México. His will also listed an impressive wardrobe, imported fabrics, books, swords, trunks, chests, table linens and tableware, and silver candlesticks, among other items. (In 1694 he reported several luxury items that had been stolen from a storage room in the Palace of the Governors, including soap, sweets, boots, and elegant silver-trimmed coconut shells, which were used as chocolate cups.)

Vargas's full name was Diego de Vargas Zapata y Luján Ponce de León y Contreras y Salinas. In the last years of his life he used the title conferred on him by the king of Spain: Marqués de la Nava de Barcinas.

Read: "The Palace of the Governors: A Witness to History," by Frances Levine, in *Santa Fe: History of an Ancient City*, edited by David Grant Noble, School for Advanced Research Press, 2008.

This vessel, with a locking iron lid, served as a storage jar for chocolate and attests to the value of that commodity during the Spanish Colonial period. Mayólica *chocolatero*, Puebla, Mexico, 1700s. Courtesy of History Collections, NMHM, DCA, museum purchase.

74. What was the name of the Santa Fe school for girls that operated from 1853 to 1968 and stressed "ladylike comportment and moral behavior"?

The Loretto Academy for Girls, first called the Academy of Our Lady of Light, was run by the Sisters of Loretto, a Catholic religious order originally founded by an Englishwoman, Mary Ward, in 1609. The Sisters of Loretto were invited to Santa Fe by Bishop Lamy in 1852. They came from Kentucky, where they had been part of one of the first U.S. communities of sisters dedicated to teaching. "La Casa Americana" was how people referred to the home of Bishop Lamy, which he turned over to the Sisters of Loretto shortly after they arrived in Santa Fe. The building was called that because it had a pitched, shingled roof, whereas adobe buildings had flat roofs.

Read: *Loretto: The Sisters and Their Chapel*, by Mary Jean Straw Cook, Museum of New Mexico Press, 2002; *Beyond the Adobe Wall: The Sisters of Loretto in New Mexico, 1852–1894*, by Patricia Jean Manion, Two Trails, 2001; *Loretto and the Miraculous Staircase*, by Alice Bullock, Sunstone Press, 1978; "Loretto Academy Reunion Sparks Fond Memories," by Anne Constable, *Santa Fe New Mexican*, July 23, 2000; and *Loretto: Annals of the Century*, by Anna Catherine Minogue, Kessinger, 2007 (first published 1912).

75. Where was Billy the Kid jailed in Santa Fe in 1881, and what map shows the jail?

An early Sanborn map shows the jail, off Water Street and west of Galisteo Street. There is a plaque on the wall of the Collected Works bookstore, on Water Street, to show where the jail was located. (There has been another plaque elsewhere in the downtown area claiming the same, but it is not accurate.)

See the digital Sanborn map, October 1883, sheet 2, in the Southwest Collections at the New Mexico State Library.

76. In what year was New Mexico's first penitentiary built, and where was it located?

Construction began in 1885 on the state penitentiary on Pen Road, near what is now the intersection of Cerrillos Road and St. Francis Drive, then the outskirts of town.

Read: "Necessity for a Penitentiary," *Santa Fe New Mexican*, February 25, 1884; and "The New Mexico Penitentiary," by Marc Simmons, *Santa Fe Reporter*, July 29, 1998.

Buildings under construction at the state penitentiary on Pen Road. Photograph by Thomas J. Curran, c. 1890. Courtesy of Palace of the Governors Photo Archives (NMHM/DCA), #015208.

77. In 1884 Santa Fe's mammoth new roller-skating rink was lit with what?

Gaslights.

Read: "Beauty on Wheels," *Santa Fe New Mexican*, December 6, 1884; and *The Book of Non-Electric Lighting: The Classic Guide to the Safe Use of Candles, Fuel Lamps, Lanterns, Gas Lights, and Fireview Stoves*, by Tim Matson, Countryman Press, 2008.

78. Who was the rich land baron from the east who founded the first bank established in New Mexico?

Charles Lucien B. Maxwell was an Illinois fur trapper. In 1864 Maxwell and his wife, Luz Beaubien, became sole owners of land that had originally been territory of the Apaches, Utes, and later the Comanche. This land had been granted in 1843 by Governor Manuel Armijo to Luz's father, Charles Beaubien, and Guadaloupe Miranda. After consolidation, the Maxwells owned one of the largest privately controlled parcels of land in the world, known as the Maxwell Land Grant. Maxwell founded the First National Bank of Santa Fe in 1870, when there was no other bank within four hundred miles.

Read: *The Man Who Owned Too Much: Maxwell's Land Grant. Together with an 1895 Newspaper Account of the Life of Lucien Maxwell*, by Jack DeVere Rittenhouse, Stagecoach Press, 1958; and *Maxwell Land Grant*, by William A. Keleher, Sunstone Press, 2008 (first published 1942).

Cartoon by Ricardo Caté, part of a series called "Without Reservations," which has appeared in the *Santa Fe New Mexican*. Caté is from Santo Domingo/Kewa Pueblo. Courtesy of the artist.

79. Sena and Apodaca are surnames of people who worked in what important profession in Santa Fe?

Blacksmithing.

Bernardino de Sena arrived in the Santa Fe area as a child in about 1694, after travelling north from Mexico City with his foster parents. The Sena family originally owned property on the south side of the Santa Fe River, east of San Miguel Church. Bernardino probably apprenticed to become a blacksmith as a young man. He married Tomasa Gonzalez, invested in real estate, and was a respected member of Santa Fe society. He and his only son, Tómas, started a blacksmithing dynasty that continued with several of Tómas's sons and beyond.

In the 1830s a descendent, Ramón Sena, and another smith, José Castillo, taught the craft to several Navajo men who wanted to make their own horse bits. The art of blacksmithing spread rapidly among the Navajo tribe and led to their skills as fine silver jewelry artisans. The last of the Sena blacksmith clan was Abrán Sena, who closed his shop across from Guadalupe Church in the 1920s.

Manuel Apodaca had a blacksmith shop off Upper Canyon Road, on what came to be called Apodaca Hill. He used the shop for over forty years, starting in the 1930s. Although horseshoeing was his main work, his mastery included the rare skills of wheelwright, which involve the construction of wooden wagon wheels and the "shrinking on" of iron tires. Many Santa Fe burro carts rolled on wheels made on Apodaca Hill. A great-nephew, Andres (Andy) Apodaca, has followed in Manuel's footsteps.

Read: *Southwestern Colonial Ironwork: The Spanish Blacksmithing Tradition*, by Marc Simmons and Frank Turley, Sunstone Press, 2007; *Blacksmithing: Basics for the Homestead*, by Joe DeLaRonde, Gibbs Smith, 2008; *The Sena Family: Blacksmiths of Santa Fe*, by Marc Simmons, Press of the Palace of the Governors, 1981; and "The Blacksmith Is Alive and Well," by George W. Emlen, *Santa Fe New Mexican*, April 16, 1972.

Santa Fe blacksmith Manuel Apodaca.
Photograph by Bob LaRouche, 1958.
Courtesy of Palace of the Governors Photo Archives
(NMHM/DCA), #006996.

80. Why did the Harrington Junior High School Drum and Bugle Corps return to Santa Fe earlier than planned from a trip to celebrate Governor's Day at Carlsbad Caverns in 1939?

When a racist comment singled out some darker-skinned students who were members of the Drum and Bugle Corps, at a municipal pool where the group had stopped on the way home, Kermit Hill, the teacher in charge, organized an immediate departure in protest. Later an appropriate apology was issued.

See photograph of the Harrington Junior High School Drum and Bugle Corps, 1938–39.

The Harrington Junior High School Drum and Bugle Corps, 1938–39.
Photographer unknown. Courtesy R. Kermit Hill Jr.

81. Who was among the first citizens from the United States to surreptitiously enter, as an illegal, undocumented visitor, the Spanish province of New Mexico, and to describe what he saw?

Explorer Lieutenant Zebulon Montgomery Pike Jr. was perhaps the first Anglo American "tourist" to visit the dramatic Southwest and to write about Santa Fe. In around 1806 he was arrested in what is now Colorado, by Spanish soldiers from Santa Fe. Under guard, he and his men were led south, first to Santa Fe, where he was entertained, still under guard, at dinner in the Palace of the Governors, then on to Chihuahua, during which time he saw the settlements of New Spain along the Rio Grande. Later, Pike and his men were released into U.S. custody at the Louisiana border.

Pike was the first writer from the United States to describe Santa Fe to readers. (He never climbed the peak in Colorado named for him.) The trading expeditions of Baptiste La Lande, Laurent Durocher, and James Purcell all made it to Santa Fe from 1804 to 1805 before being arrested, but they left no written material describing their travels.

Read: *The Southwestern Journals of Zebulon Pike, 1806–1807*, edited by Stephen Harding Hart and Archer Butler Hulbert, University of New Mexico Press, 2006; and *The Expedition of Zebulon Montgomery Pike to the Headwaters of the Mississippi River through Louisiana Territory, and in New Spain during the Years 1805–1807*, edited by Elliott Coues, Ross & Haines, 1965 (first published 1895).

82. Who was the citizen from the United States who "trespassed" into what he thought was Spanish territory only to discover that the area had become part of the recently independent country of Mexico, and that trade with the United States would be welcome?

William Becknell was the "trespasser" and entrepreneur, and the year was 1821. Becknell is considered the "father of the Santa Fe Trail" since he was the first to gain by legal trade after travelling back along the Santa Fe Trail from Santa Fe to Missouri.

Read: *Southwest on the Turquoise Trail: The First Diaries on the Road to Santa Fe*, edited by Archer Butler Hulbert, Colorado College, 1933; and "Remembering William Becknell, The Father of the Santa Fe Trail," by Marc Simmons, *Santa Fe New Mexican*, July 9, 2005.

83. Who said "See America First" and meant New Mexico?

Charles F. Lummis. He made a name for himself when he walked all the way from Cincinnati, Ohio, to Los Angeles, California, on his attention-getting "tramp across the continent." He arrived in February of 1885, after walking for 143 days over more than thirty-five hundred miles, wearing the one set of clothes he had selected for the trip, which included a white flannel shirt tied at the neck with a blue ribbon, knickerbockers, red knee-high stockings, a wide-brimmed felt hat, and low-cut dress shoes. He was an eccentric and charming character who didn't mind if people made fun of him. But he also championed Native American rights and Hispanic culture and helped found the School of American Research (now the School for Advanced Research). He was a colleague of Adolph Bandelier, a good friend of Amado Chaves (son of don Manuel Antonio Chaves), and a friend of Teddy Roosevelt, who admired his gumption. And he was a journalist, a poet, a librarian, a photographer, and an author. Perhaps his most famous book is *The Land of Poco Tiempo*. He was also the folklorist who wrote *The Man Who Married the Moon, and Other Pueblo Indian Folk-Stories*.

Read: *American Character: The Curious Life of Charles Fletcher Lummis and the Rediscovery of the Southwest*, by Mark Thompson, Arcade, 2001; *Charles F. Lummis: Author and Adventurer, A Gathering*, by Marc Simmons, Sunstone Press, 2008; and *The Land of Poco Tiempo*, by Charles Fletcher Lummis, University of New Mexico Press, 1952 (first published 1893).

Charles F. Lummis wearing the Orden de Isabel la Católica, 1917. Courtesy of Palace of the Governors Photo Archives (NMHM/DCA), #007700.

84. What transformative event in 1680 centered on Santa Fe?

The Pueblo Revolt, which is sometimes referred to as "the Pueblos' Holy War," officially began on August 10, 1680. The Spaniards were driven from Santa Fe and northern Nuevo México south to El Paso del Norte (now Juarez, Mexico); they did not return until 1692. Some historians have said that the Pueblo Revolt was the first successful battle for independence fought against a European colonial power (in this case, Spain) in what was to become the United States.

In 1682 the Spanish royal attorney in Mexico City, Martín Solís de Miranda, stated that he thought the oppression of the Native Americans by the Spaniards was the main reason for the rebellion.

Read: *Indian Uprising on the Rio Grande*, by Frank Folsom, University of New Mexico Press, 1996; *Pueblos, Spaniards, and the Kingdom of New Mexico*, by John L. Kessell, University of Oklahoma Press, 2008; *The Pueblo Revolt*, by Robert Silverberg, University of Nebraska Press, 1994; *Pueblo Nations: Eight Centuries of Pueblo Indian History*, by Joe S. Sando, Clear Light, 1992; *The Pueblo Revolt: The Secret Rebellion That Drove the Spaniards Out of the Southwest*, by David Roberts, Simon & Schuster, 2005; and "The Pueblo Revolt: Why Did It Happen?" by Marc Simmons, in *Spanish Pathways: Readings in the History of Hispanic New Mexico*, University of New Mexico Press, 2001.

85. Who was the Pueblo leader from Ohkay Owingeh (formerly called San Juan Pueblo) who is famous for coordinating and leading the 1680 uprising against the Spanish colonizers that led to the protracted Pueblo-Spanish War of 1680 to 1696?

Po'pay. He was the respected medicine man who coordinated the revolt with more than a dozen leaders from about twenty-five pueblos. He was a fierce, dynamic, and charismatic leader who inspired a core group of followers; little else is known about him.

Spanish rule of the Pueblo people had begun in 1598, and suppression of dissent and occasionally severe treatment led to unrest. In 1675 Po'pay and more than forty other spiritual leaders were taken to Santa Fe to be punished for participating in their own religious and cultural ceremonies, which some Spaniards considered "witchcraft." After this humiliation, a rebellion was planned.

The date chosen was August 11, 1680, but the Pueblo Rebellion began a day earlier because the timing was betrayed to the Spaniards. Of special note is the successful use of knotted ropes delivered by runners to each pueblo involved in the planned uprising. (The longest distance was the 400 miles to the Hopi mesas.) The number of knots corresponded to the number of days left before the revolt was to begin. An unknown number of Pueblo people perished in the combat with the besieged colonists in Santa Fe. The revolt cost about four hundred Spanish lives, including twenty-one of the thirty-three priests in New Mexico.

Most of the remaining Spaniards made the long trek to what is now Juarez, Mexico. The rebellion drove the Spanish from what is now Colorado, Arizona, and New Mexico.

Although the Spanish did eventually succeed in returning to reclaim Santa Fe and New Mexico in 1692, relations were far different after the war: the *encomienda* system of tribute that had often illegally used forced labor was prohibited, and Pueblo warriors and Spanish soldiers were brought together against their common enemies, including the Apaches, Navajos, Utes, and Comanche. And not all Spaniards and Pueblos had been in opposition to each other, since there were many ties of family and kinship between them.

The Pueblo-Spanish War lasted about sixteen years, beginning with the initial rebellion by the Pueblos in 1680, through the reconquest effort by the Spaniards in 1692, and ending with a second revolt in 1696. Ultimately, Spaniards and Pueblos developed a kind of tolerable coexistence in order to share the kingdom of New Mexico. As a result, more blending of Pueblo and Spanish cultures in New Mexico has occurred.

Po'pay died in about 1688.

Read: *Po'pay: Leader of the First American Revolution*, edited by Joe S. Sando and Herman Agoyo, Clear Light, 2005; "Ohkay Owingeh: New Mexico's First Capital," by Storyteller Kaafedeh–Blowing Leaf (Herman Agoyo), in *White Shell Water Place*, Sunstone Press, 2010; "New Mexico Under Popé," in *The Pueblo Revolt*, by Robert Silverberg, University of Nebraska Press, 1994; *Pueblos, Spaniards, and the Kingdom of New Mexico*, by John L. Kessell, University of Oklahoma Press, 2008; and *Pueblo Nations: Eight Centuries of Pueblo Indian History*, by Joe S. Sando, Clear Light, 1992.

Po'pay. Carved marble statue by Cliff Fragua, 2005. The seven-foot tall statue was donated by New Mexico to the National Statuary Hall Collection, in the U.S. Capitol. A bronze statue of Dennis Chavez, by Felex W. de Weldon, is the other statue representing New Mexico in Washington, D.C. Photograph courtesy of Clear Light Publishing.

86. Why was the Santa Fe Trail important?

The Santa Fe Trail, opened in 1821, was one of the first established international routes of commerce and travel in North America. After the strict Spanish control of trade, the relative freedom to travel and trade under the Mexican government encouraged more than the exchange of commercial goods; interest in new social mores and shared appreciation of each other's cultures blossomed between Mexico and the United States. This mutual exchange of ideas and commerce, however, was at first not open to Texas. It was Mexican governor Manuel Armijo who supposedly lamented, in 1841, "Poor New Mexico! So far from Heaven, so close to Texas!" (Later another version of this sentiment was reportedly stated by General Porfirio Díaz, president of Mexico from 1877 to 1880 and again from 1884 to 1911, about the United States' war with Mexico, from 1846 to 1848: "Poor Mexico! So far from God and so close to the United States!")

Santa Fe has been described as eclectic; this quality was also present in the 1800s, when travel and trade over the Santa Fe Trail provided opportunities to obtain the best items available from foreign sources, and different cultures intermingled.

Read: *Following the Santa Fe Trail: A Guide for Modern Travelers*, by Marc Simmons and Hal Jackson, Ancient City Press, 2001; *The Santa Fe Trail in American History*, by William R. Sanford, Enslow Publishers, 2000; *The Santa Fe Trail: Its History, Legends, and Lore*, by David Dary, Knopf, 2000; *Along the Santa Fe Trail*, by Joan Myers, University of New Mexico Press, 1986; *Tracing the Santa Fe Trail: Today's Views, Yesterday's Voices*, by Ronald J. Dulle, Mountain Press, 2011; *Eating Up the Santa Fe Trail: Recipes and Lore from the Old West*, by Samuel P. Arnold, Fulcrum Publishing, 2001; and *Changing National Identities at the Frontier: Texas and New Mexico, 1800–1850*, by Andrés Reséndez, Cambridge University Press, 2004.

After a long journey on the Santa Fe Trail, the caravan arrival in Santa Fe was a relief and exciting for all travelers who had successfully completed the arduous trip. The townspeople of Santa Fe looked forward to the wagon trains and caravans arriving from foreign lands with news and trade goods.
Courtesy of Palace of the Governors Photo Archives (NMHM/DCA), #045011.

Santa Fe Trail marker along Old Santa Fe Trail.

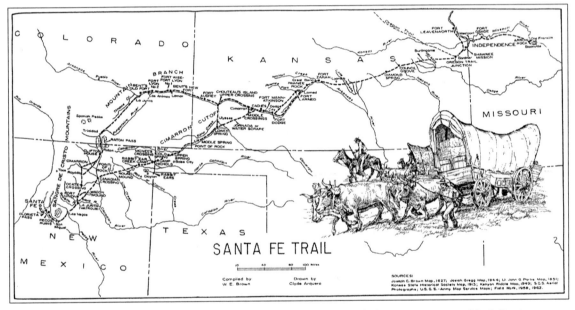

Map of the Santa Fe Trail, compiled by W. E. Brown and drawn by Clyde Arquero, National Park Service 1963 Historic Sites Survey. The Santa Fe Trail was proclaimed a National Historic Trail in 1987.

87. About how long is the Santa Fe Trail, and how much time would it take to ride its length in a stagecoach?

The Santa Fe Trail is about nine hundred miles long, stretching from Franklin, east of Westport, Missouri, to Santa Fe; it took about two weeks to travel all the way by stagecoach.

Read: "The Lost World of Stagecoaching: A Lurching Ride in a Picturesque Icon," by Marc Simmons, *Santa Fe New Mexican*, November 13, 2004; and *Stagecoach: Wells Fargo and the American West*, by Philip L. Fradkin, Simon & Schuster Source, 2002.

88. Why and when did the Santa Fe Trail lose its importance?

The railway system arrived in Santa Fe in 1880, replacing wagon and foot travel. The Santa Fe Trail officially ran between the head of navigation on the Missouri River, at Westport (later called Kansas City), and Santa Fe. Once railroad construction began, the trail was between the railhead, wherever it happened to be, and Santa Fe. The day the first train pulled into Santa Fe was the day the Santa Fe Trail died.

Read: "When the Railroad Came to Territorial New Mexico," by Marc Simmons, *Santa Fe New Mexican*, December 3, 2005; and *The Transcontinental Railroad*, by Elaine Landau, Franklin Watts, 2005.

89. Why did the Santa Fe Tertio-Millennial Grand Mining and Industrial Exposition of 1883 take place, and where is the so-called "oldest house" popular tourist attraction located?

The Santa Fe Tertio-Millennial (one third of a thousand years) event was concocted to promote the New Mexico Territory and attract investors and tourists. The year 1883 was believed to be the 333rd anniversary of the city's founding, and the event lasted for thirty-three days. The mythical date of 1550 may have been dreamed up based on an erroneous story featuring the explorer Francisco Vásquez de Coronado establishing his headquarters in a Native American pueblo on the site of Santa Fe. Santa Fe residents took part in the pageants, two infantry bands played marches, and more than a thousand New Mexican Native Americans participated in the festivities, including Mescalero Apaches, Navajos, Utes, and many of the Pueblos. The exposition grounds were inside a third-of-a-mile long roadway for horse and burro racing, whose length continued the Tertio-Millennial theme of thirds. The racetrack was later used by Santa Fe High School. Today the streets surrounding the federal courthouse and the main U.S. Post Office follow the old racetrack (South Federal Place, Grant Avenue, Paseo de Peralta, and Washington Avenue).

The so-called "oldest house," on East De Vargas Street, near Old Santa Fe Trail, was part of the tourist promotion then, as it continues to be today. Dendrochronological studies of the beams in the house date the structure to around 1763, but it was erroneously imagined to be the remains of part of an ancient Native American settlement. Very few standing structures or walls in Santa Fe predate the early 1700s.

The flamboyant celebration of the city, complete with falsehoods and various entertaining misconceptions, drew thousands of visitors from all parts of the nation.

Read: "N.M. Had Hearty Festival on Imagined Anniversary," by Marc Simmons, *Santa Fe New Mexican*, July 29, 2006; *Santa Fe Tales and More*, by Howard Bryan, Clear Light, 2010; *The Myth of Santa Fe: Creating a Modern Regional Tradition*, by Chris Wilson, University of New Mexico Press, 1997; and "Urban Legends," by Barbara Harrelson, *Santa Fe New Mexican*, May 18, 2011.

A wood-engraved illustration, based on a photograph by Henry Brown, showing the Exposition Hall, part of the Santa Fe Tertio-Millennial events of 1883. The image appeared in *Frank Leslie's Illustrated Newspaper,* on June 28, 1883. Illustrations were a popular way of conveying information during the late-nineteenth century. According to the newspaper, "The Exposition . . . illustrated the growth of American ideas, the progress of American ingenuity, in an essentially foreign community under peculiarly unfavorable conditions . . . . [T]hree civilizations are more or less strikingly represented—the Pueblo Indians, with their surviving Aztec customs, the quaint architecture and curious manners of Spain, and the magic industrial triumphs of our own country and time."

A romantic drawing of the "oldest house" that was circulated at the time of the Tertio-Millennial.

"Oldest house in the United States," 1888. Photograph by Dana B. Chase.
Courtesy of Palace of the Governors Photo Archives (NMHM/DCA), #14044.

"Oldest house," 2011, in the shadow of San Miguel Mission Church.

90. Where is the "oldest church in the United States"?

According to the tourism promotion begun during the Tertio-Millennial of 1883, the "oldest church in United States" is San Miguel Chapel, first mentioned in about 1636 and located in the Barrio de Analco, south of the Santa Fe River, along Old Santa Fe Trail, at De Vargas Street. This promotion has been widely accepted as true, and it is the oldest remaining church in Santa Fe. Although the mission church is old, however, the parish church of Saint Francis, originally on the site of today's cathedral basilica, was first mentioned in 1613.

Read: "A Window to the Past: The San Miguel and La Conquistadora Chapels and Their Builders, 1610–1776," by Cordelia Thomas Snow, in *All Trails Lead to Santa Fe*, Sunstone Press, 2010; *The Myth of Santa Fe: Creating a Modern Regional Tradition*, by Chris Wilson, University of New Mexico Press, 1997; *Caballeros: The Romance of Santa Fe and the Southwest*, by Ruth Laughlin, Sunstone Press, 2007 (first published 1931); and *The Rebuilding of San Miguel at Santa Fe in 1710*, by George Kubler, Taylor Museum of the Colorado Fine Arts Center, 1939.

San Miguel Mission Church. Photograph by Ben Wittick, 1880.
Courtesy of Palace of the Governors Photo Archives (NMHM/DCA), # 015856.

91. A Santa Fe myth about "the earliest bell in New Mexico" claims there is a bell that dates to 1356. What is the actual date, and where is the bell?

The real date is 1856, on the old bell in San Miguel Chapel. The "8" can look like a "3" because of a flaw in the casting. A local artisan from Peña Blanca (and later Embudo) named Francisco Luján cast the bell right in front of the parish church, which stood where the cathedral basilica is today.

Read: *Popular Arts of Spanish New Mexico*, by E. Boyd, Museum of New Mexico Press, 1974; "Mistake Gave Rise to Oldest Bell Myth," by Marc Simmons, *Santa Fe New Mexican*, March 31, 2007; and *The Illustrated History of New Mexico*, by Benjamin M. Read, translated into English, under the direction of the author, by Eleuterio Baca, New Mexican Printing Company, 1912.

92. The legend about the construction of the famous "miraculous" spiral staircase of Loretto Chapel claims it was constructed by Saint Joseph, the patron saint of carpenters, but actually it was probably prefabricated where, and by whom?

The staircase was probably constructed in parts in France and then assembled in Santa Fe by master carpenter François-Jean Rochas, in about 1881. The building was modeled after the small gothic chapel Sainte-Chapelle, in Paris.

Read: *Loretto: The Sisters and Their Santa Fe Chapel*, by Mary J. Straw Cook, Museum of New Mexico Press, 2002.

The staircase in Loretto Chapel, 1966.
Courtesy of Palace of the Governors Photo Archives (NMHM/DCA), #HP.2007.20.88.

93. What part of a mammalian body is referred to in a geographical landmark southwest of Santa Fe?

Tetilla Peak. It is found on the Caja del Río Plateau. Tetilla Peak is part of an old volcano formed during the creation of the Rio Grande rift, about 15 million years ago. Nearby are the somewhat smaller hills, Las Tetillitas. "Tetilla" means nipple, sometimes a male nipple.

Read: "Tetilla Peak," by Ingrid Vollnhofer, *Day Hikes in the Santa Fe Area*, Northern New Mexico Group of the Sierra Club, 2007.

What Is It?
(See Answer Key #11)

94. What mushroom is named after the "hobo artist" and mushroom-hunter Chuck Barrows, who first came to Santa Fe in the 1920s?

Boletus barrowsii is a choice white mushroom found in the Sangre de Cristo Mountains and the Jemez Mountains.

Read: *Chanterelle Dreams, Amanita Nightmares: The Love, Lore, and Mystique of Mushrooms*, by Greg A. Marley, Chelsea Green Press, 2010.

95. What and where are the Segesser hide paintings?

The two hide paintings (*reposteros*) are panoramic images that reside in the collection of the New Mexico History Museum. They may depict military expeditions sent out from the Palace of the Governors during the Spanish colonial period.

They are most likely painted on bison hides that first were tanned and made supple, then worked with pumice so the grain would not be visible, and then sewn together to make a large canvas. They may have been painted in Santa Fe after 1720 by master painters, including Tomas and Nicolas Jiron de Tejeda. They are characteristic of indigenous or folk-art paintings.

The second of the two paintings depicts an exact moment in history: an August 13, 1720, skirmish at the expedition camp of don Pedro de Villasur, a Spanish military expedition meant to check the growing French presence on the Great Plains. (Segesser is the last name of the Swiss family that sold the hides to the museum.)

Read: *The Segesser Hide Paintings: Masterpieces Depicting Spanish Colonial New Mexico*, Museum of New Mexico Press, 1991 (first published 1970). Also, see the paintings at the New Mexico History Museum, Palace of the Governors, on the Plaza.

Segesser hide painting detail, right side of Painting I. Courtesy of Palace of the Governors Photo Archives (NMHM/DCA), #179800.

96. What did Katherine Stinson Otero and Winabelle Rawson Pierce Beasley have in common?

They were early women pilots (aviatrices).

Katherine Stinson Otero became a celebrated pilot during aviation's initial age. She was the fourth woman to receive a pilot's license in the United States, in 1912. Born in 1891, she was the first female precision flyer, the first woman to conduct pre-flight inspections, the first woman to fly solo at night, and the first woman to conduct a loop-de-loop; she also invented night skywriting. Her husband was airman Miguel Otero, son of territorial governor Miguel Antonio Otero. They met at Sunmount Sanatorium, where they both were patients recovering from tuberculosis.

Winabelle Rawson Pierce, known as "Winnie," pursued her childhood dream of becoming a pilot. After college and secretarial school in the East, she joined the Royal Air Force in 1940 as part of the Women's Air Transport Auxiliary, and her name was linked with other female pilots such as Amelia Earhart and Beryl Markham. She married Colonel Peter Beasley and moved to Santa Fe with her children. Winnie Beasley was known for her flamboyant style and zest for life. She drove a motorcycle with a sidecar throughout Santa Fe. She was honored as a Santa Fe Living Treasure in 1986.

The Santa Fe Living Treasures Program was started by Mary Lou Cook in 1984 to honor the city's elders.

Read: *Living Treasures: Celebration of the Human Spirit, A Legacy of New Mexico,* by Joanne Rijmes, Western Edge Press, 1997; *Santa Fe Living Treasures: Our Elders, Our Hearts,* by Richard McCord, Sunstone Press, 2009; *Aces, Heroes, and Daredevils of the Air,* by LeRoy Hayman, J. Messner, 1981; and *Katherine Stinson: The Flying Schoolgirl,* by Debra Winegarten, Eakin Press, 2000.

Miguel (Mike) Antonio Otero Jr., son of Governor Miguel Antonio Otero, is the center of attention at his birthday party with friends at his family's house in Santa Fe, in about 1899. The future airman met his wife-to-be about twenty years later, at Santa Fe's Sunmount Sanatorium when they were both recovering from tuberculosis. Photograph by P. L. Weitfle. Courtesy of Palace of the Governors Photo Archives (NMHM/DCA), #025569.

97. When did Santa Fe experience a small earthquake during which the bell tower at the San Miguel Mission crumbled?

1870. The earthquake was minimal, and the tower probably crumbled as a result of other causes. The Santa Fe area experienced another earthquake in October 2011; the quake was centered near Chupadero, north of Santa Fe.

Read: "A Past Full of Awe and Wonder: Following the Mission Trail," by Marc Simmons, *Santa Fe New Mexican*, March 29, 2003; and "Officials Cite No Damage From 3.8 Magnitude Earthquake," *Santa Fe New Mexican*, October 17, 2011.

98. After New Mexico was taken by the United States from Mexico in 1846, Fort Marcy was built on a rise overlooking Santa Fe. Which rise, and why?

Fort Marcy was placed on the hill north of the Plaza, overlooking Santa Fe; the fort had cannons to deter a Mexican revolt. The cannons were never used.

Read: "Fort Marcy Loomed over Santa Fe for Years," by Gussie Fauntleroy, *Santa Fe New Mexican*, February 28, 1999.

Headquarters Military District of New Mexico, Fort Marcy, Santa Fe, looking northeast from the corner of Grant Avenue and Palace Avenue, 1885. Courtesy of Palace of the Governors Photo Archives (NMHM/DCA), #001738.

99. The pink Scottish Rite Temple, completed and dedicated in 1912, the year of statehood, was designed to resemble what?

The Alhambra, a fortified, Arabic palace in Granada, Spain, which was constructed in the mid-fourteenth century (*Al-Hamra* is Arabic for "the red one"). The Scottish Rite Temple, sometimes called the Masonic Lodge of Perfection, or the Scottish Rite Cathedral, is located on the corner of Washington Avenue and Paseo de Peralta, northeast of the Plaza. The

Masonic Lodge is the world's oldest and largest fraternity. The historical information that makes up an important part of the Masonic brotherhood is presented in stages, using plays. There are sixty-four lodges in New Mexico. The original architect of the Scottish Rite Temple was Myron Hunt, of Los Angeles, California (additions to the building were made in 1951). Arrangements may be made to visit the building, which is also often rented out for public events such as concerts and plays.

Other clubs, lodges, and fraternities in the Santa Fe area include the Elks Lodge, the Fraternal Order of Eagles, the Fraternal Order of Police, the Independent Order of Oddfellows & Rebekahs, Kiwanis International, Knights of Columbus, the Lions Clubs International, the Pajarito Lodge, Pilot International, and the Rotary Club International.

Many of these kinds of organizations developed from or were inspired by pre-industrial, fourteenth-century trade guilds formed by craftsmen who associated by type of craft and supported and protected each other, sharing money, and also regulating prices of their products. The guilds consisted of masters, journeymen, and apprentices. (The word *guild* comes from the early 1200s word *yilde*, which meant payment and derived from old German and old French. The Saxon word *gilden* meant "to pay" and was often associated with tribute.) In the United States, the practice of law, where each state maintains its own bar association, and real-estate brokerage, which uses standard pricing, self-regulation, and cultural identity, are two examples of modern versions of guilds. Architecture, engineering, geology (including oil, gas, and mining), dentistry, medicine, and land surveying require apprenticeships. Some online computer games involve players who can form groups called player guilds.

Read: *A History of Masonry in New Mexico*, by LaMoine "Red" Langston, Hall-Poorbaugh Press, 1977; and "Fort Marcy Area Holds History," by Paul Weideman, *Santa Fe New Mexican*, August 5, 2001; *Wage Labor and Guilds in Medieval Europe*, by Steven Epstein, University of North Carolina Press, 1991; *The Crafts and Culture of a Medieval Town*, by Joann Jovinelly and Jason Netelkos, Rosen Publishing, 2007; and *Town and Country Life*, by Peter Chrisp, Lucent Books, 2004.

Looking south out of a window in the tower of the Masonic Scottish Rite Temple, near the northwest corner of Paseo de Peralta and Washington Avenue. A glimpse of the old Palace Hotel can be seen; beyond it is St. Francis Cathedral. Photograph by Jesse Nusbaum, 1912. Courtesy of Palace of the Governors Photo Archives (NMHM/DCA), #061382.

100. The first Cross of the Martyrs monument, established by the Historical Society of New Mexico in 1920, commemorated what event, and where is it located?

The first of two crosses commemorating the twenty-one Franciscan friars who were slain during the Pueblo Revolt of 1680 was dedicated during Fiesta on September 15, 1920. The seventy-six-ton concrete cross is twenty-five feet tall and located north of the post office, up off Old Taos Highway, on Paseo de la Loma. Access is limited by surrounding houses in the residential area. The cross was donated to the Historic Santa Fe Foundation in 1993 by the Near North Neighborhood Association.

Read: "Saving the Cross: Neighborhood Would Like the 1920 Original to Stay," by John Marino, *Santa Fe New Mexican*, January 22, 1993; and "Crosses of the Martyrs Commemorate Franciscan Friars," by Emily Van Cleve, *Santa Fe New Mexican*, May 18, 1997.

101. When and where was the second Cross of the Martyrs erected, and by whom?

The second Cross of the Martyrs was erected in 1977 on the hill near the ruins of Fort Marcy. Like the first cross, it is a memorial to the twenty-one Franciscan friars killed during the Pueblo Revolt of 1680. Twenty feet tall and made of steel painted white, it was erected by the American Revolution Bicentennial Commission and the Santa Fe Fiesta Council. A short but steep walkway leads up to the cross. Accessed from Paseo de Peralta, the walkway begins as a stairway; plaques along the way provide an overview of Santa Fe's history. From the top are views of the city and the surrounding mountains.

Read: "Crosses of the Martyrs Commemorate Franciscan Friars," by Emily Van Cleve, *Santa Fe New Mexican*, May 18, 1997.

102. In 1942 physicist Klaus Fuchs passed atomic bomb secrets to Soviet spy Harry Gold at what bridge that crossed the Santa Fe River downtown?

The Castillo Street Bridge. In the early 1900s, Castillo Street ran between Marcy Street and De Vargas Street, where Paseo de Peralta runs now. The secrets were microfilmed and put on tapes that Fuchs carried around in Jello boxes.

Read: *A Spy's Guide to Santa Fe and Albuquerque*, by E. B. Held, University of New Mexico Press, 2011. Also, see the 1912 survey map (King's Map) of the City of Santa Fe, at City Hall.

103. Who was the woman from the "Banana Hill" barrio whose voice became synonymous with the Santa Fe Fiesta for nearly forty years, and for whom Santa Fe's largest physical fitness center is named, and what was her musical specialty?

Genoveva Chávez was one of Santa Fe's most popular mariachi singers and performers. She died in 1997 at the age of fifty-five. Carrying on in her tradition, the first professional all-female mariachi group in Santa Fe, Mariachi Buenaventura, was formed in 2005. (Chávez's "Banana Hill" barrio got its nickname because Gonzales Road is "as slippery as a banana peel" when the steep street is icy in the winter.)

Read: "Genoveva Chávez's Life Remembered," by Denise Kusel, *Santa Fe New Mexican*, December 15, 1999; and *Mariachi*, by Patricia Greathouse, Gibbs Smith, 2009.

Close-up of Genoveva Chávez's Fiesta dress.
Courtesy of María Martínez,
El Museo Cultural.

104. What popular Spanish colonial art form is referred to as "the poor man's gilding"?

Straw appliqué, which can be as shiny as gold. It has often been used to decorate crosses and picture frames. It was popular during the eighteenth and nineteenth centuries. The straw appliqué art form was reintroduced to Santa Fe by Eliseo and Paula Rodriguez after Eliseo was encouraged to resurrect the art form during the 1930s, with the help of the Federal Art Project, a federal work-relief program that had evolved from the Works Project Administration (WPA) during the Great Depression.

Read: *Conexiones: Connections in Spanish Colonial Art*, by Carmella Padilla and Donna Pierce, Museum of Spanish Colonial Art, 2002; "Conversations with Eliseo and Paula: Spanish Market," by Carmella Padilla, *Santa Fe New Mexican*, July 22, 2009; *Eliseo Rodriguez: El Sexto Pintor*, by Carmella Padilla, Museum of New Mexico Press, 2001; and *Survival along the Continental Divide: An Anthology of Interviews*, edited by Jack Loeffler, University of New Mexico Press, 2008.

105. One of Santa Fe's most eccentric artists had a great love of dogs and cats. Who was he?

Tommy Macaione, "El Diferente," who kept more than thirty dogs and perhaps seventy cats as pets during the 1970s. There is a small statue of him in Hillside Park. He was a barber before becoming an artist. He came to Santa Fe in 1952 to paint; he died in 1992, just before his eighty-fifth birthday.

Read: *Santa Fe Bohemia: The Art Colony, 1964–1980,* by Eli Levin, Sunstone Press, 2007.

106. In 1891 a coal-fired steam plant was the first facility to generate electric power for the city. Where was it located?

It was located downtown, at Don Gaspar and Water Streets.

Read: "The Little Building That Could," by Paul Weideman, *Santa Fe New Mexican,* September 3, 2006.

107. What is one of the oldest roads of commerce on the North American continent, and what does the word *hacienda* mean?

El Camino Real de Tierra Adentro (the Royal Road to the Interior, also known as the Silver Route) was one of many *caminos reales* in New Spain. A *camino real* connected chartered towns to one another, and the *villas reales* were given privileges and responsibilities commensurate with their prestige.

The Camino Real came up from what is now central Mexico, entered Santa Fe from south of town along what is now Agua Fria Street, and then entered the Santa Fe Plaza by way of Calle Real, or what is now San Francisco Street, where it converged in front of the Palace of the Governors with what was later to be called the Santa Fe Trail. The legislated national historic trail extends to Ohkay Owingeh/San Juan Pueblo. The Bureau of Land Management and the National Park Service are joint administrators in the United States.

After Mexican independence, the government forbade the use of the name Camino Real because of the reference to royalty and previous control by Spain; authorities urged use of the name Camino Nacional instead. The old name was preferred by most residents, however, until the Anglos introduced the name Agua Fría, in reference to the small community just south of Santa Fe. Other older roads of commerce in North America connecting Mexico City—the capital of the viceroyalty of New Spain—with the Intercontinental Camino Real are the camino real Vera Cruz–Mexico City, which connected to the European trade, and the camino real Acapulco–Mexico City, which connected to the Asian trade. Silver was one of the most important items of trade, and mercury was brought over from Europe to process it.

The word *hacienda* has come to mean a large estate, usually in a Spanish-speaking country, or the main building of a farm or ranch, and it has an almost romantic connotation today. But *hacienda*, which comes from the Spanish verb *hacer* (to make), originally meant the compound, usually rural, where family members, servants, and *peons* worked making commodities such as woolens, hides, and *mantas* (cotton cloth) for trade. And the big haciendas near silver mines were similar to factories, with forced labor. The word *hacienda* derives from the Latin *facienda* (things to be done) and *facere* (to do). Confusion of the initial "h" and "f" was common in sixteenth-century Spanish.

Read: *The Royal Road: El Camino Real from Mexico City to Santa Fe*, by Christine Preston, Douglas Preston, and José Antonio Esquibel, University of New Mexico Press, 1998.

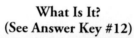

What Is It?
(See Answer Key #12)

108. Which modern painter's worldwide popularity placed Santa Fe in the limelight yet again as a city for the arts when a museum was created in 1997 that was the first of its kind in the United States?

Georgia O'Keeffe. A museum focusing on her work and American Modernism (art of the late nineteenth century to the present) opened in 1997 on Johnson Street in downtown Santa Fe. It is the first major museum in the United States named for a woman artist. Her iconic paintings and drawings feature imagery highlighting the "wildness and wonder of the world" she lived in. Her work includes abstractions and large-scale depictions of flowers, leaves, rocks, shells, bones, and other natural forms, as well as New York cityscapes and paintings of her view of the landscape and adobe architecture of northern New Mexico.

O'Keeffe was born in 1887 in a farmhouse near Sun Prairie, Wisconsin, where her parents were dairy farmers. Among the places she worked and painted are Williamsburg, Virginia; Lake George, in upstate New York; Chicago; Amarillo, in the Texas panhandle; Columbia, South Carolina; and New York City. She met the photographer and gallery owner Alfred Stieglitz in 1916 and married him in 1924. She first explored New Mexico in 1929. She spent much of each year in New Mexico from then on, and in 1934, after recuperating from a nervous breakdown, she decided to move to the state. She bought property in Abiquiu,

north of Santa Fe, in 1940. She said about the area, which has become known as O'Keeffe country, "such a beautiful, untouched, lonely feeling place, such a fine part of what I call the 'Faraway.'" She died in Santa Fe in 1986.

Read: *From the Faraway Nearby: Georgia O'Keeffe As Icon*, edited by Christopher Merrill and Ellen Bradbury, Addison-Wesley, 1992; *Georgia O'Keeffe and New Mexico: A Sense of Place*, by Barbara Buhler Lynes, Georgia O'Keeffe Museum, 2004.

Georgia O'Keeffe, with Siamese cat. Photograph by John Candelario, 1939. Courtesy of Palace of the Governors Photo Archives (NMHM/DCA), #165660.

109. Were there Harvey Girls in Santa Fe?

Yes, at La Fonda, a hotel on the southeast corner of the Santa Fe Plaza. La Fonda was owned by Fred Harvey and the Fred Harvey Corporation for more than forty years, until it was sold to Sam Ballen and his family in 1968. It was one of more than eighty facilities Harvey owned. The Harvey Girls were young women he hired to be guides and waitresses; they were required to be eighteen to thirty years of age, of good character, attractive, and intelligent. In 1883 they were paid $17.50 a month, plus room, board, and tips. Makeup and chewing gum were forbidden while on duty.

Today many guides are available to help visitors and locals alike learn more about the City of Santa Fe. Sponsored by the New Mexico History Museum/Palace of the Governors, the Downtown Walking Tours meet at the Blue Gate on Lincoln Avenue; there is a charge. The New Mexico Museum of Art sponsors tours that are free (inquire at the museum gift shop, on Palace Avenue).

Read: *The Harvey Girls: Women Who Opened the West*, by Lesley Poling-Kempes, Marlowe, 1991; *A Short History of Santa Fe*, by Susan Hazen-Hammond, Lexikos, 1988; *Santa Fe: Then and Now*, by Sheila Morand, Sunstone Press, 2008; *Walking in the Path of the Artists: A Guide to the Artists' Homes*, by Stacia Lewandowski, Salska Arts, 2011; *Walks in Literary Santa Fe: A Guide to Landmarks, Legends, and Lore*, by Barbara Harrelson, Gibbs Smith, 2007; *Romantic Days and Nights in Santa Fe: Romantic Diversions in and around the City*, by Lynn Cline, Globe Pequot, 2001; *Santa Fe on Foot: Adventures in the City Different*, by Elaine Pinkerton, Ocean Tree Books,

1994; *Enchanted Lifeways: The History, Museums, Arts, and Festivals of New Mexico*, New Mexico Office of Cultural Affairs, New Mexico Magazine, 1995; *Santa Fe*, by Larry Cheek, Compass American Guides, 2008; *New Mexico: A Guide to the Colorful State*, compiled by the Workers of the Writers' Program of the Work Projects Administration in the State of New Mexico, Hastings House, 1953; and *Through the Lens: Creating Santa Fe*, edited by Mary Anne Redding, Museum of New Mexico Press, 2008.

Tea time at the south portal of La Fonda. Photograph by T. Harmon Parkhurst, c. 1920s.
La Fonda was a Fred Harvey hotel until 1968.
Courtesy of Palace of the Governors Photo Archives (NMHM/DCA), #054316.

Tourists enjoyed touring in a Fred Harvey Car, which might take guests to see a Native American pueblo or to explore the landscape around Santa Fe. The car is parked in front of New Mexico's third state capitol. Photograph by T. Harmon Parkhurst, c. 1920–1925. Courtesy of Palace of the Governors Photo Archives (NMHM/DCA), #010385.

110. Where did Santa Fe obtain its water supply during colonial times?

For centuries Santa Feans drew their domestic water from the *acequias*, which were fed by the Santa Fe River. An acequia is an irrigation ditch or gravity chute, usually hand dug, that serves as a community-operated waterway for distributing water.

Read: *Acequia: Water-Sharing, Sanctity, and Place*, by Sylvia Rodríguez, School for Advanced Research Press, 2006; *Acequia Culture: Water, Land, and Community in the Southwest*, by José A. Rivera, University of New Mexico Press, 1998; *Mayordomo: Chronicle of an Acequia in Northern New Mexico*, by Stanley Crawford, University of New Mexico Press, 1993; "Acequia Agriculture: Water, Irrigation, and Their Defining Roles in Santa Fe History," by Tara M. Plewa, in *Santa Fe: History of an Ancient City*, edited by David Grant Noble, School for Advanced Research Press, 2008.

Burros at Acequia Madre. Photograph by T. Harmon Parkhurst, 1915.
Courtesy of Palace of the Governors Photo Archives (NMHM/DCA), #011047.

What Is It?
(See Answer Key #13)

What Is It?
(See Answer Key #14)

What Is It?
(See Answer Key #15)

A control gate on the
Acequia Madre near
Camino del Monte Sol.

An irrigation flume across the Santa Fe River near
Cristo Rey Church. Photograph by Sallie Wagner, 1960.
Courtesy of Palace of the Governors Photo Archives
(NMHM/DCA), #010566.

111. When was Santa Fe's traditional water system supplemented with water piped into homes?

The latter half of the nineteenth century saw the beginnings of efforts to dam the Santa Fe River at the canyon and to install pipe to bring running water into homes, supplementing water supplied by the acequia system.

Read: "The Little Building That Could," by Paul Weideman, *Santa Fe New Mexican*, September 3, 2006; and *Flushed: How the Plumber Saved Civilization*, by W. Hodding Carter, Atria Books, 2006.

112. Who was the world-famous explorer who crossed the Pacific Ocean in 1947 in a reed raft and lived in Santa Fe while finishing his book about the expedition?

Thor Heyerdahl. He was a Norwegian voyager, explorer, and writer. His book *Kon-Tiki* describes his experimental trip to prove that mariners from the Americas could have crossed the Pacific. While in Santa Fe from 1948 to 1949, he enjoyed visiting the School of American Research (now the School for Advanced Research), where he met the archaeologist Edwin Ferndon, who joined Heyerdahl on one of his treks. Heyerdahl was convinced that cultures of the ancient world were sometimes linked by sailors, who could have crossed oceans. He and a five-person crew sailed their reed raft from Peru to Polynesia, traveling 4,300 miles in 101 days. Heyerdahl had learned about small reed boats on Lake Titicaca, in Peru, and then realized that the inwardly curled stern of boats in ancient Egyptian pictures was not ornamental but necessary for a vessel's elasticity. His experiences supported his belief that the growth of knowledge is never neatly linear.

Inspired by *Kon-Tiki* and the vast amount of plastic trash in the world's oceans, *Plastiki*, the world's first plastic catamaran, measuring sixty feet and made of 12,500 reclaimed plastic bottles, was sailed from San Francisco, California, to Sydney, Australia, in 2010.

Read: *Kon-Tiki: Across the Pacific by Raft*, by Thor Heyerdahl, Skyhorse, 2010 (first published 1950); *Kon-Tiki Man: An Illustrated Biography of Thor Heyerdahl*, by Thor Heyerdahl, Chronicle Books, 1990; *Plastiki: Across the Pacific on Plastic, An Adventure to Save Our Oceans*, by David de Rothschild, Chronicle Books, 2011; and *Oceans: The Threats to Our Seas and What You Can Do to Turn the Tide*, by Jon Bowermaster, PublicAffairs, 2010.

What Is It?
(See Answer Key #16)

113. Who founded La Sociedad Folklórica de Santa Fe, and when, and why?

Cleofas Jaramillo founded La Sociedad Folklórica de Santa Fe (the Folklore Society of Santa Fe) in 1935 to preserve Spanish culture and traditions. The society presents two main events each year: La Merienda y Exhibición, a vintage fashion show with *chocolate* and *bizcochitos*, during Santa Fe Fiesta, and El Baile de los Cascarones, a dance party for all ages, held the Friday after Easter.

Semana Santa (Holy Week) and Pascua (Easter) are the two holidays celebrated beginning on Palm Sunday, the week before Easter, and usually continuing after Easter for about six days. On the Friday before Easter, Good Friday, many northern New Mexicans and visitors make a pilgrimage to the Santuario de Chimayó, a shrine in the town of Chimayó, about thirty miles north of Santa Fe. Starting their pilgrimages in various places, some pilgrims travel short distances while others travel more than a hundred miles over several days. Easter is celebrated on the Sunday following the first full moon after the vernal equinox (springtime, when day and night are the same length). The time of *cuaresma* (from the Latin *quadragesima*, meaning "forty days"), called Lent in English, ends on Easter morning, after approximately forty days of penance, ideally consisting of prayer, fasting, and charitable deeds. The English word Lent comes from the German word for spring—*lenz*, meaning "long," since the days of spring grow longer.

The Spanish word *pascua* derives from the Latin word meaning "grazing" and before that from the Greek; the roots of the word go back to the Hebrew *pésakh*, for "pass over." In biblical times the Jews were slaves to the pharaoh in Egypt. According to the Exodus narrative, God tried to make the pharaoh free the Jews by inflicting suffering on the Egyptians. The worst punishment was slaying the firstborn of the Egyptians; the homes of the Jews were passed over, or spared this fate. Passover commemorates this event, when the ancient Israelites were freed from slavery in Egypt. The Last Supper of Jesus was apparently a Passover seder.

The English word for Pascua is Easter; it may have derived from Eostre, the name of an Old English version of a German goddess of springtime, fertility, and renewal. The days after Easter leading up to the following Sunday are called Easter Week, or Renewal Week, a celebration of renewal and a release from Lent. Pascua, Easter, and Passover, for Christians and for Jews, is a time of remembrance, thankfulness, and renewal of faith.

Partygoers who attend the Baile de los Cascarones the Friday after Easter, an event open to anyone of any faith, often head home with confetti in their hair and all over their clothes. The *cáscarones* are confetti-filled eggshells that are broken over the head of the person invited to dance.

Read: *La Sociedad: Guardians of Hispanic Culture along the Rio Grande*, José A. Rivera, University of New Mexico Press, 2011; and *Romance of a Little Village Girl*, by Cleo Jaramillo, Naylor Company, 1955.

Cleofas Martínez Jaramillo in her wedding hat. Photography by Anderson Santa Fe, 1901. Courtesy of Palace of the Governors Photo Archives (NMHM/DCA), #009920.

114. What two Santa Fe institutions were founded to study the cultures of man?

The School of American Research, now the School for Advanced Research, was founded in 1907 originally as the School for American Archaeology. Its emphasis was on the study of the Southwest's prehistoric cultures. Anthropologist and ethnographer Alice Cunningham Fletcher, who served on the American Committee of the Archaeological Institute of America, in Boston, persuaded the institute to establish the School of American Archaeology in Santa Fe to study the American Southwest; the territorial government had offered the historic Palace of the Governors as a permanent home.

In 1909 the Museum of New Mexico was established as an agency of the school. In 1917 the school changed its name to the School of American Research. It moved to its current campus, on Garcia Street, in 1973. In 2006 the school again changed its name to reflect the broadening of its scope: the School for Advanced Research on the Human Experience. Its mission is to provide a place for advanced study and communication of knowledge about human culture, evolution, history, and creative expression.

The Laboratory of Anthropology was founded in 1930 by Kenneth Chapman, Alfred Kidder, H. P. Mera, and Anna Shepard, among many others, to advance the study of man and cultures on a global basis. Under the direction of Jesse Nusbaum, the lab was one of the earliest institutions in the United States to systematically record archaeological sites in New Mexico and surrounding states. It pioneered pipeline and salvage archaeology, which is now the basis for cultural resource management, mandated by federal law since the 1970s.

Archaeology developed out of the study of antiquities, or things of the past; this practice was fashionable in Europe from the sixteenth through the nineteenth centuries. Modern archaeology was born in the second half of the nineteenth century. It examines artifacts, bones, and architectural remains excavated from the past.

Anthropology is the study of human beings. The term was first used by German philosopher Magnus Hundt in 1501. Because there are many approaches to studying human beings, the field of anthropology is varied and complex. Basically, curiosity about the differences and similarities between people over space and time led to the study of human beings. Modern anthropology is an outgrowth of fourteenth-century colonization and increased awareness and systematic study of the varieties of human behavior, using the concept of culture.

Read: *The School of American Research: A History, The First Eighty Years*, by Melinda Elliott, School of American Research Press, 1987; *A Peculiar Alchemy: A Centennial History of SAR, 1907–2007*, by Nancy Owen Lewis and Kay Leigh Hagan, School for Advanced Research Press, 2007; *The Cambridge Illustrated History of Archaeology*, edited by Paul G. Bahn, Cambridge University Press, 1999; *Kenneth Milton Chapman: A Life Dedicated to Indian Arts and Artists*, by Janet Chapman and Karen Barrrie, University of New Mexico Press, 2008; and *Anthropology and Modern Life*, by Franz Boas, Transaction Publishers, 2004 (first published 1928).

Board meeting of the School of American Research, at Puye, New Mexico, 1909. Charles Lummis is third from the right. Photograph courtesy of Palace of the Governors Photo Archives (NMHM/DCA), #013328.

115. What prehistoric Native American settlement was located near present-day Agua Fría Village?

The Pindi Pueblo. *Pindi* is Tewa for "turkey"—the birds were pre–European-contact domesticated animals. Turkey pens and the remains of the birds were found at that location. There are at least two other early settlement sites near Santa Fe and about sixteen settlement sites in the surrounding area.

Read: "Down at the Shell-Bead Water," by David Snow, in *All Trails Lead to Santa Fe*, Sunstone Press, 2010; *Pueblo Nations: Eight Centuries of Pueblo Indian History*, by Joe S. Sando, Clear Light, 1992; and *7,000 Years on the Piedmont: Excavation of Fourteen Archaeological Sites along the Northwest Santa Fe Relief Route, Santa Fe County, New Mexico*, by Stephen S. Post, Office of Archaeological Studies, 2011.

116. In postcolonial New Mexico, to which district did the Mexican government assign Santa Fe—Rio Arriba (Upper River) or Rio Abajo (Lower River)?

Rio Arriba. The river is the Rio Grande. The demarcation of the upper and lower parts of the river is the escarpment known as La Bajada.

Read: *The Great River: The Rio Grande in North American History*, by Paul Horgan, Wesleyan University Press, 1984 (first published 1954); and *Reining in the Rio Grande: People, Land, and Water*, by Fred M. Phillips, G. Emlen Hall, and Mary Black, University of New Mexico Press, 2011.

Car descending La Bajada hill before I-25 was built.
Courtesy of Palace of the Governors Photo Archives (NMHM/DCA), #008231.

117. When do Pueblo people commemorate the 1680 Pueblo Indian Revolt?

Annually, on August 10, the day when the revolt commenced. The revolt has also been called the Pueblo Rebellion or Revolution. It was considered an act of restoration by the ancestors of today's Pueblo people.

Read: "Twelve Days in August: The Pueblo Revolt in Santa Fe," by Joseph P. Sánchez, in *Santa Fe: History of an Ancient City*, edited by David Grant Noble, School for Advanced Research Press, 2008; and *Pueblo Profiles: Cultural Identity through Centuries of Change*, by Joe S. Sando, Clear Light, 1998.

118. When did the *ayuntamiento* (town council), under the viceroyalty of New Spain, decree that Santa Fe would hold a fiesta every year to commemorate the reestablishment of the town after the reconquest by the Spaniards in 1692?

On September 16, 1712.

We do not know how consistently Fiesta was celebrated following that first Fiesta. After lapses in celebration, Fiesta was "reinvented" in the early 1900s during a conversation between James Mythen (an Episcopal deacon) and James and Ruth Seligman (a Santa Fe businessman and his wife). The idea caught on, and Fiesta was revived a few years later, in 1919, by the Museum of New Mexico. The modern Fiesta has taken place every year since 1924.

The preparation for Santa Fe's Fiesta pageantry begins in the spring, with the competition for a Fiesta Queen, a don Diego de Vargas, a Native American Princess, and their courts, organized by the Fiesta Council. In June, La Conquistadora (renamed Nuestra Señora de la Paz, or Our Lady of Peace), the revered symbol of Catholic faith and hope, is carried in procession from her home in Conquistadora Chapel, in St. Francis Cathedral Basilica, to Rosario Chapel (she is returned a week later).

In September, on the Thursday night after Labor Day, Will Shuster's Zozobra (a giant puppet, more than thirty feet tall, nicknamed "Old Man Gloom") is burned in Fort Marcy Park, with large crowds enjoying the (at least temporary) demise of gloom. Many families, friends, and visitors bring picnic suppers and enjoy the entertainment, the music, the Fire Dance, the glooms (little ghosts), Zozobra's groaning end, and a grand display of fireworks.

Then Fiesta officially begins on Friday morning, with the Pregón (Proclamation) and later the Entrada (a reenactment of the first, ritual reentry of don Diego de Vargas). The free music and entertainment on the Plaza bandstand, including mariachi bands and dance performances, continues all day and into the evening. There are plenty of food booths, and everyone seems to be eating "Indian tacos" and chile and beans or fry bread with cinnamon or honey.

On Saturday morning the Desfile de los Niños (Children's Parade), also known as the Pet Parade, is held on the Santa Fe Plaza, with children and their pets participating. A traditional *merienda* (fashion show) is sponsored by La Sociedad Folklórica in the afternoon. There are private parties all around town all weekend. On Saturday night, the city hosts the Gran Baile (large dance) for everyone at the Community Convention Center.

At the Santa Fe Playhouse (Santa Fe's oldest continuously running theater), the annual Fiesta Melodrama pokes fun at Santa Fe's political, societal, and cultural foibles around Fiesta time. The Hysterical/Historical Parade on Sunday afternoon does the same, as well as promoting all kinds of social topics—political and otherwise—with many floats and several bands. Sunday evening at dusk everyone is invited to join the solemn and religious candlelight procession that makes its way from St. Francis Cathedral Basilica up to the Cross of the Martyrs on top of Fort Marcy hill.

On Monday everyone cleans up and goes back to work.

Read: "The First Santa Fe Fiesta Council, 1712," by Fray Angélico Chávez, *New Mexico Historical Review*, July 1953; *¡Vivan las Fiestas!* edited by Donna Pierce, Museum of New Mexico Press, 1985; *The Lore of New Mexico*, by Marta Weigle and Peter White, University of New Mexico Press, 2003; *The Santa Fe Fiesta, Reinvented: Staking Ethno-Nationalist Claims to a Disappearing Homeland*, by Sarah Bronwen Horton, School for Advanced Research, 2010; *Elvis Romero and Fiesta de Santa Fe, Featuring Zozobra's Great Escape*, by Andrew Lee Lovato, Museum of New Mexico Press, 2011; *The Myth of Santa Fe: Creating a Modern Regional Tradition*, by Chris Wilson, University of New Mexico Press, 1997; *Symbol and Conquest: Public Ritual and Drama in Santa Fe, New Mexico*, by Ronald L. Grimes, University of New Mexico Press, 1992; and

"Small-Town Jubilation: Fiesta de Santa Fe, Shared Spirit of Community on Parade," by Robert Nott, *Santa Fe New Mexican*, September 12, 2011.

A procession of La Conquistadora, in 1897, along San Francisco Street. Photograph by Philip E. Harroun. Courtesy of Palace of the Governors Photo Archives (NMHM/DCA), #011326.

Zozobra burning, September 9, 2010. Photograph by Jane Phillips, *Santa Fe New Mexican.* Courtesy of the photographer.

Street dancing during Fiesta, 1938. Courtesy of Palace of the Governors Photo Archives (NMHM/DCA), #135044.

Two children, their dog, and a cart in the Santa Fe Fiesta Children's Pet Parade. Photograph in New Mexico Magazine Collection. Courtesy of Palace of the Governors Photo Archives (MNHM/DCA) #HP.2007.20.325.

The 1948 Fiesta Queen marching in a parade. Photograph by Robert H. Martin. Courtesy of Palace of the Governors Photo Archives (NMHM/DCA), #041384.

The Toonerville Trolley Fiesta float, 1929. A large version of this photograph is on the wall in the entrance hallway of the New Mexico Museum of History. Photograph by T. Harmon Parkhurst. Courtesy of Palace of the Governors Photo Archives (NMHM/DCA), #117681.

The "Bizness Wimmen" Fiesta float. Photograph by T. Harmon Parkhurst, c. 1928. Courtesy of Palace of the Governors Photo Archives (NMHM/DCA), #117676.

Tesuque Pueblo dancers in front of the Palace of the Governors, Fiesta, 1912. Photograph by Jesse Nusbaum. Courtesy of Palace of the Governors Photo Archives (NMHM/DCA), #022615.

What Is It?
(See Answer Key #17)

119. Who wrote the proclamation (*pregón*) that is read at the start of Santa Fe Fiesta?

Juan Páez Hurtado. He influenced city officials to draft the proclamation, which was signed by Governor José Chacón Medina Salazar y Villaseñor, the marqués de la Peñuela, in 1712, eight years after don Diego de Vargas had died. Hurtado was acting governor from 1704 to 1705 and then acting governor again from 1716 to 1717.

Read: *The Juan Páez Hurtado Expedition of 1695*, by John B. Colligan, University of New Mexico Press, 1995.

120. Who were the four authors of the original Santa Fe Historic Ordinance, in 1957, with the mission to preserve and protect historic architecture in the oldest part of town?

Oliver La Farge (author, anthropologist), John Gaw Meem (architect), Samuel Z. Montoya (city attorney and later chief justice of the state supreme court), and Irene von Horvath (architect, urban planner) were the four people who crafted the city's historic ordinance, one of the nation's first.

Read: *Old Santa Fe Today*, by the Historic Santa Fe Foundation, University of New Mexico Press, 1991.

What Is It?
(See Answer Key #18)

121. What was Paseo de Peralta informally called when it was first designed?

"Irene's Street" was the nickname for Paseo de Peralta in the 1960s, since Irene von Horvath had conceived the idea of the ring road. It was intended to alleviate traffic congestion in the historic downtown area so that the narrow streets could be preserved.

Will Rogers's comment about the layout of the town on his first visit to Santa Fe, in the early 1900s, supposedly was this: "Whoever designed this town did so while riding on a jackass, backwards and drunk."

Read: *¡El Boletín!*, Old Santa Fe Association newsletter, Spring 2010; and *The Best of Santa Fe and Beyond*, by Elizabeth Thornton, Adobe Publishing, 1999.

122. Who spearheaded the founding of the Museum of New Mexico?

Edgar Lee Hewett, who was the first director of the museum, in 1909. An archaeologist and anthropologist, he was most famous for bringing about the important conservation legislation called the Antiquities Act, which helped to preserve Bandelier National Monument and Chaco Culture National Monument. He was the first president of the New Mexico Normal School, in Las Vegas, New Mexico (now New Mexico Highlands University). He was also a friend of Maria Martinez, the great potter from San Ildefonso Pueblo, and he helped focus interest in pottery as a significant art form. He founded the Museum of Anthropology (now called the Maxwell Museum of Anthropology) at the University of New Mexico.

Hewett first came to Santa Fe because his wife, Cora Whitford, had tuberculosis. His wife died, and he later married Donizetta Jones Wood. Hewett died in 1946 and was buried next to his long-time friend Alice Fletcher, an important force in American archaeology. His autobiography is called *Campfire and Trail*.

Read: *Hewett and Friends: A Biography of Santa Fe's Vibrant Era*, by Beatrice Chauvenet, Museum of New Mexico Press, 1983; *Ancient Life in the American Southwest, With an Introduction on the General History of the American Race*, Edgar Lee Hewett, Bobbs-Merrill Company, 1930; *Indian*

Games and Dances with Native Songs: Arranged from American Indian Ceremonials and Sports, by Alice C. Fletcher, University of Nebraska Press, 1994 (first published 1915); and *Campfire and Trail*, by Edgar Lee Hewett, University of New Mexico Press, 1943.

Edgar Lee Hewett in his office at the Palace of the Governors, c. 1900–1910.
Courtesy of Palace of the Governors Photo Archives (NMHM/DCA), #007344.

Maria Martinez, noted potter from San Ildefonso Pueblo. Photograph by Tyler Dingee, c. 1950.
Courtesy of Palace of the Governors Photo Archives (NMHM/DCA), #073449.

123. What Santa Fe builder helped World War II veterans purchase a pueblo-style house in Santa Fe for a modest price?

Allen Stamm built close to 2,800 houses, from 1939 to 1980. The best-known Stamm neighborhoods are Casa Linda, Casa Alegre, Casa Solana, and Lovato Heights.

Read: *The Small Adobe*, by Agnesa Reeve, Gibbs Smith, 2001.

124. What was El Jardín del Obispo, where was it, and what happened to the springs that fed the ponds there?

In reminiscences by Anita González Thomas of her childhood, there are descriptions of the Bishop's Garden, which was located southeast of the cathedral, between Paseo de Peralta and Cathedral Place, north of the Alameda. It had been laid out by Bishop Lamy in the 1850s with rock-bordered ponds and walks, many kinds of fruits trees, berry bushes, and flowers.

The springs that fed the ponds were still active in the mid-twentieth century but dried up when the water table was lowered as a result of overdevelopment. The Santa Fe River had been impounded in the Santa Fe Canyon at that time.

Read: "Anita González Thomas Remembers," by Anita González Thomas, *Bulletin of the Historic Santa Fe Foundation*, July 1985; and *Turn Left at the Sleeping Dog: Scripting the Santa Fe Legend, 1920–1955*, by John Pen La Farge, University of New Mexico Press, 2001.

The carp pond in Archbishop Lamy's garden, near St. Francis Cathedral, c. 1887. Courtesy of Palace of the Governors Photo Archives (NMHM/DCA), #015264.

125. On a rise above Santa Fe, a few miles south of the city limits on Interstate Highway 25, is a rest stop for vehicles approaching Santa Fe that features a cluster of five New Mexico historical markers. What do they mention?

They are markers that honor New Mexican women: doña Gertrudis Barceló; three generations of one family: Eva Scott Muse Fényes, Leonora Muse Curtin, and Leonora Frances Curtin Paloheimo; the Sisters of Loretto; Laura Gilpin; and Amelia White. The rest stop was paid for with funds from the American Revolution Bicentennial Commission in 1976.

Read the information on the historical markers (both front and back) for yourself next time you visit that rest stop. Also read *Historical Markers in New Mexico*, by Stanley M. Hordes and Carol Joiner, Delgado Studios, 1984.

What Is It?
(See Answer Key #19)

126. Who is Nava Elementary School named after?

Francis X. Nava, the first New Mexican combat casualty of the Vietnam War; he died on September 10, 1966.

Read: "Salute to Sacrifices," by Steve Terrell, *Santa Fe New Mexican*, November 11, 2009.

127. During the Mexican period, why were the children of some wealthy Santa Feans sent to boarding schools in the United States, and who was doña Mercedes Chaves de Lamy?

Wealthy Mexicans chose to enable their children to obtain a better education in a safer and more comfortable place, away from diseases such as cholera.

For example, Francisco Perea was educated at St. Louis University, in Missouri; he was later elected delegate from New Mexico Territory to the U.S. Congress, in 1863. Dámaso López, originally from Spain, married María del Carmen Seferina Esparza, from Chihuahua. After she died, probably during a cholera epidemic in the mid-1800s, López chose to send their three sons and one daughter to St. Louis. By then a busy Santa Fe and Abiquiu trader, he wanted his children safely cared for as well as exposed to a good Catholic education. His daughter, Francesca López, who had been born in Chihuahua, was sent to the Visitation Academy in St. Louis, and his sons attended St. Louis University. Other Santa Fe families who sent children to St. Louis include the Bacas, the Armijos, and the Oteros. Donaciana Waldo was a friend of Francesca López at the Visitation Academy in St. Louis. Beatrice Perea was one of the only girls from Nuevo México to finish the course. She graduated in 1885.

Mercedes Chaves, daughter of Governor José Francisco Chaves, was sent to the Visitation Academy in Washington, D.C., for her education. She was not only the daughter of a governor, but the granddaughter of another, Francisco Xavier Chávez, and the niece of two others, Mariano Chaves and Manuel Armijo. She married the Frenchman John B. Lamy, Archbishop Lamy's nephew.

Another Frenchman, François Mallet, was the architect brought over by the archbishop to help design and build a new chapel in the gothic revival style for the Sisters of Loretto. The chapel was patterned after the famous gothic chapel Sainte-Chapelle, in Paris, erected by Louis IX, king of France in the thirteenth century. The architect was shot, probably because Lamy's nephew was jealous of a possible relationship between his wife, Mercedes, and Mallet. The weekly *New Mexican*, on September 6, 1879, reported that ". . . Francis Mallet, while standing in the door of the Exchange Hotel, was shot dead from behind by John B. Lamy." Lamy gave himself up, and his wife attempted suicide. Lamy stood trial and was acquitted by reason of temporary insanity. The Lamys later reconciled.

Read: *Deep Roots and Golden Wings: 150 Years with the Visitation Sisters in the Archdiocese of St. Louis*, by William B. Faherty, River City Publishers, 1982; and *Santa Fe Tales and More*, by Howard Bryan, Clear Light, 2010.

Francesca López.
She was born in Chihuahua in 1841, daughter of María del Carmen Seferina Esparza, of Chihuahua, and Dámaso López, of Spain. After her mother died when Francesca was a young girl, she was sent to St. Louis, Missouri, along with her brothers, for their education. Her father was a friend and a partner of Manuel Álvarez, and after López died, Álvarez stayed in touch with the López children. Francesca grew up in St. Louis and remained there. She married Benjamin Kimball. She never returned to Santa Fe. Photographer unknown. Courtesy of Mary Kimball Outten.

128. Who was the café owner in the 1950s who made a political statement about taxes by regularly taking all his sales tax money to the state capitol in the form of pennies, which he had collected in a large can kept by the cash register?

Tony Mitchell, of "Tony's U and I Steakhouse," was a feisty man with a good sense of humor. He was one of many Greek immigrants who came to Santa Fe and worked in the restaurant business, often specializing in traditional New Mexican as well as Greek food. Many Greek immigrants had originally come to New Mexico to work in the mines.

Other Greek restauranteurs include Daniel Razatos, who bought the Plaza Café from the Pomonis family, and Serando "Ike" Kalangis, who started the Faith Café, which the Klonis family changed into Evangelo's Cocktail Lounge. Nick Klonis tells the story of his illegal immigrant father, Evangelo Klonis, who at age seventeen sewed himself into a bag of coal, which was loaded onto a freighter bound for Los Angeles; he jumped off the ship in northern

California and eventually came to Santa Fe. When the U.S. government offered citizenship to illegal immigrants who enlisted in the service during World War II, he signed up with the army and eventually received his citizenship papers, during the Battle of the Bulge. (W. Eugene Smith shot a photograph of Evangelo that was used for a *Life* magazine book about World War II; another Smith image of Evangelo was later used for a postage stamp.)

Another Greek immigrant, Anthony "Tony" Maryol, arrived from Greece in 1930 and started a food dynasty that began very simply with an ice-cream cart on the Santa Fe Plaza. Eventually, with the help of his wife, Sophia, and family, including their daughter, Georgia Maryol, Ignatios "Iggy" Patsalis, and cousins, the family restaurants included the Mayflower Café (now closed), Tomasita's, Tia Sophia's, Athena's Grecian Table (now closed), and Diego's, which was replaced by Atrisco Café and Bar in 2009 (*atrisco* is an Aztec word for "by the water's edge"; the restaurant is named after the large Spanish land grant on the south side of Albuquerque along the Rio Grande).

Perhaps the first Greek immigrant in northern New Mexico was Juan Griego, who is mentioned on the muster roll for Oñate in 1597; he was born in Candia, Greece.

Read: "Greek Ideals," by Julia Linder Bell, *Santa Fe New Mexican*, April 23, 2008; and *Origins of New Mexico Families: A Genealogy of the Spanish Colonial Period*, by Fray Angélico Chávez, Museum of New Mexico Press, 1992 (first published 1954).

129. What was the first Protestant church built in New Mexico, and what became of the property?

The Baptists in Santa Fe built the first Protestant church in New Mexico, in about 1854. It was an adobe building located at what is now the corner of Grant and Griffin streets. The Presbyterians bought the property in 1866, and the church became the first continuously functioning Protestant church in New Mexico. The building was first remodeled in 1867; over the years it has undergone numerous renovations, including a large addition in 2006 by Lloyd & Associates, architects. The 1939 John Gaw Meem design was retained.

Santa Fe is a city of many faiths and belief systems that coexist peacefully and often help each other. Among these belief systems are various indigenous, Native American spiritual traditions; Catholicism, including Roman Catholicism, Eastern Orthodoxy, and Anglicanism; Protestantism; Judaism; Islam; Sufism; Bahá'í; Buddhism; Hinduism; Taoism; Pantheism; Panentheism; Gnosticism; Mormonism; Unitarianism; Polytheism; Mysticism; Paganism; Agnosticism; and Atheism.

Read: *Santa Fe: Then and Now*, by Sheila Morand, Sunstone Press, 2008; "First Presbyterian Marks 140 Years," *Santa Fe New Mexican*, January 16, 2007; *Protestantism in the Sangre de Cristos, 1850–1920*, by Randi Jones Walker, University of New Mexico Press, 1991; *National Geographic Concise History of World Religions: An Illustrated Time Line*, edited by Tim Cooke, 2011; and "Where Diverse Beliefs Are Welcome," by Anne Constable, in *Santa Fe, Its 400th Year: Exploring the Past, Defining the Future*, edited by Rob Dean, Sunstone Press, 2010.

An early image of Guadalupe Catholic Church, first built as a small adobe shrine in 1777. Photograph by F. A. Nims. Courtesy of Palace of the Governors Photo Archives (NMHM/DCA), #015145.

What Is It?
(See Answer Key #20)

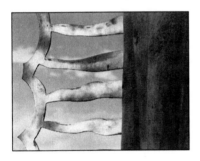

What Is It?
(See Answer Key #21)

What Is It?
(See Answer Key #22)

What Is It?
(See Answer Key #23)

What Is It?
(See Answer Key #24)

What Is It?
(See Answer Key #25)

"Coexist" is a bumper sticker seen around town. Copyright Peacemonger.org. Used with permission.

130. Who is Grant Avenue named for?

For President Ulysses S. Grant. In 1880, then General Grant and his wife, Julia, visited Santa Fe.

Read: *Grant,* by John Mosier, Palgrave Macmillan, 2006.

131. Who was the eighteenth-century French fur trader friendly with the Native Americans of the plains who was given the name Manitou, which means "Great Walker"?

Pedro Vial. Born in Lyon in about 1750, he traveled extensively and mapped many trails. He was employed by Spain to explore a route connecting San Antonio, Texas, to Nuevo México. He also explored a route north and east of Santa Fe, which later became known as the Santa Fe Trail; he did this for the Spaniards, who wanted to keep track of intruders from France and England. He later settled in Santa Fe. He died in 1814.

Read: *Pedro Vial and the Roads to Santa Fe,* by Noel Loomis and Abraham Nasatir, University of Oklahoma Press, 1967; and "My View: Blazer of Historic Santa Fe Trail All But Forgotten," by Jose Garcia, *Santa Fe New Mexican,* May 31, 2009.

132. Where are the original papers that don Pedro de Peralta was given by the viceroy with the instructions to establish a *villa* in 1610?

The original papers are at the Archivo General de las Indias (AGI), in Seville, Spain. A copy is at the Palace of the Governors, at the New Mexico History Museum, in Santa Fe.

Read: *The Threads of Memory: Spain and the United States = El Hilo de la Memoria: Espana y los Estados Unidos*, edited by Frances Levine, René Harris, and Josef Díaz, Fresco Fine Art, 2010.

133. When did the telegraph reach Santa Fe, delighting local newspaper editors, who previously had waited weeks for news to come by horseback?

The telegraph came to Santa Fe on July 8, 1868. The *Santa Fe New Mexican* became a daily paper that very day.

Read: "Telegraphs Ushered in the Communications Age," by Marc Simmons, *Santa Fe New Mexican*, March 30, 2002.

134. Bataan Death March survivor Errett Luján opened one of Santa Fe's first bowling alleys when, and under what name?

In 1958 Errett Luján opened the Coronado Lanes Bowling Alley in what became the Cordova Road shopping center. Near it was Santa Fe's small, indoor ice-skating rink. The first bowling alley was the Zia Bowling Alley, on Marcy Street, where the Gottliebs sold baloney sandwiches for fifty cents in the early 1940s.

Read: "Roll Call: Memories of WWII," by Errett Luján, *Santa Fe New Mexican*, July 10, 2005.

What Is It?
(See Answer Key #26)

135. What is the Spanish word for "cemetery," and where were the first non-Catholic cemeteries in Santa Fe, in which the Protestants, Jews, and people of other faiths were buried?

Since 1610 Santa Fe Catholics have traditionally buried their dead in *camposantos* (churchyards) near their churches. The site of the old Santa Fe cemetery that served San Miguel Mission church was east of the church, where the parking lot for the PERA building is, along East De Vargas Street.

In the 1840s, two cemeteries for non-Catholics were located side by side, north of the Plaza, just south of where the Masonic Temple is now, at Washington Street and the northern part of the Paseo de Peralta. The Masons were buried in the northwest cemetery and the Odd Fellows in the northeast cemetery. Governor Charles Bent, who had been buried for a brief time in Taos after his assassination, was moved and reburied in the Masons' cemetery in Santa Fe; later his body was moved again, to the National Cemetery, established in 1875 and situated on two parcels of land donated by Archbishop Lamy. Part of the land became the Rosario Cemetery, southeast of the National Cemetery.

Fairview Cemetery, founded in 1884, is on the west side of Cerrillos Road, opposite the western end of Cordova Road; it has been the resting place for the indigent, the destitute, the penniless, and the homeless, as well as at least three governors, ten mayors, the composer of "Little Joe the Wrangler," a few members of the Santa Fe Ring, and many affluent citizens. Buried there are such prominent non-Catholic Santa Fe families as the Gold family, who were among Santa Fe's earliest Jewish merchants, including Louis Gold, who arrived in 1849 and died in 1880; the Hayes-Moore family, including the Presbyterian minister Reverend William Hayes-Moore, who died in 1904; and the Slaughter family, including the first Black graduate of Santa Fe High School, Valdera Elvira Slaughter, who graduated with the third graduating class in 1902.

Read: "Homeless in Santa Fe: The Dead," by Christine Barber, *Santa Fe New Mexican*, November 17, 2004; "Graveyard Shift," by Tom Sharpe, *Santa Fe New Mexican*, September 15, 2006; *Fairview Cemetery, Santa Fe, NM*, by Corinne P. Sze, Fairview Cemetery Preservation Association, 2004; "Old Cemetery May Hold Answers to Santa Fe History," by Ron Longto, *Santa Fe New Mexican*, June 26, 1966; *Archbishop Lamy: An Epoch Maker*, by Louis H. Warner, New Mexican Publishing Company, 1936; and *American Military Cemeteries: A Comprehensive Illustrated Guide to the Hallowed Grounds of the United States, Including Cemeteries Overseas*, by Dean W. Holt, McFarland & Company, 1992.

Valdera Elvira Slaughter Roberts, 1934.
Courtesy of Palace of the Governors Photo
Archives (NMHM/DCA), #111081.

136. What is the name of the bridge that crosses the Santa Fe River west of the Guadalupe Church?

The De Fouri Street bridge is named for the French priest Father James de Fouri, who renovated the Guadalupe Church. It crosses the river, connecting the Alameda and Agua Fria Street. De Fouri came to Santa Fe in 1881 to be Archbishop Lamy's secretary. He died in Las Vegas, New Mexico, in 1901.

Read: *Historic New Mexico Churches*, by Annie Lux, with photographs by Daniel Nadelbach, Gibbs Smith, 2007; and *Historical Sketch of the Catholic Church in New Mexico*, by James H. Defouri, Yucca Tree Press, 2003 (first published in 1887).

137. The Lensic, El Paseo, Cassell's Oñate Theatre, the Alley, and the Paris are names of movie theaters once in Santa Fe; all are gone except the Lensic, which is no longer simply a movie theater. What was considered the best place to attend Spanish-language movies? And what was the name of the last outdoor drive-in movie theater in the Santa Fe area?

The Alley, across from the Lensic on San Francisco Street, was the place to go for Spanish-language movies in the 1940s and 1950s. The Yucca Drive-in, with its neon sign in the shape of a towering yucca plant, was the last outdoor drive-in movie theater to remain open in Santa Fe; it closed in the late 1980s. Another popular outdoor movie theater, the Pueblo Drive-in, was built at the northern end of Tesuque in 1949 and featured a giant mural on the back of the large screen, part of a pueblo-style adobe structure; the mural, of a warrior on a bucking horse scared by a skunk, was painted by Quincy Tahoma, a Navajo artist who had studied at the Santa Fe Indian School along with classmates Harrison Begay and Andy Tsihnahjinnie. The Pueblo was torn down in the 1960s, and then a drive-in of that name was located on Cerrillos Road for about a decade. In the early 1980s the El Paseo Theatre, on San Francisco Street, was restored to its earlier glory, complete with huge murals featuring Native Americans and comfortable couches for cozy movie viewing. The theater was gutted to make room for a retail store.

Read: *Santa Fe: A Pictorial History*, by John Sherman, Donning Company, 1996; *Quincy Tahoma: The Life and Legacy of a Navajo Artist*, by Charnell Havens and Vera Marie Badertscher, Schiffer Books, 2011; and *The American Drive-in Movie Theater*, by Don Sanders and Susan Sanders, Motorbooks International, 2003.

138. Who were some of the first Jewish merchants to arrive in Santa Fe?

Solomon Jacob Spiegelberg arrived in New Mexico from Germany and set up business in Santa Fe in 1846. His five brothers, as well as the Gold, Staab, Seligman, Bibo, Ilfeld, and Zeckendorf families, among others, soon followed. By 1852 Spiegelberg was such a successful businessman that he was able to loan the territorial legislature $4,000 to cover the legislators' salaries when the territory was strapped for money.

Abraham Staab was involved in Santa Fe's business and cultural activities. He cofounded and became first president of the Santa Fe Chamber of Commerce, was a director of the First National Bank in Santa Fe, served as a member of the county commissioners' board, was secretary of the First Capitol Building Commission, and was influential in bringing the Denver & Rio Grande Railroad line from Denver into Santa Fe. He was one of the prominent citizens of Santa Fe who successfully fought the move promoted by Mayor Thornton in the 1890s to relocate the capital of the territory from Santa Fe to Albuquerque.

Staab also loaned money to help build the Santa Fe cathedral (now a basilica). He forgave the loan, and most people agree that Archbishop Lamy probably intended the Tetragammaton (the four consonants of the ancient Hebrew name for God) inscribed within a triangle (a common Christian symbol for the Trinity) above the entrance to the cathedral to honor his friendships within the Jewish community of Santa Fe.

Read: *A History of the Jews in New Mexico*, by Henry J. Tobias, University of New Mexico Press, 1992; *Jewish Pioneers of New Mexico*, compiled and edited by Tomas Jaehn, Museum of New Mexico Press, 2003; *To the End of the Earth: A History of the Crypto-Jews of New Mexico*, by Stanley M. Hordes, Columbia University Press, 2005; and *Jewish Pioneers of New Mexico*, volumes 1–10, New Mexico Jewish Historical Society, 2004–2006.

Abraham Staab, c. 1880. Courtesy of Palace of the Governors Photo Archives (NMHM/DCA), #011040.

139. What was the Cradle House, and when did it open?

Santa Fe's first "nursing" home, the Cradle House was started in the 1940s by Dr. Laurence Boatman to care for new mothers and others in need of recuperation from medical procedures. It was on Don Gaspar Street.

Read: "Women Who Made a Difference," by Emma Moya, *La Herencia*, Summer 2003.

140. What is a "wayside pulpit," and where can you see one in Santa Fe?

A wayside pulpit is a small structure that functions as a roadside bulletin board where thought-provoking messages reflecting various universal truths may be posted frequently throughout the year. The concept of the wayside pulpit was introduced to North American churches in 1919 by a Unitarian minister inspired by European wayside shrines. The Unitarian Universalist Church's wayside pulpit, along Galisteo Street, has been in service since 1987. Many other churches and organizations use this method to share uplifting or instructive messages. Some typical quotations are, "All people smile in the same language," by Anonymous; "Forgiveness is the final form of love," by Reinhold Niebuhr; "I tremble for my country when I reflect that God is just," by Thomas Jefferson; "An idea is salvation by imagination," by Frank Lloyd Wright; "To be blind is bad, but worse to have eyes and not to see," by Helen Keller; "If you want peace, work for justice," by Pope Paul VI; and "No act of kindness, no matter how small, is ever wasted," by Aesop.

Walk, bike, or drive slowly along Galisteo Street north of Coronado Street to see what the wayside pulpit says.

What Is It?
(See Answer Key #27)

141. In the 1860s the Santa Fe bandstand was situated where on the Plaza, and what happened to usurp this position?

The gazebo bandstand was at the center of the Plaza until a monument for soldiers was erected there in 1868. A new bandstand, or community stage, designed by architect Beverly Spears, was built in 2004.

Read: "Staging Ground," by Doug Mattson, *Santa Fe New Mexican*, July 4, 2004.

142. Who was born in 1881, became a suffragist, was a political leader, educator, state superintendent, environmentalist, writer, and land homesteader, as well as a prominent social leader?

Adelina "Nina" Otero-Warren. Her life straddled the time when New Mexico was mostly Hispanic and rural into the time of increasing Anglo emigrant influences and challenges, as New Mexico went from being a U.S. territory to statehood. She wrote a book about Hispanic social life and customs in New Mexico, stressing Spanish cultural influence and inheritance, titled *Old Spain in Our Southwest*. (She also disarmingly declared herself a widow right after getting divorced although the stuffy, unfaithful man was still among the living.)

Read: *Nina Otero-Warren of Santa Fe*, by Charlotte Whaley, Sunstone Press, 2007; and *Old Spain in Our Southwest*, by Nina Otero-Warren, Sunstone Press, 2006 (first published 1936).

"Nina" Otero-Warren, whose full name was Adelina Isabel Emilia Otero-Warren. Courtesy of Palace of the Governors Photo Archives (NMHM/DCA), #089756.

143. Which Santa Feans in 1922 helped kill the infamous Bursum Bill, which had been introduced by New Mexico senator Albert Bacon Fall, under President Warren Harding?

The Bursom Bill aimed to take more land and water rights from Native Americans and would have unfairly legalized squatters' rights. Although the bill passed in the U.S. Senate, it was killed in the House of Representatives after strong lobbying opposition from many friends of the Native Americans, including members of the Taos and Santa Fe art colonies, John Collier, Oliver La Farge, the Indian Welfare Department of the National Federation of Women's Clubs, Nina Otero-Warren, Mamie Meadors, Alice Corbin Henderson, and others, as well as the well-organized All Indian Pueblo Council, which took their case directly to Washington, D.C.

John Collier, originally from Georgia, was educated at Columbia University and the Collège de France, in Paris; in the 1920s he came to Santa Fe and Taos, where he became a social reformer and Native American advocate. He rejected the contemporary policies of forced assimilation and worked to enable preservation of Native American culture. He served as commissioner of Indian affairs from 1933 until he retired in 1945, the longest tenure in U.S. history.

Read: *Talking Back to Civilization: Indian Voices from the Progressive Era*, edited by Frederick E. Hoxie, Bedford/St. Martin's, 2001; *The Assault on Assimilation: John Collier and the Origins of Indian Policy Reform*, by L. C. Kelly, University of New Mexico Press, 1963; *From Every Zenith: A Memoir, and Some Essays on Life and Thought*, by John Collier, Sage Books, 1963; and "Indian Man," by Marc Simmons, *Santa Fe Reporter*, February 1, 1979.

Indian with Ponies at the Water Hole. **Linoleum block cut by Harold E. West, 1930s.**

Indian Paintbrush. **Pen and ink drawing by Cathie Sullivan, 2011, based on her original screen print, 1996. Courtesy of the artist.**

The artist talks about Indian paintbrush as follows:

"In Northern New Mexico the semiarid foothills of the Southern Rocky Mountains are home to junipers and piñon and ponderosa pine trees. In the early spring a vanguard of red to orange Indian paintbrush adds a colorful footnote to the wide horizons of the Southwest, with their blue skies, towering clouds, and purple mountain ranges. Paintbrush is a member of the Figwort plant family and lives as a parasite on the roots of grasses, which it taps for nourishment. The red 'petals' are not flower petals in the usual flower structure but colored leaves called bracts. This is also the case for Christmas poinsettias. The paintbrush's tiny yellow flowers are tucked deep between the red bracts."

144. Who were the founding members of the Spanish Colonial Arts Society?

In 1925 Mary Austin, Frank Applegate, Eva Scott Muse Fényes, Leonora Muse Curtin, and Leonora Frances Curtin helped found the society that preserves and perpetuates Spanish colonial art forms produced in New Mexico and southern Colorado since colonization by Spain in 1598.

Read: *Conexiones: Connections in Spanish Colonial Art*, edited by Carmella Padilla, Museum of Spanish Colonial Art, 2002.

145. Who was the longest-serving governor in New Mexico state history?

Bruce King. He served three separate terms as governor—from 1971 to 1975, from 1979 to 1983, and from 1991 to 1995. A rancher and consummate politician, he was also known for his malapropisms, the most famous of which occurred when he said that a legislative proposal would "open a whole box of Pandoras." He was a working cowboy to boot.

Read: "A Box of Pandoras: Bruce King's Malapropisms," by Steve Terrell, *Santa Fe New Mexican*, November 14, 2009; and *Cowboy in the Roundhouse: A Political Life*, by Bruce King, Sunstone Press, 1998.

What Is It?
(See Answer Key #28)

146. Where was Santa Fe's first public park located?

The first public park in Santa Fe, in the mid-1840s, was located along the river. The area became known as La Alameda.

Read: "Alameda Park Was Place of Beauty," by Marc Simmons, *Santa Fe New Mexican*, February 17, 2001.

147. The nationwide League of Women Voters, founded in 1920, was organized to educate women to use the vote; the Santa Fe chapter was started in what year?

1951.

Read: "Voters' Group at 90 Is Strong As Ever," by Judy Williams and Meredith Machen, *Santa Fe New Mexican*, January 31, 2010.

148. When was the Rodeo de Santa Fe founded, why does it begin on a Wednesday, and what is the mascot?

The rodeo was organized and founded in 1949 by Freddie Baca, Roy Butler, Austin "Slim" Green, Gene Petchesky, Paul Ragle, Paul Rutledge, and others. One of the first structures to be built on the south side of town, it was originally situated where the public softball fields are, in what is now called Ragle Park, at Yucca Street and West Zia Road. Soon afterwards Roy Butler, of Butler & Foley Plumbing, bought close to a hundred acres for a larger arena, off what is now called Rodeo Road, and the Rodeo de Santa Fe found its permanent home. Sadly, shortly thereafter, Butler died, on a Wednesday. To honor him, the rodeo has since always opened on a Wednesday. The Rodeo Parade kicks off the events the week before.

The mascot is a bull, El Toro Diablo, originally created by artist Will Shuster, who also helped create Zozobra.

Read: "Freddie Baca: A Cowboy for all Time," by Walter K. Lopez, *La Herencia*, Summer 1996; and "A Love of Bull," by Natalie Storey, *Santa Fe New Mexican*, June 18, 2005.

The Bronc Threw Him. Linoleum block cut by Harold E. West, c. 1930s.

Best Friends. Linoleum block cut by Harold E. West, c. 1930s.

149. What famous female photographer was known for her photographic landscapes and portraits of the Navajo people, and what famous male photographer was almost as serious a cook as a photographer?

Laura Gilpin was famous primarily for her photographs of the Navajo people and vast Southwestern landscapes; she died in Santa Fe in 1979.

Beaumont Newhall's friends, including Bernice Abbott, Ansel Adams, Paul Strand, and Edward Weston, all knew he considered the preparation, appreciation, and enjoyment of food almost as important as his work with photography and its history. He died in Santa Fe in 1993.

Read: *Laura Gilpin: An Enduring Grace,* by Martha Sandweiss, Amon Carter Museum, 1986; *The Pueblos: A Camera Chronicle,* by Laura Gilpin, Hastings House, 1941; *Beaumont's Kitchen: Lessons on Food, Life, and Photography with Beaumont Newhall,* essay by David Scheinbaum, Radius Books, 2009; and *The History of Photography: From 1839 to the Present,* by Beaumont Newhall, Museum of Modern Art, 1982.

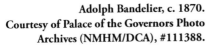

150. A Santa Fe resident from 1880 to 1892, renowned anthropologist and archaeologist Adolph Bandelier regarded the Pueblo peoples' history as what?

He determined that that the history of the Pueblo people was worthy of study, and he challenged the supposedly expert notion that indigenous people were lesser beings.

He helped instigate the field of study known as modern archaeology, which includes studies of the earliest Paleo-Indians of twelve thousand years ago, the thousands of years of archaic foragers, and the more than fifteen hundred years of Pueblo farming communities. His work helped reveal the Santa Fe area's history of continuity and adaptation in relation to farming. Ancestral Pueblo people depended on agriculture to sustain them in their predominantly non-nomadic lifestyle; corn, beans, and squash were the most important crops.

Farming, ranching, and growing gardens have long been part of the fabric of life in Santa Fe, as elsewhere. The history of farming in northern New Mexico includes the agricultural practice of sharecropping (*aparcería*), which dates to thirteenth-century Spain; by the eighteenth century sharecroppers were working together along the Rio Grande. A man who owned no land could make an agreement with a large landholder to farm a piece of his property on shares. The owner provided seed, tools, and plow oxen, while the worker (*mediero*) provided the labor; they shared the crop equally. Sometimes a worker with his own seed and equipment would in effect rent needed land; this man was called an *arendatario* in rural New Mexico, and he would take a larger share of the final crop. This kind of sharing also eventually occurred between Pueblo landholders and landless Spaniards, and vice-versa. Sharecropping continued into the twentieth century, with informal agreements between the land-rich and the land-poor, and has contributed to flexible versions of sharing still used today.

Read: *Bandelier: The Life and Adventures of Adolph Bandelier*, by Charles H. Lange and Carroll L. Riley, University of Utah Press, 1996; *Before Santa Fe: Archaeology of the City Different*, by Jason S. Shapiro, Museum of New Mexico Press, 2008; *The Medieval Heritage of Mexico*, by Luis Weckmann, Fordham University Press, 1992; and "A Fragment of Medieval History: Sharecropping Became Common Practice in N.M. by the 18th Century," by Marc Simmons, *Santa Fe New Mexican*, July 23, 2011.

Adolph Bandelier, c. 1870.
Courtesy of Palace of the Governors Photo
Archives (NMHM/DCA), #111388.

151. The first recycling program began in Santa Fe when, and because of the efforts of whom?

In the 1960s Billie Schaumberg, working with the Santa Fe chapter of the American Association of University Women, began a recycling program. The City of Santa Fe Public Utilities Department is responsible for recycling under the solid-waste section and also is in charge of refuse collection in the city as well as the treatment of wastewater. Under the Sangre de Cristo Water Division, the city is also in charge of the delivery of fire suppression water and potable water.

Read: "Schaumberg Known for Her Community Activism," by Ana Pacheco, *Santa Fe New Mexican*, February 18, 2007; *Waste and Recycling*, by Janine Amos, Raintree Syeck-Vaughn, 1993; and *Recycling: Reducing Waste*, by Buffy Silverman, Heinemann Library, 2008.

152. What are the requirements to sell jewelry and other art under the portal at the Palace of the Governors, on the Santa Fe Plaza?

The items for sale must be handmade and stamped by the artist, who must be a member of a Native American tribe. Usually the seller is the artist or a member of the artist's family.

Read: *Under the Palace Portal*, by Karl Hoerig, University of New Mexico Press, 2003.

Pueblo vendors under the portal at the Palace of the Governors. Photograph by T. Harmon Parkhurst, c. 1920. Courtesy of Palace of the Governors Photo Archives (NMHM/DCA), #069973.

153. Where was the site of the Civilian Conservation Corps in Santa Fe during the Great Depression?

In 1933 the Civilian Conservation Corps (CCC) established a camp consisting of forty-two buildings on eighty acres in the area that is now the Casa Solana subdivision, in northwest Santa Fe. The CCC was designed to provide employment for unemployed, unmarried men from ages eighteen to twenty-five who were part of relief families. The CCC was also intended to aid in implementing natural-resource conservation programs throughout the United States. It was the most popular of President Franklin Delano Roosevelt's New Deal programs, which also included the Works Project Administration (WPA); the programs often collaborated on projects. The CCC's camp trained young men to work and provided jobs on public-works projects, including the construction and repair of public buildings, roads, rock walls, campgrounds, dams, and furniture. In the City of Santa Fe streets, sidewalks, sewers, and bridges were repaired by CCC workers.

One example of their work is the National Park Service building, on Old Santa Fe Trail, constructed in 1937 and decorated by New Deal artists and craftsmen. A National Historic Landmark building, it is one of the country's largest adobe office buildings, occupying about 24,000 square feet. Out of town, at the Bandelier National Monument welcome center, some of the work done by CCC craftsmen includes chandeliers, wall sconces, and wooden furniture.

After the attack on Pearl Harbor, the CCC camp was taken over and used for the Santa Fe Japanese Internment Camp. The CCC program ended in 1942, though it became a model for other conservation programs, such as the National Civilian Community Corps, a part of AmeriCorps.

Read: *Coming of Age in the Great Depression: The Civilian Conservation Corps Experience in New Mexico, 1933–1942*, by Richard Melzer, Yucca Tree Press, 2000; *The New Deal: A 75th Anniversary Celebration*, by Kathryn A. Flynn, with Richard Polese, Gibbs Smith, 2008; and "New Deal's Legacy," by Tom Sharpe, *Santa Fe New Mexican*, April 6, 2008. Also visit the CCC exhibit at Bandelier National Monument.

154. Where were Japanese-Americans imprisoned in a Department of Justice internment camp in Santa Fe during World War II?

The Federal Immigration and Naturalization Service took over the same camp and barracks previously used by the Civilian Conservation Corps, in what is now the Casa Solana neighborhood. The Santa Fe Japanese Internment Camp was established as a high-security camp. After the entire West Coast of the United States was declared a "potential military area" in early 1942, forcible removal of Japanese-Americans from their homes and placement in relocation centers as "enemy aliens," without a trial, became legal. The relocation program was modeled on the Native American reservation system, and there was tension in New Mexico about it, especially since it was implemented in so much haste and secrecy.

The average age of the internees was fifty-two. Farmers and fishermen were the first to arrive. Later the camp's occupants included doctors, journalists, actors, and college professors. The Santa Fe camp was run more smoothly than were camps in the rest of the United States because of the experience and tolerance of the camp administration and guards; this better treatment led to more cooperation from the prisoners. The Santa Fe camp closed in April 1946, after having detained 4,555 men throughout the war.

A plaque commemorating the Japanese-American detainees is on the north ridge (in the Frank S. Ortiz Park) overlooking the area where the sprawling internment camp once was.

Read: *Silent Voices of World War II: When Sons of the Land of Enchantment Met Sons of the Land of the Rising Sun*, by Evertt M. Rogers and Nancy R. Bartlit, Sunstone Press, 2005; "Casualties of Caution and Fear: Life in Santa Fe's Japanese Internment Camp, 1942–46," by Richard Melzer, in *Essays in Twentieth-Century New Mexico History*, edited by Judith Boyce DeMark, University of New Mexico Press, 1994; "Santa Fe in World War II, 1940–1947," by Judy Reed, in *All Trails Lead to Santa Fe*, Sunstone Press, 2010; *Now Silence: A Novel of World War II*, by Tori Warner Shepard, Sunstone Press, 2008; and *The Internment of Japanese Americans during World War II: Detention of American Citizens*, by John Davenport, Chelsea House, 2010.

155. Who was the first Mexican-born U.S. senator?

Octaviano Ambrosio Larrazolo was born in Allende, Mexico, in 1859 and came to the United States in 1870. He attended Saint Michael's College, in Santa Fe. In 1918 he became the fourth governor of the State of New Mexico (and the second Hispanic governor). He served as a state representative before becoming a U.S. senator in 1928.

Read: "A Long Journey for Mexico-Born Governor," by Marc Simmons, *Santa Fe New Mexican*, January 26, 2008.

156. When did the radio show *Ripley's Believe It or Not* broadcast live from Santa Fe?

On April 16, 1940, host Robert Ripley featured guest-speaker Elfego Baca, who related that he was once sentenced to thirty days in a jail where he happened to be the jailer, and that as jailer he earned 75 cents a day for feeding the prisoner, himself—believe it or not!

In 1958 Walt Disney released a movie titled *The Nine Lives of Elfego Baca*.

Read: *Incredible Elfego Baca: Good Man, Bad Man of the Old West*, by Howard Bryan, Clear Light, 1993; and *Fun and Games*, from the series Ripley's Believe It or Not! Mind Teasers, Capstone Press, 1991.

157. In what countries does Santa Fe have sister cities?

Santa Fe has sister cities in at least seven countries: China (Zhang Jai Jie), Cuba (Holguín), Italy (Sorrento), Japan (Tsuyama), Mexico (Hidalgo de Parral), Spain (Santa Fe), and Uzbekistan (Bukhara). The United States Sister Cities Program was started by President Dwight D. Eisenhower to "promote peace through mutual respect, understanding, and cooperation—one individual, one community at a time." In Santa Fe there is a mayor-appointed, city council–approved Sister Cities Advisory Committee. St. Michael's High School, in Santa Fe, New Mexico, has a sister cities partnership program with El Instituto de Ensenanza Secundaria "Hispanidad" de Santa Fe de la Vega de Granada (in Santa Fe, near Granada, Spain.)

Find Santa Fe's sister cities on a map.

Read: *Creative Tourism: A Global Conversation*, edited by Rebecca Wurzburger, Tom Aageson, Alex Pattakos, and Sabrina Pratt, Sunstone Press, 2009; and *Mapping the World by Heart*, by David J. Smith, FableVision Learning, 2010.

158. What is a "ghost grant," and in what year did New Mexico's congressional delegation request that the U.S. General Accounting Office (GAO) investigate land-grant claims?

A ghost grant is a grant with a fictitious legal description that could not be located on the ground and usually one that is not challenged because it has not come to trial. The U.S. GAO, the investigative arm of the U.S. Congress, was invited to investigate land-grant claims in 1999. Then, in January 2001, the GAO solicited public comment about both its list of Spanish and Mexican land grants and the process it followed for identifying the 295 grants in New Mexico.

The GAO was directed to study the land-grant issue, involving more than a hundred and fifty years of history. Many scholars and land-grant heirs had determined that the federal government had not adequately lived up to its commitment to respect land grants, as addressed in the Treaty of Guadalupe Hidalgo, which ended the Mexican-American War, in 1848. Specifically, President James Polk had objected to the provision in the treaty that protected land-grant claims; he feared the provision might jeopardize the land grants that had already been settled in Texas. The U.S. Congress established the Court of Private Land Claims in 1891 to evaluate the outstanding land claims. In 1897 Congress ruled that Mexico, not local communities, held title to the communal lands in the community land grants and therefore Mexico could transfer all communal lands to the United States.

The work done by the Court of Private Land Claims did not clear up the controversy connected to the loss of the common lands. The controversy is ongoing.

Read: "A City Different Than We Thought: Land Grants in Early Santa Fe, 1598–1900," by Malcolm Ebright, in *All Trails Lead to Santa Fe*, Sunstone Press, 2010; "New GAO Report Answers Inquiries on Land Grants," by Ben Neary, *Santa Fe New Mexican*, January 25, 2001; *Mercedes Reales: Hispanic Land Grants of the Upper Rio Grande Region*, by Victor Westphall, University of New Mexico Press, 1983; *The Court of Private Land Claims: The Adjudication of Spanish and Mexican Land Grant Titles, 1891–1904*, by Richard Wells Bradfute, University of New Mexico Press, 1975; and "Private Land Claims in the Southwest" by J. J. Bowden, unpublished thesis in bound form at the New Mexico Supreme Court Law Library.

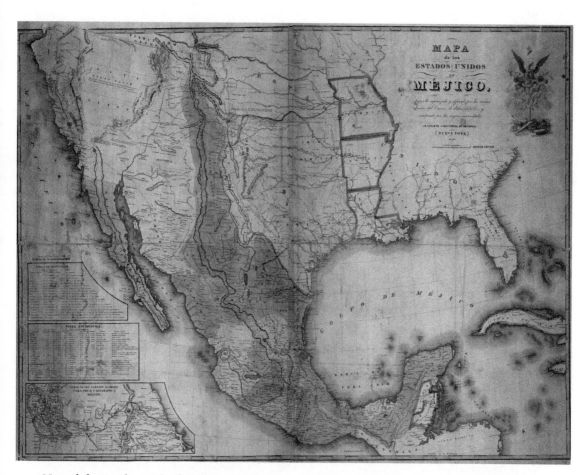

Mapa de los Estados Unidos de Méjico. This 1847 map of the U.S.–Mexico border was a lithograph made by John Disturnell shortly after the United States, under President James K. Polk, declared war on Mexico, in 1846. Disturnell used plates from an earlier map of the border area and copied some previous errors. The timing was right, however, and the map became popular and was regarded as the geographic authority. It was used during negotiation of the Treaty of Guadalupe-Hidalgo, 1848.
Photograph courtesy of the Fray Angélico Chávez History Library.

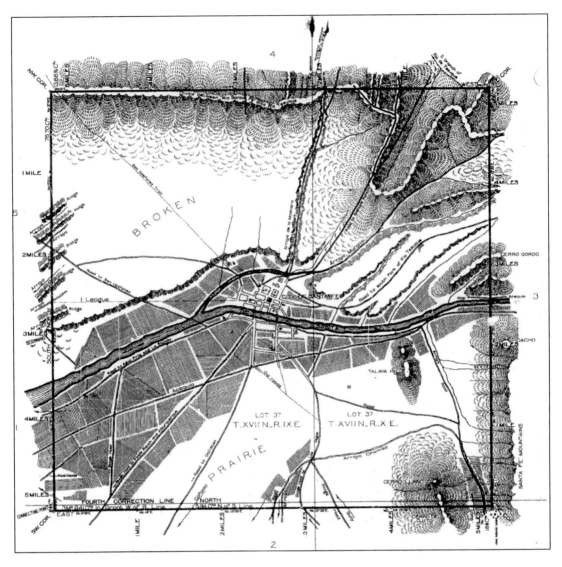

Plat of the Santa Fe Grant, encompassing approximately 17,000 acres, surveyed by Griffin and McMillin in 1877. Bureau of Land Management, Santa Fe.

159. When smallpox ravaged Santa Fe and the surrounding area in the late 1800s, how did people notify others of the danger?

They posted a yellow ribbon on their front doors as a warning that someone in the house had smallpox. Dr. Cristóbal María Larrañaga was the Santa Fe military surgeon who brought the smallpox vaccine from New Spain in 1804.

Read: "Smallpox Epidemics Plagued NM throughout 19th Century," by Marc Simmons, *Santa Fe New Mexican*, October 6, 2001.

160. When did the territorial legislature allocate funds for a library in a room in the Palace of the Governors?

In 1850 the U.S. Congress appropriated $5,000 to establish a territorial library. Books were freighted by ox wagon over the plains and placed in a room in the Palace of the Governors. This was the first public library in the Southwest. John Ward was named the first territorial librarian, in 1853. Later the Women's Board of Trade helped keep the project going.

The Santa Fe Public Library now has three branches: the main branch, located at the corner of Washington Avenue and Marcy Street, northeast of the Plaza; the La Farge branch, on Llano Street, off St. Michael's Drive; and the Southside branch, on Jaguar Drive, near Airport Road. There are many other libraries in Santa Fe.

Read: *One Book at a Time: The History of the Library in New Mexico*, by Linda G. Harris, New Mexico Library Foundation, 1998; and "A Santa Fe Tradition since 1850, Public Libraries Deserve Attention," by Marc Simmons, *Santa Fe New Mexican*, April 9, 2005.

Women's Board of Trade Library, on Washington Avenue. Photograph by Jesse Nusbaum, 1912.
Courtesy of Palace of the Governors Photo Archives (NMHM/DCA), #056603.

161. What word, deemed offensive, was chiseled away in 1974 by an unknown person in the dead of night from the soldier's monument (an obelisk) in the center of the Santa Fe Plaza?

The word *savage*, which had been used in reference to the Native Americans of the plains, who had raided both the Spanish settlements and the Indian Pueblos alike. The word was an English translation of the Spanish word *salvaje*. The Spanish used *salvaje* to mean "nomadic peoples," while *pueblo* meant "settled peoples."

Read: "Soldiers Monument on Plaza Has Survived Repeated Controversies," by Marc Simmons, *Santa Fe New Mexican*, October 14, 2000; *The Man with the Calabash Pipe: Some Observations*, by Oliver La Farge, Sunstone Press, 2011 (first published 1966); "The True Story of the Monument on the Plaza," by Thomas E. Chávez, *The Best of* From the Plaza: *Interviews and Opinions from the Plaza of Santa Fe*, by Matt Kelly, Lone Butte Press, 1998; *Nations of the Southwest*, by Amanda Bishop and Bobbie Kalman, Crabtree, 2003; and *The Pueblo: Farmers of the Southwest*, by Mary Englar, Bridgestone Books, 2003.

Obelisk. Drawing by Anita H. Lehmann, 2011. Courtesy of the artist.

162. Who is Hyde Memorial State Park named after?

The park, located on the road up to the ski basin, was established in 1938 on land donated by Benjamin Talbot Babbitt Hyde's widow, Helen Chauncey Bronson Hyde, to honor her husband. He was a Santa Fe educator, scientist, and naturalist.

Read: *The Place Names of New Mexico*, by Robert Julyan, University of New Mexico Press, 1998.

163. Bishop's Lodge Road is named for whom?

Archbishop Jean Baptiste Lamy had a comfortable out-of-town house at what is now the resort called Bishop's Lodge. His small, personal chapel and his gardens from the late 1800s have been carefully preserved; the house and the gardens nearby can be visited daily for free at the resort on Bishop's Lodge Road.

Read: *Wake for a Fat Vicar: Father Juan Felipe Ortiz, Archbishop Lamy, and the New Mexican Catholic Church in the Middle of the Nineteenth Century*, by Fray Angélico Chávez and Thomas E. Chávez, LPD Press, 2004.

The ivory handle of Archbishop Lamy's black umbrella, one of possibly several he had acquired in the 1870s from the Paris store Grands Magasins du Louvre, with his name engraved on the handle. Lamy was described as preaching or dining under his umbrella on rainy days. Courtesy of François-Marie Patorni.

164. Where was the Bruns Army Hospital, which opened on April 19, 1943, in anticipation of World War II casualties?

The main hospital complex was near the intersection of Cerrillos Road and St. Michael's Drive, close to the very edge of town in 1943, at what is the present campus of the Santa Fe University of Art and Design. The annex was located across town, not far from the Old Santa Fe Trail intersection with Camino del Monte Sol. The hospital was named for Colonel Earl Harvey Bruns, of the Army Medical Corps, who was an authority on pulmonary disease and who ironically died of pulmonary tuberculosis. The hospital was closed by the end of 1946. (The Christian Brothers bought the land, and St. Michael's College moved there in 1947.)

Read: "Santa Fe in World War II, 1940–1947," by Judy Reed, in *All Trails Lead to Santa Fe*, Sunstone Press, 2010.

165. Los Conquistadores was the name of what group that provided free entertainment from 1909 to 1940?

They were a group of volunteer musicians from the Santa Fe area who provided free band concerts for the public. Daniel McKenzie, a popular band leader for many years, composed the first official City of Santa Fe song, "La Villa de Santa Fe."

The Santa Fe Community Concert Band continues one of Santa Fe's oldest traditions, that of free public concerts by volunteer musicians. This tradition dates back more than a hundred and forty years, to when Francisco Pérez, after serving as a Confederate Army bugler in the ill-fated invasion of New Mexico by Texas forces during the Civil War, returned to Santa Fe, decided to stay, and formed La Banda de Santa Fe. This musical tradition continues to this day. The Santa Fe Community Concert Band, formally incorporated in 1983 under the directorship of Greg Heltman, plays on the Santa Fe Plaza and at Federal Park.

Other free musical entertainment includes the summer Santa Fe Bandstand series and several concerts during the year by the Santa Fe Community Orchestra, founded in 1982 and directed by Oliver Prezant.

Read: "Buried Music Unearthed for Palace Concert Band," by Emily Van Cleve, *Santa Fe New Mexican*, September 1, 1995.

166. One of the bloodiest prison riots in the history of the United States started at the State Penitentiary of New Mexico when?

February 2, 1980.

Read: *The Devil's Butcher Shop: The New Mexico Prison Uprising*, by Roger Morris, University of New Mexico Press, 1988.

167. Who was the "writer in the window"?

Georgelle Hirliman was a writer who set up her writing studio behind a big window in a shop on San Francisco Street, near the Plaza. Hirliman accepted notes and questions from the public during the 1980s. She published *Dear Writer in the Window: The Wit and Wisdom of a Sidewalk Sage* in 1992. She also wrote *The Hate Factory*, about the New Mexico prison riot.

Read: *The Hate Factory: A First-Hand Account of the 1980 Riot at the Penitentiary of New Mexico*, by Georgelle Hirliman, based on interviews with inmate W. G. Stone, iUniverse, 2005; and *Dear Writer in the Window: The Wit and Wisdom of a Sidewalk Sage*, by Georgelle Hirliman, Penguin Books, 1992.

168. Who owned the first motorcycle in Santa Fe, and in what year?

Jesse Nusbaum rode his Excelsior motorcycle into Santa Fe in 1909. He was later hired as an archaeologist by Edgar Lee Hewett, and he was one of the people most directly involved in instigating the push for what has become the Santa Fe style of architecture, a combination of Pueblo and Mexican influences. A hard worker, he was also famous for his sense of humor and his willingness to play pranks.

Nusbaum Street, in downtown Santa Fe, was not named for Jesse but for Simon Nusbaum, one of the Jewish settlers who came to the area in the 1880s. He worked in the surveyor general's office, became territorial treasurer, and later became the postmaster, a position he was so dedicated to that he lived in the post office for a while. He married Dora Rogers Rutledge, and they raised children in a house at the corner of Washington Avenue and what was later called Nusbaum Street. Simon Nusbaum died in Santa Fe in 1921.

The Simon Nusbaum property was razed for a parking lot in 1960, and public outrage about this led to the establishment of the Historic Santa Fe Foundation, in 1961, to prevent further loss of historic buildings.

The Historic Santa Fe Foundation, which was started by its parent organization, the Old Santa Fe Association, is an architectural conservation group specializing in the physical preservation of historic buildings. The organization raises money to purchase historic properties and to preserve the properties they own. Their headquarters are at El Zaguan, on

Canyon Road, the first property they acquired. In addition to their conservation efforts, HSFF promotes education about historic architecture and building methods, protects properties through historic easements (which can protect everything from a significant doorway to an entire home), and maintains a historic property registry. Properties on the registry have bronze, shield-shaped plaques on their facades.

The original organization, called the Old Santa Fe Association, was established in 1926 by Mary Austin, John Gaw Meem, Carlos Vierra, Gustave Baumann, Alice Corbin, William Penhallow Henderson, and others with the intent to preserve historic buildings and the historic nature of Santa Fe. It uses political and legal methods to monitor the Santa Fe scene.

The two organizations have a close working relationship but focus on different aspects of historic preservation.

Read: *Tierra Dulce: Reminiscences from the Jesse Nusbaum Papers*, by Jesse L. Nusbaum, Sunstone Press, 1980; *The City Different and the Palace: The Palace of the Governors, Its Role in Santa Fe History, Including Jesse Nusbaum's Restoration Journals*, by Rosemary Nusbaum, Sunstone Press, 1978.

Jesse Nusbaum, dancing with a mannequin, c. 1915. Courtesy of Palace of the Governors Photo Archives (NMHM/DCA), #028784.

ANOTHER VICTIM OF SANTA FE STYLE

"Another Victim of Santa Fe Style," cartoon by Jerome Milord, 1989. Used with permission.

The Simon Nusbaum house, on Washington Avenue, was torn down in 1960 to make room for a parking lot. The photograph was taken by Tyler Dingee just before the building was razed. Courtesy of Palace of the Governors Photo Archives (NMHM/DCA), #091901.

169. Who renamed La Conquistadora "Our Lady of Peace," and why?

In the late 1980s Archbishop Robert Sánchez renamed Santa Fe's Madonna in order to change the historic association of her name from the "conquest of peoples" to the "conquest of hearts."

Read: *Our Lady of the Conquest*, by Fray Angélico Chávez, Sunstone Press, 2010 (first published 1948); and "La Conquistadora Now Called Our Lady of Peace," *Santa Fe New Mexican*, July 13, 1992.

170. In the 1880s, where was Santa Fe's Italian neighborhood?

Directly south of the capitol building, along what is now Paseo de Peralta. The neighborhood was developed by the stonemasons, stone cutters, and architects recruited by Archbishop Lamy in 1876 to build St. Francis Cathedral. Several historic brick houses remain from this period. The Digneos, the Palladinos, and the Berardinellis were among the first from Italy; later family names include Palermo, Domenici, Gardi, Fiorina, and Pertusini. These names are associated with business people, judges, and a U.S. senator.

Read: "Italian Heritage: Religion, Work Forged Families," by Cheryl Wittenauer, *Santa Fe New Mexican*, April 20, 1986.

171. What and where was Saint Michael's College?

Saint Michael's College, founded in 1859 by the Christian Brothers to educate young men, was first located in a modest adobe building on Santa Fe Trail, which was renamed College Street in honor of the college. After the college moved to the former site of the Bruns Hospital, off Cerrillos Road, in the 1970s, the name College Street was changed to Old Santa Fe Trail.

Read: *75 Years of Service, 1859–1934: An Historical Sketch of Saint Michael's College*, Saint Michael's College, 1934.

172. Who was Francisco "Pancho" Villa's gunsmith, and what was his connection to Santa Fe?

Victor Vera was born in San Lois Potosí, in central Mexico, in the 1880s and was taken prisoner of war in his early twenties by Villa. He was forced to become the guerilla leader's gunsmith. After several months he escaped and walked into the United States. He worked as a machinist, a plumber, a boilermaker, and a welder. Vera eventually came to Santa Fe, where he made furniture hardware and did blacksmithing. He worked in Santa Fe into the 1970s. He was also a silversmith, and he played the clarinet as well. He was about ninety-five years old when he moved to Las Cruces in 1982, where he died after only three months.

During the Mexican Revolution, Villa felt betrayed by the United States when it no longer backed him. Perhaps he wanted revenge when he attacked the U.S. military camp and small border town of Columbus, in southern New Mexico, on March 9, 1916. General John J. "Black Jack" Pershing led nearly five thousand troops for almost a year in an unsuccessful retaliatory pursuit of Villa into Mexico, but the general was called back to the United States to lead the U.S. armies in Europe. Pershing noted in private that "having dashed into Mexico with the intention of eating the Mexicans raw, we turned back at the first repulse and are now sneaking home under cover, like a whipped curr with its tail between its legs."

Meanwhile, after having at first tried a policy of nonintervention in World War I, the United States under President Woodrow Wilson entered the war in April of 1917, when Germany resumed unrestricted submarine warfare. The U.S. decision to enter the war may have also been influenced by strained relations with Mexico since the Mexican-American War, only seventy years earlier. The Zimmerman telegram, from the German foreign minister in early 1917, inviting Mexico to join forces with Germany against the United States, was made public by President Wilson and became part of the cause for declaring war on Germany.

A large wall clock that was shot during Pancho Villa's Columbus, New Mexico, raid may be seen in Santa Fe in the New Mexico History Museum; in Columbus the Pancho Villa State Park honors the colorful revolutionary.

Read: *Pancho Villa at Columbus*, by Haldeen Braddy, Texas Western College Press, 1965;

Pancho Villa and Black Jack Pershing: The Punitive Expedition in Mexico, by James W. Hurst, Praeger, 2008; and *Southwestern Colonial Ironwork: The Spanish Blacksmithing Tradition,* by Marc Simmons and Frank Turley, Sunstone Press, 2007.

173. Who has been called one of the most intriguing characters in New Mexico colonial history, a diplomat who helped establish lasting peace and fair trade amongst the Comanche, Pueblo, and Hispanic peoples?

Juan Bautista de Anza was born in Fronteras, Sonora, Mexico, in 1736; his father was from the Basque area of Spain. Anza was considered one of Spain's ablest servants and military men. Known for his brilliance and integrity, he was an explorer who mapped more than 11,000 miles of New Spain's northern frontier, including what would become the Spanish Trail. (A National Historic Trail named for him, in Arizona and California, honors the Sonora-California trail he pioneered. He established the Presidio in San Francisco, California, in 1776.) Anza was governor of New Mexico from 1778 to 1787.

The largest military expedition ever mustered on the plains by Spain was the one Anza organized in 1779, at the request of the Spanish commanding general, Teodoro de Croix, to control the warring Comanches, led by Cuerno Verde, in northern New Spain. Anza mustered about six hundred presidial soldiers, militias, and Native American auxiliaries; each man was given a good horse. As the group headed north, about two hundred Utes and Jicarillas joined in. The complete success of Anza's attack on the Comanches, coupled with the hostilities that had started between the Comanches and the Kiowas and other nations with whom there was trade, forced the Comanches to consider peace with the Spanish. The final and perhaps most devastating catastrophe for the Comanche Nation was the 1779 to 1780 smallpox epidemic, a continent-wide epidemic that particularly affected nomadic populations who had not been previously exposed to the virus. In 1783 the western Comanches opened peace talks in Santa Fe.

Spain at this time was interested in forming alliances with the Native Americans to help protect her borders, and the instructions for Indian policy shifted from conversion and coercion to treaties, gifts, and trade. Spain hoped to create an extensive alliance network that would cover the area under dispute with the United States. On February 25, 1786, Governor Anza welcomed the Comanche chief Ecueracapa at the Palace of the Governors. Chief Ecueracapa represented the majority of the Comanches. The agreement to work together for peace and trade was in part a result of Anza's decision to embrace the Native American idea that trade was for sharing and helping each other as well as for profit-making. At the Comanches' request, Anza sponsored a trade fair that served to solidify peaceful relations. The Navajo Nation was invited to join in a treaty that was expanded to include the Utes. This new peaceful coalition was made possible by the Comanche-Spanish alliance and the extraordinary leaders of each group: Chief Ecueracapa and Governor Anza, who forged a close personal bond.

Juan Bautista de Anza died in Sonora in 1788. Of his many accomplishments, perhaps the most important was his skilled diplomacy as a frontiersman.

Read: *Juan Bautista de Anza*, by John Bankston, Mitchell Lange Publishers, 2004; *Juan Bautista de Anza: Basque Explorer in the New World*, by Donald Garate, University of Nevada Press, 2003; *Anza and the Northwest Frontier of New Spain*, by J. N. Bowman and Robert F. Heizer, Southwest Museum, 1967; *Forgotten Frontiers: A Study of the Spanish Indian Policy of Don Juan Bautista de Anza, Governor of New Mexico, 1777–1787, From the Original Documents in the Archives of Spain, Mexico, and New Mexico*, University of Oklahoma Press, 1932; "Church-State Relations in Anza's New Mexico: 1777–1787," by Rick Hendricks, *Texas Catholic Historical Society*, vol. 9, 1998; *New Mexico: An Interpretive History*, by Marc Simmons, University of New Mexico Press, 1988; and *The Comanche Empire*, by Pekka Hämäläinen, Yale University Press, 2009.

Juan Bautista de Anza.
Courtesy of New Mexico State Records Center and Archives.

174. What science-fiction novel addresses issues such as genetic engineering, totalitarianism, and psychological passivity, and also features a rocket that lands in Santa Fe?

Aldous Huxley's *Brave New World*, written in 1931, set in the year A.D. 2540.

Read: *Brave New World*, by Aldous Huxley, Perennial Classics, 1998.

What Is It?
(See Answer Key #29)

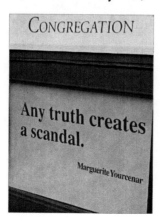

175. The *dicho* (Spanish saying) painted into Olive Rush's WPA mural at the Fray Angélico Chávez History Library says what in Spanish?

Con buenos libros no estás solo (with good books you are not alone). The mural's title is *Life in Northern New Mexico.*

WPA stands for Works Progress Administration, later Works Project Administration, part of President Franklin Delano Roosevelt's New Deal during the Great Depression of the 1930s. Olive Rush is one of many artists who benefited from New Deal programs.

See the mural and a clipping file at the Fray Angélico Chávez History Library. Also read *A More Abundant Life: New Deal Artists and Public Art in New Mexico*, by Jacqueline Hoefer, Sunstone Press, 2003.

Olive Rush on horseback in a garden on Canyon Road, 1930.
Courtesy of Palace of the Governors Photo Archives (NMHM/DCA), #019270.

What Is It?
(See Answer Key #30)

176. What important rescue did a New Mexico State historian make?

Myra Ellen Jenkins held the position of state historian from 1967 to 1980. She rescued the 1695 journals of don Diego de Vargas, which were water-damaged from a leaky roof at the Palace of the Governors.

Read: *A Brief History of New Mexico*, by Myra Ellen Jenkins and Albert H. Schroeder, University of New Mexico Press, 1974; and *Turn Left at the Sleeping Dog: Scripting the Santa Fe Legend, 1920–1955*, edited by John Pen La Farge, University of New Mexico Press, 2001.

177. Returning World War II veterans frequented what popular nightclub, which had the only lighted dance floor in the 1940s in Santa Fe?

The Rumba Club, located at the northwest corner of what is now Paseo de Peralta and Cerrillos Road. The club was owned and operated by Arthur Bonal, who also brought the first Hammond organ to Santa Fe for the nightclub. Bonal had operated a gasoline station there but in 1946 turned it into a nightclub; he later opened the restaurant La Joya immediately to the north of the bar. Before the Bonals owned it, the property had been the Frances Willard School for Girls, the only women's temperance union school for girls west of the Mississippi River. Today, the Hotel Santa Fe occupies the property.

Read: "Santa Fe in World War II, 1940–1947," by Judy Reed, in *All Trails Lead to Santa Fe*, Sunstone Press, 2010; *Chicken Soup for the Veteran's Soul: Stories to Stir the Pride and Honor the Courage of Our Veterans*, compiled by Jack Canfield, Mark Victor Hansen, and Sidney R. Slagter, Health Communications, 2001; and *Now Silence: A Novel of World War II*, by Tori Warner Shepard, Sunstone Press, 2008.

178. Santa Fe is one of the centers of New Mexico's film industry; the roots of this work go back to 1898, with what picture?

Indian Day School, made by Edison Motion Pictures, was a Thomas Edison silent black-and-white movie shot on location at Isleta, Laguna Pueblo. Edison had come to the Santa Fe area to inspect his investment in the minerals of the Ortiz Grant; the Edison mill was built in 1900 but torn down in 1907. A one-minute movie called *Santa Fe Politicians* was made in 1914. Another early movie, shot in 1916, was called *Trip to Santa Fe*. (The movie *Salt of the Earth*, also filmed in New Mexico, in 1954, and based on true events that occurred in the state, is the only movie ever to have been banned by the U.S. federal government.)

These are just a few of the many films that were at least partially filmed in Santa Fe: *The Texas Rangers* (1936), with Fred MacMurray and Jack Oakie; *Strange Lady in Town* (1955), with Greer Garson; *The Man from Laramie* (1955), with Jimmy Stewart; *Easy Rider* (1969), with

Dennis Hopper, Peter Fonda, and Jack Nicholson; *A Gunfight* (1971), with Kirk Douglas and Johnny Cash; *The Ballad of Gregorio Cortez* (1982), the American Playhouse TV series, with Edward James Olmos; *Lust in the Dust* (1985), with Tab Hunter and Divine; *Powwow Highway* (1989), with Gary Farmer; *Wyatt Earp* (1994), with Kevin Costner, Dennis Quaid, and Gene Hackman; *The Tao of Steve* (2000), based on local writer Duncan North's youthful experiences; *All the Pretty Horses* (2000), based on the novel by Santa Fe resident Cormac McCarthy, with Matt Damon and Penelope Cruz; the Academy Award–winning *No Country for Old Men* (2007), with Tommy Lee Jones, Javier Bardem, and Josh Brolin; and *True Grit* (2010), with Jeff Bridges.

The city also hosts the annual Santa Fe Film Festival, highlighting New Mexican-made films as well as new U.S. and foreign films. The festival usually takes place in the fall.

Read: *Before Hollywood: From Shadow Play to the Silver Screen*, by Paul Clee, Clarion Books, 2005; and *The Suppression of* Salt of the Earth: *How Hollywood, Big Labor, and Politicians Blacklisted a Movie*, by James J. Lorence, University of New Mexico Press, 1999. Also, see *Salt of the Earth*, available on DVD.

179. What is the "Black Legend," and how did Charles Lummis dismiss it?

The so-called Black Legend exaggerated the once-accepted propaganda that Spaniards were innately cruel and depraved people. Lummis dismissed the prejudicial stories as myth. His book *The Land of Poco Tiempo*, written in 1893, defends Spanish rule in the New World and attracted tourists to New Mexico. A Spanish translation of another one of Lumis's books, *The Spanish Pioneers*, was widely read and respected by Spanish speakers around the world.

Read: *Tree of Hate: Propaganda and Prejudices Affecting United States Relations with the Hispanic World*, by Philip Wayne Powell, University of New Mexico Press, 2008 (first published 1971); *Nina Otero-Warren of Santa Fe*, by Charlotte Whaley, Sunstone Press, 2007; *The Land of Poco Tiempo*, by Charles F. Lummis, University of New Mexico Press, 1952 (first published 1893); and *The Spanish Pioneers*, by Charles Lummis, Bibliographical Center for Research, 2011 (first published 1893).

180. What was the Old Seminary Building, and where was it located?

It was originally a one-story building built by a young priest, Father Carlos Brun, in 1853. It housed the first seminary Bishop Lamy attempted to open in Santa Fe. Subsequently remodeled to two stories, it became part of the hospital complex operated by the Sisters of Charity. The building was located between the St. Francis Cathedral and Marion Hall; it was torn down in the early 1900s and replaced with a parking lot.

Read: *The Hospital at the End of the Santa Fe Trail*, by Marcus J. Smith, Rydall Press, 1977.

181. In 1850, four prominent Santa Fe citizens gathered: Donaciano Vigil, former New Mexico governor; Francisco Ortiz y Delgado, mayor of Santa Fe; Manuel Álvarez, former U.S. consul; and Samuel Ellison, court clerk and territorial librarian. What was the occasion?

They were all witnesses to the signing of the will of doña María Gertrudis Barceló, the famed Doña Tules. She died in Santa Fe on January 17, 1852, and had a Catholic funeral, with the highest honors, in the south chapel of the parish church, site of the present day St. Francis Cathedral Basilica. Vicar Apostolic Lamy (later archbishop) presided at the extravagant funeral service, the cost for which exceeded $2,000, a fortune in those days. The Barceló residence was demolished in 1939, when the county courthouse was constructed. According to a local historian, Doña Tules' gambling *sala* was located diagonally across Palace Avenue from the Barceló home, at the eastern corner of Burro Alley, where Frank's Lounge was until the early 1960s, next door to the Palace Restaurant.

Read: *Santa Fe Tales and More*, by Howard Bryan, Clear Light, 2010; and "A True Picture of Doña Tules," by Barbara Harrelson, *Santa Fe New Mexican*, October 21, 2007.

A gathering of men having their picture taken at the southeast corner of the Santa Fe Plaza, c. 1855.
The Exchange Hotel is in the center, behind the group, and the Seligman & Clever store is to the right.
Courtesy of Palace of the Governors Photo Archives (NMHM/DCA), #010685.

182. Who gave to a Santa Fe library her significant book collections relating to the theater and art?

The late actress Greer Garson donated her extensive collection in the 1990s to Fogelson Library, now part of the Santa Fe University of Art and Design. She also gave a large sum of money to the Garson Communications Center and Studios.

Visit the Fogelson Library and the campus of the Santa Fe University of Art and Design, off St. Michael's Drive, near Cerrillos Road.

183. Who wrote a classic Western novel before ever coming out West?

Jack Schaefer wrote *Shane*, an iconic Western and perhaps his most famous book, while he lived in New England, at least six years before having been West. After moving to Santa Fe, in 1955, he wrote *Monte Walsh*, *Old Ramon*, *Stubby Pringle's Christmas*, and many other books. He died in Santa Fe in 1991.

Read: *Collected Stories*, by Jack Schaefer, Arbor House, 1985 (first published 1966); "'Shane' Author Stops Writing after His 'Loss of Innocence,'" *Santa Fe New Mexican*, July 8, 1984; *Cowboys North and South*, by Will James, Mountain Press, 1995 (first published 1924); *Cowboy Small*, by Lois Lenski, Random House, 1949; *Riders to Cibola: A Novel*, by Norman Zollinger, Museum of New Mexico Press, 1977; and *Enduring Cowboys: Life in the New Mexico Saddle*, edited by Arnold Vigil, New Mexico Magazine, 1999.

Man and Horse. **Linoleum block cut by Harold E. West, c. 1930s.**

184. When there was only one public high school in Santa Fe, what downtown location did it occupy?

Before Santa Fe High moved to Siringo Road, it was located where the Community Convention Center and City Hall are now. Mid-High, for ninth and tenth grades, utilized the old high school beginning in 1966, but after several years the ninth and tenth grades rejoined Santa Fe High. Today the city has several public high schools: SER Career Academy, Capitol High School, and Santa Fe High School, as well as Tierra Encantada Charter High School (TECHS) and the Academy for Technology and the Classics. Two of Santa Fe's private high schools are St. Michael's and the Santa Fe Preparatory School.

Read: *Santa Fe High School, 1899–1999: Centennial History*, by Marian Meyer, published by Marian Meyer, Santa Fe, 1999.

185. The stone on the Santa Fe Plaza marking the end of the Santa Fe Trail was installed over a hundred years ago by what organization?

The Daughters of the American Revolution. Founded in 1898, the Santa Fe chapter of DAR is the oldest in New Mexico.

Find the stone marker near the southeast corner of the Santa Fe Plaza. Also, read: "Santa Fe Trail Monument Marks Centennial Anniversary," by Marc Simmons, *Santa Fe New Mexican*, February 27, 2010; and *New Mexico State Organization of the National Society of the American Daughters of the Revolution*, vol. 3, Daughters of the American Revolution, 1972–1987.

What Is It?
(See Answer Key #31)

186. Gospel music was promoted at an informal restaurant in the 1990s by which cook?

Santa Fe icon and enigma Carlos White served his Hangover Stew, along with generosity to those in need, in a safe haven called Carlos' Gospel Cafe, which closed in November 2010.

Read: "Good Food, Gospel Truth," by Robert Nott, *Santa Fe New Mexican*, November 24, 2010; and *Seasons of Santa Fe: A Cookbook*, Kitchen Angels, 2000.

187. The popular flower known as the hollyhock, found in abundance in Santa Fe and northern New Mexico, is part of what Spanish folklore?

According to La Vara de San José legend, God gave his approval of marriage between Joseph and Mary by turning Saint Joseph's staff into hollyhocks. *Vara* means "staff" or "rod" and also "measuring stick."

Read: "The Legend of *La Varita de San José*," by Bertha Quintana, *La Herencia*, Summer 2005.

188. What Mexican legislative decree may have been used by José Francisco Ortiz to crowd out a mining partner in a gold-mining venture south of Santa Fe, in 1836?

Ortiz and a partner, Ignacio Cano, employed a seldom-used Mexican decree that was intended to banish foreigners from the Republic of Mexico, especially those born in Spain (*peninsulares*). The Mexican National Congress had instigated the law in 1827 and then had amended and reiterated it in 1829. It was often disregarded.

Dámaso López, a Spaniard, had come up from Chihuahua to Santa Fe in 1820 to secure the repayment on a loan his family had made to Ortiz. In 1833, partly because of his mining experience in Spain, López was appointed mining expert by the Santa Fe *alcalde* (mayor), Francisco Baca y Ortiz. López and the *alcalde*, along with Manuel Salustiano Delgado and others, went to El Real de Nuestra Señora de los Dolores, a mining camp south of Santa Fe, where they validated Ortiz's and Cano's new gold mine. The following year López was listed as a partner in that mine. By 1836 López was no longer a partner. Josiah Gregg reports that Ortiz had employed the expulsion decree to force López out.

But López didn't completely leave New Mexico. Instead, he joined up with his friend Manuel Álvarez, a respected Santa Fe businessman who, although he was a Spaniard, had returned to New Mexico. Álvarez served as the U.S. consul in Santa Fe and was thereby exempt from the decree. Governor Manuel Armijo could be inconsistent in following the law, perhaps especially with friends; Armijo was godfather to one of López's sons.

Delgado returned to El Real de Dolores in 1844 as "justice," having been appointed by Governor Mariano Chaves. El Real de Dolores was described as a crude place where the labor consisted of peonage, almost slavery. It was there that Delgado, in an attempt to instill law and order, formulated the first mining regulations in the Southwest; those regulations were never used, probably because of the unsettled times. There were four different governors of New Mexico during the year 1844: Manuel Armijo, Mariano Chávez, Felipe Sena, and Mariano Martínez de Lejanza.

Read: "The Spanish Exiles," by Marc Simmons, in *Spanish Pathways: Readings in the History of Hispanic New Mexico*, University of New Mexico Press, 2001; *The Gold of the Ortiz Mountains: A Story of New Mexico and the West's First Major Gold Rush*, by William Baxter, Lone Butte Press, 2004; *Las Carneradas: Sheep Trade in New Mexico, 1700–1860*, by John O. Baxter, University of New Mexico Press, 1987; *Commerce of the Prairies*, by Josiah Gregg, University of Oklahoma Press, 1954 (first published 1844); *Nuevas Leyes de las Minas de España: 1625 Edición de Juan de Oñate*, edited by Homer Milford, Sunstone Press, 1998; and *History of Mexico*, by Hubert Howe Bancroft, Brancroft, 1883.

The Prince and Princess of Asturias, His Royal Highness,
Felipe de Borbon y Grecia, and Her Royal Highness, Letizia
Ortiz Rocasolano, in St. Francis Cathedral Basilica,
during their visit to Santa Fe in 2010.
Photograph by Leroy Sanchez.
Courtesy of Maurice Bonal.

189. Who is Santa Fe's most famous hotel-haunting ghost?

Julia Staab's ghost is said to roam the halls of what is now La Posada de Santa Fe Resort and Spa, part of which had been her family's home in the 1880s. Julia was the wife of Abraham Staab, the wealthy supply contractor for the U.S. Army during the Civil War. She loved the Staab family home, which her husband had built, but she probably succumbed to major depression after the death of her seventh and last child shortly after his birth.

Another famous ghost is La Llorona; however, she does not haunt hotels. While the veracity of a ghost's existence may be debated, the stories about them are truly entertaining.

Read: "Intrepid Reporter Explores Spooks of Santa Fe," by Robert Nott, *Santa Fe New Mexican*, October 29, 1999; *Adobe Angels: The Ghosts of Santa Fe*, by Antonio R. Gárcez, Red Rabbit Press, 1992; *Ghosts-Murder-Mayhem, A Chronicle of Santa Fe: Lies, Legends, Facts, Tall Tales, and Useless Information*, by Allan Pacheco, Sunstone Press, 2004; and *Santa Fe Ghosts: Mystery, History, and Truth*, by Susan Blumenthal, Schiffer, 2009.

190. What Santa Fean received the Pulitzer Prize, and for which novel, in 1930?

Oliver La Farge, for his book *Laughing Boy*, published in 1929.

In 1969 N. Scott Momaday was the first Native American to be awarded the Pulitzer Prize. It was for the novel *House Made of Dawn*.

Read: "An Appreciation of a Father," by John Pen La Farge, in *Behind the Mountains*, by Oliver La Farge, Sunstone Press, 2008 (first published 1956); *Laughing Boy*, by Oliver La Farge, Mariner Books, 2004 (first published 1929); and *House Made of Dawn*, by N. Scott Momaday, Harper Perennial, 2010 (first published 1968).

Oliver La Farge, c. 1950. Courtesy of Palace of the Governors Photo Archives (NMHM/DCA), #016741.

191. Where was one of the best-known *parajes*, or stopping places, on the Camino Real for trade caravans heading toward Santa Fe?

El Rancho de las Golondrinas, now a living history museum, was a popular *paraje* on the Camino Real. It was also a working hacienda.

Read: *El Rancho de las Golondrinas: Living History in New Mexico's La Ciénega Valley*, by Carmella Padilla, Museum of New Mexico Press, 2009; "The Namesake at La Cienega," by Craig Smith, *Santa Fe New Mexican*, June 5, 2009; *On the Edge of Empire: The Taos Hacienda of los Martínez*, by David J. Weber, Museum of New Mexico Press, 1996; and *The New Hacienda*, by Karen Witynski and Joe E. Carr, Gibbs Smith, 2003.

192. How and when did Tibetan refugees come to Santa Fe?

Through the U.S. government–sanctioned Tibetan Resettlement Project, begun in 1992. His Holiness, the Dalai Lama (Tenzin Gyatso) visited Santa Fe in 1991 and met with leaders of the fourteen Pueblo Nations, paving the way for the resettlement program to include Santa Fe.

Read: "Tibet Culture in Exile," by Hollis Walker, *Santa Fe New Mexican*, March 6, 1998; and *Freeing Tibet: 50 Years of Struggle, Resilience, and Hope*, by John B. Roberts, AMACOM, 2009.

What Is It?
(See Answer Key #32)

193. Where was the Catholic Maternity Institute located?

On Palace Avenue, where what was Castillo Street (now Delgado Street) ends. The hospital was intended to serve the poor. It opened its doors in 1944 and became the first choice for many women as the place to give birth.

Read: *Santa Fe: A Modern History, 1880–1990,* by Henry Tobias and Charles E. Woodhouse, University of New Mexico Press, 2001.

194. Which chief justice was shot in 1867 in the lobby of the old Exchange Hotel, where La Fonda is now?

John P. Slough. He was a brigadier general who had commanded the Union forces at the Battle of Glorieta Pass. Andrew Johnson (who became the seventeenth president of the United States when President Abraham Lincoln was assassinated) appointed him chief justice of the New Mexico Supreme Court in 1865, at the end of the Civil War. Slough became increasingly unpopular in Santa Fe since he was so out of touch with the locals.

Read: "Tragic History Underfoot at Modern-day La Fonda," by Marc Simmons, *Santa Fe New Mexican*, August 4, 2001.

195. Who was the solar-energy pioneer of the 1950s who retrofitted a home off Garcia Street with what is arguably the country's oldest passive-solar heating system?

Peter van Dresser was a solar innovator, architect, ecologist, decentralist, proponent of regional-based economies, and humanist. In 1973 he suggested a model for resurrecting self-sufficient New Mexican villages. Another local solar architect, Betty Stewart, built adobe houses; she also donated land for hiking trails and helped start the first animal shelter in Santa Fe.

Read: *Passive Solar House Basics*, by Peter van Dresser, Ancient City Press, 1995; *A Landscape for Humans: A Case Study of the Potentials for Ecologically Guided Development in an Uplands Region*, by Peter van Dresser, Biotechnic Press, 1972; "A Landscape for Humans," by Peter van Dresser, *Santa Fe New Mexican*, October 14, 1974; "Solar Pioneers" (two-part article), by Tom Sharpe, *Santa Fe New Mexican*, November 16, 2006; *Solar Revolution: The Economic Transformation of the Global Energy Industry*, by Travis Bradford, MIT Press, 2006; and *Catch the Wind, Harness the Sun: 22 Super-Charged Science Projects for Kids*, by Michael J. Caduto, Storey Publishing, 2011.

One of several windmills within Santa Fe city limits, 2011. Photograph by E. West.

196. Legislators in Santa Fe passed the first solar-rights law in the nation. Who was the legislator who sponsored the bill?

Representative Vernon Kerr, of Los Alamos, in 1977.

Read: "Solar Law Opposition Predicted," *Santa Fe New Mexican*, October 8, 1978; and *Got Sun? Go Solar: Harness Nature's Free Energy to Heat and Power Your Grid-Tied Home*, by Rex A. Ewing, PixyJack Press, 2009.

197. Who was the architect who wore a flat-brimmed Stetson hat, was a proponent of passive-solar architecture, and founded the Santa Fe Arts Institute in 1985?

William Lumpkins was known for his passive-solar architecture; he was also a member of the Taos and Santa Fe Transcendental Painting Group, along with Raymond Jonson and Emil Bisttram. He was influenced by Zen Buddhism in both his painting and his architecture.

Another famous hat known around Santa Fe belonged to a writer and journalist who was named for an Irish warrior king: Brian Ború Dunne, or B. B. Dunne. He could often be found in La Fonda lobby interviewing someone important and fascinating. He first arrived in Santa Fe in 1909 to "work for statehood." His hat was said to be as big as a manhole cover.

Read: *Casa del Sol: Your Guide to Passive House Designs*, by William T. Lumpkins, Santa Fe Publishing Company, 1981; *William Lumpkins: Pioneer Abstract Expressionist*, by Walt Wiggins, Pintores Press, 1990; and "Beloved Eccentric," by Marsha McEuen, *Santa Fean*, June 1999.

198. A home could be purchased on Canyon Road for how much money in 1955?

Eight hundred and fifty dollars.

Read: "Solar Pioneers: The Builder," by Tom Sharpe, *Santa Fe New Mexican*, November 16, 2006.

199. What was the name of the snacks and candy store that was located near what elementary school in the 1940s and 1950s, and what color was it painted?

Della's store was located on East Booth Street, in the alley behind Wood Gormley Elementary School, in a dark green shack run by a red-haired woman named Della Collier. Wood Gormley and Harrington Junior High School students were her customers. Many hundreds, perhaps thousands, of students wrote their names on any wooden surface inside the shack with Della's permission and their signatures covered every available inch. Some favorite items for sale were jawbreakers and various candies, popsicles, piñon nuts, candied apples, Della's mustard dogs (hot dogs), and cinnamon toothpicks. A partial replica of the shack is in the Wood Gormley school cafeteria now.

Read: "Changing Faces," by Todd Bailey, *Santa Fe New Mexican*, February 25, 2007.

Students crowding into Della's, date unknown. Photograph courtesy of the *Santa Fe New Mexican*.

200. How is Santa Fe connected to a first North Pole trip in 1958?

Santa Fean and 1952 St. Michael's High School graduate Albert J. Herrera was a crew member on the nuclear submarine USS *Nautilus* (SSN-571) when it accomplished the first successful voyage under the North Pole on August 3, 1958. He later said of his trip, "It was the shortest way home."

Read: "SF Submariner Says Pole Trip 'Routine,'" *Santa Fe New Mexican*, December 22, 1958; and *Submarine*, by Neil Mallard, with the U.S. Submarine Force Museum, DK Publishers, 2003.

201. What peace accord did the Pueblos offer the Spanish before the siege of Santa Fe began during the Pueblo Revolt in 1680?

A choice between a white and a red cross. White meant the Spanish would peaceably leave and red meant war. The Spanish did not choose the white one.

Read: *The Pueblo Revolt of 1680: Conquest and Resistance in Seventeenth-Century New Mexico*, by Andrew L. Knaut, University of Oklahoma Press, 1995.

202. What were some of the reasons Santa Fe escaped the worst aspects of the Great Depression?

The city was relatively isolated, it offered steady government jobs, it lacked the industrial jobs that were being lost around the country, it was popular with wealthy tourists, and family and friends supported each other.

Read: "Refuge from the Crash," by Tom Sharpe, *Santa Fe New Mexican*, November 16, 2008; and *Living through the Great Depression*, edited by Tracy Brown Collins, Greenhaven Press, 2004.

Black Range Waltz. **Linoleum block cut by Harold E. West, c. 1930s.**

Home. **Pen and ink drawing by Harold E. West, in *Broadside to the Sun*, by Don West, 1946.**

203. When and where did Willa Cather write much of her novel *Death Comes for the Archbishop?*

In 1926, at the home of Mary Austin, and also in a room at La Fonda. The historical accuracy of the novel, supposedly based on Archbishop Lamy of Santa Fe in the mid-1800s, may be evaluated by reading *Wake for a Fat Vicar: Father Juan Felipe Ortiz, Archbishop Lamy, and the New Mexican Catholic Church in the Middle of the Nineteenth Century*, by Fray Angélico Chávez and Thomas E. Chávez.

Read: "In a Different Land," by Lynne Cline, *Santa Fe New Mexican*, June 6, 2003; *Death Comes for the Archbishop*, by Willa Cather, Vintage Classics, 1990 (first published 1928); *Death Comes for the Archbishop: Historical Essay and Explanatory Notes*, by John J. Murphy, University of Nebraska Press, 1999; *Wake for a Fat Vicar: Father Juan Felipe Ortiz, Archbishop Lamy, and the New Mexican Catholic Church in the Middle of the Nineteenth Century*, by Fray Angélico Chávez and Thomas E. Chávez, LPD Press, 2004; and *Lamy of Santa Fe*, by Paul Horgan, Wesleyan University Press, 2003 (first published 1975).

204. Who is Fred Kabotie, and what two high schools did he attend in Santa Fe?

A Hopi artist whose name was Qa'avotay had an elementary school teacher who spelled his name "Kabotie," which stuck with him for the rest of his life. He attended the Santa Fe Indian School, where the superintendent, John DeHuff, went against the prevailing policy at the time of suppressing American Indian culture; as a result DeHuff was demoted and forced to leave the school. He persuaded Kabotie to leave the Indian School and attend Santa Fe High School. Kabotie played the flute and was a talented artist. During many summers he worked with archaeologist Edgar Lee Hewett.

Read: *Indian Painters of the Southwest: The Deep Remembering*, Katherine Chase, School of American Research Press, 2002; *Field Mouse Goes to War = Tusan Homichi Tuwvöta*, by Edward A. Kennard, with Hopi text by Albert Yava, illustrated by Fred Kabotie, Filter Press, 1999; and *Designs from the Ancient Mimbreños, with a Hopi Interpretation*, by Fred Kabotie, Northland Press, 1982.

Fred Kabotie, c. 1930. Courtesy of Palace of the Governors Photo Archives (NMHM/DCA), #030714.

205. What was the Domínguez-Escalante Expedition, and when did it take place?

The Domínguez-Escalante Expedition was led by fray Francisco Atanasio Domínguez and fray Silvestre Vélez de Escalante; it left the Santa Fe Plaza on July 29, 1776, with the intention of discovering a route from New Mexico to California via Utah. Although they did not reach California, the expedition may not have been considered a failure by the two Franciscans, who were interested in possible future mission sites, since much was learned about the vast area they explored and the people who lived there. Fathers Domínguez and Escalante promised the Native Americans they met on their journey that they would revisit within a year, but circumstances prevented their return.

Read: *The Domínguez-Escalante Journal: Their Expedition through Colorado, Utah, Arizona, and New Mexico in 1776*, by Francisco Atanasio Domínguez, translated by Fray Angélico Chávez and edited by Ted J. Warner, Brigham Young University Press, 1976; and *In Search of Domínguez and Escalante: Photographing the 1776 Spanish Expedition through the Southwest*, by Greg MacGregor and Siegfried Halus, Museum of New Mexico Press, 2011.

206. Fray Francisco Atanasio Domínguez led inspections of what after he returned from the Expedition of 1776?

The missions of New Mexico.

Read: *The Missions of New Mexico, 1776: A Description, with Other Contemporary Documents*, by Francisco Atanasio Domínguez, translated and annotated by Eleanor B. Adams and Fray Angélico Chávez, University of New Mexico Press, 1956.

207. When was the first Santa Fe ski area built, and what kind of seats were used in the first ski lift?

In the 1930s, when skiing was starting to become popular in the United States, a small ski area was built at Hyde Park.

Later, after World War II, another run was built at Big Tesuque picnic area. Ernie Blake (later of Taos), Bob Nordhaus, and Buzz Bainbridge worked together to create the larger ski area, which opened in 1950 as the Santa Fe Ski Basin. Seats salvaged from World War II B-24 bomber planes (on their way to the wrecking yard in Albuquerque) were used in the first ski lift at the Santa Fe Ski Basin.

The ski basin was built largely on an old fire burn, from a fire that occurred in the spring of 1887; after starting in Big Tesuque canyon, it burned across the mountains and spread east toward Wagon Mound, New Mexico, lasting about two months.

Read: *The Mountains of New Mexico*, by Robert Julyan, University of New Mexico Press,

2006; *Cross-Country Skiing in Northern New Mexico: An Introduction and Trail Guide*, by Kay Matthews, Acequia Madre Press, 1993; *Two Planks and a Passion: The Dramatic History of Skiing*, by Roland Huntford, Continuum, 2009; and *Fire Season: Field Notes from a Wilderness Lookout*, by Philip Connors, Ecco, 2011.

What Is It?
(See Answer Key #33)

208. Which important Spanish merchant, trader, statesman, and diplomat does not have a building, plaza, or street in Santa Fe named for him?

Manuel Álvarez.

Born in Abelgas, in the province of León, in northern Spain, in 1794, Álvarez came to northern New Spain at age twenty-four in search of adventure. He witnessed the chaos leading to Mexican independence from Spain, and then, in 1823, he went to Cuba, where in Havana he somehow received a U.S. passport. He sailed to New York and from there went to Missouri and then on to Santa Fe via the newly opened Santa Fe Trail.

Álvarez became a merchant and was also a trapper with the American Fur Company (started by John Jacob Astor in 1808) in the Rocky Mountains, where he was one of the first to report seeing geysers in what is now Yellowstone Park, in 1833. He was a "mountain man" similar to others such as Jedidiah Smith, Joe Meek, Jim Beckworth, and Jim Bridger. He was also a stockman, a judge, a diplomat, a building commissioner, and a politician. He served as U.S. consul in Santa Fe from 1836 to 1841. He was known for his bravery on the Santa Fe Trail. He was acting governor briefly in 1850.

Álvarez played a pivotal role in the development of early New Mexico, leading the initial movement for statehood. He was fluent in French and English as well as his native Spanish. Álvarez adapted to the fluid circumstances that transpired in Santa Fe during its time as part of Mexico and later as part of the territorial United States. He died in Santa Fe in 1856.

Read: *Manuel Alvarez, 1794–1856: A Southwestern Biography*, by Thomas E. Chávez, University of Colorado Press, 1990; *Abelgas: Paisajes, Evocaciones y Remembranzas*, by

Román Álvarez Rodríguez, Ediciones Almar, 2003; *Yellowstone National Park: Its Exploration and Establishment*, by Aubrey L. Haines, National Park Service, 1974; *Conflict and Acculturation: Manuel Alvarez's 1842 Memorial*, edited and annotated by Thomas E. Chávez, Museum of New Mexico Press, 1989; "Report of Manuel Álvarez, 1842," in *On the Santa Fe Trail*, edited by Marc Simmons, University Press of Kansas, 1986; and *New Mexico Historical Biographies*, by Don Bullis, Rio Grande Books, 2011.

Manuel Álvarez. Pencil sketch by E. West based on Álvarez's passport description. Courtesy of the artist.

209. *The Hoop Dancer* and *The Gift* are two sculptures made by a blind Santa Clara Pueblo artist and Vietnam veteran; who is the artist, and where are the two works displayed?

The artist is Michael Naranjo. *The Hoop Dancer* is at the west side of the state capitol building, on Don Gaspar Street, and *The Gift* is at the entrance of the State Library, Archives and Records Center, off Camino Carlos Rey.

Read: *Michael Naranjo*, by Mary Carroll Nelson, Dillon Press, 1975.

Bird's Nest in a Bell. The photograph by Cody Brothers, 2008, shows a detail of the bronze sculpture *Apache Mountain Spirit Dancer*, by Craig Dan Goseyun, 1995, a gift of Sam and Ethel Ballen in remembrance of the spirited Nina Telsa Ballen. Looking closely, you can see straw from a bird's nest in the bell below the dancer's knee. See the sculpture at Museum Hill, between the Museum of Indian Arts and Culture and the Laboratory of Anthropology. Image courtesy of the photographer.

210. Cerrillos Road is named for what?

The road's name refers to the hills south of Santa Fe. Or does it?

The original Los Cerrillos were the cluster of rocky crags east of La Cienega and I-25; they are marked on maps today as Bonanza Hill, southeast of Cerro de la Cruz. Just south of those crags was the mining camp El Real de los Cerrillos, established in 1695 to service the silver and lead mines in the nearby hills. (The camp was abandoned about a year later.) Originally, the mining camp probably took its name from a leading ranch, on record in late 1600s, that had been located there. The Los Cerrillos and Sitio de los Cerrillos Grants, and the name of the road leading to them from Santa Fe, are all that have survived of the original El Real de los Cerrillos camp. The hills now named Los Cerrillos and the town of Cerrillos adopted the name later.

Cerro means "hill" in Spanish; *cerrito,* a diminutive, refers to a little hill. However, *cerrillo* does not derive from *cerro* and has various meanings that may only indirectly refer to a hill, such as "a little eminence" or prominence. The singular *cerrillo* is a masculine Spanish word whose botanical meaning is "grama," a grass that is a member of the genus *Bouteloua* (named for Claudio and Esteban Boutelou, nineteenth-century Spanish botanists). The plural, *cerrillos*, means "dies," as in the dies used for milling coined metal. The verb *cerrillar* means "to mill" coins, by marking them at the edge to show that none of the metal was shaved off. (The earliest machine known for producing coins is the screw press, invented by Leonardo da Vinci in the fifteenth century and powered by a water mill.)

Perhaps the original *ranchero*, in naming his property, liked the word *cerrillos* because of these associations: coinage, and a little eminence. However, the answer may simply be that "illo" was used instead of "ito" making "cerritos" (little hills) into "cerrillos."

Read: *The Place Names of New Mexico,* by Robert Hixson Julyan, University of New Mexico Press, 1998; *Cultural Resource Survey for the Real de los Cerrillos Abandoned Mine Lands Project, Santa Fe County, New Mexico,* by Homer E. Milford, Energy, Minerals, Natural Resources Department, 1996; *A New Pronouncing Dictionary of the Spanish and English Languages,* compiled by Mariano Velázquez de la Cadena, Prentice-Hall, 1973 (first published 1852); and *Cassell's Spanish-English, English-Spanish Dictionary,* Macmillan, 1978.

Cerrillos Hills. Photograph by Edward Ranney, 1973. Courtesy of the photographer.

211. Which library in Santa Fe is named for a local priest, historian, author, and poet?

The Fray Angélico Chávez History Library, which is part of the Palace of the Governors and the New Mexico History Museum. The entrance is on Washington Street, just north of the Plaza.

Fray Angélico Chávez was born in 1910 in Wagon Mound, New Mexico, the first of ten children of Fabián Chávez and María Nicolasa Roybal de Chávez; his parents named him Manuel Ezequiel. The rigorous seminary training he underwent in preparation for his ordination did not dampen his impish sense of humor. Ordained at St. Francis Cathedral in 1937, he was the first native-born New Mexican to become a Franciscan friar. He was a poet, a historian, an artist, and an author of numerous books. His book *The Virgin of Port Lligat,* about Salvador Dali's painting *The Madonna of Port Lligat* as an allegory of the divine, joining themes from art, theology, classical mythology, nuclear physics, and astronomy. *La Conquistadora: The Autobiography of an Ancient Statue* is one of his most popular books. He died in 1996 in Santa Fe.

Read: *The Life and Writing of Fray Angélico Chávez: A New Mexico Renaissance Man,* by Ellen McCracken, University of New Mexico Press, 2009.

Fray Angélico Chávez. Photograph by Robert H. Martin, 1950. Courtesy of Palace of the Governors Photo Archives (NMHM/DCA), #041436.

212. What might Santa Fe have looked like in 1776 if one could have flown over it then?

A painting by Wilson Hurley, *Santa Fe, July, 1776,* shows a view of Santa Fe from above, based on the plat map by José de Urrutia.

See the photo on page 55 of *Santa Fe: History of an Ancient City,* second edition, edited by David Grant Noble, School for Advanced Research Press, 2008.

213. What popular short but steep hike is named the Spanish word for "watchtower" or "vantage point"?

Atalaya is the name of a hill that rises just east of Santa Fe; it is usually reached from the trailhead near St. John's College, on Camino Cruz Blanca, where there is parking. From the top are great views of the city.

Many other walking and biking trails popular with locals and visitors alike connect different parts of town and provide some hint of wilderness within the city. Some of these include Arroyo de los Chamisos Recreational Trail (connecting the Santa Fe Rail Trail southwest along the arroyo, past the Genoveva Chavéz Community Center, to the Nava Ade Tails, near Governor Miles Road); the Santa Fe River Trail (connecting densely populated neighborhoods with downtown via the Alameda Street and Agua Fría corridors, including Camino Don Jose to the Barrio de La Canada neighborhood and Frenchy's Field Park to Camino Alire); the Acequia Bike Trail (connecting from the Railyard, across St. Francis Drive, and following the Acequia de los Pinos behind the New Mexico School for the Deaf and the Santa Fe Indian School to San José Avenue); the Dale Ball Trail System (some are off Hyde Park Road and others are off Upper Canyon Road); the Nature Conservancy Trail and Randall Davy Audubon Center (both off Upper Canyon Road); the Dorothy Stewart Trail (from St. John's College, on Camino Cruz Blanca); and the Santa Fe Rail Trail (beside the historic Atchison, Topeka & Santa Fe Railway line, beginning in the Railyard Park, heading south).

The nonprofit Trails Alliance of Santa Fe organizes volunteer projects to help maintain many of Santa Fe's trails.

Read: *Day Hikes in the Santa Fe Area,* Northern New Mexico Group of the Sierra Club, 2007; *Santa Fe on Foot: Adventures in the City Different*, by Elaine Pinkerton, Ocean Tree Books, 1994; "Bike and Hike: Arroyo Chamiso Trail," by Craig Martin, *Santa Fe New Mexican*, June 11, 1998; and *100 Hikes in New Mexico*, by Craig Martin, Mountaineers Books, 2001.

What Is It?
(See Answer Key #34)

214. Which book takes place in a pueblo near Santa Fe and reveals legends told by someone's grandfather or great-grandfather to an eager audience of Pueblo children?

Old Father Story Teller is the title of the book with a series of winter stories told in Santa Clara Pueblo, based on tribal legends handed down orally through generations. The author/illustrator of the book was sent to St. Catherine Indian School in Santa Fe at age five, before she knew English, and her given name, Tse Tsan (which means "Golden Dawn" in the Tewa language), was replaced by her teachers with "Pablita." Pablita Velarde graduated from the Indian School in Santa Fe in 1936 and eventually became a successful artist, muralist, illustrator, and lecturer, as well as a mother, grandmother, and great-grandmother.

Read: *Old Father Story Teller*, by Pablita Velarde, Clear Light, 1989.

Pueblo Dance Clowns. **Pen and ink drawing by Cathie Sullivan, 2011, based on her original screen print, 2011. Courtesy of the artist.**

The artist discusses the meaning of this image:

"When you attend a Pueblo Indian ceremonial dance in New Mexico or Arizona, you will be in the company of clown dancers with painted bodies and horned corn-husk caps. Although referred to as 'clowns,' they, like all the dancers, are sacred figures, and the dances themselves are community prayers rather than entertainment. But the duties of the clowns (called Koshares, or K'osha, in Tewa pueblos) are light-hearted as well as practical. On the practical side they help other dancers keep their costumes in good order during the dances. But they also pull visiting women from the onlookers for a dance step or two, chase each other around whooping and hollering, pour water on guests, temporarily relieve visitors of their cameras (not allowed at most dances anyway), and borrow coats from onlookers. Clown clan responsibilities are with rain. Paintings often show the clowns on rainbows or with water snakes."

215. What fictional character who lived near Santa Fe in 1824 is featured in a series of children's books?

Josefina Montoya is the young heroine of a series of stories that take place when Santa Fe was part of Mexico. The first book is called *Meet Josefina: An American Girl*. In the books, her father's ranch is based on El Rancho de las Golondrinas, south of Santa Fe.

Read: *Meet Josefina: An American Girl*, by Valerie Tripp, Pleasant Company, 1997, first of a series; *Welcome to Josefina's World, 1824: Growing Up on America's Southwest Frontier*, by Yvette La Pierre, Pleasant Company, 1999; and *Josefina's Cookbook: A Peek at Dining in the Past with Meals You Can Cook Today*, by Tamara England, Pleasant Company, 1998.

Josefina, an American Girl doll, was modeled after a local Santa Fe girl. The stories are usually set in and around Santa Fe, as well as Las Golondrinas. The series had an advisory board of New Mexicans and others that authenticated the Josefina stories. Some of the local advisors included Rosalinda Barrera, Sandra Jaramillo, Skip Keith Miller, Felipe Mirabel, Tey Diana Rebolledo, Orlando Romero, and Marc Simmons.

216. What coming-of-age novel follows the maturing of a teenage boy and is set in Santa Fe against the backdrop of racism and World War II?

Red Sky at Morning, written by Santa Fe author Richard Bradford. It was made into a film in 1971.

Read: *Red Sky at Morning*, by Richard Bradford, Perennial Classics, 1999 (first published 1968).

217. Which cowboy who was also a Pinkerton detective has a major road in Santa Fe named after him?

Siringo Road is named for cowboy and author Charlie Siringo (1855–1928), who was famous for being one of the first agents to use undercover work in the capture of fugitives, when he worked for the Pinkerton Detective Agency, in Chicago. He owned a ranch near Santa Fe but moved to Los Angeles toward the end of his life.

Read: *Riata and Spurs: The Story of a Lifetime Spent in the Saddle as Cowboy and Detective*, by Charles Siringo, Sunstone Press, 2007 (first published 1927).

Paying a Visit. **Linoleum block cut by Harold E. West, c. 1930s.**

218. In what year, and why, was Caballeros de Vargas formed?

The men's organization was reformed in 1956 to perpetuate the memory of don Diego de Vargas, and to honor their patroness, Nuestra Señora del Rosario, La Conquistadora (often called "Our Lady of Peace"). The group is also known as La Cofradía de María de Santísima. They honor and protect La Conquistadora and also help preserve the statue. Gustave Baumann mended and restored her in 1930. The fraternity of La Cofradía also helps promote Spanish culture in Santa Fe.

The first *mayordomo* of La Cofradía was don Diego de Vargas, beginning in 1692.

Read: "Los Caballeros de Vargas: A Tradition of Culture," by Roger D. Martínez y Mondragón, *La Herencia*, Fall 2000; "Statue Recalls Labor of Fray Chávez," by Ellen McCracken, *Santa Fe New Mexican*, July 19, 2011; and *La Conquistadora: The Autobiography of an Ancient Statue*, by Fray Angélico Chávez, Sunstone Press, 1983 (first published 1954).

219. La Conquistadora was taken care of by which *mayordomo* for over thirty years?

Born and raised in Santa Fe, Pedro Ribera Ortega was a writer, a teacher, and a linguist. As well as being *mayordomo* of Caballeros de Vargas, he was involved in Santa Fe Fiesta for over sixty-five years, since he was five years old. He died in Santa Fe in 2003.

Read: "Pedro Ribera Ortega, Hijo de Santa Fe," by Ana Pacheco, *La Herencia*, Spring 2003; *La Guadalupana and La Conquistadora in Catholic History of New Mexico*, by Pedro Ribera Ortega, self published, 1997; *Cancionero Fiesta*, by Pedro Ribera Ortega, self-published, 1970; *Christmas in Old Santa Fe*, by Pedro Ribera Ortega, Sunstone Press, 1973; and *La Conquistadora: America's Oldest Madonna*, by Pedro Ribera Ortega, Sunstone Press, 1975.

220. Who was Luis Tupatú, and what was remarkable about what he did?

From Picuris Pueblo, Luis Tupatú, also known as Luis el Picurí, was the primary Pueblo leader to conduct peace negotiations with don Diego de Vargas in October of 1692, when Vargas returned to Santa Fe with the intent to secure a peaceful agreement with the Pueblo communities after the Pueblo Rebellion of 1680.

Achieving peace and stability in New Mexico required sustained effort for several years to overcome distrust by both Pueblo Indian and Spanish leaders. Some of the other Indian leaders who contributed to reconciliation included Domingo of Tesuque, Cristóbal Yope, Antonio Bolsas, Bartolomé de Ojeda, and Juan de Ye. There were people with Vargas who had relatives in the Pueblo communities and vice versa, and these people also helped urge reconciliation. Tupatú and his people looked forward to the Spaniards' help in uniting in peace his pueblo with the hostile Pecos and Taos Pueblos, who were friendly with Tupatú's enemies, the Farán Apache.

There were challenges to peaceful negotiations and mistrust on both sides during 1694 and 1695, which led to a revolt in 1696, when most of the Pueblos turned against the colonists. But some Pueblo and Spanish leaders and families persevered in order to restore stable relations. Finally, 1697 saw the end of the Pueblo-Spanish War, which had begun in 1680. Complicated alliances were required to sustain negotiations in order to achieve the relatively peaceful accord, which has helped shape development of both Pueblo and Spanish societies in New Mexico to this day.

Read: "The Tupatu and Vargas Accords," by Jose Antonio Esquibel, *El Palacio*, Spring 2006; *To the Royal Crown Restored: The Journals of Don Diego de Vargas, 1692–1694*, edited by John Kessell, Rick Hendricks, and Meredith D. Dodge, University of New Mexico Press, 1995; *Blood on the Boulders: The Journals of Don Diego de Vargas, 1694–1697*, by John Kessell, Rick Hendricks, and Meredith D. Dodge, University of New Mexico Press, 1998; and *When Jesus Came, the Corn Mothers Went Away: Marriage, Sexuality, and Power in New Mexico, 1500–1846*, by Ramón A. Gutierrez, Stanford University Press, 1991.

221. Who was the noted Black drummer and herald with don Diego de Vargas?

Sebastián Rodríguez Brito, who was born in Angola, Africa, in about 1642, and was a free son of slaves. Once he arrived in New Spain, the relative geographic isolation made economic and social mobility possible. Eventually, after serving as drummer for Governor Pedro Reneros Posada of El Paso del Norte for more than three years, Rodríguez joined the Vargas expedition, in 1691, and became Vargas's trusted servant and drummer. He was asked by Vargas to proclaim the day of departure for the return to Santa Fe, which happened on October 4, 1693, from El Paso del Norte. He led columns of troops through their drills, opened ceremonies and proclamations, and cheered on the military forces. Rodríguez's drumming became an omnipresent feature among the Spanish soldiers, at El Paso del Norte, along the route north along the rough remnants of the Camino Real, and at the presidio in Santa Fe.

Later, Rodríguez rose from being a servant to a wealthy landholder, one of the first property owners in the Santa Fe area. He married Isabel Olguín, an Española widow. (His son, Melchor Rodríguez, was one of the first twelve Black settlers with Hispanic surnames to start families in the village of Las Trampas, which was established as a buffer zone in an effort to curtail raids on Spanish settlements.)

Read: "Don Diego de Vargas' Negro Drummer," by Fray Angélico Chávez, *The Black Military Experience in the American West*, edited by John M. Carroll, Liveright Publishing, 1971; and *By Force of Arms: The Journals of Don Diego de Vargas 1691–1693*, edited by John Kessell and Rick Hendricks, University of New Mexico Press, 1992.

Sebastián Rodríguez Brito. Pen and ink drawing by José Cisneros (1910–2009). Image from the Adair Margo Gallery, El Paso, Texas.

222. What was the so-called "Sweeney" Opera House?

The Santa Fe Opera was demolished by fire during their 1967 season; the company moved to Santa Fe High School's Sweeney Gym and successfully completed the season.

Read: *The First Twenty Years of the Santa Fe Opera*, by Eleanor Scott, Sunstone Press, 1976.

223. Santa Feans have been served what for Fourth of July breakfast on the Plaza, and for how many years?

Pancakes! And music is served up from the bandstand. The Chamber of Commerce started the "Pancakes on the Plaza" tradition in 1975. United Way supported the festivities for many years, and now the Rotary Club Foundation of Santa Fe is a partner in planning the event. Proceeds from the July Fourth Pancakes on the Plaza are donated to local humanitarian and social-needs organizations.

Read: *Pancake: A Global History*, by Ken Albala, Reaktion Books, 2008.

224. How did the De Vargas Mall get its name?

The De Vargas Mall sits near the area where the colonists camped before don Diego de Vargas's reconquest of Santa Fe in 1693. The actual campsite was located where Rosario Chapel is now, across from the mall.

Read: *To the Royal Crown Restored: The Journals of Don Diego de Vargas, New Mexico, 1692–94,* edited by John L. Kessell, Rick Hendricks, and Meredith D. Dodge, University of New Mexico Press, 1995; and "Rosario Chapel: An Ode to Santa Fe," by Inez Russell, *Santa Fe New Mexican,* May 23, 2004.

225. Very few women traveled the Santa Fe Trail before 1850; who was the first woman to make the journey?

Mary Donoho, in 1832. Susan Shelby Magoffin was on the trail in 1846. In 1852, when she was seven, Marion Sloan Russell traveled the trail with her mother and her brother.

Read: *Mary Donoho: New First Lady of the Santa Fe Trail,* by Marian Meyer, Ancient City Press, 1991; *Down the Santa Fe Trail and into Mexico: The Diary of Susan Shelby Magoffin, 1846–1847,* edited by Stella M. Drumm, University of Nebraska Press, 1962; *Along the Santa Fe Trail: Marion Russell's Own Story,* by Marion Russell, adapted by Ginger Wadsworth, Albert Whitman & Company, 1993; and *Twenty Thousand Roads: Women, Movement, and the West,* by Virginia Scharff, University of California Press, 2002.

226. What surprised some Anglo traders about New Mexican women when they first came to Santa Fe in the 1820s and 1830s?

Hispanic women in Santa Fe and other places could own property and conduct business, and some of them even smoked cigarettes in public!

Read: "The Independent Women of Hispanic New Mexico, 1821–1846," by Janet Lecompte, *Western Historical Quarterly,* No. 12, January 1981.

227. When and why was the Commission of Public Records created in Santa Fe?

The commission was created in 1959 to preserve, protect, and provide access to the state's public records; in 1960 it opened the first State Records Center and Archives, at the Charles Ilfeld warehouse, on Montezuma Street.

Visit them in their building off Cerrillos Road, on Camino Carlos Rey, next to the State Library.

Montezuma and Hickox Streets.
Courtesy of Palace of the Governors Photo Archives (NMHM/DCA), #026073.

228. Santa Fe has about two hundred public and private art galleries; where is Santa Fe's oldest Indian art gallery?

In the Wheelwright Museum of the American Indian, on Camino Lejo, at Museum Hill. The Case Trading Post was built in 1937 to resemble an early Navajo trading post.

Read: *The Native American Curio Trade in New Mexico*, by Jonathan Batkin, Wheelwright Museum of the American Indian, 2008.

229. When did Santa Fe join the UNESCO Creative Cities network?

Santa Fe was appointed a United Nations Educational, Scientific and Cultural Organization "City of Crafts and Folk Art" in 2005. The city's many colorful markets showcase the arts and crafts of artists and people with shared heritage and culture in Santa Fe; these events feature locals and others from around New Mexico as well as national and international participants and guests. Some of the summertime events include the International Folk Art Market (the largest folk art market in the world, in early July), the traditional Spanish Market (the oldest and largest juried Spanish market in the United States, in late July), and Indian Market (the oldest and largest juried Native American Indian art show and market in the world, in August).

A group called the Santa Fe Council on International Relations, a nonprofit organization founded in 1965 and not connected to UNESCO, promotes the understanding of international issues and cultural affairs in the community through hosting foreign visitors and discussion.

Read: *Creative Tourism: A Global Conversation*, edited by Rebecca Wurzburger, Tom Aageson, Alex Pattakos, and Sabrina Pratt, Sunstone Press, 2009; "The Art of Being Santa Fe," by Henry Shukman, *New York Times*, February 4, 2010; *Santa Fe International Folk Art Market*, special supplement in the *Santa Fe New Mexican*, July 6, 2011.

230. What Santa Fe scientific think tank met to discuss complexity science in what former convent?

The Santa Fe Institute, founded in 1984, met for several years at the Cristo Rey convent.

Read: *Manhattan Project to the Santa Fe Institute: The Memoirs of George Cowen*, by George A. Cowen, University of New Mexico Press, 2010; *The Quark and the Jaguar: Adventures in the Simple and the Complex*, by Murray Gell-Mann, W. H. Freeman & Company, 1994.

231. How many adobes were used to make Cristo Rey Church?

More than 180,000 adobes were used to build one of the largest adobe churches in the Americas. The archdiocese had the church built to house the extraordinary *retablo* (altar screen) carved by don Bernardo de Miera y Pacheco. The church was designed by John Gaw Meem. Construction began in 1939 and was completed in 1940. Most of the adobes were made by the parishioners.

The campus of St. Catherine Indian School includes the oldest three-and-a-half-story handmade adobe building in New Mexico. The private Catholic boarding school was built at the instigation of Katherine Drexel, an heiress from a strongly religious, wealthy, philanthropic family. She had became a nun in her thirties and started a new order called the Sisters of the Blessed Sacrament, dedicated to the education of Native Americans and Blacks. Sister Mary Katherine purchased land for nearly sixty schools in many states in the United States, including Pennsylvania, Virginia, Louisiana, Tennessee, and Arizona, near the Navajo Reservation. St. Catherine Indian School was situated on eighteen acres one mile northwest of the Santa Fe Plaza and contiguous to the National Cemetery. It opened in 1887 primarily for Native American students. After more than a century of successful and respected instruction, the school closed, with its final graduating class in 1998.

Tonita Peña (San Ildefonso Pueblo), Maria Martinez (San Ildefonso Pueblo), Pablita Verlarde (Santa Clara Pueblo), and Chris Thomas (Laguna Pueblo) are some of the well-known Native American artists who attended St. Catherine Indian School. Manuel "Bob" Chávez (Cochiti Pueblo) was a member of the first graduating class, in 1935. He credited his supportive and challenging experience at the school with helping him to survive the Bataan Death March and four years in a prison camp during World War II.

Katherine Drexel was canonized in the fall of 2000, becoming the second U.S.-born saint of the Roman Catholic Church.

Read: *Cristo Rey: A Symphony in Mud*, by Reverend Daniel Krahe, Lourdes School Press, 1940; *Historic New Mexico Churches*, by Annie Lux, with photographs by Daniel Nadelbach, Gibbs Smith, 2007; "Celebration Marks 70th Anniversary of Cristo Rey Catholic Church, Raises Funds for Repairs," *Santa Fe New Mexican*, November 21, 2010; "St. Catherine Indian School: The Hallways Hold Memories," by Julie Ann Grimm, *Santa Fe New Mexican*, December 13, 2010; "Gone but Not Forgotten: St. Catherine Indian School," by Corrinne P. Sze, *Bulletin of the Historic Santa Fe Foundation*, Spring 2003.

232. The "Frito pie" was originated by whom in Santa Fe?

Carmen Ornelas is credited with making the first Frito pie, in the 1950s, which she served at the old bus depot café on Water Street, before moving to F. W. Woolworth's, on the Plaza.

The "official" version of Frito pie is made by opening a small bag of Frito chips and pouring red chile made with hamburger meat over the chips and then adding toppings such as cheese, chopped onions, lettuce, and jalapeño peppers. (The first Frito chip was created in 1932.) Teresa Hernandez is one of many who carried on the tradition at the counter of Woolworth's and later elsewhere around town. Now hungry folks can get a Frito pie at many places that serve New Mexican food.

Read: "A Wonderful Life: Red Chile Memories," by Ana Pacheco, *Santa Fe New Mexican*, April 10, 2010.

233. When was the New Mexico Veterans' Memorial monument dedicated, and where is it?

The State of New Mexico Veterans' Services Memorial monument was dedicated on July 4, 2005, to honor the achievements of all the sons and daughters of New Mexico who have served in the military. The semicircular concrete structure is located downtown, on the lawn of the Bataan Building, on Galisteo Street.

One of many New Mexico veterans, Sergeant First Class Leroy Petry was honored with the Medal of Honor, awarded to him by President Barack Obama in a ceremony at the White House in July 2011.

On Veterans day in Santa Fe there is a patriotic Plaza parade and a solemn ceremony at the Bataan Memorial Building, on Galisteo Street.

Other sites that honor veterans in Santa Fe include the Wall of Honor, in the state capitol rotunda; the Bataan Memorial Monument and eternal flame, on Don Gaspar Avenue; the Bataan Memorial Museum, on Old Pecos Trail; the John F. Griego Vietnam Veterans Memorial Park, on Paseo de la Conquistadora; the Santa Fe National Cemetery, on Guadalupe Street; and the Veterans Memorial Highway, Route 599, a state highway located entirely within Santa Fe County.

Read: *Patriotic Holidays of the United States: An Introduction to the History, Symbols, and Traditions behind the Major Holidays and Days of Observance*, by Helene Hendersen, Omnigraphics, 2006; and *Chicken Soup for the Veteran's Soul: Stories to Stir the Pride and Honor the Courage of Our Veterans*, compiled by Jack Canfield, Mark Victor Hansen, and Sidney R. Slagter, Health Communications, 2001.

234. How did members of the Santa Fe Presidio assist the American Revolution?

Their donations were sent through the French military to aid the colonies back east, at the request of the Spanish Crown. Spain had agreed to join France as an ally against England, hoping to regain land that had been lost. Spain began covertly shipping arms, munitions, cattle, uniforms, medicine, blankets, and money to the American colonies, using France as the go-between. Spain declared war on England in 1779. In 1780 Carlos III decreed that in order to sustain war against England, a contribution, a one-time *donativo* (donation), was to be collected from all his "vassals" in America. *Alcaldes* (mayors) and military commanders were the collectors.

Read: *Spain and the Independence of the United States: An Intrinsic Gift*, by Thomas E. Chávez, University of New Mexico Press, 2002; and "On Establishing a Presidio at Santa Fe, 1678–1693," by Barbara De Marco, in *All Trails Lead to Santa Fe*, Sunstone Press, 2010.

235. What early seventeenth-century Spanish book with typical household guidance for *casas reales* (royal or privileged households) was used during Governor Diego de Vargas's tenure?

A copy of *Arte de Cocina* (Madrid, 1611), by Francisco Martínez Montiño, chef to Philip III, was listed in don Diego de Vargas's will. The cookbook, although directed toward the upper classes, included simple as well as refined recipes for stuffing meats and vegetables, and for elegant pies, pastries, chorizos, little meatballs, empanadas, and other foods that could be picked up and eaten by hand—perhaps the ancestors of tapas.

See *Arte de Cocina, Pastelería, Vizcochería y Conservería*, by Francisco Martínez Montiño, Cocinero Mayor del Rey Nuestro Señor, a facsimile reproduction of the original edition, Barcelona L. Tusquets, 1982–86. A copy is often on display at the New Mexico History Museum, Palace of the Governors. Also, read *Food in Early Modern Europe*, by Ken Albala, Greenwood Press, 2003.

236. What is the soothing Mexican-American gruel still used by many households and offered at meals in Santa Fe's largest hospital?

Atole is a thin blue cornmeal gruel; it is cooked in water and sometimes has milk, a pinch of salt, and a sweetener such as maple syrup added. *Chaqueweh* is another term for a similar, thicker mixture, a sort of porridge served with milk or cream and sometimes with fruit or red chile.

Find the recipes in *Historic Cookery*, by Fabiola Cabeza de Baca Gilbert, Gibbs Smith, 1997 (first published 1931); *Pueblo Indian Cookbook: Recipes from the Pueblos of the American Southwest*, by Phyllis Hughes, Museum of New Mexico Press, 1977; *Southwest Indian Cookbook: Pueblo and Navajo Images, Quotes, and Recipes*, by Marcia Keegan, Clear Light, 1987; *Foods of the Southwest Indian Nations: Traditional and Contemporary Native American Recipes*, by Lois Ellen Frank, Ten Speed Press, 2002; and *Cooking Vegetarian with Melonie Mathews,* by Melonie Mathews, Gathering of Nations Publishing, 2002. Also, read "Long Before Starbucks, Atole Was the Beverage of Choice," by Marc Simmons, *Santa Fe New Mexican*, September 18, 2010.

237. Where is the mural series that depicts the judicial history of Santa Fe, beginning with Native Americans and ending with what?

The four-panel mural painted by Zara Kriegstein is in the lobby of the municipal court building; in the last panel, at the far right side, Judge Tom Fiorina is shown receiving a turkey, one of many he accepted as payment for traffic fines, and then donated to the needy. (The Pantry Restaurant, on Cerrillos Road, features Kriegstein's artwork on their menu. The diner was started in 1948 on the original Santa Fe spur of Route 66, by George Myers and his sister. After George married local Santa Fean Dolores Apodaca, his wife helped him run the restaurant, which has been in continuous service, under various family ownerships, for over sixty years.)

Read: "'Turkey Court' Gets Makeover, Mural Stays," by Jason Auslander, *Santa Fe New Mexican*, August 23, 2009. Also, see the murals and the information displayed with them at the municipal court building, 2511 Camino Entrada, off Cerrillos Road, south of Airport Road.

Panel I, Pre-colonial Native American Judicial System, Prehistoric Era to 1598

Panel II, Spanish and Mexican Period, 1598–1846

Panel III, Territorial Period, 1846–1912

Panel IV, Statehood, 1912–1995

The Judicial History of Santa Fe is a series of four acrylic murals painted by Zara Kriegstein in 1995, in the Santa Fe Municipal Court House. The commentary that appears with the murals was written by Alfonso Ortiz, Adrian Bustamante, and Nancy Owen Lewis. The commentary follows below. The images were photographed by Melanie West.

Panel I
Pre-colonial Native American Judicial System
Prehistoric Era to 1598
(This text was prepared with the assistance of Alfonso Ortiz, Ph.D.)

Prior to Spanish arrival the Santa Fe area was inhabited by the ancestors of the Pueblo tribes, who were descendants of the Anasazi cultural tradition. Pueblo Indians and the visiting nomadic peoples traded their goods, which often was also a means to settle differences.

In Native American tribal life, the harmony of religious, spiritual, and social life was the basis for a tribe's survival; the judicial system was thus a structure of meditative justice. Small offenses often were corrected by clowns mocking the offender during the religious feasts and dances, in this way embarrassing the individual before the entire community. Disciplinary Kachinas would catch children who misbehaved with a long stick and put them into a basket on their backs. Their mothers would later ransom them, a practice anthropologists recorded in their accounts of Pueblo life.

In such societies everyone knew that if you violated the rules, the authority figures of these small, close-knit communities would discipline you. For serious offenses such as violence, adultery, stealing, or failing to perform community duties, the accused and the accuser and their clans would be called before the council of elders to state their cases and work out a settlement. If a man killed the breadwinner of a family, for example, he would be required to support the family for the rest of his life.

If a tribal member continued to step out of line and did not make an effort to integrate into the harmonious social and spiritual life of the tribe, he could be banished from society. This was comparable to a death sentence, as an individual could not normally survive by himself in the world outside the community.

In 1535 don Alvar Nuñez Cabeza de Vaca was the first Spanish explorer to report the existence of towns in what is now New Mexico. Based on his report, as well as a later one by fray Marcos de Niza, the Coronado expedition was launched in 1540. This became the first real contact that the Pueblos had with the Europeans. In 1598 don Juan de Oñate founded the first permanent Spanish colony in New Mexico, at San Gabriel, near San Juan Pueblo.

Panel II
Spanish and Mexican Period
1598–1846
(This text was prepared with the assistance of Adrian Bustamante, Ph.D.)

Don Juan de Oñate brought the first settlers accompanied by missionary friars to New Mexico in 1598. The secular laws of the colony were administered by the governor aided by *encomenderos*, to whom he assigned areas of tribute (*encomiendas*) to govern. After don Pedro de Peralta established Santa Fe as the capital in 1610, the governor, together with the *alcalde* (mayor) and the selected *cabildo* (town council), administered the secular laws in Santa Fe. Civil and criminal cases were brought to trial.

The missionaries had legal power over the colonists only as granted by the Inquisition regarding faith and morals. The Inquisition did not apply to the Indians, who were subject to the rules set down by the Franciscan friars, especially once they converted to Christianity. Indian converts built the adobe missions and supplied them with food, blankets, and other goods, but when the governor tried to use Indian labor in the same way, a bitter conflict arose between him and the friars.

This conflict agitated the Indians and colonists alike and lasted until 1680, when the Pueblo tribes united and revolted against the harsh treatment by both the church and state. Priests and settlers were killed, and the remaining colonists were driven from New Mexico.

Don Diego de Vargas was ordered to reconquer New Mexico, and he set out from El Paso del Norte (Juarez) in the spring of 1692 with a small group of soldiers. Upon his arrival in Santa Fe, he found the Palace of the Governors had been converted into a multistoried pueblo inhabited by members of the Tano tribe. After some tense moments, he held peaceful negotiations with the inhabitants about the return of the Spanish colonists. When he returned with settlers the following year, the Indians were not willing to vacate Santa Fe for the winter and did not welcome them. Vargas then took the pueblo by force. After their return the missionaries did not try to force the Indians to convert, and the Catholic Church enforced only one judicial power—the right to grant sanctuary in the church to those who were fleeing from the law.

After the reconquest the *encomienda* system was eradicated and the society was administered by the governor and district *alcaldes*, who held civil and judicial powers. They dealt with legal issues involving land, boundaries, water-rights violations, and crime. The new settlers were given land grants in the name of the crown as long as the land did not infringe on the Indian land. When the *alcalde* issued the land grant (the Act of Possession), the settlers would set piles of stones as boundaries and joyfully throw rocks and grass in the air praising the king in celebration.

Serious crimes were handled by the governor, and sentences could be appealed to him. Women had the same civil and judicial rights as men. Many of the cases brought before the officials dealt with the honor of a lady's name, which was a serious issue. In one case a woman who had insulted a prominent couple was sentenced to be led on horseback around the Plaza, gagged and naked from the waist up. Then she was exiled to Albuquerque for two years. In cases involving robbery, the thieves were sentenced to the *picota* (pillory) on the Plaza, and if the thieves were members of a *casta* (mixed ancestry), the stolen goods were hung around their necks.

While Indian tribes maintained their own governments, they also had the right to complain to the governor of the province about their mistreatment. They frequently took advantage of that right.

In 1821, when Mexico won independence from Spain, New Mexico became a province under the Mexican government. Mexico continued to bestow land grants and also began trading with the United States when the Santa Fe Trail opened in 1821. An increasing number of wagon trains arrived from Missouri, and the Santa Fe Trail became a lifeline of goods and riches, which changed the economic structure of this formerly poor and isolated area. It also brought American immigrants and fostered the subsequent occupation by the United States.

Panel III

Territorial Period

1846–1912

(This text was prepared with the assistance of Adrian Bustamante, Ph.D.)

In August 1846 General Stephen Watts Kearny, leading the Army of the West against northern Mexican forces, entered New Mexico. Governor Manuel Armijo responded by setting up a defense at Cañoncito with 5,000 men but decided not to fight. Kearney then entered Santa Fe and established a government of occupation with a governor (Charles Bent), law enforcement officer, district attorney, and judicial officials.

Many New Mexicans, resenting the occupation and fearing that their religion, culture, and personal safety were imperiled, planned to rebel against the Americans, but the conspiracy was betrayed and several people were arrested. Although the Americans believed that the insurgency had been squelched, in January 1847 Governor Bent and others were assassinated in Taos by Mexicans and Pueblo Indians. Guerrilla incidents against the U.S. Army continued for several months throughout northern New Mexico, finally ending in July 1847.

In the first jury trial held in New Mexico, the Mexican and Indian prisoners were tried as traitors to the United States by Judge Joab Houghton. Some forty-eight insurgents were hanged. This trial was unjust because the insurgents had not sworn loyalty to the United States.

The U.S. judicial system was adopted in 1850, and the newly established territorial assembly passed laws for New Mexico. As a U.S. territory, New Mexico was allowed to have a non-voting delegate to Congress.

Not everyone was hostile to the Americans. Doña Tules (Gertrudes Barceló), a rich and powerful woman who had been Governor Armijo's advisor and owner of a very profitable gambling house, lent money to the U.S. Army so that they could pay the soldiers. Understanding the new nature of things, she remained friends with both the local population and the newcomers. Gambling remained legal in New Mexico until 1912.

Under the new sovereignty a group of politicians and lawyers known as the "Santa Fe Ring" conspired to gain control of the natural wealth of New Mexico by acquiring Spanish land grants by questionable means. By ignoring provisions of the Treaty of Guadalupe Hidalgo, which referred to the protection of land and property, American "shysters" gained wealth, land, and power while Washington stood by. When they began to sell and fence these lands, a group of New Mexicans known as Gorras Blancas (White Caps) took the law into their own hands. They cut fences and burned haystacks in order to discourage settlers on their traditional community land.

In 1880 the railroad reached Santa Fe from Kansas and a *Santa Fe New Mexican* newspaper headline read: "Santa Fe's Triumph! The Last Link Is Forged in the Iron Chain Which Binds the Ancient City to the United States, and the Old Santa Fe Trail Passes into Oblivion." The railroad accelerated change in New Mexico, bringing yet another influx of people, goods, and a whole new culture to Santa Fe.

Panel IV
Statehood
1912–1995
(This text was prepared with the assistance of Nancy Owen Lewis, Ph.D., and Adrian
Bustamante, Ph.D.)

New Mexico attained statehood in 1912, and during the following eighty years Santa Fe grew
from a small town capital of 5,000 to a city of over 60,000. As the seat of government during
the early years of statehood, the town always had enough jobs for its citizens. Santa Fe was also a
commercial center for the surrounding villages, with goods coming in by rail and later by trucks,
while many gardens and cultivated fields dotted the area.

This was also the era when Americans fell in love with the "primitive" cultures that existed
in the area. Artists began to relocate to Santa Fe to draw inspiration from these cultures, the clear
desert light, and dramatic landscapes. Ultimately, Santa Fe became one of the premier art centers
in the United States. Archeologists and other interested persons soon followed, endeavoring to
study the cultural landscape of bygone days. Together with the artists they helped to revive and
foster the Indian and Hispanic arts and crafts of northern New Mexico.

With the arrival of immigrants, including persons suffering from tuberculosis seeking the
benefits of New Mexico's dry air, Santa Fe began to grow yet again. Further growth occurred after
World War II owing to the baby boom and tourism, with its associated jobs, developing into a
major industry. This newest influx altered inexorably the slow paced character of the town. The
1960s brought urban renewal, and in an effort to protect Santa Fe's charm and uniqueness a
historical district overseen by citizen representatives was established.

In response to this unprecedented growth, Santa Fe's judicial system also changed. Until
the 1930s all petty civil and criminal cases within the county were still brought before a justice of
the peace, who drew his salary from fees collected during the proceedings. A new law, however,
made possible the establishment of a "police magistrate court," later known as municipal court, to
handle cases occurring within the city limits. The justice of the peace continued handling county
cases until 1966, when a constitutional amendment abolished this system. It was replaced by the
magistrate court, which has jurisdiction over county cases.

In 1938, Joseph Berardinelli, a state police officer, became the city's first municipal judge,
with a salary paid by the city. Judge Berardinelli's caseload consisted primarily of domestic violence,
disorderly conduct, and public drunkenness offenses. Court was conducted at the old city hall
building, which housed city court until 1985. Named in his honor, the Berardinelli Building is
now occupied by the Santa Fe Public Library.

In 1958, Romualdo E. "Cuate" Chavez succeeded Berardinelli as judge, a position he held
until his retirement in December 1982. Reflecting the philosophy of his predecessor, Judge Chavez
believed that "people who come before my court are not criminals; they are people with problems,"
and he conducted his court accordingly. "Wife beaters" generally received a jail sentence—and a
lecture. Juvenile offenders might get a day in jail—to teach them a lesson—or were handed over
to their parents or school principal to impose punishment. Traffic offenses, such as driving while
intoxicated (DWI), became increasingly common, and parking violations emerged as a major issue
owing to lack of available spaces in the downtown area.

Appointed by the city council to succeed Judge Chavez, Thomas A. Fiorina became the third city judge in January 1983. Known for his creative sentences, Judge Fiorina was one of the first in the state to initiate an alcohol screening program for DWI offenders. He also started a community service program, which included his Thanksgiving "turkeys for tickets" for parking violators (a popular practice that came to an end in the spring of 1995). Calling himself a "people's court judge," Fiorina often adapted his sentences to the particular needs of the offender. When a British citizen, calling himself the "last American cowboy," was cited for riding his horse across the Plaza, Judge Fiorina told him, "There will be no fine as long as your horse is out of town by sundown." In another case, a speeding opera diva was sentenced to "sing" before the court. She performed an aria—to a standing ovation, no less—an appropriate measure for a city which owes so much history to its wealth of cultural riches.

238. During the 1940s, how did Gormley's grocery store help an important local businessman with a popular but erratic crop?

Frank Gormley had a knack for predicting good piñon crops, which he would do for his friend Daniel T. Kelly, president of Gross, Kelly & Company, whose mercantile business thrived in what is now the Railyard district.

Many Santa Feans believe a good crop of pine nuts comes about every seven years. The piñon nut is rich in calories and is also valuable nutritionally since it has all twenty amino acids that make up complete protein. Tewa Pueblo tradition holds piñon nuts to be their most ancient food.

Read: *The Buffalo Head: A Century of Mercantile Pioneering in the Southwest*, by Daniel T. Kelly, with Beatrice Chauvenet, Vergara Publishing Company, 1972; and *Wild Plants of the Pueblo Province: Exploring Ancient and Enduring Uses*, by William Dunmire and Gail Tierney, Museum of New Mexico Press, 1995.

Piñon nut shipment from Gormley's General Store, in front of the Palace of the Governors. Photograph by Jesse Nusbaum, 1913. Courtesy of Palace of the Governors Photo Archives (NMHM/DCA), #061440.

The Piñon. Pen, ink, and colored crayon. Drawn at Puye, New Mexico, by Harold E. West, 1941.

239. What is the earliest known time of occupation by what archeologists call Archaic peoples in the Santa Fe area?

Circa 2000 B.C. The Archaic peoples were foragers who stayed in one place because they became proficient at growing corn, beans, and squash. The Paleo-Indian culture before them was nomadic, following the game they hunted.

Read: *Before Santa Fe: Archaeology of the City Different,* by Jason Shapiro, Museum of New Mexico Press, 2008.

240. "El Zaguán" means what and is the name of which vintage-1800s property on Canyon Road?

Zaguán means "hallway," or passageway. The building at 545 Canyon Road is named for the 175-foot-long hallway that leads to a garden with two pre–Civil War chestnut trees and some peony bushes imported from China over a hundred years ago.

Originally the property was a hacienda, the earliest parts dating to 1816, with a corral where Santa Fe Trail freighters kept their oxen, horses, and mules while they stayed in town. Santa Fe merchant James L. Johnson bought the property in 1849, and in 1875 El Zaguán was considered "one of the finest villas on the edge of the city." It was said that Johnson had the largest personal library west of the Mississippi River at the time. Artist Dorothy Stewart's sister, Margretta Stewart Dietrich, purchased the property in 1928 and converted it to apartments.

El Zaguán still houses several private apartments and is home to a small artists' colony. The offices of the Historic Santa Fe Foundation are there as well. Willa Cather told Margretta Dietrich that El Zaguán inspired the scene for the dinner party in Cather's novel *Death Comes for the Archbishop.* Brinton Turkle, an author and an illustrator, lived there during the 1960s.

Read: *El Zaguán: The James L. Johnson House, 545 Canyon Road; A Social History*, by Corinne Sze, Historic Santa Fe Foundation, 1997; "The Bones of El Zaguan Date to 1816," *Santa Fe New Mexican*, January 6, 2008; *Death Comes for the Archbishop*, by Willa Cather, Vintage Classics, 1990 (first published 1928); and *Do Not Open* and *Thy Friend Obadiah*, children's books by Brinton Turkle.

Interior hallway at El Zaguán. Photograph by Charles F. Lummis.
Courtesy of Palace of the Governors Photo Archives (NMHM/DCA), #136252.

241. What did Spanish colonizer don Juan de Oñate accomplish when he led an expedition of settlers north into New Mexico's Upper Rio Grande valley in 1598?

Don Juan de Oñate y Salazar, born in Spain in 1550, was ordered by King Philip II in 1595 to colonize the northern frontier of New Spain. The stated objective was to establish new missions and spread Catholicism, but Oñate probably hoped to find a mining bonanza similar to one his father and associates had found in Zacatecas; he must have been disappointed to discover that New Mexico would not yield mineral riches for him and his financial backers. Oñate did, nonetheless, establish New Mexico's first capital, in 1598, at San Juan de los Caballeros, as well as a system of governance that would be used for the rest of the Spanish colonial period in New Mexico. Along with the office of the governor, the *cabildo* (town council meeting), Spanish law and religion, and Spanish as a predominant language, Oñate established the first Spanish families of New Mexico. The capital was moved from San Juan de los Caballeros to San Gabriel in 1599 and finally to Santa Fe in 1610.

Oñate and his settlers were also involved in the war at Acoma, when the warriors there killed his nephew and several other Spaniards. The confrontation at Acoma has two sides and remains controversial. The battle of Acoma was fought by the Acomans in an attempt to drive out the Spaniards. By the same token, it was fought by the Spanish settlers to protect themselves from an all-out war and possible annihilation by the pueblos.

Oñate had married Isabel de Tolosa Cortés de Moctezuma in Mexico several years before he left for northern New Spain. Her father was a wealthy, Spanish-born Basque who discovered silver mines in Zacatecas, and on her mother's side she was the granddaughter of Hernán Cortés and great granddaughter of the Aztec emperor Moctezuma Xocoyotzin. Oñate was the first governor of the province of New Mexico, a position he held for about twelve challenging years. He died in 1626.

Gaspar Pérez de Villagrá, one of Oñate's captains, wrote about the 1598 expedition in the epic poem *Historia de la Nuevo México, 1610*, an account that reveals perhaps unintended or covert sympathy for the Native Americans who were mistreated during the expedition.

Read: "Juan de Oñate: Colonizer, Governor," by Rick Hendricks, in *Telling New Mexico: A New History*, edited by Marta Weigle, with Francis Levine and Louise Stiver, Museum of New Mexico Press, 2009; *Don Juan de Oñate: Colonizer of New Mexico, 1595–1628*, by George P. Hammond and Agapito Rey, University of New Mexico Press, 1953; *The Last Conquistador: Juan de Oñate and the Settling of the Far Southwest*, by Marc Simmons, University of Oklahoma Press, 1991; *Juan de Oñate's Colony in the Wilderness: An Early History of the American Southwest*, by Robert McGeagh, Sunstone Press, 1990; *New Mexico and Politicians of the Past: True Tales of Some of New Mexico's Founding Fathers and a Few Other Office Seekers and Holders*, by Don Bullis, Rio Grande Books, 2009; *Historia de la Nueva Mexico, 1610*, by Gaspar Pérez de Villagrá, translated and edited by Miguel Encinias, Alfred Rodriguez, and Joseph P. Sánchez, University of New Mexico Press, 1992; and *The Daring Flight of My Pen: Cultural Politics and Gaspar Pérez de Villagrá's "Historia de la Nueva Mexico, 1610"*, by Genaro M. Padilla, University of New Mexico Press, 2010.

242. LeBaron Bradford Prince was an affable, ambitious, and progressive politician most proud of what?

He was a historian as well as a chief justice and a territorial governor in the late 1800s, but he was particularly proud of helping to introduce a modern public school system to New Mexico.

Read: *The Student's History of New Mexico*, facsimile of 1921 second edition, by L. Bradford Prince, Sunstone Press, 2008.

Governor L. Bradford Prince residence on Palace Avenue, not far from the Plaza, looking east. This 1919 photograph shows an automobile sharing the muddy street with a horse and buggy. Photograph by Charles F. Coffin. Courtesy of Palace of the Governors Photo Archives (NMHM/DCA) #088800.

243. What was the precursor to Santa Fe's annual summertime Spanish Market?

"Native Market" was created during the Depression by Leonora Curtin, who had been a member of the Spanish Colonial Arts Society, which incorporated in 1929. The society cooperated with the Normal School in El Rito and with country schools under Nina Otero-Warren to preserve the vanishing traditional-craft production of Spanish-speaking artisans and to present opportunities to market their work.

Other people who helped support Native Market were Brice Sewell, state director for vocational education and training; Henry Gonzales, woodworker; Dolores Perrault, weaver and teacher; Carmen Espinoza, Spanish teacher and authority on traditional Spanish culture; and William Lumpkins, art student and furniture maker. Beginning in 1952, the Spanish Colonial Arts Society sponsored the Spanish Market, on the Plaza on the last weekend in July each year.

Some of the groups and events that showcase the different cultures that enrich Santa Fe include La Sociedad Folklórica, Los Caballeros de Vargas, and the Santa Fe Indian Market.

Read: *The Native Market of the Spanish New Mexican Craftsman, 1933–1940*, by Sarah Nestor, Sunstone Press, 2009 (first published 1928); and *Popular Arts of Spanish New Mexico*, by E. Boyd, Museum of New Mexico Press, 1974.

Going to Saturday Market. **Linoleum block cut by Harold E. West, c. 1930s.**

244. What is *sabanilla labrada,* which is often seen during Santa Fe's Spanish Market?

It is wool-on-wool *colcha* embroidery work, a textile art developed and made in New Mexico during the Spanish colonial period. *Sabanilla* usually means "small sheet" or bedcovering, and *labrada* means "worked," or manufactured. Often the decorated woolen sheets are used as bed coverings or quilts; sometimes smaller ones are used as altar cloths. Some are all a natural white, and many incorporate colored wool.

In colonial times, and sometimes still today, the colorful embroidery wool was created using dyes made from local desert plants such as the chamisa plant (yellow) as well as traded dyes made from indigo (blue), brazil-wood chips (brown), and cochineal (red). Cochineal dye is made from extractions of the cochineal insect, which lives on prickly pear and other cacti. One of the more unusual domestications in the New World, cochineal was used throughout Peru, Chile, Mexico, and Central America in payment of tribute from one individual to another, or one nation to another. In addition to being used in dye, it was made into inks and paints for codices and murals for centuries before the arrival of the Spanish. Shortly after the conquest of the New World, the production of cochineal became a monopoly controlled by Spain. It was not until the early nineteenth century that cochineal became widely available.

Traditionally, the wool used for *sabanilla labrada* is from the *churro* sheep. (*Churro* is the Americanized version of the word, which means "rough.") The *churro* sheep is a sturdy, adaptable old breed of Spanish sheep, brought to New Spain by the Spaniards in the late 1500s; eventually they became popular in the Upper Rio Grande area and were acquired by the Navajo Indians through raids and trade. They have a long protective top coat of wool and a soft undercoat. Some rams have four fully developed horns.

The Portuguese returning from Ming Dynasty China brought new culinary techniques, including their version of a rough bread stick, called *You tiao,* which evolved into the Spanish churro, a long prism-shaped fried snack that may be straight, curled, or spirally twisted, resembling the *churro* sheep's horns. Churros are often served at breakfast and dipped in a cup of thick hot chocolate or rolled in cinnamon sugar.

Read: *Traditional Arts of Spanish New Mexico*, by Robin Farwell Gavin, Museum of New Mexico Press, 1994; *New Mexico Colcha Club: Spanish Colonial Embroidery and the Women Who Saved It*, by Nancy C. Benson, Museum of New Mexico Press, 2008; *A Perfect Red: Empire, Espionage, and the Quest for the Color of Desire*, by Amy Butler Greenfield, HarperCollins, 2006; and *To Walk in Beauty: A Navajo Family's Journey Home*, by Stacia Spragg-Braude, Museum of New Mexico Press, 2009.

**A five-horned *churro* sheep.
Photograph by Robert Nymeyer, 1940.
Courtesy of Palace of the Governors
Photo Archives (NMHM/DCA), #059014.**

245. What summer choral company performs in various historic places in Santa Fe?

The Santa Fe Desert Chorale was founded in 1982. It brings in professional singers to perform a cappella choral music in such places as the Loretto Chapel, St. Francis Cathedral, the Randall Davey Audubon Center, and Cristo Rey Church.

Listen to *Live from Loretto Chapel*, by the Santa Fe Desert Chorale, Clarion Records, 2007, available at the Santa Fe Public Library.

**What Is It?
(See Answer Key #35)**

246. When was a railroad line to Santa Fe first opened?

On February 9, 1880, the first train arrived at the Santa Fe depot, on tracks that connected the Atchison, Topeka & Santa Fe to the capital.

Read: "When the Railroad Came to Territorial New Mexico," by Marc Simmons, *Santa Fe New Mexican*, December 13, 2005.

247. What were the three earliest railroads that served Santa Fe?

The Denver & Rio Grande, the Atchison, Topeka & Santa Fe (AT&SF), and the Santa Fe Central, which became the New Mexico Central. The last spike on the Santa Fe Central Railroad was driven at Kennedy, New Mexico, on August 13, 1903. The flyover of the AT&SF at Kennedy was the most difficult piece on the Santa Fe to Torrance (near Corona) line, and it was the last part to be completed. The New Mexico Central Railroad was subsequently acquired by the AT&SF. The popular New Mexico Rail Runner Express trains, connecting Santa Fe with Albuquerque and Belen, with stops in between, began commuter rail service in 2006.

Read: *New Mexico's Railroads: A Historical Survey*, by David F. Myrick, University of New Mexico Press, 1990 (first published 1970).

The Denver & Rio Grande engine northbound on a trestle in front of Guadalupe Church. Photograph by Margaret McKittrick, 1941. Courtesy of Palace of the Governors Photo Archives (NMHM/DCA), #041833.

248. Heading south from Santa Fe, where did the New Mexico Central Railroad join the Union Pacific, which later became the Atchison, Topeka & Santa Fe Railroad?

At Willard, New Mexico. It carried commodities such as pinto beans and piñon nuts.

Read: *New Mexico's Railroads: A Historical Survey*, by David F. Myrick, University of New Mexico Press, 1990 (first published 1970).

249. Hopewell Street is named for what far-ranging entrepreneur?

Willard Samuel Hopewell was a territorial representative (from 1892 to 1893) and a friend of Governor Miguel Otero. He was also a captain of the cavalry in the New Mexico National Guard. He was involved in mining, land speculation, cattle, and railroads. Willard, New Mexico, was named for his son, Willard Junior.

See the Willard S. Hopewell Papers, at the Center for Southwest Research, University of New Mexico Libraries, in Albuquerque. Also, read *New Mexico Place Names: A Geographical Dictionary*, edited by T. M. Pearce, University of New Mexico Press, 1965.

250. Which Santa Fe artist's property was donated to a national conservation organization?

Randall Davey's house and extensive grounds on Upper Canyon Road were donated to the National Audubon Society in 1983. Randall Davey came to Santa Fe in 1919 at the recommendation of his art teacher, Robert Henri. He loved to play polo, and many of his paintings feature polo ponies and polo matches. He also loved cars, but unfortunately he died in an automobile accident in 1964.

Read: *Turn Left at the Sleeping Dog: Scripting the Santa Fe Legend, 1920–1955*, by John Pen La Farge, University of New Mexico Press, 2001; and *The Audubon Ark: A History of the National Audubon Society*, by Frank Graham Jr., with Carl Buchheister, Random House, 1990.

251. Who was the first collector, in the early 1900s, of early cowboy songs and culture who wrote "Little Joe the Wrangler"?

Jack Thorp (Nathan Howard Thorp). He and his wife Annette settled in Santa Fe in 1940. He wrote *Tales of the Chuck Wagon*, a novel based on his work as a cowboy.

Read: "From Buried Treasure to Desperados, Jack Thorp Kept Cowboy Life Alive," by Marc Simmons, *Santa Fe New Mexican*, August 13, 2005: and *Jack Thorp's Songs of the Cowboys*, edited by Mark L. Gardner, Museum of New Mexico Press, 2005.

Cowboy Dreaming of Home. Pen and ink drawing by Harold E. West, c. 1930s.

252. Where was the little burro sculpture stationed before it was moved to its proper place, at Burro Alley, between San Francisco Street and Palace Avenue?

The burro stood patiently at the corner of Water and Sandoval Streets for a while. Burro Alley is the correct place for the sculpture since the alley was named for the area where many traders and wood-sellers would station their burros, until the early 1900s, when people began using pickup trucks instead.

Read: City of Santa Fe Arts Commission booklet; and *The Burro*, by Frank Brookshier, University of Oklahoma Press, 1974.

Burro Alley, looking north from San Francisco Street. Notice the *carreta* on top of the building at the left. Photograph by C. G. Kaadt, c. 1895–1898. Courtesy of Palace of the Governors Photo Archives (NMHM/DCA), #011070.

Homage to the Burro. Steel sculpture by Charley Southard, 1988, in Burro Alley at San Francisco Street. Courtesy of the artist.

253. The first animal shelter in Santa Fe was founded by whom and when?

Disheartened by the number of abandoned animals in the city, Amelia Elizabeth White donated her family home for an animal shelter, in honor of her late sister Martha. She and Betty Stewart founded the first official animal shelter in Santa Fe, in 1939. Today the Santa Fe Animal Shelter and Humane Society is on the southwestern edge of town, on Caja del Rio Road (named for the Caja del Rio, a dissected plateau of volcanic origin, managed by the Santa Fe National Forest, where ranchers have permits to run cattle), north of the Veterans' Memorial Highway. The Animal Shelter and Humane Society coordinates its work with animal control in both the city and the county.

The Frank S. Ortiz Park, commonly referred to as the Dog Park, in the Casa Solana neighborhood, is one of the most visited parks in Santa Fe since dogs are permitted to roam free and off leash there.

Wildlife that have been seen in Santa Fe because of climate changes and loss of habitat include bears, mountain lions, snakes, coyotes, deer, raccoons, skunks, and various birds of prey.

Read: *Artists of the Canyons and Caminos: Santa Fe, Early Twentieth Century,* by Edna Robertson and Sarah Nestor, Ancient City Press, 2006 (first published 1976); *Animal Happiness: A Moving Exploration of Animals and Their Emotions,* by Vicki Hearne, Skyhorse Publishing, 1994; and "Living with Wildlife: Climate Changes, Loss of Habitat Force Wild Critters into Urban Areas," by Ben Swan, *Santa Fe New Mexican,* August 24, 2011.

What Is It?
(See Answer Key #36)

Many Santa Feans live with dogs and/or cats, and often with bugs too. Some of these animals are pets, some are wild. All have been seen within the city limits of Santa Fe. The horse standing in the wind and the cow being milked are by Harold E. West. All the other drawings are by Anita H. Lehmann and are courtesy of her.

What Is It?
(See Answer Key #37)

John Sloan, painting, with Dolly Sloan in the car, near Santa Fe. Photograph by T. Harmon Parkhurst, c. 1926. Courtesy of Palace of the Governors Photo Archives (NMHM/DCA), #028835.

254. What summer activity still enjoyed by locals and visitors on the Santa Fe Plaza was depicted by which artist in 1920?

Music in the Plaza, an oil painting by John Sloan, shows this popular activity for Santa Feans on summer evenings. Santa Feans and visitors alike enjoy the free Summer Bandstand series, cofounded by David Lescht, which presents music on the Plaza weekday nights from after the Fourth of July until Indian Market, in late August.

Local musicians may obtain a permit from City Hall to perform on the Plaza.

Attend free musical events on the Santa Fe Plaza, and see John Sloan's painting at the New Mexico Museum of Art. Also, read "Music on the Plaza," a poem by Joan Logghe, City of Santa Fe Poet Laureate, 2010–2012.

Musicians performing on the Santa Fe Plaza.
Photographs by E. West, 2012

Music in the Plaza. Oil on canvas, by John Sloan, 1920. New Mexico Museum of Art.
Photograph courtesy of Palace of the Governors Photo Archives (NMHM/DCA), #040881.

"Music on the Plaza," by Joan Logghe

Then there was that evening on Plaza Fatima,
little circle tucked between Acequia Madre
and Canyon Road. Behind the ravens settling down
for night, beneath the scent of basil and roses
we could hear the music from the Plaza, free

music filling in the distance, traveling up
Paseo de Peralta and turning left and music
turning right at Delgado and right again, and we heard
as if from long times ago, a tune. We stopped,
put down our pens, our water glasses filled

with juice of watermelon, and we either wept
or smiled, depending on how our families
found themselves that season. Myself, I strained
to hear and then leaned back, received.
This city has been my Santa Fe for years, holy

as we ourselves are music, driven streets and faith,
walked more than a few miles. Music for the meals
I've eaten, grace notes for the friends I've made.
I ate my first enchilada at The Shed. Red.
I met men with languages I speak and those
whose language I can't. Men with state jobs and

at my bank, my money floating in and out
of hands, tellers, Josephine, now gone, she was
rooting for me. My shopping life, the goods
and jewelry, my taxes going for the public good.
That music. Every time I buy a stamp downtown,
this music from the Plaza, this town grown city
right before my years. That music from the bandstand
that summer night. That night, the voice of city.

(Printed with permission of the poet.)

255. A mural at City Hall shows a bird's-eye view of Santa Fe with various scenes, including a procession, some musicians in blue, and a clock; what are these scenes and where is the clock actually located now?

The scenes are a long parade that includes a Corpus Christi procession, three men from the 9th Cavalry Buffalo Soldiers Band, and the Spitz clock, now located east of the entrance to the New Mexico Museum of Art, at the northwest corner of the Santa Fe Plaza.

See the mural at a side entrance to City Hall, on Marcy Street. (A photograph of the mural is on the cover of this book, and a key to some sections of the mural is at the back of the book.)

What Is It?
(See Answer Key #38)

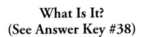

256. What was presented in 1912 to the Wood-Davis hardware store, on the Plaza, to honor which special event?

A version of the Great Seal of the State of New Mexico, made by the Shapleigh Hardware Company of Missouri using an assortment of hardware, including hooks, keys, knives, and silver spoons, was presented to the Wood-Davis hardware store to commemorate New Mexico's entrance into the Union as the forty-seventh state.

President William Howard Taft signed a proclamation on January 6, 1912, admitting the New Mexico territory as a state, saying "Well, it is all over. I am glad to give you life. I hope you will be healthy."

President Taft had more than a year earlier begun the process of enabling statehood when he signed the Enabling Act, in June of 1910. There was much celebrating, and the *Santa Fe New Mexican* announced that "Santa Fe is wild with joy." The celebrations in 1912 for actual statehood were more sedate.

(Taft is the only person to have served as both president of the United States and chief justice of the Supreme Court. Taft and Millard Fillmore are the only U.S. presidents who have been Unitarians, and Taft is the only Unitarian chief justice.)

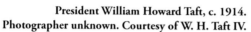

Read: "Where N.M.'s March to Statehood Begins," by Tom Sharpe, *Santa Fe New Mexican*, November 27, 2010; *William Howard Taft: Confident Peacemaker*, by David H. Burton, Fordham University Press, 2004; and *The Life and Times of William Howard Taft: A Biography*, by Henry F. Pringle, American Political Biography Press, 1998. Also, see the hardware version of the state seal in the New Mexico History Museum.

President William Howard Taft, c. 1914.
Photographer unknown. Courtesy of W. H. Taft IV.

257. Who was the first civil governor of New Mexico, appointed by General Kearny in August 1846, and what was the name of the governor's slave?

The first civil governor was the celebrated Santa Fe Trail trader Charles Bent. He was assassinated within six months of his appointment, in the January 1847 Taos uprising, and eventually was buried in what became the National Cemetery, in Santa Fe. One of the people who wanted to avenge Charles Bent's death was Dick Green, who, along with Green's wife Charlotte, were African-American slaves who had been brought from Missouri by the Bent brothers, William and Charles, to help at their huge adobe trading post. The brothers had established the post in 1833, with Céran St. Vrain, along the Santa Fe Trail, in what is now southeastern Colorado.

When Charles Bent was appointed governor in the summer of 1846 by Kearny, he came to Santa Fe and brought Dick Green with him. In January Governor Bent traveled home to Taos for a visit, but a mob of rebellious New Mexicans stormed his home and killed him. When Green heard of his master's murder, he was grief-stricken and begged for and received permission to join the troops who were dispatched to put down the uprising. For his bravery and heroism, William Bent granted freedom to Dick Green and his family.

Read: *The Massacre of Governor Bent*, by Don Turner, Humbug Gulch Press, 1969; *New Mexico Mavericks: Stories from a Fabled Past*, by Marc Simmons, Sunstone Press, 2005; and *Following the Santa Fe Trail*, by Marc Simmons and Hal Jackson, Ancient City Press, 2001.

258. What famous female architect designed the interior of which hotel restaurant still in use today?

Mary Jane Colter, born in 1870, was a follower of the American arts and crafts movement. She used Native American, Spanish colonial, and Mission revival elements and motifs in designing La Cocina (now a French restaurant), at La Fonda. She was hired by the owner, Fred Harvey, in 1910 and influenced the design concept throughout the hotel. It was said of this dynamic, visionary architect/designer that "she could teach masons how to lay adobe bricks, plasterers how to mix washes, and carpenters how to fix viga joints."

Read: *Mary Colter: Architect of the Southwest*, by Arnold Berke, Princeton Architectural Press, 2002.

259. Which philanthropists with a keen interest in archaeology donated land in the early 1900s for which notable Santa Fe properties?

Amelia Elizabeth White, along with her sister, Martha Root White, provided the land for the School of American Research (now the School for Advanced Research), the Laboratory of Anthropology, the International Folk Art Museum, the Wheelwright Museum of the American Indian, and the Garcia Street Club, among others. Their house on Garcia Street was incorporated into the design for the School of American Research; the first swimming pool, first billiards room, and first clay tennis court in Santa Fe were all built on their property. During their parties and events, the beloved Afgan hounds and Irish wolfhounds raised and bred by the sisters would mingle with the guests. Martha died in 1933, and Amelia Elizabeth died in 1972.

Read: *El Delirio: The Santa Fe World of Elizabeth White*, by Gregor Stark and E. Catherine Rayne, School of American Research Press, 1998; and *Artists of the Canyons and Caminos: Santa Fe, Early Twentieth Century*, by Edna Robertson and Sarah Nestor, Ancient City Press, 2006 (first published 1976).

260. Who takes care of dressing La Conquistadora, and how many dresses does she have?

The *sacristana* is voted in every other year by the lay group La Cofradía de la Conquistadora; this person cares for the wardrobe of more than a hundred dresses.

Some of the dresses are decorated with family heirlooms and donations of valuable items, including rings, gold and silver filigree, well-used rosary beads, and various religious medals. Many local people have made dresses for her, working with their neighbors and teaching each other how to sew if necessary. She is admired from far away as well: a group of Native Americans in Holy Cross, Alaska, made an ermine cape for La Conquistadora; the cape was passed from home to home in the community until every family had added stitches, and when it was finished it was sent to Santa Fe. A Spanish ceremonial cape she wears sometimes was fashioned from a stole belonging to the first archbishop of Santa Fe, Jean Baptiste Lamy. One of her dresses is an authentic Native American costume made by Dorothy Trujillo of Cochiti Pueblo; La Conquistadora usually wears this dress during Santa Fe Indian Market.

Read: *La Conquistadora: The Autobiography of an Ancient Statue*, by Fray Angélico Chávez, Sunstone Press, 1983 (first published 1954); and "Dressing La Conquistadora with Care and Devotion," by Camille Flores, *La Herencia*, Summer 1994.

261. Who led a Pecos delegation of fifty men into Santa Fe in 1702 to assure Governor Pedro Rodríguez Cubero of support?

Felipe Chistoe, a determined American Indian leader and governor of Pecos, persuaded most of the Pecos factions to join together and show loyalty to the Spanish governor in Santa Fe since it seemed to be the best option. Chistoe spoke Spanish and chose loyalty to Spain as the better path, although not all the Native Americans agreed. Chistoe's main rival was Diego Umviro, who was intent on stirring up anti-Spanish feeling.

Read: *Pueblos, Spaniards, and the Kingdom of New Mexico*, by John L. Kessell, University of Oklahoma Press, 2008.

262. What is the longest continuously running theater company west of the Mississippi River?

The Santa Fe Playhouse, located on De Vargas Street, in the Barrio de Analco, was incorporated in 1922 and supported by Mary Austin. The playhouse presents a variety of plays and is especially noted for its annual Fiesta Melodrama, which pokes fun at everything and everyone that Santa Feans consider sometimes funny or offensive and in need of ridicule.

Another year-round theater group is the alternative company Theaterwork, which has put on innovative plays, including a *zarzuela* (a traditional Spanish lyric-dramatic genre that alternates between spoken and sung scenes), as well as plays by Sophocles to Shakespeare and various contemporary, sometimes local playwrights. Where silence is found is one very important part of the company's focus.

Read: *Mary Austin and the American West*, by Susan Goodman and Carl Dawson, University of California Press, 2008.

263. Metropolitan Avenue was renamed what, after which Santa Fe historian?

The name of the street (which runs between Sandoval and South Guadalupe Streets) was changed to Read Street in the early 1900s, for Benjamin Read, a lawyer and historian who published *Historia Ilustrada de Nuevo México* in 1911; the English edition, *The Illustrated History of New Mexico*, translated by Eleuterio Baca, was published in 1912.

Benjamin Read believed that Santa Fe was founded by Juan de Oñate, and he was involved in a lengthy debate with historian Lansing Bloom, who believed it was founded by Pedro de Peralta.

Read: *The Illustrated History of New Mexico*, by Benjamin M. Read, translated into English, under the direction of the author, by Eleuterio Baca, New Mexican Printing Company, 1912; and "When Was Santa Fe Founded?" by Lansing B. Bloom, *New Mexico Historical Review*, 1929; and *Who Discovered New Mexico?* by Lansing B. Bloom, Santa Fe, 1940.

264. Who founded the Santa Fe Opera?

John Crosby, a New York conductor, founded Santa Fe's open-air opera in 1956. It is now one of the world's leading summer opera festivals. The first opera performed was *Madame Butterfly*.

Read: *The Santa Fe Opera: An American Pioneer*, by Philip Huscher, Sunstone Press, 2006.

265. Who was the last governor in Santa Fe to serve under the administration of the Republic of Mexico?

Manuel Armijo is often mentioned as the last Mexican governor, but Juan Bautista Vigil y Alarid served briefly in that capacity in 1846.

Read: "'She Was Our Mother': New Mexico's Change of National Sovereignty and Juan Bautista Vigil y Alarid, the Last Mexican Governor of New Mexico," by Samuel E. Sisneros, in *All Trails Lead to Santa Fe*, Sunstone Press, 2010.

266. What ex-slave worked for a territorial governor in Santa Fe and wrote a memoir of his boyhood life as a slave, his escape, and his youthful adventures as a muleteer and mess servant in the Civil War?

John McCline ("Mac") worked for Governor Herbert J. Hagerman, who encouraged him to write about his life. McCline lived in Santa Fe from 1906 until he died, in 1948.

Read: *Slavery in the Clover Bottoms*, by John McCline, edited by Jan Furman, University of Tennessee Press, 1998.

267. Who was the first native New Mexican Hispano to serve as governor under the U.S. military occupation following New Mexico's takeover by the United States in 1846, and where did he live?

Donaciano Vigil, who served as governor in 1847 and 1848, managed to be on good terms with the people from the United States and the Mexicans equally. He lived at 518 Alto Street, a property he had inherited from his father, Juan Cristóbal Vigil. In 1856 he sold the property to Vicente García and retired to his Pecos ranch on some of the land he and others in the 1850s and 1860s managed to own during a time of confusion in disputation of land grants; this may be understood as an early version of the land-grant manipulation that occurred in the Santa Fe area in the late nineteenth century. Years later, in 1999, the U.S. General Accounting Office (GAO), the investigative arm of the U.S. Congress, was invited to look into disputed land-grant claims in New Mexico, but no resolution was achieved.

Vigil wrote "Arms, Indians and Mismanagement of New Mexico" in 1846, a report critical of the Mexican central government.

Read: *The Military Career of Donaciano Vigil*, by J. Richard Salazar, Center for Land Grant Studies, 1994; *Biographical Sketch of Donaciano Vigil*, by William C. Ritch, in the Donaciano Vigil papers, New Mexico State Records Center and Archives, Santa Fe; *Los Patrones: Profiles of Hispanic Political Leaders in New Mexico History*, by Maurillo E. Vigil, University Press of America, 1980; and *Four Leagues of Pecos: A Legal History of the Pecos Grant, 1800–1933*, by G. Emlen Hall, University of New Mexico Press, 1984.

Donaciano Vigil, governor of New Mexico in 1847 and 1848. Photograph taken in the Albright Art Parlors, c. 1880–1882. Courtesy of Palace of the Governors Photo Archives (NMHM/DCA), #011405.

What Is It?
(See Answer Key #39)

268. Who were Lars and Belle Larson, and what school did they start in 1885 that still accepts New Mexican children free of charge?

The Larsons were a deaf pioneer couple who taught deaf students in their small adobe house; the New Mexico School for the Deaf was officially established in 1887, the only land-grant school for the deaf in the United States, and the first public school in New Mexico.

Read: *A Century of Progress: History of the New Mexico School for the Deaf,* by Marian Meyer, New Mexico School for the Deaf, 1989; *Sign Language for Kids: A Fun and Easy Guide to American Sign Language,* by Lora Heller, Sterling, 2004; and *Talking Hands: What Sign Language Reveals about the Mind,* by Margalit Fox, Simon & Schuster, 2007.

269. What was Santa Fe's first attempt at what we now call urban renewal?

In about 1620 the *cabildo* (town council) requested permission to move the *villa* to a better location, but the viceroy denied the request and instead sent tools and equipment to fix up and complete the town.

Read: "Parientes," by José Antonio Esquibel, *La Herencia,* Summer 2008; "Thirty-eight Adobe Houses: The Villa de Santa Fe in the Seventeenth Century, 1608–1610," by José Antonio Esquibel, in *All Trails Lead to Santa Fe,* Sunstone Press, 2010.

270. Where can more than 200,000 photographs of historic Santa Fe be found, and which image is the most popular?

The most popular photograph at the Photo Archives of the Palace of the Governors is negative number 061456, Jesse Nusbaum's *Plaza in Winter,* from about 1912.

Visit the Palace of the Governors Book, Print, and Photo Archives Shop, on Washington Avenue.

Plaza in Winter. Photograph by Jesse Nusbaum, 1914. A popular image of the Plaza. Courtesy of Palace of the Governors Photo Archives (NMHM/DCA), #061463.

Plaza in Winter. Photograph by Jesse Nusbaum, 1912. This is the most requested photograph. Courtesy of Palace of the Governors Photo Archives (NMHM/DCA), #061456.

271. Which future governor spent seven weeks in jail with his attorney, who was later appointed chief justice of the Territorial Supreme Court?

In about 1883 young Miguel Antonio Otero and others were sent to the county jail on Water Street by former governor and then chief justice S. B. Axtell when they disputed the order to keep them off the premises of the "Big Copper" mine, in the Cañón del Agua grant, in Santa Fe County. Otero's attorney, William A. Vincent, was one of his roommates in jail; he was later appointed chief justice, when Axtell was removed. Otero became governor from 1897 to 1906.

The Cañon del Agua grant was fraudulently represented by members of a powerful organization called the Santa Fe Ring so as to include the very valuable Big Copper mine; Otero's efforts were in part to remedy that. He was ultimately vindicated, and the grant lines were relocated.

Read: *New Mexico's Troubled Years: The Story of the Early Territorial Governors*, by Calvin Horn, with foreword by John F. Kennedy, Horn & Wallace, 1963; *The Far Southwest, 1846–1912: A Territorial History*, by Howard Roberts Lamar, University of New Mexico Press, 2000 (first published 1966); and *My Life on the Frontier, 1864–1882: Incidents and Characters of the Period When Kansas, Colorado, and New Mexico Were Passing through the Last of Their Wild and Romantic Years*, by Miguel Antonio Otero, Press of the Pioneers, 1935.

Brigadier General José María Chávez (1801–1902) witnessed about a century of New Mexico history. He was a military officer or civil servant under every New Mexican governor from 1814, under Alberto Máynez, to the end of the nineteenth century, under Miguel Antonio Otero.

272. Which prominent Native American artist first began his studies in 1934 at Dorothy Dunn's famed art studio at the Santa Fe Indian School, became a sculptor, and was also the grand-nephew of Geronimo?

Allan Houser. He became a long-time teacher at the Indian School and was a painter and an illustrator as well as a sculptor in wood, stone, and bronze. (Harrison Begay, the prominent Navajo painter, was Houser's classmate.)

Read: *Allan Houser (Ha-o-zous)*, by Barbara H. Perlman, Smithsonian Institution Press, 1992; *The Sacred Mountains of the Navajo: In Four Paintings by Harrison Begay*, by Leland Clifton Wyman, Northern Arizona Society of Science & Art, 1967; and *Allan Houser: An American Master (Chiricahua Apache, 1914–1994)*, by W. Jackson Rushing III, Abrams, 2004.

Allan Houser Haozous, 1914–1994, detail. Bronze sculpture by Phillip M. Haozous, 2001.
This life-size portrait of the artist's father stands on the sidewalk on Lincoln Avenue, south of Marcy Street.
Photograph by E. West. Used with permission of the artist.

273. In 1922 Museum of New Mexico director Edgar Lee Hewett said, "The hour has arrived." To what was he referring?

With these dramatic words, Hewett opened the first Southwest Indian Fair and Arts & Crafts Exhibition, the future Santa Fe Indian Market.

The fair and exhibition was at first sponsored by the Museum of New Mexico, but in 1936 the New Mexico Association of Indian Affairs took over the event, and now it is organized by the Southwestern Association for Indian Arts (SWAIA). Each year it showcases more than a thousand top American Indian artists from across the country. It is the oldest and largest juried Native American art showcase and market in the world.

All artists must show proof of enrollment in a federally recognized tribe, and their work must meet very strict quality and authentic materials standards. The work is judged by art experts. Coveted awards and prize money are distributed in various categories.

The Santa Fe Indian Market is a weekend event held in late August. It features pottery, weaving, sculpture, jewelry, beadwork, painting, basketry, and other work, both traditional and contemporary.

Read: *Santa Fe Indian Market: Showcase of Native American Art*, by Sheila Tryk, Tierra Publications, 1993; "From Indian Fair to Indian Market," by Bruce Bernstein, *El Palacio*, Summer 1993; and "Culture Warriors: Market Legacy Continues to Inspire Families of Artists," by Kim Baca, *SWAIA Official Guide: Indian Market, 90th Anniversary*, special supplement in the *Santa Fe New Mexican*, August 14, 2011.

274. Who founded the Wheelwright Museum of the American Indian, and when?

It was founded jointly in 1937 by Mary Cabot Wheelwright, of Los Luceros and Boston, and Hosteen Klah, an important Navajo singer and weaver. The design for the building was created by artist-architect William Penhallow Henderson; it was inspired by the Navajo ceremonial hogan and features an interlocking, whirling log ceiling.

Read: *Hosteen Klah: Navajo Medicine Man and Sand Painter*, by Franc Johnson Newcomb, University of Oklahoma Press, 1964.

Hostiin (or Hosteen) Klah, Navajo singer. Photograph by T. Harmon Parkhurst. Courtesy of Palace of the Governors Photo Archives (NMHM/DCA), #004330.

275. Who was the only woman in the early twentieth-century Pueblo group of artists who were called the Self-Taught Artists?

Tonita Peña, originally from San Ildefonso Pueblo but raised with her aunt and uncle in Cochiti Pueblo, was an easel painter whose original and innovative work was shown all over the United States. (Some of the men in the group were Crencencio Martinez, Julian Martinez, Alfredo Montoya, Encarnación Peña, Alfonso Roybal, and Abel Sanchez.)

Read: "Where Credit Is Due," *Santa Fean*, February/March 2009; *Tonita*, by Samuel L. Gray, Avanyu Publishing, 1990; and *Between Indian and White Worlds: The Cultural Broker*, edited by Margaret Connell Szaaz, University of Oklahoma Press, 1994.

Tonita Peña and baby, Cochiti Pueblo. Photograph by T. Harmon Parkhurst, c. 1935. Courtesy of Palace of the Governors Photo Archives (NMHM/DCA), #047480.

276. When was the Palace of the Governors built?

The oldest building in the United States that has been in continuous use since it was built, the Palace of the Governors was constructed probably shortly after 1610. "Palace of the Governors" is a mistranslation of *Palacio del Govierno* (Government Palace), the name used during the Mexican period. Earlier, during the Spanish colonial period, the building was one of several official buildings lining the original Plaza called *Las Casas Reales* (the Royal Houses).

Read: *New Mexico's Palace of the Governors: History of an American Treasure*, by Emily Abbink, Museum of New Mexico Press, 2007.

What Is It?
(See Answer Key #40)

277. When was a presidio (a fortified base or fortress) established in Santa Fe?

1694. Santa Fe had a presidio during the don Diego de Vargas era. A Spanish colonial presidio may have occupied the area where a *fuerte* (fort) existed as early as 1620, somewhere downtown, between what became the Palace of the Governors and what is now the Federal Building.

Read: *The Presidio: Bastion of the Spanish Borderlands*, by Max L. Moorhead, University of Oklahoma Press, 1975; *Presidio, Mission, and Pueblo: Spanish Architecture and Urbanism in the United States*, by James Early, Southern Methodist University Press, 2004; and *Blood on the Boulders: The Journals of Don Diego de Vargas, New Mexico, 1694–1697*, by Diego de Vargas, edited by John L. Kessell, Rick Hendricks, and Meredith D. Dodge, University of New Mexico Press, 1998.

278. Who was the "gatekeeper" for Los Alamos during the Manhattan Project, in the 1940s?

Dorothy McKibben, a widow, controlled the censorship office at 109 Palace Avenue. Her job was to greet the scientists and others who were to work on the project as they arrived, check their identification, and arrange for their transport to the "secret city" of Los Alamos on "the hill."

Read: *109 East Palace: Robert Oppenheimer and the Secret City of Los Alamos*, by Jennet Conant, Simon & Schuster, 2005.

279. What were some of the tall tales shared by Santa Feans about the "secret city," Los Alamos, during World War II, when there was wild speculation about what was going on up there?

One of the stories concerned the manufacture of special windshield wipers being made for submarines, and another was about a secret submarine base being built in the Los Alamos duck pond with a secret passage to the Rio Grande! A later story involved Emit J. "Chief" Bowles, the star pitcher for the Madrid Miners baseball team in the 1920s and '30s, who said, after the war, that it was really he who had created the bomb; he claimed the U.S. Army had employed him for his expertise in picking out the exceptionally combustible pieces of coal in Madrid, New Mexico, and that the bomb had been made out of that.

The noted managing editor of the *Santa Fe New Mexican* newspaper, Will Harrison, found out the truth earlier but kept the 1940s Manhattan Project a secret, as he was required to do by the U.S. government.

Edith Warner provided a peaceful respite for the Manhattan Project scientists, who were permitted to visit her adobe home in the train depot where she was a caretaker, along the river at the base of Los Alamos. She served them chocolate cake, homemade bread, chokecherry jam, and tea.

Read: "Now They Can Be Told Aloud, Those Stories of 'The Hill,'" by William McNulty, *Santa Fe New Mexican*, August 6, 1945; *The House at Otowi Bridge: The Story of Edith Warner and Los Alamos*, by Peggy Pond Church, University of New Mexico Press, 1960; and the foreword, by Carmella Padilla, in *Santa Fe, Its 400th Year: Exploring the Past, Defining the Future*, edited by Rob Dean, Sunstone Press, 2010.

280. Which famous cub had his own zip code for fan mail, and who was the Santa Fe conservationist who promoted him?

Elliott Barker, the first game warden in New Mexico, was instrumental in popularizing a cub rescued from a fire, Smokey Bear, in the 1950s. Barker died in Santa Fe at age 103. His younger brother was Squire Omar Barker, who wrote the poem "A Cowboy's Christmas Prayer."

Read: *Smokey Bear 20252: A Biography*, by William Clifford Lawter Jr., Lindsay Smith Publishers, 1994; and *Rawhide Rhymes: Singing Poems of the Old West*, by S. Omar Barker, Doubleday, 1968.

281. Where can one make a large bubble while standing inside it?

At the Santa Fe Children's Museum, on Old Pecos Trail, there are opportunities for local and visiting children to learn and explore while playing.

Visit them at 1050 Old Pecos Trail, next door to the Bataan Military Museum. Also, read *The Teacher's Almanack: A Complete Guide to Every Day of the School Year*, by Dana Newmann, Center for Applied Research in Education, 1973.

282. Who made a horseback ride in record time from Santa Fe to Independence, Missouri, in 1848?

Francis X. Aubry, an explorer, rode 780 miles in five days and sixteen hours, riding six horses through twenty-four-hour rain and six hundred miles of mud.

One of the saddest bar fights in Santa Fe history happened in 1854, at Mercure's Saloon, on the Plaza. In an argument over an abusive news article about Francis X. Aubry written by Colonel Richard Weightman, Aubry and Weightman, who had been drinking, became increasingly angry with each other. Weightman threw his drink at Aubry and Aubry pulled a gun, which fired at the ceiling. In reaction Weightman mortally stabbed the twenty-nine-year-old trader. He then left Santa Fe and regretted the act for the rest of his life.

Read: *The Beginning of the West: 1540–1854*, by Louise Barry, Kansas State Historical Society, 1972; and *Santa Fe Tales and More*, by Howard Bryan, Clear Light, 2010.

283. What is the name of the prominent Lebanese builder and businessman from the 1960s who developed an early subdivision in Santa Fe?

Abdul Hamid "Dale" Bellamah, whose given name means "servant of God."

Some other Lebanese families who have settled in Santa Fe, and in many cases have become prominent business people, include the names Adelo (derived from Abdallah, which also means "servant of God"); Anton; Budagher (the Budaghers exit off I-25, near Santo Domingo Pueblo, slightly north of the halfway point between Santa Fe and Albuquerque, is named for the brothers John, Robert, George, and Saith, who had two gas stations, one with a trading post, a café, and a tavern in the 1930s through the 1980s); Fidel; Francis; Harroun;

218

Koury; Maloof; Najjar; Salmon (anglicized from Na' Aman Soleiman Farah); Shaya (their jewelry store in the 1950s was similar to a mercantile store, and it carried everything from rosaries to Zippo lighters and gold Zia symbols); and Younis.

Many of the immigrants came in the late 1800s and early 1900s from near Beirut, in Lebanon, originally part of Syria, to escape the then-repressive Turkish government. Some local Lebanese families organized what was called the Syrian-American Club, which often met upstairs in the Lensic Theater, owned by the Greers, who were also Lebanese. The ritual of meeting for coffee also occurred at the Canton Café and then later at Tia Sophia's.

Read: "New Mexico's Lebanese Influence," by Arnold Vigil, *Santa Fe New Mexican*, September 24, 2007; and "Into the Fabric of Santa Fe: The Salmons and the Greers," *Santa Fean*, May 1978.

284. What is the "call to prayer," and where can one hear it in Santa Fe?

Adhan (الأَذَان) is the Arabic term for the call to prayer, a melodic, vocal announcement of the times of prayer; it can be heard sung on a recording from the TaHa Mosque, on East Barcelona Street, not far from the Santa Fe Children's Museum. (The bell ringing of the *Angelus*, Latin for "angel," is a Christian version of the call to prayer.)

Read: *Encyclopedia of Islam in the United States*, Greenwood Press, 2007; and *The Bezels of Wisdom*, by Ibn Al 'Arabi, translated by R. W. J. Austin, Paulist Press, 1980.

285. How much was the wagon train fare from Fort Leavenworth, Kansas, to Santa Fe in 1852?

$250 for adults and half-fare for children.

Read: *Land of Enchantment: Memoirs of Marian Russell along the Santa Fe Trail*, University of New Mexico Press, 1985.

286. Which Santa Fe parking lot was the location for the first official Santa Fe Farmers' Market?

Saint Anne's Church parking lot, on Hickox Street, was the first formal location of the outdoor farmer's market, in 1971. The Santa Fe Farmers' Market now has a permanent building in the Railyard district. Other cities in New Mexico with farmers' markets include Corrales, Las Cruces, Los Alamos, Los Ranchos, and Silver City.

Read: "The Santa Fe Farmers' Market: A Vital Link between Northern New Mexico Vendors and Consumers" *Santa Fe New Mexican*, June 16, 2010; *The Farmers' Market Book: Growing Food, Cultivating Community*, by Jennifer Meta Robinson and J. A. Hartenfeld, Indiana University Press, 2007; and *Farmers Market, Día de Mercado*, by Carmen Parks, Houghton Mifflin Harcourt, 2010.

Apache Plume. **Pen and ink drawing by Cathie Sullivan, 2011, based on her original screen print, 1996.
Courtesy of the artist.**

The artist made these comments about apache plume:

"This lovely shrub, a member of the Rose family, likes dry lower mountainsides and drainages throughout the Southwest. The curved pink tails do double-duty for the tiny attached seed—they carry it on the wind and they bury it in the soil. This mechanism is amazing—the tail is spiraled like a drill, and when it absorbs ground moisture, it erects itself and drills into the soil, driving the seed in ahead. Thinking this turning must be too slow to see, I marked the position of the tail on a needle-and-thread grass seed and could watch it turning within minutes.

"Ancestors of roses go back to the early history of flowering plants in the Cretaceous Period, 146 million to 65 million years ago. Imagine rose ancestors growing on the north *shore* of New Mexico, close to a huge inland sea stretching from Alaska to the Gulf of Mexico and full of exotic marine reptiles. Such was our landscape in the late Cretaceous Period. The oldest flower fossils go back 120 million years, and the oldest pollen, 127 million years old, is difficult to distinguish from today's evergreen tree pollen. Speaking of pollen, note that in some wild roses, pollen is released only at certain times of the day. This is also true of nectar; honey bees learn the schedule for each species and time their rounds accordingly."

287. Who was the nineteen-year-old nun who may have died of fright on her way to Santa Fe in the mid-nineteenth century?

Sister Mary Alphonsa Thompson died en route to Santa Fe on July 24, 1867. The young woman was a member of a group of Sisters of Loretto who were travelling with Bishop Lamy's caravan, part of one of the last large wagon trains that came from Missouri to Santa Fe after the Civil War. Although some reports state that she died of fright because of the stress of two Indian raids, many historians conclude that she probably died of the cholera that had also taken the lives of twelve other members of the wagon train. Her death and burial took place along the Santa Fe Trail, somewhere west of present-day Dodge City, Kansas.

A recent painting inspired by a faked photograph shows a nun, Lamy, and various other people associated with the nun's death. The photograph, a composite of several others, was meant to show the circumstances of her death. In the photograph, look at the size of the snake and the gun, and notice the awkward positioning of the bishop. The composer of the composite photograph is unknown.

Read: *American Caravan*, by Alice Anne Thompson, Two Trails Press, 2006; *Lamy of Santa Fe: His Life and Times*, by Paul Horgan, Wesleyan University Press, 2003 (first published 1975); and *At the End of the Santa Fe Trail*, by Sister Blandina Segale, Bruce Publishing Company, 1948.

Here is the composite photograph, from the files of the St. Vincent Regional Medical Center archives.

The Bishop. **Painting by Christopher Benson, 1992. The work was "inspired" by the composite photograph. Courtesy of Edward Ranney.**

288. Why did Helen Keller come to Santa Fe in 1942?

Santa Fean Albert Torres Gonzales, a blind state representative, invited Helen Keller to Santa Fe to help promote a bill to establish a division of services for the blind. She came, and the bill passed. In 1929 Mr. Gonzales had become the first blind person to practice law in Santa Fe.

Read: *Albert: Behind the Dark Glasses*, by Alexander Andrews, Andrews Publisher, 2004; the book is also available as a recorded book for the blind at the State Records Center and Archives, on Camino Carlos Rey.

289. What were some of the trade items sent west on what is now called the Old Spanish Trail, which began and ended where?

Woolen and leather goods, as well as horses, mules, and some sheep, were sent west over what is now called the Old Spanish Trail, which ran from Santa Fe and northern New Mexico to Los Angeles via what is now Utah. However, most of the *commerciantes* (businessmen and traders) who took sheep to California used the southern route, along the Gila River, and crossed the Colorado River at what is now Yuma, Arizona, and then headed up to Los Angeles across the desert in what is now southern California.

Read: *In Search of the Spanish Trail: Santa Fe to Los Angeles, 1829–1848*, by C. Gregory Crampton and Steven K. Madsen, Gibbs Smith, 1994; *Old Spanish Trail: Santa Fe to Los Angeles*, by LeRoy R. Hafen, University of Nebraska Press, 1993; and *Las Carneradas: Sheep Trade in New Mexico, 1700–1860*, by John O. Baxter, University of New Mexico Press, 1987.

What Is It?
(See Answer Key #41)

290. Where did the popular outdoor theater group Shakespeare in Santa Fe first begin showing its performances, and to where did it move?

The first performances were held in the Amelia White Rose Park in 1987. Later the group moved to St. John's College, where it stayed for several years, until the group suspended operations in 2003, with a final project featuring a Federico Garcia Lorca play. Support for producing plays by William Shakespeare is ongoing and includes interest in the Shakespeare authorship conundrum. One of the people on the list of possible authors of the Shakespearean canon is Mary Sidney, the Countess of Pembroke; the Mary Sidney Society was founded in 2005 and has its international headquarters in Santa Fe. A local group called the Santa Fe Shakespeare Society meets for discussion and production of Shakespeare works. (It is interesting to note that both Miguel de Cervantes Saavedra, in Spain, and William Shakespeare, in England, were writing in the early 1600s, when Santa Fe became an official *villa* of New Mexico, in northern New Spain.)

Read: "Parting Is Such Sweet Sorrow," by Robert Nott, *Santa Fe New Mexican*, August 2, 2002; *Sweet Swan of Avon: Did a Woman Write Shakespeare?* by Robin P. Williams, Wilton Circle Press, 2011; *Who Wrote Shakespeare?* by John Michell, Thames & Hudson, 1996; "Lorca's Dream of Puppets," by Robert Nott, *Santa Fe New Mexican*, May 16, 2003; *The Complete Works of Shakespeare*, edited by David Bevington, Longman, 2008; and *Don Quixote*, by Miguel de Cervantes, introduction by Harold Bloom, Ecco, 2003.

William Shakespeare, as sketched by the author Paul Horgan on a library book date-due card pocket. The sketch is one of more than two hundred Horgan made of the authors in the collection at the library where he worked, at the New Mexico Military Institute in Roswell, before World War II. The series of ink and watercolor drawings is called "One Week Only," referring to the length of time a book could be checked out. Courtesy of the Fray Angélico Chávez History Library, Palace of the Governors, New Mexico History Museum.

291. When did the all-black 9th Cavalry Band, part of the famed Buffalo Soldiers, play on the Santa Fe Plaza for the first sitting U.S. president to visit New Mexico?

On October 28, 1880, they played for President Rutherford B. Hayes and his wife, Lucy Webb Hayes, along with other dignitaries, on the Santa Fe Plaza during the president's one-day visit to Santa Fe. The band also played for other special occasions, including Fourth of July festivities. They were extremely popular.

Read: *Santa Fe Tales and More*, by Howard Bryan, Clear Light, 2010; and *Rutherford B. Hayes*, by Hans L. Trefousse, Times Books, 2002.

The 9th Cavalry Band performed on the Plaza and other places in Santa Fe and the surrounding area.
Photograph by Ben Wittick, 1880.
Courtesy of Palace of the Governors Photo Archives (NMHM/DCA), #050887.

292. Which general is reported to have suggested that the United States should go to war with Mexico again, to make her take back New Mexico?

General of the U.S. Army William Tecumseh Sherman, who visited Santa Fe with President Hayes in 1880. The president, his wife, and all his entourage except Sherman seemed to enjoy their visit. Sherman had very little that was positive to say about Santa Fe and New Mexico. The newspapers reported that he announced to the local citizens: "You must improve your land, and make the most of the resources that your location affords you, and get rid of your burros and goats. I hope ten years hence there won't be any adobe houses in the territory. I want to see you learn to make them of brick, with slanting roofs. Yankees don't like flat roofs, nor roofs of dirt."

Sherman was not the only prominent easterner to deride aspects of the Southwest. Daniel Webster, who died in 1852 having never been to Santa Fe and the Southwest, was a successful lawyer, a leading conservative statesman and a representative from New Hampshire for ten years, a senator from Massachusetts for nineteen years, and secretary of state for three presidents. He was also an acknowledged elitist, who said about the southwestern United States: "What do you want of that vast and worthless area, that region of savages and wild beasts, of deserts, of shifting sands and whirling winds, of dust, of cactus and prairie dogs?"

Read: *Santa Fe Tales and More*, by Howard Bryan, Clear Light, 2010; *Citizen Sherman: A Life of William Tecumseh Sherman*, by Michael Fellman, Random House, 1995; and *Daniel Webster: The Man and His Time*, by Robert Vincent Remini, Norton, 2009.

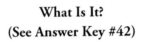

What Is It?
(See Answer Key #42)

293. Who was the original creator of what has become the Zozobra spectacle, and when did the event first occur?

Noted Santa Fe artist Will Shuster, along with Gustave Baumann, E. Dana Johnson, and others, built a giant puppet in Shuster's backyard in 1925. The puppet was burned to usher out gloom at Santa Fe Fiesta. Baumann fashioned the head out of cardboard boxes, and Johnson is credited with the name Zozobra.

Read: *Will Shuster: A Santa Fe Legend*, by Joseph Dispenza and Louise Turner, Museum of New Mexico Press, 1989; *Zozobra: The Story of Old Man Gloom*, by Jennifer Owings Dewey, University of New Mexico Press, 2004.

294. What does "Zozobra" mean?

The Spanish word *zozobra* means "worry" or "anguish"; "the Gloomy One" was the translation E. Dana Johnson and Will Schuster gave for Zozobra. The burning of Zozobra begins with the Fire Dancer (first played by Witter Bynner in the 1920s, later by Jacques Cartier, and then by Chip Lilienthal). The initial public burning of Zozobra, behind the old courthouse on Washington Avenue in 1926, began a new Fiesta tradition that continues today at Fort Marcy Park. Today Santa Feans refer to Zozobra as Old Man Gloom.

Read: "Santa Fe's Own: A History of Fiesta," by Thomas E. Chávez, *¡Vivan las Fiestas!*, edited by Donna Pierce, Museum of New Mexico Press, 1985.

295. What religious event begins at the cathedral basilica and proceeds to the hilltop Cross of the Martyrs during the annual Fiesta in September?

The somber candlelight procession of hundreds of people carrying lighted candles concludes Santa Fe Fiesta, on Sunday evening.

Read: *¡Viva la Fiesta! A Promise Made, a Promise Kept,* by Diane O. Alvarado, Santa Fe Fiesta Council, 2003.

296. Who was the only woman in the labor force that restored San Miguel mission in 1710?

Magdalena Ogama was a Mexican Indian who arrived with Vargas in 1693 and cooked meals for the laborers. She eventually became a property owner. In 1711 she sold property she owned on the Plaza. Her property was mentioned as having roses on its western boundary, and they were identified as Roses of Castile.

Read: "A Window to the Past: The San Miguel and La Conquistadora Chapels and Their Builders, 1610–1776," by Cordelia Thomas Snow, in *All Trails Lead to Santa Fe*, Sunstone Press, 2010.

297. Who were the three black soldiers reburied with full military honors in the Santa Fe National Cemetery in July 2009?

Privates David Ford, Levi Morris, and Thomas Smith had belonged to what was called the U.S. Colored Troops (the Buffalo Soldiers), the African-American military regiments created after slavery was abolished. Another reburial involves Charles Bent, the first territorial governor, who was assassinated at his home in Taos in 1847. He was first buried in Taos, and then his body was moved to Santa Fe, in 1864, to the Masonic Cemetery, which was located south of where the Masonic Temple is now; later Charles Bent's body was moved again, to the Rosario Cemetery (in an area that is now southeast of the National Cemetery).

Read: *New Mexico's Buffalo Soldiers: 1866–1900,* by Monroe Lee Billington, University Press of Colorado, 1991; and "National Cemetery Goes Way Back," by Howard Bryan, *Albuquerque Tribune*, February 21, 1969.

298. What occurred far away in 1810 that led to a new beginning in Santa Fe?

On September 16, 1810, *El Grito de Dolores*, the famous "Cry of Independence," the call to mobilize and engage in a war for independence from Spain, was announced by Miguel Hidalgo y Costilla, a Roman Catholic priest, who had ordered the church bells to be rung to gather his congregation at the church of Dolores Hidalgo, in Dolores, near Guanajuato. The Battle of Guanajuato, the first major engagement of the insurgency, occurred four days later. The Declaration of Independence of the Mexican Empire was not declared until September 27, 1821, after a decade of war. Mexico's independence paved the way to open trade with the United States.

The exact wording of the most famous of all Mexican speeches is unknown, although the general meaning is understood to be a call to revolt and to throw off the yoke of Spain.

Read: *New Mexico: Past and Future*, by Thomas E. Chávez, University of New Mexico Press, 2006; and *The Story of Mexico: The Mexican War of Independence*, by R. Conrad Stein, Morgan Reynolds Publisher, 2008.

What Is It?
(See Answer Key #43)

299. What grocery store has served Santa Feans since the 1890s?

In 1896 Henry Spencer Kaune established Kaune Food Town, on College Street (now Old Santa Fe Trail, near Paseo de Peralta), featuring items from dried beans to caviar.

Read: *Santa Fe: A Pictorial History*, by John Sherman, Donning Company, 1996.

A New Mexican woman baking outdoors. Photograph by Christian G. Kaadt, c. 1898–1900. Courtesy of Palace of the Governors Photo Archives (NMHM/DCA), #069106.

300. The Yom Kippur holiday was first formally observed in Santa Fe when?

A Yom Kippur service was first held in Santa Fe in 1860, at the home of Levi Spiegelberg.

Read: *Pioneer Jews: A New Life in the Far West,* by Harriet Rochlin and Fred Rochlin, Houghton Mifflin Harcourt, 2000; *A History of the Jews in New Mexico,* by Henry J. Tobias, University of New Mexico Press, 1992; *Jewish Pioneers of New Mexico,* compiled and edited by Tomas Jaehn, Museum of New Mexico Press, 2003; and *Rosh Hashanah and Yom Kippur: Sweet Beginnings,* by Malka Drucker, Holiday House, 1981.

301. What place established in 1610 has been and still is a physical, commercial, social, and cultural center in Santa Fe?

La Plaza de Santa Fe was established by don Pedro de Peralta, who followed the *reales ordenanzas* (royal laws) issued by King Phillip II of Spain in 1573. The physical center of *la villa de Santa Fé* in 1610 was the Santa Fe Plaza, but as of 2010 the physical center of the city was located three miles south of the Plaza, approximately where the Santa Fe University of Art and Design is located, near the intersection of Cerrillos Road and St. Michael's Drive.

The population in 1610 was probably about 300 colonists, but exact data are not available. In fray Alonso de Benavides's memorial, written twenty years later, in 1630, the author, who had been the Franciscan *custos* (custodian) from 1626 to 1629, stated that the approximately 250 Spaniards had about 700 persons in service, so that "counting Spaniards, Mestizos and Indians, the total is about a thousand." (*Mestizo* refers to a person with one Spanish parent and one American Indian parent.) Santa Fe had a population of 67,947 in the 2010 census.

Read: "The History of the Santa Fe Plaza, 1610–1720," by Stanley M. Hordes, in *All Trails Lead to Santa Fe*, Sunstone Press, 2010; *The Plazas of New Mexico*, edited by Chris Wilson and Stefanos Polyzoides, Trinity University Press, 2011; "Southwest Shift Continues," by Julie Ann Grimm, *Santa Fe New Mexican*, April 3, 2011; and *Benavides' Memorial of 1630*, edited by Cyprian J. Lynch, Washington Academy of American Franciscan History, 1954.

La Ciudad de Santa Fe. **Lithograph based on a field sketch by Lieut. J. W. Abert, 1848.**

Street view of Santa Fe, with La Fonda in the foreground, looking east to the Parroquia. Sketch by Theodore R. Davis, for *Harper's Weekly*, April 21, 1866.

Burros loaded with corn fodder, on Santa Fe Plaza. Stereoscopic photograph by George C. Bennett, 1880.
Courtesy of Palace of the Governors Photo Archives (NMHM/DCA), #132160.

The Plaza with planted fields, looking east. Photograph by Nicholas Brown, 1866.
Courtesy of Palace of the Governors Photo Archives (NMHM/DCA), #038025.

South side of the Plaza, San Francisco Street, looking east, with covered wagons, tired oxen. Part of a stereograph, c. 1868–1869. Courtesy of Palace of the Governors Photo Archives (NMHM/DCA), # 011329.

San Francisco Street, looking east, with *carretas*, wagons, mules, and oxen, c. 1869. Courtesy of Palace of the Governors Photo Archives (NMHM/DCA), #070437.

Cathedral being built. San Francisco Street, looking east, c. 1885.
Courtesy of Palace of the Governors Photo Archives (NMHM/DCA), #091416.

Wood venders with burros packed and loaded, looking east toward the cathedral. Photograph by
Aaron B. Craycraft, 1910. Courtesy of Palace of the Governors (NMHM/DCA), #011340.

Santa Fe Plaza, looking northeast. The obelisk appears in the center, with the bandstand moved to the west, c. 1887. Courtesy of Palace of the Governors Photo Archives (NMHM/DCA), #011299.

Winter scene, the Plaza in the snow, looking east along San Francisco Street. Central Photographic Studio, c. 1925. Courtesy of Palace of the Governors Photo Archives (NMHM/DCA), #134573.

United States and New Mexico flags fly over the Palace of the Governors. Photograph by E. West, 2011.

302. Who was the first priest born in New Mexico to serve in Santa Fe?

Santiago Roybal was ordained and started serving in Santa Fe in 1730.

Read: *Origins of New Mexico Families: A Genealogy of the Spanish Colonial Period*, by Fray Angélico Chávez, Museum of New Mexico Press, 1992 (first published 1954).

303. What is the name of the college whose curriculum utilizes the "great books" program, and when did it open its Santa Fe campus?

St. John's College opened its Santa Fe campus in 1964, on 250 acres donated by John Gaw Meem. The original campus, in Annapolis, Maryland, opened in 1784 and is the third-oldest college in the United States. Both campuses offer undergraduate and graduate degrees focusing on enduring questions of human existence through the study of primary sources in philosophy, literature, history, theology, mathematics, and science in the Western tradition. (One of the most frequently borrowed books from the Santa Fe campus library is *The Republic of Plato*.) The Graduate Institute offers the Liberal Studies Program, a master's degree program based on the undergraduate curriculum, as well the Eastern Classics Program, which it initiated in 1994.

The Santa Fe campus of St. John's College also offers community seminars, free concerts, and a lecture series open to the public.

Read: *The Colonization of a College: The Beginnings and Early History of St. John's College in Santa Fe*, by Richard D. Weigle, St. John's College Print Shop, 1985; *Three Dialogues on Liberal Education*, edited by William A. Darkey, St. John's College Press, 1979; and *The Republic of Plato*, translated, with notes, an interpretive essay, and a new introduction by Allan Bloom, Basic Books, 1991.

304. Canyon Road is named for what canyon?

The long Santa Fe road approximately follows a canyon made by the Santa Fe River; it was first called El Camino del Canyon and later became Canyon Road.

But a reference book about stories behind street names suggests that the road was named for Apache Canyon, which is about ten miles east of Santa Fe and is on a different watershed, one that flows into Glorieta canyon. Apache Canyon?!

When this incorrect origin of the name for Canyon Road was printed in the *Santa Fe New Mexican*, on September 22, 2010, with the inaccurate answer to the question above, several people complained. One person wrote the following: "Regarding the 400 Facts feature on September 22, 2010: Are you sure that Canyon Road is named for Apache Canyon? I have always been told it is so named because from its start to its end, it runs along the path of the canyon of the Santa Fe River. If you project Canyon Road to the east, it goes into the Sangre de Cristo Mountains. If you project it to the west, it hits the Rio Grande. No way could it reach Apache Canyon. My answer seems to make more sense." This letter to the editor, from Richard McCord, was printed in the paper on September 24, 2010, and is quoted here with permission of the author.

It is wise to check your sources.

It is obvious that Canyon Road follows the Santa Fe River's canyon, but read *Stories Behind the Street Names of Albuquerque, Santa Fe, and Taos*, by Donald A. Gill (Bonus Books, 1994), and find the incorrect reference, on page 174. The rest of the book is apparently accurate.

What Is It?
(See Answer Key #44)

305. Which crop was added to the traditional Native American staple crops of squash, corn, and beans and was especially compatible with Santa Fe's short growing season?

Winter wheat, introduced by don Juan de Oñate in 1598, was planted in autumn and harvested in spring. Winter wheat is "soft" wheat, with less protein and therefore less gluten than "hard" wheat, which is planted in the spring and harvested before frost. Winter wheat makes lighter breads, necessary for communion wafers.

Read: *Don Juan de Oñate: Colonizer of New Mexico, 1595–1628*, by George Hammond and Agapito Rey, University of New Mexico Press, 1953; *Life in the Pueblos*, by Ruth Underhill, Ancient City Press, 1946; *The Last Conquistador: Juan de Oñate and the Settling of the Far Southwest*, by Marc Simmons, University of Oklahoma Press, 1991; and "Juan de Oñate: Colonizer, Governor," by Rick Hendricks, in *Telling New Mexico: A New History*, edited by Marta Weigle, with Frances Levine and Louise Stiver, Museum of New Mexico Press, 2009.

What Is It?
(See Answer Key #45)

306. "XXX" was a pseudonym for which New Mexican poet, educated more than a century ago at Saint Michael's College, in Santa Fe?

Luis Tafoya. In 1911, on the eve of New Mexico statehood, he created the official state poem, "A Nuevo Mexico."

Read: *Speaking for Themselves: Neomexicano Cultural Identity and the Spanish-Language Press, 1880–1920*, by Doris Meyer, University of New Mexico Press, 1996.

307. How did the black stenographer who worked all night long in Santa Fe's Palace Hotel help establish the University of New Mexico?

In one night in 1889, Fred Simms transcribed all sixty sections of the bill dictated to him by congressmen to create the charter establishing the University of New Mexico.

Read: *Pueblo on the Mesa*, by Dorothy Hughes, University of New Mexico Press, 1939.

308. What obelisk is located in front of the federal courthouse on Federal Place, at the north end of Lincoln Avenue?

The Carson Monument, commemorating Kit Carson, was donated in 1885 by the Grand Army of the Republic, an organization composed of veterans of the Union Army, who had served in the Civil War. One of the earliest monuments dedicated in the western United States, it is in front of the U.S. district courthouse building. The building, which had simply been called the U.S. courthouse, was named in 2004 for Santiago E. Campos, a federal district court judge who had been nominated by President Jimmy Carter to a seat on the U.S. District Court for the District of New Mexico. Campos died in 2001. Other federal courthouses in New Mexico are located in Albuquerque, Las Cruces, and Roswell.

The building was originally supposed to be the territorial capitol building of New Mexico. Construction began in 1853, but Civil War problems, lack of workmen, and lack of funds slowed construction, and eventually the project was essentially abandoned. Later the building was completed and used for various federal courts. The building's stone was quarried in the Hyde Park area of the Sangre de Cristo Mountains.

Six large landscape paintings by William Penhallow Henderson may be seen on the first floor, and three scenes of Native American life by Warren E. Rollins are located on the second floor. The Rollins paintings were originally exhibited in Gallup, New Mexico, but were moved to Santa Fe to be shown in the capital city. Both artists were working through the Public Works of Art Commission in the 1930s.

Read: *The Life and Adventures of Kit Carson: The Nestor of the Rocky Mountains, From Facts Narrated by Himself,* by De Witt C. Peters, W. R. C. Clark & Company, 1858.

What Is It?
(See Answer Key #46)

309. What is the difference between a cathedral and a cathedral basilica, and what is Santa Fe's largest Catholic building called?

A cathedral is dedicated to a saint (Santa Fe's cathedral is dedicated to Saint Francis) and is the chief church of a diocese in which the bishop has his throne. A basilica not only is a major building but also has received the title of "basilica" from the Holy See—the ecclesiastical jurisdiction of the Catholic Church in Rome. A basilica is dedicated to the Virgin Mary. (The five great patriarchal sees of Christian antiquity are Rome, Alexandria, Antioch, Jerusalem, and Constantinople.)

Yes, St. Francis Cathedral is also a basilica. It was officially elevated to a basilica by Pope Benedict XVI on October 4, 2005.

Read: *Roman Catholicism: The Basics*, by Michael Walsh, Routledge, 2005.

Cathedral Basilica of Saint Francis. Photograph by E. West, 2011.

310. When was the first cornerstone laid for the cathedral, and where is it today?

It was laid on October 10, 1869, but its whereabouts are unknown, since it was stolen within a week.

Read: *The Archbishop's Cathedral*, by Carl D. Sheppard, Cimarron Press, 1994.

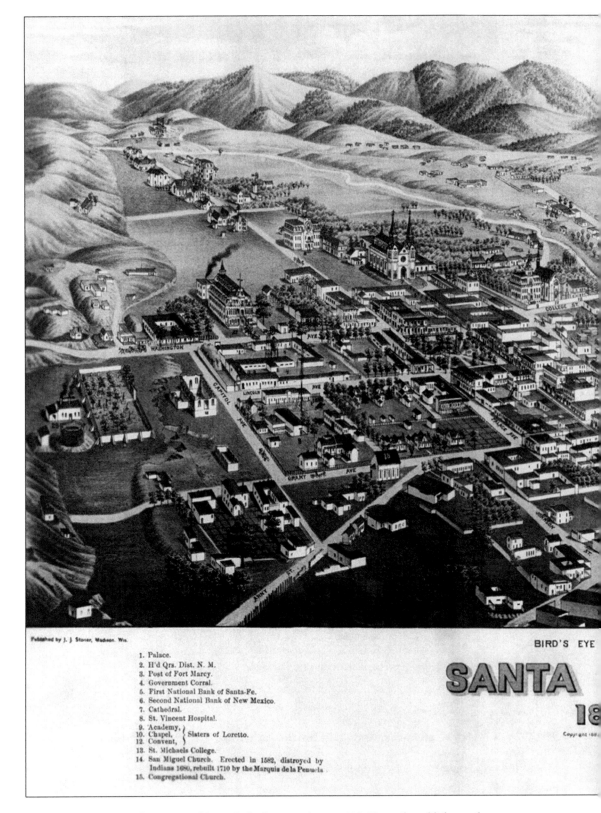

Published by J. J. Storer, Madison. Wis.

BIRD'S EYE

SANTA

18

Copyright 1882

1. Palace.
2. H'd Qrs. Dist. N. M.
3. Post of Fort Marcy.
4. Government Corral.
5. First National Bank of Santa-Fe.
6. Second National Bank of New Mexico.
7. Cathedral.
8. St. Vincent Hospital.
9. Academy, ⎫
10. Chapel, ⎬ Sisters of Loretto.
12. Convent, ⎭
13. St. Michaels College.
14. San Miguel Church. Erected in 1582, distroyed by
    Indians 1680, rebuilt 1710 by the Marquis de la Penuela
15. Congregational Church.

Bird's eye view of Santa Fe, looking southeast, 1882. Unattributed lithograph.

OF THE CITY OF

É, N.M.

2.

ff, Madison, Wis.

Beck & Pauli, Lithographers, Milwaukee, Wis.

16. Guadalupe Church.
17. M. E. Church.
18. Presbyterian Church.
19. Episcopal Church.
20. Oldest Building in Santa-Fe.
21. Palace Hotel, P. Rumsey & Son.
22. Exchange Hotel, Reed & Bishop.
23. Capitol Hotel, Gray & Bailey.
24. Herlow's Hotel, P. F. Herlow.
25. Santa-Fe Planing Mill, P. Hesch.
26. Cracker Factory, D. L. Miller & Co.
27. Post Office.
28. Depot.
29. Gas Works.
30. Fisher Brewing Co.'s Brewery.

311. Who was the former congressman from Indiana appointed by President Grover Cleveland to investigate land fraud in Santa Fe in the late territorial period?

In May of 1885, George W. Julian accepted the presidential appointment of surveyor-general of New Mexico and the job of examining land fraud in New Mexico.

The Santa Fe Ring was a group of lawyers, bankers, politicians, and powerful businessmen who dominated territorial politics, business, and land grants from the 1860s to the mid-1880s. Back east the *New York Times* had presented a case against the Santa Fe Ring that made national news, in effect saying that the ring was ruthless and stole New Mexico from New Mexicans by intimidation and oppression so that few of the victims dared to speak up.

Julian exposed members of the Santa Fe Ring and detailed how they stole land grants; he also laid blame at the feet of the U.S. Congress for basically ignoring the problems associated with land grant claims. During times of confusion it is apparently easy for people in power to take advantage of those who are not. One of the many people involved in the land grant complications was Max Frost, the "colonel" who had been sent by the U.S. Army to ensure that the crucial telegraph lines were working in New Mexico, Arizona, and Texas. Frost eventually became involved in Santa Fe politics and also became editor, publisher, and owner of the *New Mexican* newspaper, using its voice to promote and protect the Santa Fe Ring. Frost did not resist the temptation to become involved with them.

Miguel Antonio Otero, himself a member of a prominent banking family and one of the last territorial governors, later wrote about the ring's role, stating that "the territory of New Mexico was dominated by one of the most corrupt, unscrupulous, and daring organizations ever connected with its history." (It is interesting to note that Frost's second wife was Maud Pain, of Kansas City, a woman who outlived him, stayed in Santa Fe for many years, and later married Otero.)

Read: "King Maker in the Back Room, Editor Max Frost, and Hardball Politics in the Late Territorial Period," by Robert K. Dean, in *All Trails Lead to Santa Fe*, Sunstone Press, 2010; "New-Mexico's Land Ring: Gigantic Swindles Accomplished in the Territory," *New York Times*, May 18, 1884; *Maxwell Land Grant*, by William A. Keleher, Sunstone Press, 2008 (first published 1942); and *My Life on the Frontier, 1864–1882: Incidents and Characters of the Period When Kansas, Colorado, and New Mexico Were Passing through the Last of Their Wild and Romantic Years*, by Miguel Antonio Otero, Press of the Pioneers, 1935.

What Is It?
(See Answer Key #47)

312. What organization has provided more than four hundred thousand hours of free tutoring in reading, writing, and speaking English, and when did it begin providing these services?

The Literacy Volunteers of Santa Fe began their work in 1985, in partnership with the Santa Fe Community College.

Established in 1983 on a 366-acre campus on the south side of town, off Richards Avenue, the Santa Fe Community College serves more than 8,000 students per semester in its credit, noncredit, and adult-education programs. It offers over seventy degree and certificate programs, including occupational specialties such culinary arts, criminal justice, and nursing, as well as regionally and nationally recognized programs in woodworking, media arts, and fine arts. The campus is also home to KSFR, Santa Fe's public radio station, and SFCTV public television.

Read: *Literacy in America: Historic Journey and Contemporary Solutions*, by Edward E. Gordon and Elaine H. Gordon, Praeger, 2003; "Santa Fe Community College Chefs the Main Ingredient in Inspiring Student Cooks," by Miranda Merklein, *Santa Fe New Mexican*, February 15, 2011; and "Santa Fe Community College Clears Final Hurdle for Expansion," by Steve Terrell, *Santa Fe New Mexican*, August 12, 2010.

313. What was the main occupation in Santa Fe during the colonial period?

The majority of those polled in various censuses listed their occupation as farmer; other occupations mentioned include blacksmith, painter, mason, gunsmith, barber (they were also the surgeons), presidio soldier, and household servant.

Read: "Españoles, Castas, y Labradores: Santa Fe Society in the Eighteenth Century," by Adrian H. Bustamante, in *Santa Fe: History of an Ancient City*, edited by David Grant Noble, School for Advanced Research Press, 2008; *Jamestown, Quebec, Santa Fe: Three North American Beginnings*, by James C. Kelly and Barbara Clark Smith, Smithsonian Books, 2007; and *Coronado's Land: Essays on Daily Life in Colonial New Mexico*, by Marc Simmons, University of New Mexico Press, 1991.

314. When is the patron saint of Santa Fe honored?

Saint Francis of Assisi is honored on October fourth, the day after he died, according to custom. The fourth of October is his feast day.

Read: *Saints and Seasons: A Guide to New Mexico's Most Popular Saints*, by Ana Pacheco, Gran Via, 2005.

What Is It?
(See Answer Key #48)

315. The City of Santa Fe's patron saint is also associated with which state in the United States?

Saint Francis, often called "everybody's saint," is the patron saint of New Mexico as well as of Santa Fe. He is also the patron saint of children, animals, and environmentalists around the world.

Read: *Reluctant Saint: The Life of Francis of Assisi*, by Donald Spoto, Viking Compass, 2002.

316. Where can one see murals in Santa Fe featuring Saint Francis and Saint Clare?

Visit the St. Francis Auditorium, in the New Mexico Museum of Art, at the northwest corner of the Plaza. Saint Clare, an Italian saint, born Chiara Offreduccio in 1194, was one of the first followers of Saint Francis; she wrote the first monastic rule known to have been written by a woman. An order, often called the "Poor Clares," was founded in her name.

Read: *The Saint Francis Murals of Santa Fe: The Commission and the Artists*, by Carl D. Sheppard, Sunstone Press, 1989.

317. During the Spanish era, how long was the typical roundtrip expedition, using wagons conveying goods and supplies, on El Camino Real (the royal road) between Santa Fe and Mexico City?

About a year, or a year and a half, depending on time spent at the destination. The trip was estimated to take about six months one way using wagon caravans.

A full *journada* (a day's travel on foot) was traditionally seven *ligas* (leagues), a measurement not used today. A league equaled the distance a person or a horse could walk in an hour, or about three miles. The Franciscan caravans expeditions took longer, typically three years round trip, since they stayed at either end and did not turn around and come back as soon as possible. The approximately fifteen-hundred-mile trail travels from Mexico City through the Chihuahuan desert up along the Rio Grande to Santa Fe, traversing some of the most desolate and rugged terrain in western North America. The Camino Real de Tierra Adentro was established in about 1598; portions of the original track can be visited today. The road's successors and improvements, such as part of I-25 in the United States and Carretera Federal 45 in northern Mexico, are still in use today.

El Camino Real International Heritage Center, fifty miles south of Albuquerque, is open year-round (except Tuesdays) and highlights New Mexico's oldest and most historic highway. El Camino Real is a National Historic Trail.

Read: *From Mexico City to Santa Fe: A Historical Guide to El Camino Real de Tierra Adentro*, compiled and edited by Joseph P. Sánchez and Bruce A. Erickson, Rio Grande Books, 2011; *The Royal Road: El Camino Real from Mexico City to Santa Fe*, photographs by Christine Preston, with text by José Antonio Esquibel and Douglas Preston, University of New Mexico Press, 1998; *Following the Royal Road: A Guide to the Historic Camino Real de Tierra Adentro*, by Hal Jackson, University of New Mexico Press, 2006; and *New Mexico's Royal Road: Trade and Travel on the Chihuahua Trail*, by Max L. Moorhead, University of Oklahoma Press, 1994 (first published 1954).

Patient Man and Sturdy Burros. **Linoleum block cut by Harold E. West, c. 1930s.**

318. Which New Mexican governor was born in Albuquerque's Old Town but spent most of his time in Santa Fe?

Manuel Armijo, who served two terms as governor during the Mexican period (1821–1846).

Read: "Colonial Governors," by José Garcia, *La Herencia*, February 2008; and "The Rehabilitation of Governor Armijo," by Paul Kraemer, *La Crónica de Nuevo México*, No. 89, October 2011.

General and Governor Manuel Armijo. This familiar sketch perhaps does not convey the charm and stamina that must have been part of Armijo's character. When the United States entered Santa Fe and took over New Mexico in 1846, one of General Kearny's officers, Captain Philip St. George Cooke, evidently remarked after being shown to the governor's offices in the Palace of the Governors that "there was no mistaking the governor, a large, fine looking man . . . he wore a blue frock coat, with a rolling collar and a general's shoulder straps, blue striped trousers with gold lace, and a red sash." Image courtesy of Palace of the Governors Photo Archives (NMHM/DCA), #050809.

319. What and where was the only "public clock," used by public employees and the government in the 1820s?

A sundial was erected in the center of the Plaza by Governor Antonio Narbona.

Read: *Old Santa Fe: The Story of New Mexico's Ancient Capital*, by Ralph Emerson Twitchell, facsimile of 1925 edition, Sunstone Press, 2007.

320. Where was the old bus station located in downtown Santa Fe?

On Ortiz Street, off Water Street, behind the De Vargas Hotel (now the Hotel St. Francis). The old bus station had clean toilets available; you had to pay 10 cents to use one. In the early 1980s the bus station for statewide and out-of-state buses moved to St. Michael's Drive. Within ten years there was no out-of-state service depot in Santa Fe. In 2010 the city's local bus system had its downtown terminus on Sheridan Street.

Union bus depot in downtown Santa Fe. Photograph by T. Harmon Parkhurst, c. 1925–1945. Courtesy of Palace of the Governors Photo Archives (NMHM/DCA), #051111.

What Is It?
(See Answer Key #49)

321. Who was "the youngest mayor in the oldest city" and when?

Ralph Emerson Twitchell, a "progressive" from Missouri, was a historian with narrow-minded attitudes toward Hispanics and Pueblo peoples. He served as mayor one year, from 1893 to 1894, when he was thirty-four years old; he recalled that time as "365 days of grief."

Read: "Progressive Santa Fe: 1880–1912," by Robert L. Spude, in *All Trails Lead to Santa Fe*, Sunstone Press, 2010; *The Spanish Archives of New Mexico*, by Ralph Emerson Twitchell, facsimile of 1914 edition, Sunstone Press, 2008; *The Leading Facts of New Mexican History*, by Ralph Emerson Twitchell, facsimile of 1911 edition, Sunstone Press, 2007; and *Old Santa Fe: The Story of New Mexico's Ancient Capital*, by Ralph Emerson Twitchell, facsimile of 1925 edition, Sunstone Press, 2007.

Ralph Emerson Twitchell, c. 1910. Courtesy of Palace of the Governors Photo Archives (NMHM/DCA), #007902.

322. When and why did a descendant of Christopher Columbus visit Santa Fe?

The Duque de Veragua, Cristóbal Colón de Carvajal, a direct descendant of Christopher Columbus, visited Santa Fe in October of 1991, while touring the Americas at the beginning of the 500th anniversary of Columbus's first voyage.

Read: "Cristobal Colon Attempts Links, Gets Ties," by David Roybal, *Santa Fe New Mexican*, September 17, 1991.

What Is It?
(See Answer Key #50)

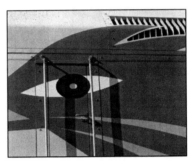

323. Preceliano Ortiz's store, nicknamed "Percy's" (a mispronunciation of "Precy's") was one of four popular stores clustered on Canyon Road in the mid-1900s; what kind of stores were they, and which lasted the longest?

All four were grocery stores: Percy's, Gormley's, the Friendly Grocery, and the Canyon Road Grocery were all within a few blocks of each other. Percy's lasted the longest.

Read: *Santa Fe Bohemia: The Art Colony, 1964–1980*, by Eli Levin, Sunstone Press, 2007.

324. During the Mexican era what was the legislative body that met in Santa Fe called?

La Asamblea Territorial, the Territorial Assembly, met from 1821 to 1846. The history of assembled meetings in representative government in Santa Fe, New Mexico, began with the introduction by don Juan de Oñate of the *cabildo*, or town council, when he arrived in northern New Spain in 1598. A version of the same town meeting is still used today.

Read: *Between Two Rivers: The Atrisco Land Grant in Albuquerque History, 1692–1968*, by Joseph P. Sánchez, University of Oklahoma Press, 2008; "Mis Tiempos: Territorial Legislature," by Julian Vigil, *La Herencia*, Winter 2006; and "Thirty-eight Adobe Houses: The Villa de Santa Fe in the Seventeenth Century, 1608–1610," by José Antonio Esquibel, in *All Trails Lead to Santa Fe*, Sunstone Press, 2010.

What Is It?
(See Answer Key #51)

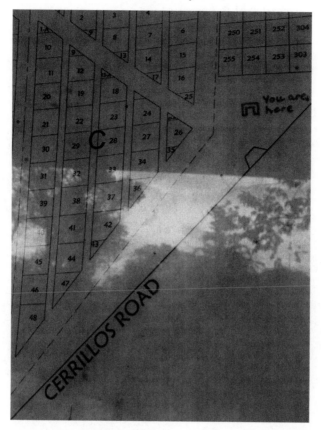

325. Under which Santa Fe mayor were the last gaslights on the Plaza replaced, and when?

Manuel Valdes was the mayor in 1892, when electric lights replaced gaslights.

Read the handwritten minutes of the 1892 Santa Fe City Council.

326. What was the name of the area where the village of Agua Fría is now?

The area was once known as Quemado (which translates as "burned"); it was first referred to as Agua Fría in 1776, when it was described by fray Francisco Atanasio Domínguez. *Agua fría* means "cold water" or "fresh water."

Read: *The Missions of New Mexico, 1776: A Description, with Other Contemporary Documents,* by Fray Francisco Atanasio Domínguez, translated by Eleanor B. Adams and Fray Angélico Chávez, University of New Mexico Press, 1956.

327. What is the significance of the name of the church in the village of Agua Fría?

San Isidro Church, built in 1835, is named for the patron saint of farmers.

Read: *Saints and Seasons: A Guide to New Mexico's Most Popular Saints*, by Ana Pacheco, Gran Via, 2005.

Iglesia de San Isidro Official Scenic Historic Marker, in Agua Fría village, once part of the far northern end of the Camino Real Adentro. The marker is written in Spanish on one side and English on the other. Photograph by E. West, 2011.

328. Where was Santa Fe's first hydroelectric plant, and what became of it?

The "powerhouse" was located across from Cristo Rey Church, on the northeast corner of Camino Cabra and Upper Canyon Road; it was owned by the Santa Fe Water and Light Company. During the Spanish colonial and Mexican eras in Santa Fe, water was community-owned, but privatization of water began in 1880. Dams were built on the Santa Fe River, and electrical power was generated by the force of the river running downhill. The hydroelectric plant was first turned on in 1895; by 1940 it was out of use. It eventually became a park, and the restored Hydro Electric Plant is now the home of the Santa Fe Water History Museum.

In 2011 the City of Santa Fe again wanted to diversify its local power sources, and a new turbine buried in a vault on city-owned land, at the same location near Camino Cabra, generates electric power from energy in the water utility's transmission pipes; the water pressure turns into velocity, which then is converted into energy. The renewable energy is sold to the Public Service Company of New Mexico and earns cash in the form of renewable-energy credits. Most of the project's cost was covered by the federal government's stimulus funds under the American Recovery and Reinvestment Act, as well as the New Mexico Finance Authority and the New Mexico Environment Department.

The Santa Fe project was the first in the nation to harness the power of treated water by a municipal hydro-generation system on its way to consumer taps.

Read: "Tapping Force of H2O" by Julie Ann Grimm, *Santa Fe New Mexican*, July 14, 2011; and "The Santa Fe River and Its Water," by Don Goldman, Santa Fe office of the Nature Conservancy, 2003.

329. Who built Sena Plaza?

Sena Plaza, downtown on Palace Avenue, was built by and for the Alarid family. In 1844 Juan Nepomuceno Alarid willed the house to his sister, María del Rosario Alarid, the wife of Juan Estevan Sena. It became the home of the family of José D. Sena, a veteran of the Civil War and a prominent Santa Fean, and it remained in the Sena family until 1927. Today there are small shops and restaurants around the interior plaza's peaceful gardens.

Browse the Santa Fe County Deed Book, G: 42–44, at the Santa Fe County courthouse. Also, read *Old Santa Fe Today*, by the Historic Santa Fe Foundation, University of New Mexico Press, 1991.

330. When was Sena Plaza remodeled and by whom?

In 1927, by William Penhallow Henderson, who organized the remodeling; a second floor was added in 1929. The Sena family heirs had sold the property to Martha and Amelia Elizabeth White that year.

Read: *Old Santa Fe Today*, by the Historic Santa Fe Foundation, University of New Mexico Press, 1991.

331. Who was the New Mexico governor appointed by Mexican dictator Antonio López de Santa Anna in 1835, and what happened to him?

Governor Albino Pérez. He was assassinated on the outskirts of Santa Fe during the Revolt of 1837.

Pérez had been unpopular because of his "outsider" status, coming from central Mexico, and because he was expected to levy taxes and impose the tightened administration of the Mexican government, thereby restructuring the regional political system. He was also unpopular because he was accused of fraud, was in an openly adulterous relationship with his housekeeper while his wife was in Mexico City, and was ostentatious about his wealth when most New Mexicans were poor.

The rebellion was organized by Juan José Esquibel and others in northern New Mexican communities, including Native Americans from surrounding pueblos. The event is sometimes called the Chimayó Rebellion since the insurrection gathered at Santa Cruz de la Cañada, near Chimayó. Pérez started to go after the rebels, but he had little support, and after failing to achieve guaranteed safety in Santa Fe, he was attacked and killed while trying to sneak out of town at night.

Manuel Armijo succeeded him as governor. The Pérez governmental mismanagement was one of many problems during the turbulent times of unrest in Mexico leading up to the takeover of northern Mexico by the United States in 1846.

Read: "It Happened in Old Santa Fe: The Death of Governor Albino Pérez, 1835–1837," by Joseph P. Sánchez, in *All Trails Lead to Santa Fe*, Sunstone Press, 2010; *Rebellion in Rio Arriba, 1837*, by Janet Lecompte, University of New Mexico Press, 1985; *Revolution and Rebellion: How Taxes Cost a Governor His Life in 1830s New Mexico*, by Frank McCulloch, Sunstone Press, 2001; and *New Mexico in the Nineteenth Century: A Pictorial History*, by Andrew K. Gregg, University of New Mexico Press, 1987.

332. Seton Village, east of Santa Fe, was named for which popular author/illustrator who became one of the first proponents of wildlife conservation?

Ernest Thompson Seton (1860–1946), who was also a cofounder of the Boy Scouts. "Seton Castle," the Seton family home, was sold to Santa Fe's Academy for the Love of Learning in 2003.

Read: *Ernest Thompson Seton: The Life and Legacy of an Artist and Conservationist*, by David L. Witt, Gibbs Smith, 2010.

Ernest Thompson Seton visited Mary Austin at her house, 1927. Photograph by Carol Stryker. Courtesy of Palace of the Governors Photo Archives (NMHM/DCA), #14348.

333. Who was the Sweeney Gym, in the old Santa Fe High School, named after?

Sports enthusiast and educator Raymond Patrick Sweeney, who had been a popular Santa Fe school superintendent, and was head of New Mexico's High School Athletic Association in the 1940s.

Read: "Turning the Page on Sweeney Gym," by Walter K. Lopez, *La Herencia*, Fall 2006.

What Is It?
(See Answer Key #52)

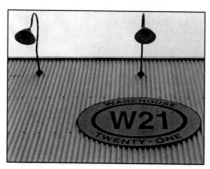

334. Which city councilor pushed to get the City of Santa Fe to buy the water company in 1995?

After twelve years of trying, Art Sanchez helped Santa Fe purchase its own water system, now called the Sangre de Cristo Water Division.

Read: "PUC OK's City Purchase of Water Company," by Ben Neary, *Santa Fe New Mexican*, May 23, 1995; *Not a Drop to Drink: America's Water Crisis (and What You Can Do)*, by Ken Midkiff, New World Library, 2007; and *A Great Aridness: Climate Change and the Future of the American Southwest*, by William Debuys, Oxford University Press, 2011.

335. Which State of New Mexico government building in Santa Fe is named for a leader of a Native American nation, and where is the building?

The Wendell Chino building, at 1220 South St. Francis Drive, is named for the influential and controversial president of the Mescalero Apache Nation. He was born in 1923 and died in 1998.

Read: *New Mexican Lives: Profiles and Historical Stories*, by Richard W. Etulain, University of New Mexico Press, 2002.

336. What popular pre-territorial gambling pastimes did women in Santa Fe particularly enjoy?

Visitors to Santa Fe often found it curious and sometimes shocking that women could participate in dancing at public fandangos and gambling just as the men did. They played the game of chance called *chuza*, similar to roulette, and they also enjoyed monte, a guessing game using sleight of hand.

Read: "Territorial Gambling," by Walter K. Lopez, *La Herencia*, Summer 2002: and *La Chicana: The Mexican-American Woman*, by Alfredo Mirandé and Evangelina Enríquez, University of Chicago Press, 1981.

What Is It?
(See Answer Key #53)

337. When and where did the first Santa Fe City Council under U.S. rule meet?

Santa Fe was incorporated in 1891 in the U.S. style, and the first territorial city council met on July 13 in the Coronado Building, on the corner of East Palace Avenue and Otero Street.

Read: "Stumbling across the Hidden History of Santa Fe Raises a Few Questions," by Marc Simmons, *Santa Fe New Mexican*, August 10, 2002.

338. Who were the "five nuts in five mud huts"?

Los Cinco Pintores, an artist group formed in 1921, included Josef Bakos, Fremont Ellis, Walter Mruk, Willard Nash, and Will Shuster, who all built adobe houses on Camino del Monte Sol. Witter Bynner instigated the teasing by calling them the "mud hut nuts." The colorful lifestyles of these and other artists and entrepreneurs went against the more modest segment of Santa Fe society at the time, which was dry during the Prohibition era.

More recently, in 1978, a group of Hispanic artists formed La Cofradía de Artes y Artesanos Hispanicos to support the contemporary revival of Southwest art outside the established Santa Fe art scene. A show at the Museum of International Folk Art in the spring of 2001 caused a major stir by featuring Our Lady of Guadalupe pictured in a rose-covered swimsuit.

Read: *Los Cinco Pintores*, by Edna Robertson, Museum of New Mexico Press, 1975; *Last Call: The Rise and Fall of Prohibition*, by Daniel Okrent, Scribner, 2010; "Frederico M. Vigil: One of a Rare Breed of Fresco Artists," by Michele Jácquez-Ortiz, *La Herencia*, Fall 2004; "War of the Roses: 'Our Lady' 10 Years On," by Casey Sanchez, *Santa Fe New Mexican*, May 5, 2011; *Viva Guadalupe! The Virgin in New Mexican Popular Art*, by Jacqueline Dunnington and Charles C. Mann, Museum of New Mexico Press, 1997; and *Our Lady of Controversy: Alma López's Irreverent Apparition*, edited by Tey Marianna Nunn, University of Texas Press, 2011. Also, see the large fresco mural by Frederico Vigil upstairs in the Santa Fe county courthouse, at the intersection of Palace and Grant Avenues.

What Is It?
(See Answer Key #54)

339. Which prominent Egyptian architect lectured in Santa Fe in the 1980s and spoke about building with what familiar sun-dried bricks?

Hassan Fathy, the architect for the Dar al Islam center and mosque near Abiquiu, spoke about adobe brick construction and using traditional, vernacular building techniques. He described how to construct a dome out of adobe bricks.

Read: *Architecture for the Poor: An Experiment in Rural Egypt*, by Hassan Fathy, University of Chicago Press, 1973; *Adobe: Building and Living with Earth*, by Orlando Romero and David Larkin, Houghton Mifflin, 1994; *Making the Adobe Brick*, by Eugene H. Boudreau, Fifth Street Press, 1971; *Architecture without Architects: A Short Introduction to Non-Pedigreed Architecture*, by Bernard Rudofsky, University of New Mexico Press, 1987 (first published 1964); and *A Pattern Language: Towns, Buildings, Construction*, by Christopher Alexander, Sara Ishikawa, and Murray Silverstein, Oxford University Press, 1977.

340. What is the etymology of the word for the predominant building material used in the construction of the Palace of the Governors in the 1600s?

The Spanish word *adobe* is derived from the Arabic *at-tube* (الطوبة), from the Coptic *tobe*, which comes from the Middle Egyptian era of about 2000 B.C. Adobe has a long history. A quarter to a third of all Spanish words is Arabic in origin. Other words from the Arabic include *acequia*, *alacrán*, *alcalde*, *alcohol*, *alfalfa*, *álgebra*, and *algodón*. There are many more.

Etymology is a kind of genealogy of a word. For example, the town about forty miles south of Santa Fe called Algodónes uses a Spanish word that comes from the Arabic: *al* = the; *godón* = cotton; *es* = place of. The town may have been named for the cottonwood trees growing there. The English word *cotton* comes from the Spanish *godón*, which in turn comes from the Arabic *qtn* (قُطْن), and they all sound almost the same.

Read: *Adobe: Building and Living with Earth*, by Orlando Romero and David Larkin, Houghton Mifflin, 1994; *American Adobes: Rural Houses of Northern New Mexico*, by Beverley Spears, University of New Mexico Press, 1986; *Mud, Space, and Spirit: Handmade Adobes*, by Virginia Gray and Alan Macrae, Capra Press, 1976; and *Word Origins and How We Know Them: Etymology for Everyone*, by Anatoly Liberman, Oxford University Press, 2005.

Making adobes.
Courtesy of Palace of the Governors
Photo Archives (NMHM/DCA), #059238.

Adobes.
Photograph by Melanie West, 2001.
Courtesy of the photographer.

341. Who was the writer, instructor, and landscape designer who was influential in broadening perceptions and perspectives on the "vernacular" landscape?

J. B. Jackson, or John Brinckerhoff "Brink" Jackson. He died in La Cienega in 1996.

Read: *Discovering the Vernacular Landscape*, by John Brinckerhoff Jackson, Yale University Press, 1984; and *Turn Left at the Sleeping Dog: Scripting the Santa Fe Legend, 1920–1955*, edited by John Pen La Farge, University of New Mexico Press, 2001.

Two Kinds of Horsepower. Pen and ink drawing by Harold E. West, c. 1930s.

342. *Es como los brujos, duerme con los ojos abiertos* is a traditional Spanish saying referencing witches, who are assumed to be constantly alert, with wide open eyes; is La Llorona a witch, or is she a ghost who, as some legends say, still roams Santa Fe looking for her children?

Both are possibilities: sometimes La Llorona is represented as a tragic witch and other times she is imagined as a yearning ghost.

Read: *Witchcraft in the Southwest: Spanish and Indian Supernaturalism on the Rio Grande*, by Marc Simmons, University of Nebraska Press, 1980; *Bruja: The Legend of La Llorona*, by Lucinda Ciddio Leyba, University of New Mexico Press, 2011; *La Llorona = The Weeping Woman: An Hispanic Legend Told in Spanish and English*, by Joe Hayes, Cinco Puntos Press, 2004; and *The Legend of La Llorona*, by Ray John de Aragón, Sunstone Press, 2006.

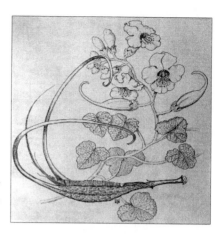

Devil's Claw, Genus Martynia family. Drawing by
G. B. T. of Plants of the Southwest, on Agua Fria Street.

343. The bells of the Cathedral Basilica of St. Francis of Assisi and other Santa Fe churches ring out in celebration of what on Todos Santos, the first of November?

Todos santos means "all saints," and all the saints are honored on November 1, All Saints' Day.

The four new bells in the cathedral basilica were installed in 2009; the largest weighs about 3,000 pounds. The bells were baptized and christened with female saints' names: Katherine, Mercedes, Sofia, and Theresa. The actual bells are rung electronically, and their peals carry for miles.

Santa Feans like hearing the ringing of bells from various churches and other places of worship and gathering throughout town. While bells have called people to gather for many reasons, most often they are a call to contemplation and prayer, and they usually suggest peace.

Read: *Saints and Seasons: A Guide to New Mexico's Most Popular Saints,* by Ana Pacheco, Gran Via, 2005; "Faith in the Royal City," by Dennis Jarrett, *Santa Fe Reporter,* December 11, 1996; *Christian Peace and Nonviolence: A Documentary History,* edited by Michael G. Long, Orbis, 2011; *Tintinnalogia, or, The Art of Ringing,* by Richard Duckworth and Fabian Stedman, Echo Library, 2007 (first published 1671); and *The Nine Tailors: Changes Rung on an Old Theme, in Two Short Touches and Two Full Peals,* by Dorothy L. Sayers, Harcourt Brace Jovanovich, 1989 (first published 1934).

What Is It?
(See Answer Key #55)

344. What is El Día de los Muertos, and how is the holiday celebrated?

The Day of the Dead, or All Souls' Day, on November 2, is a time of honoring and celebrating ancestors, as is done in Mexico, when families and friends gather to pray and celebrate in remembrance of departed loved ones, honoring the deceased with favorite foods and sugar skulls and marigolds.

Read: "Día de los Muertos," by Rita Younis, *La Herencia*, Fall 1997; and *Pablo Remembers: The Fiesta of the Day of the Dead*, by George Ancona, Lothrop, Lee & Shepard Books, 1993.

Day of the Dead Fandango. **Pencil drawing by Anita H. Lehmann. Courtesy of the artist.**

345. Who was the educated wife of Governor Bernardo López de Mendizábal, and why was she arrested by the Holy Office of the Inquisition?

Doña Teresa Aguilera y Roche was arrested at the Palace of the Governors by the Inquisition on August 27, 1662. She and her husband were both accused of practicing Judaism. Along with others, they were taken down to Mexico City, imprisoned, and eventually put into *carceles secretas* (secret jails) in the Palace of the Inquisition. Governor Mendizábal had seen the dangerous military implications of the strict policy towards the Pueblo people and was willing to stand up to the Franciscan power structure in New Mexico. This no doubt made him unpopular with the Church. The aim of the Inquisition was to secure Catholic orthodoxy and to perform as an institution at the service of the monarchy.

In Mexico City, after determinedly defending herself through a thirteen-page, handwritten defense, doña Teresa de Aguilera y Roche's case was suspended, in December of 1664. Her husband had died in the Inquisition jail in Mexico City a few months earlier, before any determination of his guilt or innocence had been made. (She was required by the Inquisitors to pay 4,000 pesos to cover the expenses she had incurred during her two years of incarceration.)

The struggles of intellectual or independent women in the seventeenth century are illuminated by Octavio Paz in his book about New Spain's most famous writer, the poet Juana Inés de la Cruz; he places her story in the historical context of the life and culture of New Spain.

Read: "In Her Own Voice: Dona Teresa Aguilera y Roche and Intrigue in the Palace of the Governors, 1659–1662," by Gerald González and Frances Levine, in *All Trails Lead to Santa Fe*, Sunstone Press, 2010; *To the End of the Earth: A History of the Crypto-Jews of New Mexico*, by Stanley M. Hordes, Columbia University Press, 2005; "Bernardo López de Mendizábal: Could He Have Prevented the Pueblo Revolt?" by Carroll L. Riley, *El Palacio*, Fall 2007; and *Sor Juana, or, The Traps of Faith*, by Octavio Paz, translated by Margaret Sayers Peden, Belknap Press, 1989.

346. Who was Miguel de Quintana, and how did he stand up to the Inquisition in colonial New Mexico?

Quintana was born in New Spain in about 1670. He was a poet whose writing was considered too liberal and independent by the Inquisition, which usually sought total control. He arrived in Santa Fe with Vargas in 1693. In 1732 he was examined by the Inquisition because he was considered to have a "damaged imagination" and was accused of being a heretic. He was eventually pardoned for lack of evidence, although he was threatened with severe punishment if he continued the "ravings" that he called "inspiration." Quintana acted contrite in order to escape punishment.

Read: *Defying the Inquisition in Colonial New Mexico: Miguel de Quintana's Life and Writings*, translated and edited by Francisco A. Lomelí and Clark A. Colahan, University of New Mexico Press, 2006; and *Pasó por Aquí: Critical Essays on the New Mexican Literary Tradition, 1542–1988*, edited by Erlinda Gonzales-Berry, University of New Mexico Press, 1989.

347. Who was the American Indian scholar and Princeton professor who came to Santa Fe to work on the *Handbook of North American Indians* at the request of the Smithsonian Institution?

Alfonso Ortiz, a native of San Juan Pueblo, now called Ohkay Owingeh, moved to Santa Fe in the early 1970s and taught anthropology at the University of New Mexico. He died in 1998.

Read: *The Tewa World: Space, Time, Being, and Becoming in a Pueblo Society*, by Alfonso Ortiz, University of Chicago Press, 1969.

348. What is the first bilingual dictionary to be produced at an American Indian pueblo?

The Tewa and English bilingual dictionary, collected at what is now called Ohkay Owingeh (formerly San Juan Pueblo). The dictionary was formulated in the 1980s.

Read: *San Juan Pueblo Tewa Dictionary*, collected by P'oe T´sa wa (Esther Martinez), with illustrations by ´P'aá Sen (Peter Povijua), San Juan Pueblo Bilingual Program, 1982.

At the Pueblo. Linoleum block cut by Harold E. West, c. 1930s.

349. Which New Mexico governor changed Route 66 so that it no longer came through Santa Fe?

As a result of political maneuvering in 1926, Governor A. T. Hannett ordered the state engineer to construct a new road directly west from Santa Rosa to Albuquerque, avoiding Santa Fe. There are signs in Santa Fe that point out the old Route 66.

Read: *Route 66 across New Mexico: A Wanderer's Guide*, by Jill Schneider, University of New Mexico Press, 1991.

350. Where are two of the best resources in Santa Fe to research New Mexico family history or New Mexico genealogy?

The Fray Angélico Chávez History Library, in the New Mexico History Museum, on Washington Avenue downtown, and the New Mexico State Records Center and Archives, next to the New Mexico State Library, on Camino Carlos Rey, are two of the best places to find out who your New Mexico connections might be.

Read: "Libraries Rich Source for Genealogy Research," by Hazel Romero, *La Herencia*, Winter 2003.

351. What are the current names for five historic roads that were considered the main arteries into and out of Santa Fe?

The roads are named Agua Fria Street, Cerrillos Road, Galisteo Street, Old Pecos Trail, and Old Taos Highway.

Read: "Caminos de Santa Fe," by Aaron Martinez, *La Herencia*, Winter 2006; and *Travel New Mexico Scenic and Historic Byways: A Travel Guide to New Mexico Roads of Distinction*, New Mexico Highway & Transportation Department, 2000.

352. What is the name of the "first lady of Southwestern archaeology," who was an expert witness for the Pueblos?

Florence Hawley Ellis. She and her field-school students verified the precise location of New Mexico's first capital, San Gabriel del Yunque, and that it was established in 1598, among other accomplishments. She produced more than three hundred articles and manuscripts during her career. In 1983 Ellis was an expert witness for the Pueblos in the lengthy dispute known as the Aamodt Case, which concerned water rights.

Read: "Florence Hawley Ellis: First Lady of Southwestern Archaeology," by Emily Abbink, *El Palacio*, Summer 2010.

353. Which architect who contributed to the "New-Old" style of architecture in Santa Fe, in the early 1900s, chose to come to Santa Fe after seeing a flashing neon sign?

John Gaw Meem, seeking advice back east about the tuberculosis he had contracted, was given a choice of three places to go for treatment in 1920; since he had not heard of any of them and couldn't decide, when he saw a flashing neon sign advertizing the Santa Fe Railroad, he decided to choose Santa Fe. He had been an engineer by training, but at Sunmount Sanatorium he became interested in adobe architecture and historic preservation.

The "New-Old" style of architecture was a result of the conscious return to an older, supposedly traditional style of architecture that included Native American and Spanish influences. Jesse Nusbaum had given initial impetus to this movement with the remodeling of the Palace of the Governors, which began in 1909 and included the reconstruction of the palace portal. This style had been strongly promoted in the "New-Old Santa Fe" exhibit of 1912, at the palace. The new Art Museum building (now called the New Mexico Museum of Art), designed in 1916 by Isaac Hamilton Rapp, of Rapp, Rapp & Hendrickson, at the northwest corner of the Plaza, was recognized as a fine example of this style, eventually called "Santa Fe style." John Gaw Meem designed the Laboratory of Anthropology at what is now called Museum Hill. He later designed the Museum of International Folk Art, also located on Museum Hill.

Read: *John Gaw Meem: Pioneer in Historic Preservation*, by Beatrice Chauvenet, Museum of New Mexico Press, 1985; "The Cure at the End of the Trail," by Nancy Owen Lewis, in *All Trails Lead to Santa Fe*, Sunstone Press, 2010; *Facing Southwest: The Life and Houses of John Gaw Meem*, by Chris Wilson, Norton, 2001; *Southwestern Ornamentation and Design: The Architecture of John Gaw Meem*, by Anne Taylor, Sunstone Press, 1989; *Tierra Dulce: Reminiscences from the Jesse Nusbaum Papers*, by Jesse L. Nusbaum, Sunstone Press, 1980; *Creator of the Santa Fe Style: Isaac Hamilton Rapp, Architect*, by Carl D. Sheppard, University of New Mexico Press, 1988; and *The Myth of Santa Fe: Creating a Modern Regional Tradition*, by Chris Wilson, University of New Mexico Press, 1997.

354. Which territorial governor said, "We have condemned and put slavery from our laws"?

The territorial governor Henry Connelly demanded and won, through legislative action, repeal of the Slave Act, on December 8, 1861. Governor Connelly was in office from September of 1861 until July of 1866; a doctor by profession, he died of an opium overdose less than a month after leaving politics. He was buried at Rosario Cemetery.

Read: *New Mexico's Troubled Years: The Story of the Early Territorial Governors*, by Calvin Horn, with foreword by John F. Kennedy, Horn & Wallace, 1963.

What Is It?
(See Answer Key #56)

355. Who persuaded artist Gustave Baumann to stay and work in Santa Fe when he was financially broke and considering leaving?

Paul Walter, a fellow German and the curator of what was then the Art Museum (now the New Mexico Museum of Art), gave Baumann support money and space to do his artwork in the museum's basement. Baumann's masterful wood-block prints, iconic depictions of Southwestern scenes, are as popular today as they were when he produced them. His carved wooden marionettes, made for the entertainment of his family and friends, are featured in puppet shows occasionally performed in the St. Francis Auditorium, in the New Mexico Museum of Art. He used several different colors of wood when he carved a *retablo* (altarpiece) for the Church of the Holy Faith Episcopal church.

Gustave Baumann was born in Germany in 1881 and came to the United States at the age of ten. He took classes at the Art Institute of Chicago and at the Kunstgewerbe Schule, in Munich, where he studied wood carving and wood-block printing. In 1918 he traveled to Taos to check out the famed art colony there; finding it too crowded, he took the train to Santa Fe, where he lived for more than fifty years, until he died, in 1971.

Read: *Artists of the Canyons and Caminos: Santa Fe, Early Twentieth Century*, by Edna Robertson and Sarah Nestor, Ancient City Press, 2006 (first published 1976); *Gustave Baumann: Nearer to Art*, by Martin F. Krause, Madeline Carol Yurtseven, and David Acton, Museum of New Mexico Press, 1993; *Hand of a Craftsman: The Woodcut Technique of Gustave Baumann*, by David Acton, Museum of New Mexico Press, 1996; *The Hand-Carved Marionettes of Gustave Baumann: Share Their World*, by Ellen Zieselman, Museum of New Mexico Press, 2000.

Morning Sun. **Wood-block print by Gustave Baumann, c. 1932. Courtesy of the Owings Gallery, Santa Fe.**

356. Who was the German immigrant who became a close associate of and business manager for the Spaniard Manuel Álvarez in Santa Fe during the mid-1800s?

Charles Blumner arrived in Santa Fe in 1836 at age thirty-one. He was a pioneer, civil servant, merchant, and friend of Álvarez. Blumner eventually became a U.S. marshal.

Read: *Germans in the Southwest: 1850–1920*, by Tomas Jaehn, University of New Mexico Press, 2005.

357. A popular Chinese restaurant in Santa Fe was opened on San Francisco Street in the early 1900s by whom?

Henry Park (Gee Gay) and his family operated the New Mexico Café, the popular Chinese restaurant known as the Canton Café. It opened in the early 1900s and did not close until the 1970s.

Read: "Smart Chinese Boys Become Good Citizens," *Santa Fe New Mexican*, December 12, 1936.

The 9th Cavalry Army band performed a wintertime concert in front of Sang Kee Laundry in the late 1800s. The laundry also sold "fancy goods" from China and Japan. Courtesy of Palace of the Governors Photo Archives (NMHM/DCA), #015289.

358. Whose Canyon Road painting studio and kitchen became an occasional hangout for local artists in the 1950s, with a place to pitch horseshoes outside and strong coffee on the cookstove inside?

Harold (Hal) West set up his Canyon Road gallery and studio in 1954. Artists and their galleries can be found all about town, and Canyon Road is still one of the most prominent art communities in Santa Fe. The gallery rental property at 601 Canyon Road is part of one of the last compounds still intact along Canyon Road and is still owned by a Santa Fe family who have been there for generations.

Read: *Artists of the Canyons and Caminos: Santa Fe, Early Twentieth Century*, by Edna Robertson and Sarah Nestor, Ancient City Press, 2006 (first published 1976); and *New Mexico Artists at Work*, by Dana Newmann, Museum of New Mexico Press, 2005.

Hal West's Studio. Etching by Eli Levin.
(The photograph shows the reverse of the etching.) Private collection.

Horses with the Windmill Brand Pull the Plow. Oil on board by Harold E. West, c. 1930s.
The small painting is tacked up in a well house.

359. What Burro Alley corner business venture, undertaken in 1862, may have been named for a Dickens novel?

The Old Curiosity Shop was started by Jake Gold and enticed customers with dramatic displays of Indian blankets for many years.

Read: *Santa Fe: A Pictorial History*, by John Sherman, Donning Company, 1996; and *The Old Curiosity Shop*, by Charles Dickens, Penguin Classics, 2001 (first published 1841).

360. What kind of cart is on the rooftop above 204 West San Francisco Street?

A *carreta* (wooden ox cart) was placed on the roof of J. C. Candelario's Curio Store in the late-nineteenth century; the current cart is reinforced with steel pipes.

Read: *Santa Fe: A Pictorial History*, by John Sherman, Donning Company, 1996.

Carreta.
**Drawing by Lachlan Allan MacLean,
c. 1846–1847. Courtesy of Palace of
the Governors Photo Archives
(NMHM/DCA), #147547.**

**San Francisco Street, looking east toward the cathedral basilica.
Note the *carreta* on the roof. Photograph by E. West, 2011.**

361. Mayor Alfredo Ortiz was asked by several Santa Feans to require dozens of boys swarming the Plaza to pay taxes during the summer of 1940. Why?

Some citizens complained that there were too many shoe-shine boys on the Plaza and that they should be required to pay taxes. Instead Mayor Ortiz decided to do nothing as long as the boys stayed out of barbershops, hotels, and established shine parlors, which were paying an annual five-dollar occupation tax.

Read: *The 1940s*, by Michael V. Uschan, Lucent Books, 1999.

362. Which speaker of the New Mexico House of Representatives was appointed the first Superintendent of Public Instruction, in 1892?

Don Amado Chaves, son of Manuel Antonio Chaves, was selected by Governor L. Bradford Prince as superintendent of public instruction. In this role he actively promoted bilingual literacy. Chaves had been a mayor of Santa Fe as well as a state senator. He was a practicing attorney at the supreme court and worked at the U.S. Pension Bureau. He was also a writer and a rancher. He ran a thriving law practice, specializing in land grant issues with the U.S. government, and he was one of the attorneys who helped solve the New Mexico/Texas boundary litigation in 1912. He traveled often to Chicago, Washington, D.C., and the San Diego area of California. He was a good friend of Charles Lummis.

Chaves was born in Santa Fe in 1851 and died in Santa Fe in 1930.

Read: *Two Southwesterners: Charles Lummis and Amado Chaves*, by Marc Simmons, San Marcos Press, 1968; *The Little Lion of the Southwest: A Life of Manuel Antonio Chaves*, by Marc Simmons, Sage Books, 1973; *Old Santa Fe: The Story of New Mexico's Ancient Capital*, by Ralph Emerson Twitchell, facsimile of 1925 edition, Sunstone Press, 2007; and *The Borderlands of Culture: Américo Paredes and the Transnational Imaginary*, by Ramón Saldívar, Duke University Press, 2006.

363. What best-selling and award-winning author reported for United Press International (UPI), edited the *Santa Fe New Mexican*, and taught journalism at the University of New Mexico?

Tony Hillerman. He was born in Oklahoma in 1925 and was a decorated combat veteran of World War II, earning the Silver Star, the Bronze Star, and the Purple Heart. He worked for newspapers in Oklahoma and Texas before coming to Santa Fe in 1953 to work for UPI. He later became editor of Santa Fe's daily newspaper. He taught journalism at the University of New Mexico after moving to Albuquerque in 1963. He died in 2008.

Although Hillerman started as a journalist, he was the author of more than thirty books, including works about the Southwest, memoirs, and anthologies. However, he is best known for his eighteen mystery novels, whose two protagonists are members of the Navajo tribal police: Joe Leaphorn and Jim Chee. He received many awards and honors, including the Navajo Tribe's Special Friends of the Dineh Award.

Tony Hillerman once commented that when his wife, Marie, observed him relaxing on the living room sofa with his eyes shut, she knew he was really hard at work, writing in his mind.

Begin with the first of the Joe Leaphorn/Jim Chee books, *The Blessing Way*, by Tony Hillerman, Harper, 2009 (first published 1970). Also read *Seldom Disappointed: A Memoir*, by Tony Hillerman, Harper Collins, 2001; and *Tony Hillerman's Landscape: On the Road with Chee and Leaphorn*, by Anne Hillerman, with photographs by Don Strel, Harper, 2009.

364. What are the original French (and Hispanicized) names for the three explorers who came to America with La Salle in 1684 and later arrived in Santa Fe after being taken prisoner by the Spanish?

Jean L'Archivêque (Juan Archibeque), Jacques Grollet (Santiago Gurulé), and Pierre Meusnier (Pedro Munier) were Frenchmen who were part of the French expedition led by René-Robert Cavelier, Sieur de La Salle. La Salle explored the Great Lakes region, the Mississippi River, and the Gulf of Mexico, claiming the entire Mississippi River basin for France. L'Archivêque turned against La Salle, and he and the others evidently lived as heros with the Hasinai (or Tejas) Native Americans in eastern Texas for about two years, until they were found by Spaniards, who were searching for any Frenchmen who they believed were trespassing. L'Archivêque and Grollet gave themselves up and were sent to Mexico City and then to Spain, where they stayed in jail for two years. They were let go and sent back to Mexico to work in the silver mines in Zacatecas. They were granted their freedom when they joined the Velasco-Farfán colonists, who were part of the Vargas colonizing and reconquest expedition of 1693.

Juan Archibeque was part of the 1720 Villasur military expedition, where he lost his life fighting for the Spanish when the group was ambushed by the French and all were killed. The Villasur expedition massacre is depicted on one of the Segesser hide paintings, on display at the Palace of the Governors.

In 1701, Juan Archibeque and his family had owned a house (along what is now known as Canyon Road) that more than two hundred years later, in 1915, was owned and restored by Ina Sizer Cassidy and her husband, the artist Gerald Cassidy.

Read: "French Make Early Appearance in NM," by Marc Simmons, *Santa Fe New Mexican*, September 20, 2008; and "History of Canyon Road Home Harkens to First Fiesta," by Charles Padilla, *Santa Fe New Mexican*, September 4, 2011.

What Is It?
(See Answer Key #57)

365. There were originally many acequias that guided water from the Santa Fe River for domestic use in the city and to outlying areas. What is the name of the most important and longest acequia in Santa Fe?

The Acequia Madre (Mother Ditch) originally ran from Upper Canyon Road to lower Agua Fría village. It is today still the longest acequia, running for about seven miles, from the diversion (*la presa*) in the Santa Fe River, near Cristo Rey Church, south to about a thousand feet past Agua Fría School, in Agua Fría.

An acequia is a gravity chute, similar to a flume. An acequia distributes water for irrigation. The Spanish word comes from, and is pronounced the same as, the classical Arabic word, which means "the water conduit"; English speakers in the Southwest are familiar with the term. Some acequias are of modern fabrication, but most are simple open ditches with dirt banks, many of which are hundreds of years old. Santa Fe's acequias take out from the Santa Fe River. The acequias that take out of other acequias are called "laterals"; the Analco and Ranchitos acequias are two laterals.

There were thirty-eight acequias listed in Santa Fe in 1919. Today four are still active: Acequia Madre, Acequia del Llano, Acequia de la Muralla, and Acequia Cerro Gordo.

In New Mexico, by state statute, acequias are political subdivisions of the state of New Mexico. They usually have three commissioners and a *mayordomo*, who are in charge of regulating and protecting the acequia for the water-right holders (*parcientes*).

Read: "Acequia Agriculture: Water, Irrigation, and Their Defining Roles in Santa Fe History," by Tara M. Plewa, in *Santa Fe: History of an Ancient City*, edited by David Grant Noble, School for Advanced Research Press, 2008; *The Essence of Santa Fe: From a Way of Life to a Style*, by Jerilou Hammett, Kingsley Hammett, and Peter Scholz, Ancient City Press, 2006; *The Santa Fe Acequia Systems: Summary Report on Their History and Present Status, with Recommendations for Use and Protection*, by David H. Snow, Planning Department, City of Santa Fe, 1988; *Mayordomo: Chronicle of an Acequia in Northern New Mexico*, by Stanley Crawford, University of New Mexico Press, 1993; *Acequia: Water-Sharing, Sanctity, and Place*, by Sylvia Rodriguez, School for Advanced Research Press, 2006; and "Water That Runs in Ditches," in *Spanish Pathways: Readings in the History of Hispanic New Mexico*, by Marc Simmons, University of New Mexico Press, 2001.

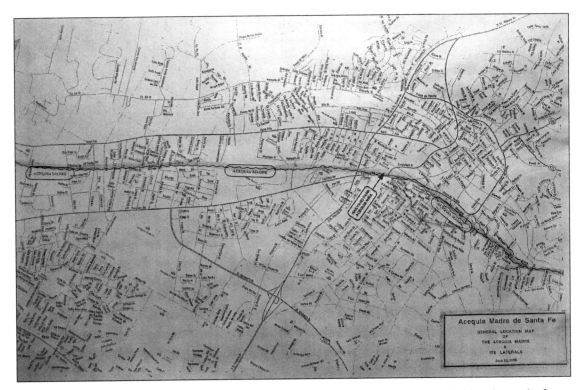

1948 map showing the Acequia Madre traveling from the northeast side of town behind and to the north of Wood-Gormley School, through the Railyard Park, and on to the south, behind the New Mexico School for the Deaf and the Santa Fe Indian School, toward Agua Fría village, between Cerrillos Road and Agua Fria Street. Courtesy of Phillip and Eleanor Ortiz Bové.

View of Santa Fe from the southwest, 1881. Photograph by Ben Wittick. Courtesy of Palace of the Governors Photo Archives (NMHM/DCA), #015820.

366. How much did a hotel restaurant meal cost at the Evans Cafe in 1929?

Hotels and places to eat have always been important to the commerce and tourism of Santa Fe. Regular meals cost 25 cents each at the cafe in the Evans Hotel, on San Francisco Street; a multilevel parking garage is on that spot now.

Santa Fe's "first hotel," the Exchange Hotel, which replaced a simple *fonda* (inn), was at the southeast corner of the Plaza (where La Fonda is now), with its entrance into the lobby at the corner and the entrance to the saloon inside. The Exchange Hotel had a long *placita*, or interior courtyard, and a high-walled corral for the patrons' horses, located roughly where La Fonda's parking lot is now—for a different kind of horsepower.

In the mid-1800s other public lodging included the Missouri House, on what was called Main Street in territorial times (San Francisco Street now); Beck and Redman's Hotel; the Santa Fe House; and the German Hotel. There were also several boarding houses, or *mesones* (small inns), where visitors and locals alike could enjoy a good noonday meal. Mrs. G. de Habile, from New Orleans, opened her boarding house in about 1847, near the Missouri House. Eliza Sloan opened the Sloan Boarding House in the abandoned Spanish military barracks at the corner of the Plaza; Archbishop Lamy was evidently a regular at lunch there, as was Kit Carson when he was in town. In the later 1800s, visitors' names and where they were from were mentioned daily in the *New Mexican*. The paper listed the registered guests in each hotel every day: The Claire Hotel, the Exchange Hotel, Herlow's Hotel, and even the Bon-Ton, where lodging could be had for as little as 25 cents a night. The Capital Hotel opened its doors in 1884; it occupied a commercial building built in about 1863 at the northeast corner of the Plaza, at Palace and Lincoln Avenues. Later, by 1898, it became the home for the *New Mexican*, and then still later the building was owned by Archbishop Lamy's nephew.

Other historic hotels include the early 1900s Palace Hotel, a grand building that was located on what is now East Marcy Street; the De Vargas Hotel (now the Hotel St. Francis), on Don Gaspar Street; and La Posada (now called the La Posada Resort and Spa), incorporating the old Staab family home on Palace Avenue.

More recently, in 1988, the Hotel Santa Fe was built as a joint venture between local Santa Fe business people and Picuris Pueblo. Majority-owned by the Picuris Pueblo people, it is the only venture of its kind in the United States. Southwest Seminars, begun in 1997, is a nonprofit educational program and lecture series that has since 1999 been based out of Hotel Santa Fe; it creates programs in Southwest studies in the fields of archaeology, Southwest history, Native American Indian culture, natural science, and the environment.

One of the oldest motels still in use along Route 66 was opened in 1936. It was called the El Rey Court, with carports that were later made into sleeping rooms in the 1950s; Alamo Lodge, a neighboring motel, was incorporated into the property, and by the late 1900s the entire place was called El Rey Inn.

There is probably no longer any hotel or motel in Santa Fe that serves a full meal for 25 cents. Allowing for inflation, the equivalent meal, a very modest one, might cost about five dollars.

Read: *Coronado's Land: Essays on Daily Life in Colonial New Mexico*, by Marc Simmons, University of New Mexico Press, 1991; and *The Food of Santa Fe: Authentic Recipes from the American Southwest*, by Dave DeWitt and Nancy Gerlach, Periplus Editions, 1998. Also, see page 108 in *Santa Fe: A Walk through Time*, by Kingsley Hammett, Gibbs Smith, 2004.

Kinsell Live-stock Meat Market, c. 1900–1905, where the Exchange Hotel
had been and where today's La Fonda would eventually be built.
Courtesy of Palace of the Governors Photo Archives (NMHM/DCA), #105576

367. Which Santa Fe institution was "dedicated" during Thanksgiving week in 1917, during the New Mexico Education Association Teachers' Convention?

The Museum of New Mexico's new Art Museum and St. Francis Auditorium were honored by Governor Washington E. Lindsey, with speeches by Edgar Lee Hewitt, Frank Springer, and Antonio Lucero. The timing was chosen because the governor, the museum dignitaries, and politicians chose to honor teachers, and many were in Santa Fe for the convention.

Read: *The Artist in the American West, 1800–1900*, Museum of Fine Arts Press, 1961.

368. Where in downtown Santa Fe could one purchase a locally made herbal salve for a child's skinned knee in the 1960s and '70s?

At Lujan's Herbal Shop, on Galisteo Street. The owner, Mr. Delfino Lujan, offered advice as well as all kinds of herbs and salves.

Read: *Los Remedios: Traditional Herbal Remedies of the Southwest*, by Michael Moore, Museum of New Mexico Press, 1990 (first published 1977); and *Medicinal Plants of the Mountain West*, by Michael Moore, Museum of New Mexico Press, 2003.

369. In what year during the territorial period did Santa Fe win its only professional baseball championship?

In 1888 the Santa Fe Ancients (named for the "ancient" city) won by default because the two other teams in the league, from Las Vegas and Albuquerque, went bankrupt and couldn't play. Years later, in the 1930s, the city had a semi-professional baseball team called the Santa Fe Stationers (named for one of their sponsors).

Read: "The New Mexico Baseball League," *Santa Fe Daily Herald*, October 4, 1888; *The Golden Years of Baseball*, by Jim Kaplan, Random House, 1992; and *New Mexico Baseball: Miners, Outlaws, Indians, and Isotopes, 1880 to the Present*, by L. M. Sutter, McFarland, 2010.

370. Who are the two people featured in the large sculpture in a little park west of the main post office, downtown?

Don Pedro de Peralta is on horseback conferring with an unidentified settler. Peralta seems to be pointing toward Española instead of Santa Fe.

See the sculpture, *The Founding of Santa Fe: Don Pedro de Peralta, 1610*, by Dave McGary, in Peralta Park, at the corner of Paseo de Peralta and Grant Avenue.

371. Which famed World War II correspondent wrote satirical comments about Santa Fe and its artists?

Ernie Pyle visited Santa Fe in the 1930s and proved kinder to individuals than toward stereotypes. He was a well-known columnist who reported on wars from Africa to Okinawa. During his visit to Santa Fe, he ridiculed the art community, though he liked individual artists.

Read: *Ernie Pyle in the American Southwest*, by Richard Melzer, Sunstone Press, 1996; and *Here Is Your War: Story of G.I. Joe*, by Ernie Pyle, Henry Holt & Company, 1945.

What Is It?
(See Answer Key #58)

372. What loss of important documents in territorial Santa Fe was compared to the "barbarous burning of the libraries of Alexandria" by the citizens of the town?

The partial dispersal and destruction of the Spanish Archives by Governor William Pile occurred in 1870.

Read: *New Mexico's Troubled Years: The Story of the Early Territorial Governors*, by Calvin Horn, with foreword by John F. Kennedy, Horn & Wallace, 1963.

373. Which Spanish-born governor welcomed U.S. traders to Santa Fe within a few months of Mexican independence from Spain in 1821?

Governor Facundo Melgares permitted foreign merchants to trade, welcoming the "gringos."

Read: *Foreigners in Their Native Land: Historical Roots of the Mexican Americans*, by David J. Weber, University of New Mexico Press, 2003 (first published 1973).

374. What was traded over the Santa Fe Trail by New Mexicans in the mid-1800s, during the Mexican period, and what was the result?

Coins, especially the eight-reales silver peso; later, horses and mules were traded in exchange for U.S. manufactured goods such as textiles and hardware and even some fashionable luxury items. Trade led to New Mexican economic dependence on the United States.

By the mid-1800s the freewheeling, colorful trading practices of many of the Santa Fe *commerciantes* (traders), which had yielded quick return on small investment, began to evolve into more highly capitalized and complex business practices increasingly linked to financial interests in St. Louis, Boston, and New York. Most successful Santa Fe trading associations, such as those belonging to the Spiegelberg Brothers, Messervy & Webb, and Webb & Kingsbury, maintained full-time connections in the East to facilitate purchasing, shipping, and collections.

John Kingsbury's correspondence during 1853 to 1861 with his senior partner, James Josiah Webb, offers details about day-to-day life in Santa Fe and some gossip, as well as the company's business dealings. It also reveals the stress experienced in Santa Fe by Kingsbury's wife, Kate Messervy Kingsbury, sister of prominent trader William S. Messervy, who was acting governor of New Mexico Territory in 1853. Messervy was apparently not very sympathetic to his sibling's depression and loneliness or her struggles taking care of a sick child. John Kingsbury (originally from the Boston area) worried about his wife's depression. Although her weak physical condition, a result of consumption (tuberculosis), was improved by living in Santa Fe, she elected to return to Massachusetts with their son. In 1856 Kingsbury wrote to Webb that he was experiencing "the most trying time of my life."

Read: *Foreigners in Their Native Land: Historical Roots of the Mexican Americans*, by David J. Weber, University of New Mexico Press, 2003 (first published 1973); and *Trading in Santa Fe: John M. Kingsbury's Correspondence with James Josiah Web, 1853–1861*, edited by Jane Lenz Elder and David J. Weber, Southern Methodist University Press, 1996.

William S. Messervy, acting governor of New Mexico Territory in 1853. Photograph c. 1849. Courtesy of Palace of the Governors Photo Archives (NMHM/DCA), #088121.

375. What illustrated children's book tells the story of a young cottonwood sapling that eventually arrives in Santa Fe in 1834 as a yoke for oxen?

Tree in the Trail, by Holling Clancy Holling, tells about two hundred years of history on the Great Plains and the Santa Fe Trail. Traveling on the Santa Fe Trail between Missouri and the Santa Fe Plaza is a popular jaunt for contemporary travelers.

Read: *Tree in the Trail*, by Holling Clancy Holling, Houghton Mifflin, 1942; "In the Steps of History, A Modern Day Journey along the Santa Fe Trail Offers Glimpses of the Past," by Robin Martin, *Santa Fe New Mexican*, February 2010; "Accepting Trail's Challenge—Minus the Hardships," by Robin Martin, *Santa Fe New Mexican*, February 2010; *The Santa Fe Trail: Its History, Legends, and Lore*, by David Dary, Knopf, 2000; *The Santa Fe Trail: From Independence, Missouri, to Santa Fe, New Mexico*, by Arlan Dean, Power Kids Press, 2003; *Peter Becomes a Trail Man: The Story of a Boy's Journey on the Santa Fe Trail*, by William C. Carson, University of New Mexico Press, 2002; *The Santa Fe Trail*, by Judy Alter, Children's Press, 1998; *Along the Santa Fe Trail*, by Joan Myers and Marc Simmons, University of New Mexico Press, 1986; and *Tracing the Santa Fe Trail: Today's Views, Yesterday's Voices*, by Ronald J. Dulle, Mountain Press, 2011.

A mature elm tree growing in the inner courtyard of the Palace of the Governors.
Drawing by Carol Stanford, 2004. Courtesy of the artist.

376. In the 1600s, when Santa Fe was the only formal municipality in New Mexico and there were few strong presidios, what was expected of the leading citizens?

They were expected to be good farmers and to join the militia in times of danger.

Read: *The Spanish Frontier in North America*, by David J. Weber, Yale University Press, 1992.

On the Frontier. Linoleum block cut by Harold E. West, c. 1930s.

377. In colonial times, sharing limited water and pasturage was a challenge for settlers and soldiers; how many animals were deemed to be needed by the Santa Fe Presidio?

An expedition-size herd (*caballada*) numbered four- to five-hundred horses and mules; the entire presidio herd could number 1,200 or more. The herd was officially owned by the King of Spain. Regulations (*reglamentos*) in 1720 show that each soldier was expected to have six horses. Later, in 1772, the requirements stated that the captains were to provide each soldier with "six serviceable horses, one colt and one mule; the captain shall not permit any animal to be kept that cannot endure the greatest hardships."

The grazing areas (*parajes para comedores*) used by the presidio included Caja del Río, Santa Cruz, La Majada de Domínguez, Las Bocas, Los Cerrillos (east of La Cienega), San Marcos, and Maragua (near Galisteo). Most of these are in various parts of what is now Santa Fe County. In 1737 Governor Henrique de Olavide y Micheleña issued a government order (*bando*) stating that these grazing areas were for the presidio animals and were not to be used by any settler.

Read: "The Pastures of the Royal Horse Herd of the Santa Fe Presidio, 1692–1740," by Linda Tigges, in *All Trails Lead to Santa Fe*, Sunstone Press, 2010.

378. What popular liquor store in the 1950s took its name from an intersection of three streets in the downtown area?

Points Drive-In, also known as Five Points, owned by Joe Hernandez, was where Agua Fria, Sandoval, and Water Streets met before the area was redesigned.

Read: *Santa Fe: A Walk through Time*, by Kingsley Hammett, Gibbs Smith, 2004.

Points Drive-In liquor store. Courtesy of Palace of the Governors Photo Archives (NMHM/DCA), #061508.

379. A hotel magnate and a movie star celebrated their wedding in what private mansion whose garden wall was designed with Chapultapec Park, Mexico City, in mind?

Conrad Hilton and Zsa Zsa Gabor used the Salmon-Greer house, built in 1910, at the corner of Don Gaspar and the Paseo de Peralta, for their wedding in 1942. Nathan Greer had built a hotel in Albuquerque for his friend Conrad, nicknamed "Connie"; it was the first of the Hilton Hotels built outside of Texas. The Albuquerque hotel was called La Posada and now is the Hotel Andaluz.

Read: *The Santa Fe House: Historic Residences, Enchanting Adobes, and Romantic Revivals*, by Margaret M. Booker, Rizzoli, 2009.

380. What do George C. Bennett, William H. Brown, William Henry Jackson, and Benjamin Wittick have in common with regard to Santa Fe's image?

They are some of the earliest photographers to see Santa Fe through the camera's lens, in the late 1800s.

Read: *Through the Lens: Creating Santa Fe*, edited by Mary Anne Redding and Krista Elrick, Museum of New Mexico Press, 2008; and *Photography in New Mexico: From the Daguerreotype to the Present*, by Van Deren Coke, University of New Mexico Press, 1979.

381. There are at least two images of Our Lady of Guadalupe within a hundred feet of each other near the Guadalupe Church. Which one is visible only on sunny days?

The design in the shade cover across the street from the church casts an image of the Patroness of the Americas on the ground when the sun shines.

Look for this in the De Vargas Park, once nicknamed "the cheese park" because of the climbing sculptures in the shape of Swiss cheese.

What Is It?
(See Answer Key #59)

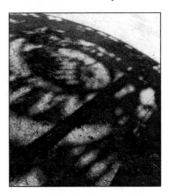

382. What army entered Santa Fe on March 10, 1862, and stayed less than a month?

The Confederate Army, under Major Henry Hopkins Sibley, left on April 7, after the defeat at Glorieta Pass.

Read: *The Civil War in New Mexico*, by F. Stanley, Sunstone Press, 2011 (first published 1960).

383. Saint Michael's College was established in 1859, chartered in 1874, and began a new program in 1947; what are two names the property has used since then?

The College of Santa Fe opened in 1966, and in 2010 the school reopened as the Santa Fe University of Art and Design.

Some other schools that are part of Santa Fe's eclectic education scene include the Academy for Technology and the Classics, Hypnotherapy Academy of America, Impact Personal Safety, Institute of American Indian Arts, New Mexico Academy of Healing Arts, New Mexico School for the Deaf, St. John's College, Santa Fe College of Beauty, Santa Fe Community College, Santa Fe Indian School, Santa Fe Institute, Santa Fe Martial Arts, Santa Fe Photographic Workshops, Santa Fe School for the Arts and Sciences, Santa Fe School of Cooking, School for Advanced Research, School of Aspen Santa Fe Ballet, Scherer Institute of Natural Healing, Southwest Acupuncture College, Southwestern College, University of Natural Medicine, and at least three extension universities: Highlands University, University of New Mexico, and University of Phoenix.

Read: *Choosing Colleges: How Social Class and Schools Structure Opportunity*, by Patricia M. McDonough, SUNY Press, 1997.

What Is It?
(See Answer Key #60)

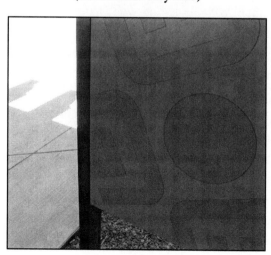

384. What were the earliest popularly elected government agencies in Santa Fe and other places in New Mexico?

Ayuntamientos were municipal councils, or town councils, also referred to as *cabildos*, instituted by Oñate in the late sixteenth century; they were modeled on medieval councils in Spain. After 1812 they became part of local government throughout New Mexico. They were composed of council members who represented the interests of their constituents and could relieve provincial governors of responsibility for issues such as water management. Except for Santa Fe's council, the *ayuntamientos* after 1836 were suppressed in favor of a more centralist government, when Nuevo México, as a department of Mexico, was divided into two prefectures: Rio Arriba (Upper River) and Rio Abajo (Lower River).

Read: *Dividing New Mexico's Waters, 1700–1912*, by John O. Baxter, University of New Mexico Press, 1997; and *Acequia Culture: Water, Land, and Community in the Southwest*, by José A. Rivera, University of New Mexico Press, 1998.

385. Concha Ortiz y Pino de Kleven was the first woman in the United States to hold a leadership position in a state legislature. What was that position?

The energetic and multitalented New Mexican became New Mexico State Democratic majority whip in 1941, after having been elected for three terms to the New Mexico Legislature.

Born María Concepción Ortiz y Pino in 1910, she was educated at Loretto Academy and was one of the first students to pursue Latin American studies; she later helped raise money for Zimmerman Library at the University of New Mexico. In order to help with her family's property in the Galisteo area, she became a rancher. She founded New Mexico's first vocational school, in Galisteo, and she taught woodworking and crafts at the school. Among the many causes she supported were letting women serve on juries, equalizing financing for urban and rural schools, and preserving traditional arts and crafts. Five U.S. presidents (Kennedy, Johnson, Nixon, Ford, and Carter) appointed her to various national boards, including the National Endowment for the Arts, the National Advisory Council to the National Institute of Health, and the National Commission on Architectural Barriers to the Rehabilitation of the Handicapped.

In 1943 she married Victor Kleven, a law professor at the University of New Mexico. She said, "Life is so interesting if you don't sit on it. . . . The worst thing, to me, is the accumulation of goods that don't help anyone."

The "Grand Dame of New Mexico" died in 2006, at age ninety-six. One of her proudest accomplishments was her suggestion of and then the establishment of what is now the familiar blue and white sign that shows handicap accessibility.

Read: ¡*Concha! Concha Ortiz y Pino, Matriarch of a 300-Year-Old New Mexico Legacy*, by Kathryn M. Córdova, bilingual edition, Gran Via, 2004; *Home Lands: How Women Made the West*, by Virginia Scharff and Caroline Brucken, University of California Press, 2010.

Concha Ortiz y Pino de Kleven, holding the handicap accessible sign she helped establish. It has become a familiar symbol worldwide. Photographer unknown. Photograph used with permission of Ana Pacheco.

386. Whom did fray Isidro de Ordóñez excommunicate in 1613, and why?

Don Pedro de Peralta, governor of New Mexico, was excommunicated and denounced by Ordóñez, the head of the Franciscan order in New Mexico, because he disliked Peralta and decided he was gaining undue power, which threatened the Church's position.

Earlier, Governor Peralta had sent troops to Taos to collect tribute, but Ordóñez had refused. Peralta and Ordóñez had a shouting match in church during mass, and later Peralta took a shot at Ordóñez. He missed. The turmoil prompted Ordóñez to relocate the custodial office to Santo Domingo. After being held in Santo Domingo on Ordóñez's orders, Peralta departed for Mexico City in August of 1613 to defend himself against the trumped up accusations; but he was ambushed, arrested, and held at Sandia convent, near Albuquerque, for about nine months; Ordóñez was in charge of New Mexico off and on until 1615, with the arrival of Bernardo de Ceballos, the governor Mexico City appointed for New Mexico.

Governor Ceballos at first appeared to side with Peralta, although Peralta was kept imprisoned while a review of his administration (*la residencia*) transpired; eventually the new governor decided to side with Ordóñez after all. Ordóñez was tyrannical and erratic, and life in the *villa* under his influence was a kind of "hell," according to one witness. It was worse for the Pueblo people. In the spring of 1614, Peralta was finally permitted to leave for Mexico City, where he successfully defended himself and was exonerated, and Ordóñez was reprimanded.

About a decade later, fray Esteban de Perea and fray Alonso de Benevides managed to have Governor Juan de Eulate sent away to Mexico City. The conflict between church and state resulted in continued friction that partially defined New Mexico's early history.

Read: "The Peralta-Ordóñez Affair and the Founding of Santa Fe," by Joseph P. Sánchez, in *Santa Fe: History of an Ancient City*, edited by David Grant Noble, School for Advanced Research Press, 2008; *Church and State in New Mexico*, by France V. Scholes, University of New Mexico Press, 1937; and "Colonial Governors, 1614–1625," by José Garcia, *La Herencia*, Summer 2008.

387. What was an early name for Cerrillos Road?

Camino de los Carros. The Spanish word *carro* means "cart," or carriage. The asterism (a group of stars that is not a true constellation) that looks like a cart or a dipper in the night sky is called *el Carro Mayor*, or the Big Dipper; it is part of the constellation Ursa Major. In Latin America and elsewhere, including New Mexico, *carro* has come to mean an automobile or car.

See the deed records at the Santa Fe County courthouse showing the road used as a boundary marker, the south boundary of the Cristóbal Nieto land grant, in the Analco barrio. Also check out *A Dictionary of New Mexico and Colorado Spanish*, by Rubén Cobos, 2003; and *Constellations: The Stars and Stories*, by Chris Sasaki, Sterling, 2003.

Sign along Cerrillos Road, part of a movable display show in 2011 called
Haiku Roadsign Project, by Axle Contemporary, a gallery that travels around in a van.
Photograph used with permission of Axle Contemporary Gallery.

What Is It?
(See Answer Key #61)

388. Which current Santa Fe wood business was begun as a wood, coal, freight-demolition, and excavation company in 1935?

Jesus Rios and Teresa Gabaldon Rios started the Rios Wood and Coal Yard, on Abeyta Street, in Teresa's grandmother's yard.

Read: "Warm Heart," by Monica Soto, *Santa Fe New Mexican*, October 29, 1996.

Rios wood yard, on Camino del Monte Sol, near Canyon Road. Photograph by E. West, 2011.

389. How many historic districts are there in Santa Fe?

As of 2012, there were five historic districts.

A historic district is an area of land to which the city has added standards to the land-use zoning to preserve the historical integrity of the neighborhood. The Santa Fe National Register Historic District was the first to be designated in the city, in 1972; it includes the core original downtown and east side neighborhoods. The second district to be designated was the Don Gaspar Area Historic District, in the South Capitol neighborhood; the third is the Transition Historic District; the fourth is the West Side–Guadalupe Historic District; and the fifth is the Historic Review Historic District, which covers part of the southeast area of town. Historic districts cover approximately 20 percent of the city's area.

Santa Fe also has three archaeological districts: the Historic Downtown Archaeological Review District, the River and Trails Archaeological Review District, and the Suburban Archaeological Review District. The last two have expanded beyond the 2010 city limits.

Read: *The Politics of Historic Districts: A Primer for Grassroots Preservation*, by William E. Schmickle, Altamira Press, 2006. Also, see Historic Design Review maps at City Hall.

390. Maria Benitez Teatro Flamenco, the Santa Fe Chamber Music Festival, the Santa Fe Concert Association, Santa Fe Desert Chorale, the Santa Fe Opera, Santa Fe Pro Musica, the Santa Fe Symphony and Chorus, and Santa Fe Stages are the groups that helped start what organization?

The Lensic Performing Arts Center, on San Francisco Street. Santa Fe's nonprofit performing arts center opened in 2001. Housed in the Lensic theater, which was built in 1931 by Nathan Salmon and John Greer and designed by the Boller Brothers architects, the building boasts an architectural style that has been called an atmospheric mixture of Spanish, Arabic, and Renaissance.

One of the organizations that regularly utilizes the Lensic is the Lannan Foundation, which offers a lecture series featuring well-known authors and political figures.

Read: "Curtain Opens on Reincarnated Lensic," by Michelle Pentz, *Albuquerque Journal*, April 22, 2001, and "Echos of Opulence: The Lensic," by Paul Weideman, *Santa Fe New Mexican*, April 15, 2011.

What Is It?
(See Answer Key #62)

391. Why was Santa Fe considered the only fireproof city in the United States in the early 1880s?

Santa Fe was widely and erroneously regarded as fireproof because of the adobe construction of its buildings. A major fire in 1892 gutted the territorial capitol building, though it was built of stone.

Read: "Yesterday's Heroes: The History of Organized Fire Fighting in New Mexico," by Marc Simmons, *Santa Fe New Mexican*, January 11, 2003; and *The Santa Fe Volunteer Fire Department: A History of Its Life and Reputation*, by Raymond Otis, Santa Fe New Mexican Publishing Corporation, 1933.

Fire on San Francisco Street, looking east toward St. Francis Cathedral, c. 1911–1920.
Courtesy of Palace of the Governors Photo Archives (NMHM/DCA), #012158.

Two young Red Cross girls in Santa Fe, date unknown.
Courtesy of Palace of the Governors Photo Archives (NMHM/DCA), #014079.

392. What is the difference between a *farolito* and a *luminaria*?

A *farolito* is a small "lantern" that can be set on a wall and grouped in decorative ways, may be carried, and is usually made by putting a votive candle in sand at the bottom of a small paper bag. Mass-produced, flat-bottomed paper bags were commonplace after 1850, and this probably contributed to the *farolito*'s widespread use. A *luminaria* is a small bonfire for light and warmth. Both *farolitos* and *luminarias* are used in Santa Fe during festive occasions, especially for Christmas Eve.

Farol is Spanish for "lantern," or lamp, and comes from the word *faro*, which means "lighthouse," or large lantern. *Faro* comes from the Latin *pharus*, which means "lighthouse," which in turn comes from the Greek word for lighthouse, referring to one of the Seven Wonders of the Ancient World, the Pharos (Lighthouse) of Alexandria, in Egypt, on the small island of Pharos, just off the coast of the Greek city of Alexandria. Constructed in about 280 B.C., the tower was about four hundred feet tall; it guided mariners in the eastern Mediterranean Sea with its fire and reflective mirrors at night and as a landmark by day.

Farolito is the diminutive of *farol*. Though the word *luminaria* is the plural form of the Latin *luminare,* it is used as if it were singular. (By the way, *bonfire* comes from the medieval "bone-fires," made of animal bones and rubbish.)

A traditional custom concerning *farolitos* existed in Mexico, and before that Spain, where the lamplighter, who was also the night watchman (*el sereno*), would call out "*Sereno, sereno*" as he lit the lanterns in the evening, announcing his availability to help people into their locked houses at night, since he was entrusted with the keys to their compounds. (*Sereno* also means "calm" or "all's well.") The lamplights on the lampposts were either ball shaped or octagonal lanterns.

A Santa Fe restaurant and bar in continuous use on Canyon Road since 1835 has been called El Farol because during the nineteenth century a lantern was hung out to announce when food and drink were ready to be served, so fishermen, sheep herders, and farmers from up the canyon would know to stop there on their way back into town.

In Santa Fe and northern New Mexico, Mexico, and Spain everyone knows what *farolitos* and *luminarias* are, but it seems the rest of the world gets them confused. The *American Heritage Dictionary of the English Language* (fourth edition, Houghton Mifflin, 2000) is an example of a good dictionary that, although it refers to New Mexico, has inaccurate, supposedly regional definitions of *farolito* and *luminaria*, confusing the two.

Read: "You Say 'Luminaria,' We Say You're Wrong," by Barbara Harrelson, *Santa Fe New Mexican*, November 26, 2005; *Santa Fe Icons: 50 Symbols of the City Different*, by Camille Flores, Globe Pequot, 2010; *The Seven Wonders of the Ancient World*, by Diana Bentley, Oxford University Press, 2001; and *The Farolitos of Christmas*, by Rudolfo Anaya, Hyperion Books for Children, 1995.

Farolitos on a Stone Wall. Pen and ink drawing by Cathie Sullivan, 2011. Courtesy of the artist.

La Fonda's *farolitos* light up the night during winter holidays. Photograph by T. Harmon Parkhurst, c. 1927. Courtesy of Palace of the Governors Photo Archives (NMHM/DCA), # 054312.

After the holidays a Pueblo-style building still displays their *farolitos,* sometimes called "electrolitos" when they are lit by electricity, while the territorial-style building on the right has put its farolitos away. These buildings are on Washington Avenue, north of Palace Avenue. Photograph by E. West, 2011.

393. What do Santa Fe waitresses and waiters mean when they ask, "Red, green, or Christmas?"

Red and green are the colors of chile sauces, and you can answer "Christmas" if you want both with your meal. All chiles start off green. The ones called "green" are picked when they are still green, roasted, peeled, and often served chopped into a sauce, or they may be stuffed. The chiles that are allowed to ripen until red are usually dried, ground, and then cooked into a fine, thickened red-chile sauce, usually served with the main course along with beans and vegetables. Chiles can be strung in a *ristra* (a rope) for drying, as can be done with garlic and onions, and these *ristras* are often hung as useful decorations.

The spicy-hot chile fruit, a stimulant and an endorphin-releaser, is a member of the nightshade family, genus Capsicum (from the Greek, meaning "to bite"); it is not technically a pepper. It retains its heat level whether cooked, dried, or frozen. Originating in the Americas perhaps as early as about 7000 B.C., chile was first brought to Spain in the 1490s. Spanish and Portuguese trade helped spread its use around the world. Chile in varying degrees of heat figures prominently in the cuisine of many countries, including Algeria, Bhutan, China, Hungary, India, Japan, Korea, Nigeria, the Philippines, Tunisia, and Turkey. New Mexico and Mexico favor hot chile, but their "mother country," Spain, does not.

"Red or green?" is the official New Mexico state question.

To learn more about this hot topic, read: *The Complete Chile Pepper Book: A Gardener's Guide to Choosing, Growing, Preserving, and Cooking*, by Dave DeWitt and Paul Bosland, Timber Press, 2009; *Red Chile Bible: Southwestern Classic and Gourmet Recipes*, by Kathleen Hansel and Audrey Jenkins, Clear Light, 1997; *Green Chile Bible: Award-Winning New Mexico Recipes*, compiled and edited by the Albuquerque Tribune, Clear Light, 1993; *A Garlic Testament: Seasons on a Small New Mexico Farm*, by Stanley Crawford, University of New Mexico Press, 1998; and *The Chile Chronicles: Tales of a New Mexico Harvest*, by Carmella Padilla, Museum of New Mexico Press, 1997.

394. Who was the director of the New Mexico Legislative Council Service who established a greenhouse on top of the capitol building rotunda?

Clay Buchanan used donated funds to start the greenhouse in the Roundhouse, which he maintained for about twenty years, until he died in office, in 1988. It was said that his favorite tree was the cottonwood.

Read: "'Capitol Gardener' Clay Buchanan Dies," by David Roybal, *Santa Fe New Mexican*, April 23, 1988; *Trees and Shrubs of New Mexico*, by Jack Carter, Mimbres Publisher, 1997;

New Mexico Gardener's Guide, by Judith Phillips, Thomas Nelson, 2005; *Plant-Driven Design: Creating Gardens That Honor Plants, Place, and Spirit*, by Scott Ogden and Lauren Springer Ogden, Timber Press, 2008; and *A Tree Is Nice*, by Janice May Udry, Harper, 1956.

395. Who said, "There are no nobodies in Santa Fe. Here everyone is *somebody*"?

Erna Fergusson. Writer, historian, and storyteller, she was sometimes referred to as New Mexico's First Lady of Letters. Fergusson may have been the first person to point out, in her 1934 *Mexican Cookbook*, that the Anglo interpretation of *frijoles refritos* as "refried beans" was incorrect. In fact, *frijoles refritos* translates to "well-fried beans," and the dish consists of beans (usually pinto beans) that have been cooked in water until soft, often mashed, and sometimes fried—but not "refried."

Read: "A Brief Encounter with JFK: New Mexico Author Met 35th President in Albuquerque," by Marc Simmons, *Santa Fe New Mexican*, May 14, 2011; *Dancing Gods: Indian Ceremonials of New Mexico and Arizona*, by Erna Fergusson, University of New Mexico Press, 1991 (first published 1931); *New Mexico: A Pageant of Three Peoples*, by Erna Fergusson, University of New Mexico Press, 1973 (first published 1951); and *Mexican Cookbook*, by Erna Fergusson, University of New Mexico Press, 1969 (first published 1934).

396. What are some of the mountains and hills Santa Feans and visitors can see from various parts of the city?

If you start by looking toward the north and sweep around clockwise, here is what you will see: the Sangre de Cristo Mountains (the southern end of the Rocky Mountains), including Aspen Peak, Santa Fe Baldy, Lake Peak, Tesuque Peak, Atalaya, Sun Mountain, and Moon Mountain; the Ortiz Mountains; Los Cerrillos; Sandia Mountain; Tetilla Peak; and the Jemez Mountains, including the distinctive Chicoma Mountain, also known as Santa Clara Peak.

Get a map and take a look. Also, read "The Sangre de Cristo Mountains," by William deBuys, in *Telling New Mexico: A New History*, edited by Marta Weigle, with Frances Levine and Louise Stiver, Museum of New Mexico Press, 2009; and *The Mountains of New Mexico*, by Robert Hixson Julyan, University of New Mexico Press, 2006.

Mountain Mahogany. **Pen and ink drawing by Cathie Sullivan, 2011, based on her original screen print, 1996. Courtesy of the artist.**

The artist comments on this shrub:

"Mountain mahogany is a hardy citizen of the foothills of the Southwest mountains. It requires little water and is happy in rocky, mineralized soils. Like the seed of another Rose family member, mountain mahogany has spiral-shaped, self-planting seeds that twist their way into the ground by absorbing soil moisture. The 'feathered' spiral erects itself on the soil and proceeds slowly to twist and bury the seed carried on its tip. Mountain mahogany has deep genealogical roots in New Mexico—roots that go back 146 million years, to the Cretaceous Period of our planet."

397. "La Villa Real de la Santa Fé de San Francisco de Asis" is sometimes said to be the official full name of New Mexico's capital. Is this name correct?

No, it is not correct. There is no documentation for the long name for Santa Fe, which is a relatively modern, touristic romanticism that has gained some popularity, including becoming part of the Santa Fe city seal. The translation for the long name is "The Royal Town of the Holy Faith of Saint Francis of Assisi." In 1609 and 1610, don Pedro de Peralta, the first official governor, was instructed to establish the town as the capital of the "Kingdom of New Mexico"; he used the name *la villa Real de Santa Fé* (the Royal town of Holy Faith). *Real* connotes the privileges (and responsibilities) that went along with the elevation to a *villa real*. The name Santa Fe, in proper Spanish, takes an accent, as in *Santa Fé*, but the accent is usually omitted in New Mexico.

Read: *The Place Names of New Mexico*, by Robert Hixson Julyan, University of New Mexico Press, 1998; and "A History of the Histories of Santa Fe," by Stanley M. Hordes, in *Santa Fe: History of an Ancient City*, edited by David Grant Noble, School for Advanced Research, 2008.

398. What do the dates and the symbols on the City of Santa Fe's seal represent?

1610 = the official founding of the city; 1821 = Mexican independence from Spain; 1846 = the beginning of the U.S. occupation; the castle and the lion = the Castile and Leon regions of Spain; the Mexican eagle = New Mexico under Mexican rule; and the stars and stripes = the U.S. government.

One image of the seal is on the floor of City Hall, at the main entrance, on Lincoln Avenue. Most of the large trash containers used by Santa Feans feature the Santa Fe shield, which is in the center of the city seal.

399. How may have the three most significant trails into and out of Santa Fe influenced the composition of the town and its people?

El Camino Real, the Spanish trails (including the so-called Old Spanish Trail), and the Santa Fe Trail are trails that lead into and away from a center where many different people and ideas have visited and existed; this convergence probably has contributed to an awareness of the importance of inclusivity and regeneration because of the multiplicity of cultures that traded with, as well as raided, each other. Santa Fe is not so much a melting pot as a meeting place. As one historian has said, "New Mexicans know and have inherited the idea that they are richer and better off because of all the cultures and people who have flourished in the state." This may be especially true of the City of Santa Fe.

Read: *Converging Streams: Art of the Hispanic and Native American Southwest*, edited by William Wroth and Robin Farwell Gavin, Museum of Spanish Colonial Art, 2010; and *New Mexico: Past and Future*, by Thomas E. Chávez, University of New Mexico Press, 2006.

400. The debate about the settlement and founding of the City of Santa Fe is ongoing; what is the range of years around which the debate occurs?

Historians ascribe the beginning of the settlement or the founding of the *villa* of Santa Fe to anywhere from 1605 to 1610. Most agree that the official founding occurred in 1610.

Read: "The Viceroy's Order Founding the Villa of Santa Fe: A Reconsideration, 1605–1610," by James Ivey, as well as the foreword, by Marc Simmons, and the introduction, by Joseph P. Sánchez, in *All Trails Lead to Santa Fe*, Sunstone Press, 2010.

Answer Key
to
What Is It? Images

What Is It?
(See Answer Key #63)

Two Burros. Linoleum block cut by Harold E. West, c. 1930s. A smaller version of this image was used as the repeated cartouche or ornamental figure between questions in this book. (They add up to more than 800 burros.) Originally, the linoleum block was inked and then used to decorate skirts, aprons, and various textiles by making a continuous pattern when printed side by side.

1) *Family.* Clay sculpture by Roxanne Swentzell, 2009. The fourteen-foot-wide bas relief sculpture is attached to a wall in the main lobby of the Santa Fe Community Convention Center. The City of Santa Fe commissioned the work as an artistic statement about community. The artist commented about what inspired her: "Santa Fe was originally a pueblo village long before the Europeans arrived. The pueblos were all about community . . . [W]hat I want all of us to remember [is] it takes a whole community to raise a child to become a healthy part of the Whole."

Roxanne Swentzell, of Santa Clara Pueblo, comes from a family of artists, potters, and sculptors. She studied at the Institute for American Indian Arts, in Santa Fe. The photograph is used courtesy of the artist and her family.

2) Route 66 sign along Old Santa Fe Trail, south of Buena Vista Street.

3) Our Lady of Guadalupe Church, at the intersection of Guadalupe and Agua Fria Streets.

4) "No Dumping—Flows to Arroyo/No Descargue Basura—Desagua al Arroyo/Only Rain in the Drain"

These words appear on a sidewalk sign along the western side of Old Santa Fe Trail, north of East De Vargas Street. The drain flows to an arroyo that in turn flows to the Santa Fe River. This sign is not seen in most U.S. cities, but there are many signs like it around Santa Fe.

5) The Fray Angélico Chávez History Library, on Washington Street, is housed in the building that used to be the Santa Fe Public Library. The edge of the almost life-size bronze sculpture of Fray Angélico Chávez by Donna Quasthoff, 1997, is on the right in the photograph. The cornerstones at ground level behind the statue show the dates of the several renovations to the building: 1907; 1932; 1963; 1996. The public library moved across the street to its current location in 1987.

6) Photograph by Charles Lee of the life-size bronze bust of Bronson Cutting, by Lee Friedlander, 1973, on the New Mexico State Capitol grounds. Photograph used with permission.

7) Painted sketch of Bernard Parachou, the French dairy farmer, part of whose property remains as a park called Frenchy's Field, on Agua Fria Street. The image is a detail from the left side of the City Hall mural by Jerry West, featured on the cover of this book. Courtesy of the artist.

8) Spitz clock face at night (at the corner of Lincoln and Palace Avenues, near the New Mexico Museum of Art).

9) Lensic Performing Arts Center, outdoor plaster wall decoration.

10) Santa Fe River watershed sign, at the corner of Galisteo Street and West Alameda, looking south. The Bataan Building is in the background.

11) View of Tetilla Peak, heading west along Airport Road.

12) The city seal, on the floor at City Hall, Lincoln Avenue entrance; the feet belong to Mayor David Coss, 2011.

13) Acequia Madre in the Railyard Park.

14) An old acequia passing under the bridge near the intersection of Third and Hopewell Streets.

15) The arroyo near Fort Marcy Park, looking west.

16) Bronze life-size bust of Miguel Chavez, by Eugenie Shonnard, in St. Michael's High School sculpture park, on Siringo Road. Although Chavez attended the school for only one year, he was inspired to become a generous donor to the institution in 1927. He died in 1928.

17) A nighttime photograph of the handicap-accessible ramp up to the Santa Fe Plaza bandstand, designed by architect Beverly Spears.

18) Plaque honoring *Oga Po Ge*, sometimes spelled *Ogapogeh* or *O'gha Po'oge*, in the sidewalk on the eastern side of the Santa Fe Plaza.

19) The St. Francis Cathedral Basilica's bronze doors were commissioned to Donna Quastoff in 1986; the twenty bas-relief images include this image of Kateri Tekakwitha, the first Native American from North America to be canonized a saint. She was a seventeenth-century Mohawk-Algonquin woman. There is also a statue of her in front of the building.

20) Close-up of the sun rays on the Shrine of Our Lady of Guadalupe, northeast of Guadalupe Church, near the northern end of the Camino Real de Adentro, the royal road that connected Mexico with northern New Spain. The life-size sculpture is by doña Georgina Farias, of Mexico City. It was placed in its permanent location in July 2008.

21) The doorway to Olive Rush's home, now the Quaker Meeting House, on Canyon Road.

22) Loretto Chapel window.

23) The church bells of First Presbyterian, on Grant Avenue.

24) A late-1800s stained-glass window showing the Star of David in the Episcopal Church of the Holy Faith. Visible from inside the church, when the sun is shining, it honors the community connection between various faiths.

25) The dove of peace sign at St. Anne Parrish, a Catholic church at Alicia and Hickox Streets.

26) Bataan Memorial Eternal Flame, on Don Gaspar Avenue.

27) Part of the sign for El Museo Cultural de Santa Fe, on Camino de la Familia, at the northern end of Railyard Park. The center showcases and supports Hispanic art, culture, and history in Santa Fe.

28) Hitching post on Washington Avenue, near the northeast corner of the Santa Fe Plaza. It is dedicated to "American Cattlemen and Their Horses, 1776–1976" by the Roadrunner Cowbelles (Santa Fe women's auxiliary of the Cattlemen's Association).

29) The Unitarian Universalist Congregation's Wayside Pulpit sign, along Galisteo Street, north of Barcelona Road.

30) Courtyard at Capital High School, on Paseo del Sol, off Jaguar Drive.

31) The wall of the Salmon-Greer house at the corner of Don Gaspar and Paseo de Peralta. The design was inspired by Mexico City's Chapultapec Park.

32) The Tibetan tower at Kagyu Shenpen Kunshab Buddhist Center and Bodhi Stupa, on Ksk Lane, off Airport Road. The Buddhist center is a member of the Tibetan Association of Santa Fe, a nonprofit organization focused on preserving Tibetan culture and committed to actively engaging with other cultures and communities.

33) El Toro, the Rodeo Bull.

34) Bike route along the Acequia Trail, near Baca Street.

35) Mural at Randall Davey House, at the National Audubon Society, on Upper Canyon Road. The two burros depicted in the mural were permitted to stop and refresh themselves, eating apples from the Daveys' orchard, in the 1920s, on their way back into town after wood-gathering expeditions with their owners.

36) Two young Santa Fe children and their spaniel (on a leash) take in the view from on top of the rock pile in the Railyard Park. A nearby sheet-metal sculpture of a twelve-foot-high, twenty-foot-long dog with a bench swing under its belly keep them company. *The Yard Dog*, by Don Kennell, was on temporary loan to the Railyard Park as part of a program aimed at displaying contemporary art in the park.

37) This is a close-up of the eye of the life-size bronze buffalo sculpture by Allan Houser and his students, now located near the center of campus at the Institute of American Indian Arts, on Avan Nu Po Road.

38) Santa Fe High School Demon Country sign, in the stadium.

39) Part of the sign on the Catron Building, on the eastern side of the Santa Fe Plaza.

40) There is always some new construction or renovation happening in Santa Fe. This is the crane at the construction site of the Santa Fe County Judicial Complex, District Court House, in 2011 and 2012. Across the street, in the foreground, is the defunct siren on top of the Old Fire Station, at the corner of Sandoval and Montezuma Streets.

41) Old Spanish Trail plaque, on the wall at 72 West Marcy Street (La Boca restaurant).

42) Scaffolding for Zozobra.

43) Detail from Frederico Vigil's large fresco mural, *Treaty of Guadalupe Hidalgo*, 1997, in the Santa Fe County Court House Chambers. This close-up features the words "Protect, Preserve, Cultural Traditions, Pristine Resources, Diverse Communities."

44) The Santa Fe Water History Museum, in the restored hydroelectric plant, at the intersection of Camino Cabra and Upper Canyon Road.

45) The Institute of American Indian Arts Museum, across from St. Francis Cathedral.

46) Santa Fe Plaza obelisk with two birds sitting on top. An obelisk is a specialized kind of stele.

47) "33" is one of the numbered spaces under the Palace of the Governors portal. Native American artisans hoping to display their wares in one of these coveted spots are chosen by lottery, under the jurisdiction of the Palace of the Governors Portal Program.

48) Perhaps the most popular image of the patron saint of the city of Santa Fe: Saint Francis, *San Francisco de Asis*, a bronze sculpture by Andrea Bacigalupa, 1980, near Santa Fe City Hall, at the corner of Lincoln Avenue and Marcy Street. The intimate, smaller than life-size sculpture features St. Francis with a prairie dog. Photograph used with permission of Andrea Bacigalupa.

49) Bus stop across from Santa Fe Prep School, on Camino de Cruz Blanca

50) Eye of the New Mexico Rail Runner Express train, seen at the Santa Fe depot, in the Railyard district.

51) Fairview Cemetery plot plat.

52) Warehouse 21 sign.

53) A Santa Fe Trail marker along Old Pecos Trail, north of Barcelona Road, across the road from the Center for Contemporary Arts, the Armory for the Arts Theater, the Bataan Memorial Military Museum, and the Santa Fe Children's Museum.

54) Carlos Vierra plaque, one of many honoring artists and writers, in the sidewalk in front of the New Mexico Museum of Art, near the Plaza. Vierra is usually credited as the first professional artist to settle in Santa Fe. He came in 1904 to recover from tuberculosis.

55) Late afternoon tree shadow on the western wall of the Santa Fe Community Convention Center, near the corner of Grant Avenue and Marcy Street.

56) Looking west across Don Gaspar Avenue, north of Paseo de Peralta. The bronze statue is a Civilian Conservation Corps worker, "Iron Mike," symbolizing the millions of young men who served in President Franklin D. Roosevelt's conservation projects. Fifty-five thousand New Mexicans were members of the CCC. The sculpture was designed by Jim Brothers and produced by Sergey Kazaryan at the Elliot Gantz & Company Foundry, in New York. It is one of more than fifty similar statues in thirty-four states. The CCC Alumni instigated the effort to place statues across the United States.

57) The mansard roof (sometimes called a "French" roof, a popular architectural style of the late 1800s) of the old New West Academy building, now offices, at the corner of Garfield and Guadalupe Streets.

58) Outdoor trash container at the New Mexico State Capitol.

59) The shadow cast on a sunny day by the steel sculpture shade cover in De Vargas park, at the corner of Guadalupe and De Vargas Streets. The sculpture is one of a two-part installation, *Trail of Dreams, Trail of Ghosts,* by Catherine Widgery. Look carefully at the shadow on the grass and you'll see the image of Our Lady of Guadalupe.

60) A Santa Fe Community College sign on campus.

61) Detail of a four-sided stele, one of several bus-stop markers along Cerrilllos Road that have been inscribed and/or decorated to recognize the many trails and roads into and out of Santa Fe. The stelae were designed and built by Juan and Patricia Navarette and made of concrete. The imagery decorating this stele is by Mary Antonia Wood and Christopher Gibson and is composed of inscribed words and images with steel and rock attached to the concrete. This approximately six-foot-tall marker, which honors Route 66, is at the bus stop in front of the Trailer Ranch on Cerrillos Road, north of Zafarano Road, and is part of the project titled *Cuentos del Camino/Road Stories* by Wood and Gibson. Santa Fe elementary school students were involved in the research for the project, which included gathering stories and learning about the history of various Santa Fe trails. This piece is one of many in the City of Santa Fe Art in Public Places Collection, commissioned by the City of Santa Fe Arts Commission, established in 1987.

62) The 1909 Santa Fe Railroad Depot station, near the terminus of the New Mexico Rail Runner Express and Lamy spur railroads.

63) It is not known who this elegant mystery woman is. The flag in the background shows 48 stars, so the year is probably after New Mexico became a state. The woman, a local or a visitor, is walking toward the Santa Fe Plaza on West San Francisco Street in the early 1900s, when cars were still sharing the roads with horses and wagons. Photograph by Wesley Bradfield, c. 1918. Courtesy of Palace of the Governors Photo Archives (NMHM/DCA), #014142.

64) Sign at the northwest corner of Palace Avenue and Washington Street, near the Plaza.

65) One of two stone sculptures about two feet high by Hanna Mecklem Smith on either side of the entry to the atrium of the Santa Fe Public Library, on Washington Street. Smith worked as a WPA artist in the 1930s.

All photographs are by E. West unless otherwise noted.

Recuerdos y Sueños de Santa Fe
Cover Image Key

This diagram relates to the mural at Santa Fe City Hall called *Recuerdos y Sueños de Santa Fe,* by Jerry West (oil on gessoed plastered wall, 1989). The mural is in the two-story entrance alcove off the building-permits offices of the Land Use Department. If you are standing in front of the mural, you will be able to use the artist's diagram and corresponding notes to learn more about the images within the work.

(If you are not in front of the mural, see the cover of this book.)

**Mural key notes written by the artist, Jerry West, in 1989,
with some revisions and corrections made for this book.**

1) This shows a building that stood on the present site of City Hall, where you can see the mural. [The city hall in use in 2010, four hundred years after the founding of the *villa* of Santa Fe, was built in the 1950s, on city land, at the corner of Lincoln Avenue and Marcy Street.] Originally all of this property north of the Plaza to the federal courthouse was part of Fort Marcy military complex. With the decline of need for a fort in the 1890s, President Theodore Roosevelt by proclamation gave over the federal land to the City of Santa Fe. The city built a major school building in 1903 to 1905. It served as a grade school from then until the late 1930s, when it was taken over as part of Santa Fe High School. The building was torn down in 1951 to make room for the present building.

2) Around the old Catron building one can see throngs of students from all times engaging in typical childhood activities, from ball playing and kite flying to jumping rope, yo-yoing, bicycle riding, and playing hopscotch, jacks, red rover, crack-the-whip, tops, and marbles. A number of the young people have animals. Note also the pigeons flying from the old building.

3) Early citizens of Santa Fe, from early conquistadors to explorers, freighters, immigrants in carts and wagons, and cowboy sorts like Rudy Sena and Anayas and their brother buddies, join up in a fantasy procession with the many students filing out of the old building.

4) This series of buildings has some slight historical references, including to Brady Majors, who for years had a business establishment on this block. There is also a glimpse at the old Batrite supermarket. Behind these buildings can be seen burros in shade, cats on a roof, an old well, dogs, children, a woman hanging up clothes, men talking, old pickup trucks, and an old woman returning from vespers. In front can be observed vintage cars and many Santa Fe people from all times.

5) This is a reference to the first Little Chief Grill, a small Santa Fe family café that became a landmark until the late 1970s.

6) This corner bakery was active from the late 1930s through the 1960s. Note the Victorian house (from the 1890s) between the bakery and the café.

7) This reference to a photograph of the 1921 Fiesta parade includes an early airplane riding on an ancient flatbed truck and a Mac truck.

8) This composite image was taken from photos and from memory. In 1926 George Armijo and Gus Baumann made the first giant *toro* for a Fiesta melodrama performance behind old St. Mike's. Later, Will Shuster developed a *toro* that became the symbol of Rodeo de Santa Fe.

9) This early, archetypal Zozobra is more a mythical character, an enigmatic person being burned. The first Zozobra was put together by local people, including artists such as Will

Shuster and Gus Bauman. They burned him in the lot [where the main branch of the Santa Fe Public Library now sits, along Washington Avenue], and afterwards they had a great *baile* [dance] in the old armory, north of the Palace of the Governors.

10) This image, based on photos from 1900 to 1920 of Corpus Cristi processions, shows young women going through first communions.

11) This image derives from a 1921 photo of a Fiesta Queen float showing a young woman with giant star behind her head and an old Ford totally draped in cloth.

12) This generalized condensed block of buildings shows where Sears, Cartrights Hardware, and the Hewitt house used to be. It is also a reference to the New Mexico Museum of Art building, finished in 1917, which served as a prototype for the development of the "Santa Fe Style."

13) This image is taken from composite photos depicting Sisters of Charity and their involvement with Santa Fe, from the 1870s to the present day.

14) In Santa Fe's early days, outdoor shrines were constructed for special occasions. This one comes from a 1910 photo showing an altar for Corpus Cristi day.

15) This is a composite complex of the Palace of the Governors.

16) This composite image was taken from 1920s photos showing governors from surrounding pueblos wearing ceremonial feathers at Fiestas.

17) During Fiestas in the 1920s, the Palace of the Governors was decorated with giant masks.

18) This image is a reference to a huge adobe building that stood on the west side of the Plaza in the late 1870s. Many persons appear from different periods of history.

19) This is Bernard (Frenchy) Parachou, with his old delivery truck. Frenchy originally came from the French Pyrennes to Cuba, then to Canada, and then, in the 1920s, to Santa Fe. For years he ran a one-man dairy on Agua Fria Street.

20) This composite image derives from many photos of the procession of La Conquistadora, from 1887 to the 1950s.

21) This image comes from many photos of orphans from St. Vincent's Orphanage. The orphanage was operated by the Sisters of Charity from 1880 to the 1960s.

22) This image comes from a 1920 photo of Los Matachines. The ceremony is extremely old and embodies elements of Catholic and pagan beliefs.

23) This is a reference to a bandstand that stood in the center of the Plaza during the 1860s.

24) This image derives from an 1880 photo of the all-Black Regimental 9th Cavalry Band. They played on the Plaza for the military as well as for citizens, and they were extremely popular.

25) This is Tito Griego, a man who served Santa Fe for many years as a neighborhood grocer. He becomes a stand-in for a whole generation of concerned, compassionate local businessmen.

26) This group of local Santa Feans, too numerous to name specifically, represent men and women who are singers and musicians, a fundamental part of the fabric of Santa Fe life.

27) This is image comes from a 1900s photograph of two girls on West San Francisco Street riding sidesaddle on burros.

28) From 1926 to the 1960s, Santa Fe conducted all of its Fiestas on the Plaza. The Tio Vivo, the old hand-operated merry-go-round, was a favorite part of some of those great celebrations. In 1943 there was also the Tio Voladero, a hand-operated revolving swing, very popular with young people.

29) For years this man, Victor Feliberto "Tisnado" Valdez, ran a café called El Monterrey on West San Francisco Street. He was also a deeply concerned community leader.

30) This image is taken from a 1930s photo of a Fiesta couple dancing in a street dance. Archie West becomes a stand-in for all dancers past, present, and into the future.

31) This is a man who grew up in Santa Fe's San Acacio area. He apprenticed under some of the Cinco Pintores, including Josef Bakos, and became a muralist, a *santero*, a furniture maker, a builder, and a theological scholar.

32) This monument was erected in the center of the Plaza after the Union was successful in the 1862 battle against Confederate soldiers at Apache Canyon. The monument was dedicated in 1867, at which time many documents and trinkets were placed underneath it.

33) The Franciscan order of missionaries were for centuries the dominant order allowed into the New World and into New Mexico. Their efforts form a colorful and important segment of New Mexico history. These are all local guys as stand-ins.

34) B. B. Dunn was for years a private secretary to U.S. senator Bronson M. Cutting. Later he was a writer and a permanent fixture sitting in the lobby of La Fonda, ready to interview almost anyone.

35) This is Shorty Martinez, local ambassador of good will, volunteer street sweeper, and carrier of boxes. (His brother was chief of police.) Nobody loved the Fiestas more than Shorty, and he symbolizes the caring and openness of Santa Fe.

36) In 1935 we had a Fiesta Queen by the name of Carmen Espinosa. This image is derived from a photo taken at that Fiesta. The women are contemporary stand-ins.

37) This group of people all have deep rural roots in and around Santa Fe.

38) These two guys symbolize the long, colorful, passionate rivalry between St. Mike's and Santa Fe High: the Horsemen and the Demons. There has been only one tie game in the entire history of their competition: the football game of 1967.

39) This is Carlos Gallegos, a stand-in for all concerned businessmen, thoughtful citizens, and city council persons.

40) In the 1880s Solomon Spitz, from Germany, rode into Santa Fe from the South Dakota goldfields. He started a jewelry store and watch-repair shop. His son Bernard followed in the business until the 1970s. When the store finally closed its doors, the family gave the old clock to the City of Santa Fe.

41) In the early 1900s Dave Gallegos and his grandfather set up a shoe shop on Burro Alley, where they also made saddles.

42) Flavio Gonzales built houses of adobe and mud plaster and shared his love and skill with others. He was one of the great old-time, classical builders in Santa Fe.

43) Jesus Rios originally came from Durango, Mexico, as a young man with his father, who was working on the railroad. He worked mines and construction and finally bought a small store near Guadalupe Church. After marrying Teresa Gabaldon, he moved to the Abeyta Street/ Canyon Road area, in the 1930s, and started a wood business that his family still runs.

44) Three generations of women exemplify the archetypal loving and giving matriarchy. The image depicts Teresa Rios, a daughter, and granddaughters. They stand as a vital symbol of the strong and enduring family-centered life so important to the strength of our city.

45) Amarante Tapia was born and raised in Agua Fría. As a boy he sold papers in Santa Fe, delivered goods from local drugstores, worked as a custodian in the local schools, and for thirty years worked at Big Jo Lumber Company, where the Eldorado Hotel is now. He remains a symbol of hard work, perseverance, and deep caring. He figured in a dream the artist had and became the inspiration for this mural.

This is the photograph the artist refers to in Note 27, above. The two girls sit on quite elegant burros, while passersby stare, in this scene on lower San Francisco Street. Photograph by C. G. Kaadt, 1900. Courtesy of Palace of the Governors Photo Archives (NMHM/DCA), #011341.

Timeline

More than a billion years ago	Igneous and metamorphic rocks form in the mountains around what is now Santa Fe.
14,000 to 10,000 years ago	Nomadic peoples exist but probably do not pass through the Santa Fe area. Clovis and Folsom peoples leave the earliest evidence of human existence in what is now New Mexico.
10,000 to 7,000 years ago	The climate in North America begins to warm. Hunter-gatherers possibly pass through Santa Fe.
4,500 years ago	The earliest corn grown in the Southwest is obtained from further south; there is evidence of occasional campsites.
3,000 years ago	Beans and squash are added to the dietary staples, and this revolutionizes Native American lifestyles. Evidence of trading.
A.D. 850–1150	Major construction is undertaken in Chaco Canyon.
1200–1500	Native Americans establish villages along the Rio Grande.
1400s	Native Americans utilize the Santa Fe area: *Oga Po Ge, Ogapogeh,* or *O'gha Po'oge* (various spellings for "White Shell Water Place").
1492	Europeans arrive in the Americas which they call the New World.
1540	The Spanish first explore what is now New Mexico.

1598	Juan de Oñate travels from El Paso del Norte through New Mexico to San Juan Pueblo, now Okay Owingeh, where he founds the first permanent Spanish settlement on the northern frontier of New Spain. El Camino Real de Tierra Adentrowill become the main road of commerce and connection between Mexico City and Santa Fe.
1610	At the request of the king of Spain, through the viceroy in Mexico City, don Juan de Peralta is appointed governor and establishes a settlement that becomes *La Villa de Santa Fé*. The population at founding is approximately one thousand people.
1616	The great writers Cervantes (Spain) and Shakespeare (England) both die in April.
1620	Plymouth Colony is established by English colonists in the area that eventually becomes New England.
1680	The Pueblo Revolt begins the Pueblo-Spanish War; Spanish colonists flee Santa Fe and New Mexico, heading south to Mexico.
1692–1693	Don Diego de Vargas leads the resettlement of Santa Fe and New Mexico by Spain.
1712	The Proclamation of Fiesta begins the Fiesta tradition.
1760	The Miera y Pacheco *retablo* (altar screen) is commissioned for the military chapel, La Castrense.
1766	Lieutenant José Urrutia creates a map of Santa Fe.
1786	Governor Anza and Chief Escueracapa agree to work together for peace.
1821	Mexico wins independence from Spain; the Santa Fe Trail is opened and used for trade with the United States.
1827	Manuel Armijo is appointed governor of New Mexico, for the first of three terms.
1834	The first printing press in New Mexico operates in Santa Fe.
1841	The Texas Santa Fe Expedition is thwarted.
1846	General Kearny invades Santa Fe and takes New Mexico for the United States, part of the U.S.-Mexican War.

1849	The *Santa Fe New Mexican* newspaper is first published.
1850	New Mexico becomes a U.S. Territory; future archbishop Jean Baptiste Lamy arrives in Santa Fe.
1861–1865	The United States undergoes civil war.
1862	In the Battle of Glorieta Pass, the Union army defeats the Confederate army, which had briefly claimed Santa Fe.
1870	Amendment XV is ratified, acknowledging citizens' right to vote; this includes Blacks but does not include Native Americans or women.
1881	The Santa Fe Railroad reaches Santa Fe.
1897–1906	Miguel Antonio Otero serves as territorial governor.
1912	The United States admits New Mexico as a state, during President William Howard Taft's term.
1914–1918	World War I takes place.
1917	The Fine Arts Museum is established in Santa Fe; the United States enters World War I under President Woodrow Wilson.
1920s	Women gain the right to vote in 1920; artists groups develop in Santa Fe.
1929	The Great Depression begins, with 1932 and 1933 being the worst years.
1933	President Franklin D. Roosevelt establishes New Deal programs such as the Civilian Conservation Corps and the Work Projects Administration.
1937	Highway 66 is paved.
1939	World War II begins.
1941	United States enters World War II; Concha Ortiz y Pino becomes first female majority whip of a state legislature.
1942	The Bataan Death March takes place, including 1,800 New Mexican guardsmen. New Mexicans serve all over the world.

1945	The United States drops atomic bombs, developed in Los Alamos, on Japan during President Harry Truman's term.
1948	Native Americans win the right to vote in the United States.
1952	The United States bans school segregation.
1966	A new state capitol building, the "Roundhouse," is dedicated.
1971	Bruce King begins his first of three separate terms as governor.
1980	The New Mexico Penitentiary riot takes place.
2009	The New Mexico History Museum opens.
2010	Santa Fe commemorates the 400th anniversary of its official founding in 1610. The U.S. census reports the population at 67,947.
2012	New Mexico celebrates the state centennial with events throughout the state and the Centennial Ball in Santa Fe on statehood day, January 6.

For more information, visit the New Mexico Office of the State Historian website (www.newmexicohistory.org), which offers extensive information on all aspects of New Mexico's history.

Study Guides

Teachers and students may find the following study guides
by E. West helpful and amusing.

Study Guide 1: Maps

Miguel de Cervantes wrote in *Don Quixote*, "Journey over all the universe in a map, without the expense and fatigue of traveling, without suffering the inconveniences of heat, cold, hunger, and thirst."

This map, titled *Le Nouveau Mexique et La Floride: Tireés de diverses Cartes, et Relations*, was created in 1656 in Paris, France, and drawn by N. Sanson d'Abbeville, geographer, at the request of the King Louis IV. Courtesy of the Fray Angélico Chávez History Library.

If you know some geography and if a map is accurate, or at least partly accurate, you can see right away what it is describing. Sometimes the first thing you notice is the design and any decorations. Sometimes you notice the words that describe the map. When you look more closely you may notice more. Some maps are very simple, while others are very complex. The cartographer (map-maker) chooses what to put in his or her map.

What in this map interests you? What appears beautiful about it? What seems to be drawn correctly, and what seems to be incorrect?

Did you notice that California is drawn as a very large island? Did you notice that what we call the Rio Grande (named R. del Norte on this map) flows to the Gulf of California (named Mar Vermeio on this map)? It should really be drawn to show that the Rio Grande flows to the Gulf of Mexico. Did you notice that the lake at Taosii (what we call Taos) is very large? Did the cartographer mean a lake near Taos, or did he perhaps mean the Great Salt Lake, which is further north, in what is now Utah? And which three of the Great Lakes are missing?

Even though the map has lots of mistakes, we still can recognize that the cartographer understood something about what we know today as northern Mexico, much of the United States, and some of Canada. You probably also noticed that the two languages used for the map are French and Spanish.

Could you draw a map of northern Mexico, most of the United States, and part of Canada that would correct the mistakes you see here? Could you do this from memory?

Two popular world maps that are quite different from each other are the Mercator map and the Peters map. The Mercator projection, the world map most people are familiar with, was developed in 1569 by Gerardus Mercator as a navigation tool. In 1974 Arno Peters introduced the Peters projection, an area-accurate map, in German (it became available in English in 1983). Placed side by side, these maps give very different impressions of the world. They are two of the thousands of map projections available.

Maps describe many types of subjects. In addition to geographical maps, there are road maps, travel-guide maps, maps of planets and stars, spy maps, mystery maps, genetic maps, historical maps, and more.

Drawing maps is fun. You might start your cartographic career by tracing maps that look interesting to you. Or you could study a map and then draw it from memory. How much of a world map can you draw from memory? Perhaps you could draw a map of your neighborhood. You might draw a kind of map of the layout of the house you live in. Draw a simple map that shows the route you would like to take to someplace at least a thousand miles away from where you live. Make a map to find things hidden for a scavenger hunt. Or draw an upside-down map. Or make up a fantasy map.

You might want to find some good map books and compare what they show you. Does your home or school have a good atlas? You could go to the local public library in your neighborhood to find books with maps or to a museum, such as the New Mexico History Museum, that displays maps.

Two useful books on cartography are David Smith's *Mapping the World by Heart* (FableVision Learning, 2010) and *The Map Book*, edited by Peter Barber (Walker, 2005). For fun look through *Strange Maps: An Atlas of Cartographic Curiosities*, by Frank Jacobs (Studio, 2009). Also visit the New Mexico Humanities Council's online atlas of historic New Mexico maps (altas.nmhum.org).

Study Guide 2: Scavenger Hunt

What Is It?
(See Answer Key #64)

A scavenger hunt is one entertaining way to team up with friends to learn about the place you live in. The hunts can have a theme or be somewhat random. You might make up a game about the different historical points of interest, or various architectural styles you can see around downtown Santa Fe. A scavenger hunt might invite the players to interact with people in order to find out answers. The following list of questions about downtown Santa Fe is taken from scavenger hunts compiled by the Pueblo of Pojoaque Boys and Girls Club. Thanks to Gwen Orona and the boys and girls who have participated in the Santa Fe scavenger hunts for their ideas. They form teams of three or four and help each other find the answers, which they write down on the paper with the questions. The answers are simple. Sometimes they are riddles. Sometimes they are not questions but instead are simple activities, such as picking up trash or getting someone's signature. Or the questions in a scavenger hunt could be linked with some of the questions and answers in this book. You might use the index to find information for the answers. In fact, this book is a kind of scavenger hunt.

1) What year was the Palace of the Governors built?
2) Get a brochure from a hotel.
3) What is the name of the alley where you can find a donkey?
4) What is the name of the statue of an Indian woman in front of the St. Francis Cathedral?
5) What year was the Delgado House built?
6) Get the signature of a police officer.
7) What is the new school called at the old St. Francis Cathedral building?
8) The more of them you take, the more you leave behind. What are they?
9) Get signatures from an employee and a guest at La Fonda.
10) What is the shape of the state capitol?
11) Sing a song to a stranger from out of town.
12) Get the bus schedule.
13) Write down an interesting fact from a history museum and name the museum.
14) Pick up trash along a street of your choice.
15) Who is the mayor of Santa Fe?
16) What is the name of the chapel at 207 Old Santa Fe Trail?
17) What belongs to you but others use it more?
18) Get the signature of a tourist from another country.
19) What monument is at the northern end of Lincoln Avenue?
20) What is the building at 145 Washington Avenue?

Some answers: 1610; Burro Alley; Kateri Tekakwitha; 1890; New Mexico School of the Arts; footsteps; Zia symbol; Loretto Chapel; your name; Kit Carson; Santa Fe Public Library

Study Guide 3: Dinner Party

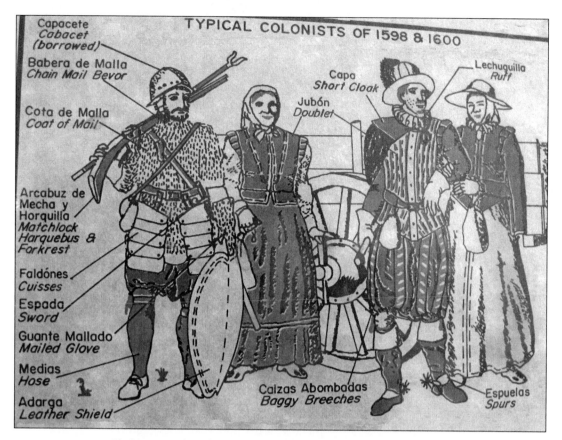

**Clothing worn by colonists in New Spain, 1500–1600s. Artist unknown.
Courtesy of María Martínez, El Museo Cultural, Santa Fe.**

Choose ten men and women from this book who you think are interesting. Make a list of them. Now imagine giving a dinner party for the ten people on your list.

Perhaps you'd like to invite a friend from your own era who could help you give the party. Would your guests all be from the same time period? Try picking people of different time periods. Imagine everyone seated around a table. Where would you place each guest? Where would you sit? Make a diagram of the seating arrangement. What food would you serve? You might ask each of your guests to bring some food from his or her culture and time, if you decide to give a pot-luck meal.

Some of the people you find interesting might like each other. Others might not get along very well. How would you help them understand each other better? What languages do your guests speak? Tewa, Spanish, English, or some other language? You might imagine that the guests can understand each other (imagine

People in costume at a Santa Fe party.
Photograph taken by T. Harmon Parkhurst at the Amelia White residence, 1928.
Courtesy of Palace of the Governors Photo Archives (NMHM/DCA), #069623.

that they are multilingual) so they will find it easier to learn about each other. Perhaps you can guide the conversation somehow. What does each guest find most curious? What would some of the guests want to know about your life? Would you provide some music in the background? What kind of music would be best for your party? If you could hire any live band or musician to play, what would you choose? Mariachis? A quartet? A guitarist? Plan to give a toast to your guests, perhaps during dessert. What would you like to say?

One way to give a good party is to know your guests. Learn a little about each of them, their history, their likes and dislikes, their hopes and fears, what they think is funny or peculiar, and introduce them to each other with a sentence or two about each person, finding something that will connect the people you introduce to each other. How would you describe your guests? How would you describe yourself to them? What do you think your guests would like best about you? After getting to know them, do you think you would have more compassion for some of the problems historical figures have had to deal with? What do you think you could learn from any of them? Would you want to give any advice to any of them since you have the perspective of history?

Take a group photograph so that you can remember everyone before they all disappear.

Study Guide 4: A Recipe and a Song

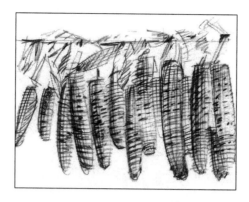

Corn. **Drawing by Anita H. Lehmann, 2011. Courtesy of the artist.**

tole is a thin blue cornmeal gruel; it is cooked in water and sometimes has milk, a pinch of salt, and a sweetener such as maple syrup added. *Chaqueweh* is another term for a similar, thicker mixture, a sort of porridge served with milk or cream and sometimes with fruit or red chile."

This is the answer to question number 236 in this book. Someone commented that the word *gruel* sounded depressing. And the word does come with some associations of deprivation and hardship; *gruel* does mean "a thin, watery porridge," and its British meaning is "severe punishment." The word is reminiscent of *gruesome* and *grueling*, words from Middle English, Old French, and Low German meaning frightful, causing repugnance, and physically or mentally demanding to the point of exhaustion.

But *atole* is a delicious, soothing drink that actually has positive connotations, including being comforted, nourished, and supported. The word comes from the Nahuatl Native American word *atolli*, which means "mush." And it is made with corn, an honored part of the Native American and Spanish southwestern diet, with a long history going back more than four thousand years. *Atole* is traditionally made with blue corn.

The recipe in Fabiola Cabeza de Baca Gilbert's *Historic Cookery* is as follows:

> Stir ½ cup of blue corn meal into ½ cup of cold water. Add this to 2 cups of boiling water. Boil until it has reached the consistency of cream. Cook. Serve in cups about half full. Add enough salted boiled milk to fill cups. This is a very common beverage for sick or old people.

Champurrado is the same drink with added spiced chocolate, usually with cinnamon. Some people like to stir their *atole* in micaceous pots, and sometimes cream and a sweetener are added. If the mixture thickens, it is called *chaqueweh* and then becomes a cereal to eat with a spoon. Try adding a little red chile caribe to the *chaqueweh*.

In her *Southwest Indian Cookbook*, Marcia Keegan says, "The sacred nature of food is everywhere evident in Indian culture. The dances, prayers, and ceremonies all reflect the significance and value of food in daily existence." Among other dances, corn dances "have been an integral part of Indian ceremonies for centuries. And when food is taken, a little is always given back—either to the fire or to the earth—in order to replenish the source in a symbolic gesture of thanks."

Corn became a staple crop in the Southwest first for Native Americans and later for the Spanish. Traditionally, during the winter dried corn is ground into flour by women in small social groups using a rounded hand-held grinder, or *mano*, against a base stone slab, or *metate*. The stone for the *metate* is usually made of volcanic rock—basalt or andesite—hard, porous stone that creates an uneven surface, which is desirable because it gives the cornmeal texture. If you grind your own cornmeal and masa, you won't need to go to the gym.

This Zuni corn-grinding song may be sung while grinding corn with friends:

E-lu ho-ma ya ya yal-lan-ne! Yal-lan-ne. A-weh-lwi-a kwai-I im-u-na kwa-gia. Lo-nan esh-to wi-ya-ne. He-ya ha-ya he-ya! Li-wa-ma-ni i-yu-te-a-pa. A-wi-ya-ne. Ha-wi-la-na li-i-tla.

The English translation is roughly as follows: "See the lovely mountain rising high, rising high. Up among the clouds see Rainmakers sitting. Rain clouds now float softly by. Heya, haya, heya! Rain comes soon to feed our sweet new corn, food for one and all, soon our sweet young corn will grow tall." You can make up your own tune that works well while grinding corn.

Atole, chaqueweh, tortillas, cornbread, and muffins: all good, even if you buy your cornmeal or masa from the market.

These four cookbooks may inspire you to begin a Southwestern cooking adventure: *Southwest Indian Cookbook: Pueblo and Navajo Images, Quotes and Recipes*, by Marcia Keegan; *Historic Cookery*, by Fabiola Cabeza de Baca Gilbert; *Los Comidas de los Abuelos*, edited by Ana Pacheco; and *Josephina's Cookbook: A Peek at Dining in the Past with Meals You Can Cook Today*, by Tamara England.

Corn Dancers. **Pen and ink drawing by Cathie Sullivan, 2011, based on her original screen print, 2011. Courtesy of the artist.**

The artist talks about this image here:

"These imaginary dance figures are based on the shapes of growing corn plants. Behind the figures, dots symbolize corn pollen, a sacred substance in the religious traditions of the Indian pueblos of the U.S. Southwest. In Mexico and in Native American pueblos of the Southwest, corn was one of the three staple foods, along with beans and squash. This image symbolizes that importance."

Santa Fe's 400th Anniversary Board and History Task Force

The Santa Fe 400th Anniversary, Inc., was a 501(c)(3) nonprofit corporation created to design and produce public events, educational initiatives, symposia, and books commemorating the City of Santa Fe, officially established by the Spanish in 1610 and therefore the oldest capital city in the United States. The intent of the more than year-long commemoration was to honor all of Santa Fe's cultures, legacies, and lasting contributions, to connect the founding past with the promise of tomorrow, and to show respect for the collective heritage of the community.

The board of directors of the Santa Fe 400th Committee included the following people:

Maurice Bonal, chairman and president of the board
Martin Aguilar
Eva Aschenbrenner
Adrian Bustamante
Jessica C. de Baca
Charles Carrillo
Pavon Dhindsa
Rudy "Froggy" Fernandez
Troy Fernandez
José Garcia
Connie Tsosie Gaussoin
Gerald T. E. González
Darlene Griego
Greg Heltman
Jennifer Hobson
Jeff Jinnette
Tony Lopez

Herman Lovato
Eric Lujan
Leslie Lujan
Paul Margetson
Mark Mitchell
Albert "Gaby" Montoya
Peter Pacheco
Gilbert Romero
Kurt Young
Mayor David Coss and the Santa Fe City Council

One of the committees assisting the board was the History Task Force, which addressed historical matters. Many people served intermittently on that committee. The three people who served the entire time, for over two years, were Maurice Bonal, Adrian Bustamante, and José Garcia.

The History Task Force included the following people:

Adrian Bustamante, chairman
Martin Aguilar
Maurice Bonal
Samuel Delgado
José Esquibel
Albert Gallegos
José Garcia
Gerald T. E. González
Rick Hendricks
Sandra Jaramillo
Michael King
Pat Kuhlhoff
Ana Pacheco
Estevan Rael-Gálvez
Orlando Romero
Joseph P. Sánchez
Cordelia Thomas Snow
Samuel Temkin
Elizabeth West

Acknowledgments

People who write or edit books say they couldn't have done such and such without the help of so and so, and I now know they mean it! I was asked to edit this book, and saying yes was quite easy. Later I discovered that how many people it takes to make a village is about the same number required to edit a book. Fortunately I live in the vibrant "village" of Santa Fe, and a lot of wonderful people have made this somewhat eccentric book possible.

The History Task Force, which supported the efforts of the Santa Fe 400th Commemoration Committee, debated, analyzed, challenged, and discussed many issues and questions that needed attention. Most of those who participated in the History Task Force are historians or are involved in Santa Fe's history in one way or another. Although I am not an historian, I was pleased to be a part of that group and observe the usually serious, sometimes amusing, always sincere way in which the group approached what it was directed to do. Our primary job was to make sure Santa Fe's history was accurately represented. There was seldom 100 percent agreement on the difficult questions, such as who might be named to a list of top ten most important people in Santa Fe's history (you give that a try!), but there was always the willingness to tackle them.

One subcommittee, chaired by Orlando Romero, worked diligently on producing the collection of essays in the award-winning *All Trails Lead to Santa Fe,* published by Sunstone Press in 2010. An anthology titled *White Shell Water Place,* also published by Sunstone Press in 2010, afforded Native American authors a book in which to express opinions and perspectives on historical and cultural aspects of Santa Fe; this project was supported by the All Indian Pueblo Council as well as Maurice Bonal and the Santa Fe 400th Commemoration Board and Committee. The book was edited by F. Richard Sanchez and is a ceremony of Native voices, commencing with a blessing composed by N. Scott Momaday.

Maurice Bonal, chairman and president of the Santa Fe 400th Anniversary Board, and Ana Pacheco, author of a weekly column for the *Santa Fe New Mexican* and a member of the History Task Force, suggested that a series of four hundred "trivia" questions about Santa Fe be presented in the newspaper, one question for each year since the Spanish founding of Santa Fe in 1610. The History Task Force liked the idea. The owner of the newspaper, Robin Martin, and the managing editor, Rob Dean, also agreed, and the Santa Fe 400th Committee supported the concept. The format consisted of presenting a question each day with the answer revealed the next day, for four hundred days in a row. Adrian Bustamante, who served on both the task force and the Santa Fe 400th Committee, and Ana were the initial contributors to the list of questions to be vetted by the task force for the newspaper.

After the four hundred questions appeared in the paper, from November 2009 into January 2011, it was decided that they might be compiled into a book. A small subcommittee was formed to propose ideas and to check and rewrite the questions and answers, as well as to add more references for each question and answer. These people were invaluable for their historical expertise, insightful support, and generous spirit as the process of putting this book together developed. The group I worked with included the following people:

Adrian H. Bustamante, an ethnohistorian who is retired from the Southwest Studies Department of Fort Lewis College, in Durango, Colorado. He has published numerous essays in various collections, including *Santa Fe: History of an Ancient City*, rev. ed., 2008. He also stepped in as chairman, with intelligence and terrific good will, to complete the job put in front of the History Task Force.

The late Gerald T. E. González, a lawyer who earned his law degree at Harvard University, where he edited the *Harvard Civil Right–Civil Liberties Law Review*. He had a private practice as well as serving in a succession of federal and state governmental positions. He worked on a translation of the Juan Martínez de Montoya documents, relating to Santa Fe's pre-founding. He was also a poet. He died on November 1, 2011.

Rick Hendricks, state historian for New Mexico. He was coeditor on the Vargas Project, which produced six volumes on the administration of seventeenth-century governor Diego de Vargas. He is also an author of several books, including *New Mexico in 1801: The Priests' Report*.

Michael King, director of education at El Rancho de las Golondrinas, a living history museum near Santa Fe highlighting life in New Mexico from 1710 through statehood in 1912.

Joseph P. Sánchez, director of the Spanish Colonial Research Center at the University of New Mexico and superintendent of Petroglyph National Monument. His many books include *The Río Abajo Frontier, 1540–1692: A History of Early Colonial New Mexico*; *Explorers, Traders, and Slavers: Forging the Old Spanish Trail, 1678–1850*; *Between Two Rivers: The Atrisco Land Grant in Albuquerque's History, 1692–1968*; and *From Mexico City to Santa Fe: A Historical Guide of Geographic Place*

Names along El Camino Real de Tierra Adentro. In 2004, he was inducted into the knightly *Order de Isabel la Católica* by King Juan Carlos of Spain for his contributions to Spanish colonial history.

Cordelia Thomas Snow, a historic sites archaeologist and a long-term employee of the Archaeological Records Management Section (ARMS) of the Historic Preservation Division of the New Mexico Department of Cultural Affairs.

The group of us was in touch occasionally by telephone but usually by email. Each of these people knows how much I have not only needed their help but welcomed their critiques and queries. I cannot imagine a kinder, more intelligent subcommittee. And we all miss Gerald.

Maurice Bonal was the perseverant and supportive liaison between the subcommittee and the Santa Fe 400th Anniversary Board. Ana Pacheco, founder and publisher of *La Herencia*, a culture and history magazine that ran from 1994 to 2009, was not on the subcommittee because of other commitments.

Many other people have helped with this book. First among them is my friend and colleague from the Santa Fe Public Library, Judy Klinger. She is a reference librarian who retired in 2011 after working thirty-four years at the Santa Fe Public Library. She has also worked at the Fray Angélico Chávez History Library, the Laboratory of Anthropology Library, and the New Mexico State Library. She assisted in doing research and also created the index for this book.

The publishers, Jim Smith and Carl Condit at Sunstone Press, must have been rather puzzled when they met the person who had volunteered to revise and edit the newspaper questions, answers, and references into a book. I had no experience in book publishing, and they were remarkably patient with me. I really do appreciate their kindnesses as well as their matter-of-fact assumption that I could do this. I steadfastly have taken their teasing as a compliment and their challenges as instructive. And Vicki Ahl is their helpful designer.

Sarah Baldwin was my terrific line editor. She began working with me in the early stages of the book project and assisted in many aspects of its development, from suggestions for additions and revisions to fact-checking and copyediting. She also accepted changes that may have sometimes seemed in endless supply.

I appreciate every suggestion, difference of opinion, question, and offer of support, all of which helped make working on this project a pleasure. Here is a partial list of friends and acquaintances who have helped in too many ways to detail here. Aside from the historians and scholars on the task force and on my subcommittee, I want to especially mention the historians Tom Chávez, John Kessell, and Marc Simmons. New Mexico is fortunate indeed to be the frequent object of their interest and research. I also would like to thank Marcia Keegan, photographer and publisher of Clear Light Books, for introducing me to the late Howard Bryan, author and long-time journalist, who impressed me with his integrity and bravery; he was inspiringly unafraid of the truth. The late Richard Rudisill, retired from the Fray Angélico Chávez History Library Photo Archives, shared several pithy comments with me during meals at the Zia Diner, where he ate most of his suppers and where I often found a comfortable booth that accommodated me and my computer.

All the hard-working people at the *Santa Fe New Mexican*, who saw me come and go during the process of presenting the vetted 400 questions and answers, are to be thanked for their tolerance of my bubbly intrusions. Rob Dean, the editor, is one of the longest-serving editors of a major newspaper in the United States, and his tact and perseverance are no doubt part of the reason for his enduring tenure there. He edited *Santa Fe, Its 400th Year: Exploring the Past, Defining the Future*, published by Sunstone Press in 2010. Cynthia Miller, Ben Swan, Camille Flores, Jane Phillips, and many others were helpful coordinators, often answering questions late at night when they were on deadline. The late Rebekah Azen also contributed her expertise.

Adriana Ortega, Andy Jimenez, Mary Prince Adams (great-granddaughter of New Mexico governor Le Baron Bradford Prince), Ray Graumlich, Tim Greer, María Valencia Finley (a descendant of Donaciano Vigil), Pat Hodapp, and many others at the Santa Fe Public Library have helped me. At the Institute of American Indian Arts Library, Sarah Kostelecky, Grace Nuvayestewa, and Jennifer James are to be thanked, as is Ryan Flahive, in the IAIA photo archives. Sandra Jaramillo, retired director of the New Mexico State Records Center and Archives, served on the History Task Force and was supportive when I needed advice.

Many other librarians, curators, and archivists were of great assistance during this process: Dennis Peter Trujillo, in the Office of the State Historian; the librarians in the Southwest Room of the state library, especially Virginia Lopez and Faith Yoman; all the librarians and archivists at the New Mexico State Records Center and Archives have helped me at some point, starting with Al Regensberg, who was patient with me years ago when I was first beginning to do New Mexico history research, and most recently Sibel Melik; Tomas Jaehn, curator at the Fray Angélico Chávez History Library; downstairs in the photography archives of the New Mexico History Museum, Palace of the Governors Photo Archives, Daniel Kosharek, photo archivist, Mary Anne Redding, curator, and Mark Scharen, imaging specialist extraordinaire, all went out of their way to help me; Mike Kelly, at the University of New Mexico Center for Southwest Research; Susan Webber, docent at St. Louis Mercantile Library; and Laura Holt, librarian at the School for Advanced Research, who generously shared her indexing expertise as well as her wit.

Others I'd like to thank include Robert J. Tórrez and Stanley F. Hordes, both retired New Mexico state historians; José Garcia, Santa Fe city historian; Quintard Taylor; Robin Williams and John Tollett; Kermit Hill, retired history teacher in the Santa Fe Public Schools, who met with me at the Santa Fe Baking Company café; Donald Gill; Mary Kimball Outten and Robert Bawell; Pat Kuhlhoff; Melanie Brown, who introduced me to Anita H. Lehmann, who contributed the *City Different Alphabet: Santa Fe* and other illustrations; Hazel Romero; Richard C. McCord; Gwen Orona and the Pueblo of Pojoaque Boys and Girls Club; Doris Vigil, librarian at Pojoaque Pueblo Community Library and translator into Tewa of the dicho in the front of this book; Dorothy G. Ulibarrí; Roxanne Sosa; Richard Trujillo; Beverly Spears; Martha Greenway; Alessa Seawright; Cecilia Rios; John Pen La Farge; David Grant Nobel; John Baxter; Andrew Smith for the great All Saints' Day story; Jesús Reveles; Nathaniel Messimer; Bill Baxter who helped me mine information I needed; Homer Milford; Julia Gomez; Eva Aschenbrenner; Rudy Fernandez; Mary Riseley; Mary Kraai; Patricia Rivera; Charles Lee; Barbara Harrelson; Roxanne Swentzell; Drew Bachigalupa; Eli Levin; Jerry West; Phillip Haozous; David McGary; Ricardo Caté; David Rasch in the Historic Preservation Division of the City of Santa Fe; Sabrina Pratt and the Santa Fe Arts Commission department; Geralyn Cardeñas; Kathy Hagerman; Cathie Sullivan; Samuel Temkin; Joe Gallegos; Elaine Bergman and Cara Evans at the Historic Santa Fe Foundation; Zeinab Benhalím; Ron and Frances Kessler; Susan and Felix Warburg; Frances Levine, director of the New Mexico History Museum; Josef Díaz; Mayor David Coss, who is able to think on his feet; Helen Pacheco; María Martínez at El Museo Cultural; Tara Gibbons; Ron and Pat Rundstrom; François-Marie Patorni; Frank Turley; Peter Cata and Anthony Rosetta; Christopher Chavez; Joan Logghe; Miriam Bobkoff; Sandra Deacon; Richard Melzer; MaLin Wilson and Greg Powell; Peter Ellzey; Peg Goldstein; Jim Mafchir; Christopher Benson; Will Taft; Melanie West; Edward and Melanie Ranney; everyone at the Camera Shop; everyone at Visions Photo Lab, especially Nikkol Brothers for her patience and savvy; Tom Leech at the Palace Press; Eleanor Ortiz Bové and Phillip Bové, who shared their respect for and knowledge about acequias in Santa Fe; and Martin Aguilar, who calmly reminded me that some of yesterday's battles are not ours to fight today.

The helpful support and understanding of my family—Archie, Melanie, Kurt, Mollie, Matt, Julia, Alison, Ben, Clara, Harold, and Arthur—have been appreciated more than they know.

Thank you all.

—Elizabeth West

Editor's Selected Reading List

Below is the editor's selected reading list of ten books providing a visual and textual introduction to Santa Fe:

New Mexico: Past and Future, by Thomas E. Chávez (University of New Mexico Press, 2006)

New Mexico: An Interpretive History, by Marc Simmons (University of New Mexico Press, 1988)

Pueblo Profiles: Cultural Identity through Centuries of Change, by Joe S. Sando (Clear Light, 1998)

Santa Fe: History of an Ancient City, edited by David Grant Noble, second edition, revised and expanded (School for Advanced Research Press, 2008)

Through the Lens: Creating Santa Fe, edited by Mary Anne Redding and Krista Elrick (Museum of New Mexico Press, 2008)

Turn Left at the Sleeping Dog: Scripting the Santa Fe Legend, 1920–1955, by John Pen La Farge (University of New Mexico Press, 2001)

Santa Fe: A Pictorial History, by John Sherman, second edition (Donning Company, 1996)

Meet Josefina: An American Girl, by Valerie Tripp (Pleasant Company, 1997)

The Essence of Santa Fe: From a Way of Life to a Style, by Jerilou Hammett, Kingsley Hammett, and Peter Scholz (Ancient City Press, 2006)

Santa Fe Icons: 50 Symbols of the City Different, edited by Camille Flores (Globe Pequot Press, 2010)

And three more:

All Trails Lead to Santa Fe: An Anthology Commemorating the 400th Anniversary of the Founding of Santa Fe, New Mexico, in 1610 (Sunstone Press, 2010)

White Shell Water Place: An Anthology of Native American Reflections on the 400th Anniversary of the Founding of Santa Fe, edited by Richard F. Sanchez (Sunstone Press, 2010)

Santa Fe, Its 400th Year: Exploring the Past, Defining the Future, edited by Rob Dean (Sunstone Press, 2010)

What Is It?
(See Answer Key #65)

Bibliography

Abbink, Emily. *New Mexico's Palace of the Governors: History of an American Treasure*. Santa Fe: Museum of New Mexico Press, 2007.

Abeita, Louise Chewiwi (E-Yeh-Shure). *I Am a Pueblo Indian Girl*. New York: William Morrow, 1939.

Acton, David. *Hand of a Craftsman: The Woodcut Technique of Gustave Baumann*. Santa Fe: Museum of New Mexico Press, 1996.

Adair, John. *The Navajo and Pueblo Silversmiths*. Norman: University of Oklahoma Press, 1944.

Adobe Conservation: A Preservation Handbook. Compiled by Cornerstones Community Partnerships. Santa Fe: Sunstone Press, 2006.

Albala, Ken. *Food in Early Modern Europe*. Westport, CT: Greenwood Press, 2003.

———. *Pancake: A Global History*. London: Reaktion Books, 2008.

Alexander, Christopher, Sarah Ishikawa, and Murray Silverstein, with Max Jacobson, Ingrid Fiksdahl-King, and Shlomo Angel. *A Pattern Language: Towns, Buildings, Construction*. New York: Oxford University Press, 1977.

All Trails Lead to Santa Fe: An Anthology Commemorating the 400th Anniversary of the Founding of Santa Fe, New Mexico, in 1610. Santa Fe: Sunstone Press, 2010.

Alter, Judy. *The Santa Fe Trail*. Danbury, CT: Children's Press, 1998.

Alvarado, Diane O. *¡Viva la Fiesta! A Promise Made, a Promise Kept*. Santa Fe: Santa Fe Fiesta Council, 2003.

Álvarez, Manuel. *Manuel Álvarez Papers 1825–1856*. New Mexico State Records Center and Archives. Santa Fe.

The American Heritage Dictionary of the English Language, 4th ed. New York: Dell, 2001.

Amos, Janine. *Waste and Recycling*. Austin: Raintree Steck-Vaughn, 1993.

Anaya, Rudolfo. *Bless Me, Ultima*. Berkeley: Quinto Sol Publications, 1972.

———. *The Farolitos of Christmas*. New York: Hyperion Books for Children, 1995.

———. *The First Tortilla: A Bilingual Story*. Albuquerque: University of New Mexico Press, 2007.

———. *The Legend of La Llorona: A Short Novel*. Berkeley: Tonatiuh-Quinto Sol International, 1984.

———. *Santero's Miracle: A Bilingual Story*. Albuquerque: University of New Mexico Press, 2004.

Ancona, George. *Come and Eat!* Watertown, MA: Charlesbridge, 2011.

———. *¡Olé! Flamenco*. New York: Lee & Low, 2010.

———. *Pablo Remembers: The Fiesta of the Day of the Dead*. New York: Lothrop, Lee & Shepard Books, 1993.

Anderson, Dwayne. *All That Glitters: The Emergence of Native American Micaceous Art Pottery in Northern New Mexico*. Santa Fe: School of American Research Press, 1999.

Anderson, Joan. *Spanish Pioneers of the Southwest*. New York: E. P. Dutton, 1989.

Andrews, Alexander. *Albert: Behind the Dark Glasses*. Santa Fe: Alexander Andrews, 2004.

Ansary, Mir Tamim. *El Día de Martin Luther King, Jr.* Chicago: Heinemann Library, 2003.

Applegate, Frank. *Indian Stories from the Pueblos*. Philadelphia: J. B. Lippincott, 1929.

Aragón, Ray John de. *The Legend of La Llorona*. Santa Fe: Sunstone Press, 2006.

————. *The Penitentes of New Mexico: Hermanos de la Luz = Brothers of the Light*. Santa Fe, Sunstone Press, 2006.

Aranda, Charles. *Dichos: Proverbs and Sayings from the Spanish*. Santa Fe: Sunstone Press, 1977.

Architects Associated. *The New Mexico State Capitol, 1963–1980: A Twenty Year Development Plan*. Privately printed. Santa Fe: 1963.

Arellanes, Kathy, ed. *Travel New Mexico Scenic and Historic Byways: A Travel Guide to New Mexico Roads of Distinction*. Santa Fe: New Mexico Highway & Transportation Department, 2000.

Arnold, Samuel P. *Eating Up the Santa Fe Trail: Recipes and Lore from the Old West*. Golden, CO: Fulcrum, 2001.

The Artist in the American West, 1800–1900. Santa Fe: Museum of Fine Arts Press, 1961.

Astrov, Margot, ed. *The Winged Serpent: American Indian Prose and Poetry*. Boston: Beacon Press, 1992. First published 1946.

Austin, Mary Hunter. *Earth Horizon*. Facsimile of 1932 edition. Santa Fe: Sunstone Press, 2007.

————. *Land of Little Rain*. Facsimile of 1904 edition. Santa Fe: Sunstone Press, 2007.

————. *Literary America, 1903–1934: The Mary Austin Papers*. Westport, CT: Greenwood Press, 1979.

Awalt, Barbe, and Paul Rhetts. *Our Saints among Us: 400 Years of New Mexican Devotional Art*. Albuquerque: LPD Press, 1998.

Aylesworth, Thomas G. *State Capitals*. New York: Gallery Books, 1990.

Baca, Elmo. *Native American Style*. Salt Lake City: Gibbs Smith, 1999.

Baca, Elmo, and Suzanne Deats. *Santa Fe Design*. Lincolnwood, IL: Publications International, 1995.

Baca, Jimmy Santiago. *Black Mesa Poems*. New York: New Directions, 1989.

————. *Breaking Bread with the Darkness*. Santa Fe: Sherman Asher, 2011.

Bachelard, Gaston. *The Poetics of Space*. New York: Omen Press, 1964.

Bacigalupa, Drew. *Journal of an Itinerant Artist*. Huntington, IN: Our Sunday Visitor, 1977.

Bahn, Paul G., ed. *The Cambridge Illustrated History of Archaeology*. Cambridge, UK: Cambridge University Press, 1999.

Bahti, Mark. *Pueblo Stories and Storytellers*. Tucson: Rio Nuevo, 2010.

Bailey, Florence Miriam. *Birds of New Mexico*. Santa Fe: New Mexico Department of Game and Fish, 1928.

Bailey, Gauvin A. *Art of Colonial Latin America*. New York: Phaidon, 2005.

Bailey, Vernon. *Mammals of New Mexico*. Washington, DC: U.S. Department of Agriculture, 1931.

Balish, Chris. *How to Live Well without Owning a Car*. Berkeley: Ten Speed Press, 2006.

Ball, Jacqueline A. *Martin Luther King, Jr.: I Have a Dream!* New York: Bearport, 2006.

Ballen, Samuel B. *Without Reservations: From Harlem to the End of the Santa Fe Trail*. Santa Fe: Ocean Tree Books, 2001.

Balthazar, Richard. *Getting Get: The Glossary of a Wild Verb*. Bloomington, IN: Authorhouse, 2006.

Bancroft, Hubert Howe. *History of Mexico*. 6 vols. San Francisco: Bancroft, 1883.

Bandelier, Adolph Francis Alphonse. *The Delight Makers*. New York: Mead, Dodd, 1890.

Bankston, John. *Juan Bautista de Anza*. Hockessin, DE: Mitchell Lane, 2004.

Barber, Peter, ed. *The Map Book*. New York: Walker, 2005.

Barker, Elliott Speer. *Smokey Bear and the Great Wilderness*. Santa Fe: Sunstone Press, 1982.

Barker, S. Omar. *Rawhide Rhymes: Singing Poems of the Old West*. New York: Doubleday, 1968.

Barry, Louise. *The Beginning of the West, 1540–1854*. Topeka: Kansas State Historical Society, 1972.

Batkin, Jonathan. *Clay People: Pueblo Indian Figurative Traditions*. Santa Fe: Wheelwright Museum of the American Indian, 1999.

———. *The Native American Curio Trade in New Mexico*. Santa Fe: Wheelwright Museum of the American Indian, 2008.

Baxter, John O. *Dividing New Mexico's Waters, 1700–1912*. Albuquerque: University of New Mexico Press, 1997.

———. *Las Carneradas: Sheep Trade in New Mexico, 1700–1860*. Albuquerque: University of New Mexico Press, 1987.

Baxter, William. *The Gold of the Ortiz Mountains: A Story of New Mexico and the West's First Major Gold Rush*. Santa Fe: Lone Butte Press, 2004.

Baylor, Byrd. *Amigo*. New York: Aladdin Books, 1963.

Beard, Sam. *Ski Touring in Northern New Mexico*. Albuquerque: Nordic Press, 1988.

Beck, Warren A., and Ynez D. Haase. *Historical Atlas of New Mexico*. Norman: University of Oklahoma Press, 1969.

Bédoyère, Camilla de la. *Farmyard Friends: Cows*. London: QEB, 2011.

Bello, A. Kyce, ed. *The Return of the River: Writers, Scholars, and Citizens Speak on Behalf of the Santa Fe River*. Santa Fe: Sunstone Press, 2011.

Benson, Nancy C. *New Mexico Colcha Club: Spanish Colonial Embroidery and the Women Who Saved It*. Santa Fe: Museum of New Mexico Press, 2008.

Benson, Richard, and Edward Ranney. *Archaeology and the Shape of Time*. Santa Fe: Fisher Press, 2011.

Bentley, Diana. *The Seven Wonders of the Ancient World*. New York: Oxford University Press, 2001.

Berg, A. Scott. *Lindbergh*. New York: Putnam, 1998.

Berke, Arnold. *Mary Colter: Architect of the Southwest*. New York: Princeton Architectural Press, 2002.

Berlo, Janet Catherine, and Ruth B. Phillips. *Native North American Art*. New York: Oxford University Press, 1998.

Bernard, Jane, and Polly Brown. *American Route 66: Home on the Road*. Santa Fe: Museum of New Mexico Press, 2003.

Bevington, David, ed. *The Complete Works of Shakespeare*, 6th ed. New York: Longman, 2008.

Bezy, John, and Joseph P. Sánchez, eds. *Pecos Gateway to Pueblo and Plains: The Anthology*. Tucson: Southwest Parks and Monuments Association, 1988.

Billington, Monroe Lee. *New Mexico's Buffalo Soldiers, 1866–1900*. Boulder: University Press of Colorado, 1991.

Bishop, Amanda, and Bobbie Kalman. *Life in a Pueblo*. New York: Crabtree, 2003.

———. *Nations of the Southwest*. New York: Crabtree, 2003.

Blea, Juan. *Butterfly Warrior: A Novel*. Santa Fe: Sherman Asher, 2006.

Bloom, Allan, trans. *The Republic of Plato*. 2nd ed. With notes, an interpretive essay, and a new introduction. New York: Basic Books, 1991.

Bloom, Lansing B. *The Vargas Encomienda*. Albuquerque: University of New Mexico Press, 1939.

———. *Who Discovered New Mexico?* Santa Fe, 1940.

Blouin, Nicole. *Road Biking New Mexico*. Guilford, CT: Globe Pequot Press, 2002.

Blumenthal, Susan. *Santa Fe Ghosts: Mystery, History, and Truth*. Atglen, PA: Schiffer, 2009.

Boas, Franz. *Anthropology and Modern Life*. New York: Transaction, 2007. First published 1928.

Bobkoff, Miriam, and Miriam Sagan, eds. *Just Outside the Frame: Poets from the Santa Fe Poetry Broadside*. Española, NM: Tres Chicas Press, 2005.

Bolton, Herbert E. *Pageant in the Wilderness*. Salt Lake City: Spanish Historical Society, 1950.

Booker, Margaret M. *The Santa Fe House: Historic Residences, Enchanting Adobes, and Romantic Revivals*. New York: Rizzoli International, 2009.

Boomhower, Ray E. *The Sword and the Pen: A Life of Lew Wallace*. Indianapolis: Indiana Historical Society, 2005.

Bork, William Albert. *Nuevos aspectos del comercio entre Nuevo Mexico y Misuri 1822–1846.* Mexico City: Universidad Nacional Autónoma de México, 1944.

Boudreau, Eugene H. *Making the Adobe Brick.* Berkeley: Fifth Street Press, 1971.

Bowden, J. J. *Private Land Claims of the Southwest.* Unpublished master's thesis from Southern Methodist University, in bound form at the New Mexico Supreme Court Library, Santa Fe, and in the New Mexico State Records Center and Archives.

Bowermaster, Jon. *Oceans: The Threats to Our Seas and What You Can Do to Turn the Tide.* New York: PublicAffairs, 2010.

Bowman, J. N., and Robert F. Heizer. *Anza and the Northwest Frontier of New Spain.* Los Angeles: Southwest Museum, 1967.

Boyd, E. *Popular Arts of Spanish New Mexico.* Santa Fe: Museum of New Mexico Press, 1974.

Boyle, Susan Calafate. *Los Capitalistas: Hispano Merchants and the Santa Fe Trade.* Albuquerque: University of New Mexico Press, 1997.

Braddy, Haldeen. *Pancho Villa at Columbus.* El Paso: Texas Western College Press, 1965.

Bradford, Richard. *Red Sky at Morning: A Novel.* New York: Harper Perennial Modern Classics, 1999. First published 1968.

Bradford, Travis. *Solar Revolution: The Economic Transformation of the Global Energy Industry.* Cambridge, MA: MIT Press, 2006.

Bradfute, Richard Wells. *The Court of Private Land Claims: The Adjudication of Spanish and Mexican Land Grant Titles, 1891–1904.* Albuquerque: University of New Mexico Press, 1975.

Braudel, Ferrand. *The Mediterranean and the Mediterranean World in the Age of Philip II.* Berkeley: University of California Press, 1996.

Briggs, Walter. *Without Noise of Arms: The 1776 Dominguez-Escalante Search for a Route from Santa Fe to Monterey.* Flagstaff: Northland Press, 1976.

Broida, Marian. *American Indians of the Southwest.* New York: Benchmark Books, 2004.

Bronson, Wilfrid Swancourt. *Coyotes.* Santa Fe: Sunstone Press, 2007. First published 1946 by Harcourt, Brace.

Brookshier, Frank. *The Burro.* Norman: University of Oklahoma Press, 1974.

Brooks, James F. *Captives and Cousins: Slavery, Kinship, and Community in the Southwest Borderlands.* Charlotte: University of North Carolina Press, 2002.

Brown, Loren W., with Charles L. Briggs and Marta Weigle. *Hispano Folklife of New Mexico: The Lorin W. Brown Federal Writers' Project Manuscripts.* Albuquerque: University of New Mexico Press, 1978.

Bryan, Howard. *Incredible Elfego Baca: Good Man, Bad Man of the Old West.* Santa Fe: Clear Light, 1993.

———. *Santa Fe Tales and More.* Santa Fe: Clear Light, 2010.

———. *True Tales of the American Southwest: Pioneer Recollections of Frontier Adventures.* Santa Fe: Clear Light, 1998.

Bryant, Kathleen. *Kokopelli's Gift.* Fort Wayne, IN: Kiva, 2003.

Bullis, Don. *New Mexico and Politicians of the Past: True Tales of Some of New Mexico's Founding Fathers and a Few Other Office Seekers and Holders.* Los Ranchos de Albuquerque, NM: Rio Grande Books, 2009.

———. *New Mexico Historical Biographies.* Los Ranchos de Albuquerque, NM: Rio Grande Books, 2011.

Bullock, Alice. *Discover Santa Fe.* Santa Fe: Rydal Press, distributed by Sunstone Press, 1973.

———. *Living Legends of the Santa Fe Country: A Pictorial Guidebook.* Santa Fe: Sunstone Press, 1978.

———. *Loretto and the Miraculous Staircase.* Santa Fe: Sunstone Press, 1978.

Bunker, Nick. *Making Haste from Babylon: The Mayflower Pilgrims and Their World, A New History.* New York: Knopf, 2010.

Burt, Elinor. *Spanish Dishes from the Old Clay Pot = Olla Podrida.* Berkeley: Ross Books, 1977.

Burton, David H. *William Howard Taft: Confident Peacemaker.* New York: Fordham University Press, 2004.

Buzan, Tony. *Use Both Sides of Your Brain.* New York: Plume, 1991.

Bynner, Witter. *Guest Book: Portraits in Poetry; If You've Ever Been a Guest, You're in This Book—Here's What Your Host Thinks of You.* New York: Knopf, 1935.

———. *Indian Earth.* New York: Knopf, 1929.

———. *Light Verse and Satires.* Farrar, Straus and Giroux, 1978.

Caduto, Michael J. *Catch the Wind, Harness the Sun: 22 Super-Charged Science Projects for Kids.* North Adams, MA: Storey, 2011.

Cajete, Greg. *Igniting the Spark: An Indigenous Science Education Model.* Skyland, NC: Kivaki Press, 1999.

Cajete, Greg, and Leroy Little Bear. *Native Science: Natural Laws of Interdependence.* Santa Fe: Clear Light, 2000.

Campa, Arthur L. *Hispanic Culture in the Southwest.* Norman: University of Oklahoma Press, 1979.

Campbell, Susan, and Suzanne Deats. *Landscapes of New Mexico.* Albuquerque: Fresco Fine Art Publications, 2006.

Canfield, Jack, Mark Victor Hansen, and Sidney R. Slagter, comps. *Chicken Soup for the Veteran's Soul: Stories to Stir the Pride and Honor the Courage of Our Veterans.* Deerfield Beach, FL: Health Communications, 2001.

Carmichael, Elizabeth, and Chloë Sayer. *The Skeleton at the Feast: The Day of the Dead in Mexico.* Austin: University of Texas Press, 1992.

Carrillo, Charles M. *Saints of the Pueblos.* Albuquerque: LPD Press, 2008.

Carroll, John M., ed. *The Black Military Experience in the American West.* New York: Liveright, 1971.

Carson, Christopher. *Kit Carson's Own Story of His Life.* Facsimile of 1926 edition. Santa Fe: Sunstone Press, 2007.

Carson, Rachel. *Silent Spring.* Boston: Houghton Mifflin, 2002. First published 1962.

Carson, William C. *Peter Becomes a Trail Man: The Story of a Boy's Journey on the Santa Fe Trail.* Albuquerque: University of New Mexico Press, 2002.

Carter, Jack. *Trees and Shrubs of New Mexico.* Albuquerque: Mimbres, 1997.

Carter, W. Hodding. *Flushed: How the Plumber Saved Civilization.* New York: Atria Books, 2006.

Carter, William B. *Indian Alliances and the Spanish in the Southwest, 750–1750.* Norman: University of Oklahoma Press, 2009.

Cash, Marie Romero. *Built of Earth and Song: Churches of Northern New Mexico.* Santa Fe: Red Crane Books, 1993.

———. *Tortilla Chronicles: Growing Up in Santa Fe.* Albuquerque: University of New Mexico Press, 2007.

Cather, Willa. *Death Comes for the Archbishop.* New York: Vintage Classics, 1990. First published 1928.

———. *Death Comes for the Archbishop.* Historical essay and explanatory notes by John J. Murphy. Lincoln: University of Nebraska Press, 1999.

Castillo, Ana. *Mi Hija, Mi Hijo, El Aguila, La Paloma: Un Canto Azteca.* New York: Dutton Books, 2000.

Cervantes, Miguel de. *Don Quixote.* Translated by Edith Grossman. Introduction by Harold Bloom. New York: Ecco, 2003. First published 1605 and 1615.

Cesari, Jocelyne, ed. *Encyclopedia of Islam in the United States.* Westport, CT: Greenwood, 2007.

Chamberlain, John. *The Heart of the Matter: The Diary of a School Year*. Santa Fe: Ginger Plum Press, 2001.

Chapman, Janet, and Karen Barrie. *Kenneth Milton Chapman: A Life Dedicated to Indian Arts and Artists*. Albuquerque: University of New Mexico Press, 2008.

Chaput, Donald. *François X. Aubrey: Trader, Trailmaker, and Voyageur in the Southwest, 1846–1854*. Glendale, CA: Arthur H. Clark, 1975.

Chase, Katherine. *Indian Painters of the Southwest: The Deep Remembering*. Santa Fe: School of American Research Press, 2002.

Chase-Daniel, Matthew, and Jerry Wellman. *Haiku Roadsign: A Project of Axle Contemporary*. Santa Fe: Axle Contemporary, 2011.

Chauvenet, Beatrice. *Hewett and Friends: A Biography of Santa Fe's Vibrant Era*. Santa Fe: Museum of New Mexico Press, 1983.

———. *Holy Faith in Santa Fe: The Story of a Pioneer Parish*. Santa Fe: Episcopal Church of the Holy Faith, 1977.

———. *John Gaw Meem: Pioneer in Historic Preservation*. Santa Fe: Museum of New Mexico Press, 1985.

Chávez, Fray Angélico. *But Time and Chance: The Story of Padre Martínez of Taos, 1793–1867*. Santa Fe: Sunstone Press, 1981.

———. *Chávez: A Distinctive American Clan of New Mexico*. Santa Fe: Sunstone Press, 2009. First published 1989.

———. *La Conquistadora: The Autobiography of an Ancient Statue*. Rev. ed. Santa Fe: Sunstone Press, 1983. First published 1954.

———. *My Penitente Land: Reflections on Spanish New Mexico*. Albuquerque: University of New Mexico Press, 1974.

———. *New Mexico Triptych*. Santa Fe: Sunstone Press, 2010. First published 1959.

———. *Origins of New Mexico Families: A Genealogy of the Spanish Colonial Period*. Santa Fe: Museum of New Mexico Press, 1992. First published 1954.

———. *Our Lady of the Conquest*. Santa Fe: Sunstone Press, 2010. First published 1948.

Chávez, Fray Angélico, and Thomas E. Chávez. *Wake for a Fat Vicar: Father Juan Felipe Ortiz, Archbishop Lamy, and the New Mexican Catholic Church in the Middle of the Nineteenth Century*. Albuquerque: LPD Press, 2004.

Chávez, Nicolasa, ed. *A Century of Masters: The NEA National Heritage Fellows of New Mexico*. Los Ranchos de Albuquerque, NM: Rio Grande Books, 2009.

Chávez, Thomas E., ed. *Conflict and Acculturation: Manuel Alvarez's 1842 Memorial*. Santa Fe: Museum of New Mexico Press, 1989.

———, ed. *An Illustrated History of New Mexico*. Albuquerque: University of New Mexico Press, 2002.

———. *Manuel Alvarez, 1794–1856: A Southwestern Biography*. Boulder: University Press of Colorado, 1990.

———. *New Mexico: Past and Future*. Albuquerque: University of New Mexico Press, 2006.

———. *Spain and the Independence of the United States: An Intrinsic Gift*. Albuquerque: University of New Mexico Press, 2002.

Cheek, Lawrence W. *Santa Fe*. Photographs by Eduardo Fuss. 5th ed. New York: Compass American Guides, 2008.

Chevalier, Jaima. *La Conquistadora: Unveiling the History of a Six Hundred Year Old Religious Icon*. Santa Fe: Sunstone Press, 2010.

Chrisp, Peter. *Town and Country Life*. San Diego: Lucent Books, 2004.

Chronic, Halka. *Roadside Geology of New Mexico*. Missoula, MT: Mountain Press, 1987.

Church, Peggy Pond. *The House at Otowi Bridge: The Story of Edith Warner and Los Alamos.* Albuquerque: University of New Mexico Press, 1960.

Clark, Ann Nolan. *In My Mother's House.* New York: Viking Press, 1941.

———. *Young Hunter of Picuris.* Walnut, CA: Kiva Publishing, 1999.

Clark, Ann Nolan, and Frances Carey. *A Child's Story of New Mexico.* Lincoln: University Publishing, 1941.

Clark, Ira. *Water in New Mexico: A History of Its Management and Use.* Albuquerque: University of New Mexico Press, 1987.

Clark, Willard F. *Recuerdos de Santa Fe, 1928–1943.* Santa Fe: Clark's Studio, 1990.

Clarke, Dwight L. *Stephen Watts Kearny: Soldier of the West.* Norman: University of Oklahoma Press, 1961.

Clee, Paul. *Before Hollywood: From Shadow Play to the Silver Screen.* New York: Clarion Books, 2005.

Cleland, Robert Glass. *This Reckless Breed of Men: The Trappers and Fur Traders of the Southwest.* New York: Knopf, 1950.

Cline, Lynn. *Literary Pilgrims: The Santa Fe and Taos Writers' Colonies, 1917–1950.* Albuquerque: University of New Mexico Press, 2007.

———. *Romantic Days and Nights in Santa Fe: Romantic Diversions in and around the City.* Guilford, CT: Globe Pequot Press, 2001.

Cobb, Mary. *A Sampler View of Colonial Life, with Projects Kids Can Make.* Brookfield, CT: Millbrook Press, 1999.

Cobos, Rubén. *A Dictionary of New Mexico and Colorado Spanish.* Rev. ed. Santa Fe: Museum of New Mexico Press, 2003.

———. *Refranes = Southwestern Spanish Proverbs.* Santa Fe: Museum of New Mexico Press, 1985.

Coke, Van Deren. *Photography in New Mexico: From the Daguerreotype to the Present.* Albuquerque: University of New Mexico Press, 1979.

Cole, M. R. *Los Pastores: A Mexican Play of the Nativity.* Boston: Houghton Mifflin, 1907.

Collier, John. *From Every Zenith: A Memoir, and Some Essays on Life and Thought.* Denver: Sage Books, 1963.

Colligan, John B. *The Juan Páez Hurtado Expedition of 1695.* Albuquerque: University of New Mexico Press, 1995.

Collins, Tracy Brown, ed. *Living through the Great Depression.* Farmington Hills, MI: Greenhaven Press, 2004.

Comfort, Charles Haines, and Mary Apolline Comfort. *This Is Santa Fe: A Guide to the City Different.* Santa Fe: Charles Haines Comfort, 1955.

Conant, Jennet. *109 East Palace: Robert Oppenheimer and the Secret City of Los Alamos.* New York: Simon & Schuster, 2005.

Connor, Seymour V., and Jimmy M. Skaggs. *Broadcloth and Britches: The Santa Fe Trade.* College Station: Texas A & M University Press, 1971.

Connors, Philip. *Fire Season: Field Notes from a Wilderness Lookout.* New York: Ecco, 2011.

Cooney, Barbara. *Miss Rumphius: Story and Pictures.* New York: Puffin Books, 1985.

Constandse, William. *A Tribute to the Women of Santa Fe.* Santa Fe: Utama, 1983.

Cook, Mary J. Straw. *Doña Tules: Santa Fe's Courtesan and Gambler.* Albuquerque: University of New Mexico Press, 2007.

———. *Loretto: The Sisters and Their Chapel.* Santa Fe: Museum of New Mexico Press, 2002.

Corbett, Katherine T. *In Her Place: A Guide to St. Louis Women's History.* St. Louis: Missouri Historical Society Press, 1999.

Córdova, Kathryn M. *¡Concha! Concha Ortiz y Pino, Matriarch of a 300-Year-Old New Mexico Legacy.* Bilingual edition. Santa Fe: Gran Via, 2004.

Coues, Elliott, ed. *The Expedition of Zebulon Montgomery Pike to the Headwaters of the Mississippi River through Louisiana Territory, and in New Spain during the Years 1805–1807.* Minneapolis: Ross & Haines, 1965. First published 1895.

Coulter, Lane, and Maurice Dixon, Jr. *New Mexican Tinwork, 1840–1940.* Albuquerque: University of New Mexico Press, 2004.

Covey, Cyclone, trans. and ed. *Cabeza de Vaca's Adventures in the Unknown Interior of America.* Albuquerque: University of New Mexico Press, 1961.

Cowen, George A. *Manhattan Project to the Santa Fe Institute: The Memoirs of George Cowen.* Albuquerque: University of New Mexico Press, 2010.

Crampton, C. Gregory, and Steven K. Madsen. *In Search of the Spanish Trail: Santa Fe to Los Angeles, 1829–1848.* Layton, UT: Gibbs Smith, 1994.

Crandall, Elizabeth. *Cities of the World Series: Santa Fe.* Chicago: Rand McNally, 1965.

Crawford, Stanley. *A Garlic Testament: Seasons on a Small New Mexico Farm.* Albuquerque: University of New Mexico Press, 1998.

————. *Mayordomo: Chronicle of an Acequia in Northern New Mexico.* Albuquerque: University of New Mexico Press, 1993.

Crayton, Sharon Louise. *One Taste: Vegetarian Home Cooking from around the World.* Santa Fe: Provecho Press, 2008.

Crozier-Hogle, Lois, and Darryl Bade Wilson, eds. *Surviving in Two Worlds: Contemporary Native American Voices.* Austin: University of Texas Press, 1997.

Crutchfield, James A. *It Happened in New Mexico: From the Pueblo Revolt to the Death of Billy the Kid, Thirty-one Events That Shaped the Land of Enchantment.* Guilford, CT: Morris, 2009.

Cuba, Stanley L. *Olive Rush: A Hoosier Artist in New Mexico.* Muncie, IN: Minnetrista Cultural Foundation, 1992.

Cunningham, Kevin, and Peter Benoit. *A True Book: The Pueblo.* New York: Children's Press, 2011.

Curtin, L. S. M. *Healing Herbs of the Upper Rio Grande.* Santa Fe: Laboratory of Anthropology, 1947.

Curtis, Edward S. *The North American Indian.* Cologne, Germany: Taschen, 2005.

Cutter, Charles R. *The Protector de Indios in Colonial New Mexico, 1659–1821.* Albuquerque: University of New Mexico Press, 1986.

Cutts, James M. *The Conquest of California and New Mexico, 1846–1848.* Albuquerque: Horn & Wallace, 1965.

Dale, Edward Everett. *The Indians of the Southwest: A Century of Development under the United States.* Norman: University of Oklahoma Press, 1949.

Dance Ceremonies of the Northern Rio Grande Pueblos. Santa Fe: High Desert Field Guides, 2005.

D'Antonio, Bob. *Santa Fe–Taos Hiking Guide: 52 Best Hiking Trails of Northern New Mexico.* Englewood, CO: Westcliffe, 2004.

Darkey, William A., ed. *Three Dialogues on Liberal Education.* Annapolis: St. John's College Press, 1979.

Dary, David. *The Santa Fe Trail: Its History, Legends, and Lore.* New York: Knopf, 2000.

Davenport, John. *The Internment of Japanese Americans during World War II: Detention of American Citizens.* Philadelphia: Chelsea House, 2010.

Davis, W. W. H. *El Gringo: New Mexico and Her People.* Lincoln: University of Nebraska Press, 1982. First published 1857.

Day Hikes in the Santa Fe Area. 6th ed. Santa Fe: Northern New Mexico Group of the Sierra Club, 2007.

Dean, Arlan. *The Santa Fe Trail: From Independence, Missouri, to Santa Fe, New Mexico.* New York: Power Kids Press, 2003.

Dean, Rob, ed. *Santa Fe, Its 400th Year: Exploring the Past, Defining the Future*. Santa Fe: Sunstone Press, 2010.

De Aragon, Ray John. *The Legend of La Llorona*. Sunstone Press, 2006.

DeBuys, William. *Enchantment and Exploitation: The Life and Hard Times of a New Mexico Mountain Range*. Albuquerque: University of New Mexico Press, 1985.

———. *A Great Aridness: Climate Change and the Future of the American Southwest*. New York: Oxford University Press, 2011.

DeBuys, William, and Alex Harris. *River of Traps: A Village Life*. Albuquerque: University of New Mexico Press, 1990.

Defouri, James H. *Historical Sketch of the Catholic Church in New Mexico*. Edited and annotated by Thomas J. Steele. Las Cruces, NM: Yucca Tree Press, 2003. First published 1887.

DeLaRonde, Joe. *Blacksmithing: Basics for the Homestead*. Layton, UT: Gibbs Smith, 2008.

Deloria, Vine. *God Is Red: A Native View of Religion*. Golden, CO: North American Press, 1994.

Deloria, Vine, and Daniel R. Wildcat. *Power and Place: Indian Education in America*. Golden, CO: Fulcrum, 2001.

DeMark, Judith Boyce, ed. *Essays in Twentieth-Century New Mexico History*. Albuquerque: University of New Mexico Press, 1994.

DePaola, Tomie. *The Night of Las Posadas*. New York: G. P. Putnam's Sons, 1999.

Deutsch, Sarah. *No Separate Refuge: Culture, Class, and Gender on an Anglo-Hispanic Frontier in the American Southwest, 1880–1940*. New York: Oxford University Press, 1987.

Dewey, Jennifer Owings. *Cowgirl Dreams: A Western Childhood*. Honesdale, PA: Boyds Mills Press, 1995.

———. *A Night and Day in the Desert*. Boston: Little, Brown, 1991.

———. *Zozobra: The Story of Old Man Gloom*. Albuquerque: University of New Mexico Press, 2004.

DeWitt, Dave, and Paul Bosland. *The Complete Chile Pepper Book: A Gardener's Guide to Choosing, Growing, Preserving, and Cooking*. Portland, OR: Timber, 2009.

DeWitt, Dave, and Nancy Gerlach. *The Food of Santa Fe: Authentic Recipes from the American Southwest*. Boston: Periplus Editions, 1998.

Dickens, Charles. *The Old Curiosity Shop*. New York: Penguin Classics, 2001. First published 1841.

Dispenza, Joseph, and Louise Turner. *Will Shuster: A Santa Fe Legend*. Santa Fe: Museum of New Mexico Press, 1989.

Di Suvero, Victor, ed. *We Came to Santa Fe*. Tesuque, NM: Pennywhistle Press, 2009.

Dobie, J. Frank. *Coronado's Children: Tales of Lost Mines and Buried Treasures of the Southwest*. Dallas: Southwest Press, 1930.

Domínguez, Francisco Atanasio. *The Domínguez-Escalante Journal: Their Expedition through Colorado, Utah, Arizona, and New Mexico in 1776*. Translated by Fray Angélico Chávez; edited by Ted J. Warner. Provo, UT: Brigham Young University Press, 1976.

———. *The Missions of New Mexico, 1776: A Description, with Other Contemporary Documents*. Translated and annotated by Eleanor B. Adams and Fray Angélico Chávez. Albuquerque: University of New Mexico Press, 1956.

Downey, Nate. *Harvest the Rain: How to Enrich Your Life by Seeing Every Storm as a Resource*. Santa Fe: Sunstone Press, 2010.

Dozier, Edward P. *The Pueblo Indians of North America*. New York: Holt, Rinehart & Winston, 1970.

Drohojowska-Philp, Hunter. *Full Bloom: The Art and Life of Georgia O'Keeffe*. New York: W. W. Norton, 2004.

Drucker, Malka. *The Family Treasury of Jewish Holidays*. New York: Little, Brown, 1994.

———. *Hanukkah: Eight Nights, Eight Lights*. New York: Holiday House, 1980.

————. *Rosh Hashanah and Yom Kippur: Sweet Beginnings.* New York: Holiday House, 1981.

Drumm, Stella M., ed. *Down the Santa Fe Trail and into Mexico: The Diary of Susan Shelby Magoffin, 1846–1847.* Lincoln: University of Nebraska Press, 1962.

Duckworth, Richard, and Fabian Stedman. *Tintinnalogia, or, The Art of Ringing.* Teddinton, England: Echo Library, 2007. First published 1671.

Duffus, Robert L. *The Santa Fe Trail.* New York: Longmans-Green, 1930.

Dulle, Ronald J. *Tracing the Santa Fe Trail: Today's Views, Yesterday's Voices.* Missoula, MT: Mountain Press, 2011.

DuMars, Charles T., Marilyn O'Leary, and Albert E. Utten. *Pueblo Indian Water Rights: Struggle for a Precious Resource.* Tucson: University of Arizona Press, 1984.

Dunmire, William W. *Gardens of New Spain: How Mediterranean Plants and Foods Changed America.* Austin: University of Texas Press, 2004.

Dunmire, William W., and Gail Tierney. *Wild Plants of the Pueblo Province: Exploring Ancient and Enduring Uses.* Santa Fe: Museum of New Mexico Press, 1995.

Dunnington, Jacqueline, and Charles C. Mann. *Viva Guadalupe! The Virgin in New Mexican Popular Art.* Santa Fe: Museum of New Mexico Press, 1997.

Dutton, Bertha P. *American Indians of the Southwest,* rev. ed. Albuquerque: University of New Mexico Press, 1983.

————. *Let's Explore Indian Villages, Past and Present: Tour Guide for Santa Fe Area.* Santa Fe: Museum of New Mexico Press, 1970.

————. *Myths and Legends of the Indians of the Southwest.* San Francisco: Bellerophon Books, 1978.

Dye, Victoria E. *All Aboard for Santa Fe: Railway Promotion of the Southwest, 1890s to 1930s.* Albuquerque: University of New Mexico Press, 2005.

Dyson, Michael Eric. *I May Not Get There with You: The True Martin Luther King, Jr.* New York: Free Press, 2000.

Early, James. *Presidio, Mission, and Pueblo: Spanish Architecture and Urbanism in the United States.* Dallas: Southern Methodist University Press, 2004.

Ebinger, Virginia Nylander. *Aguinaldos: Christmas Customs, Music, and Foods of the Spanish-Speaking Countries of the Americas.* Santa Fe: Sunstone Press, 2008.

Ebright, Malcolm. *Land Grants and Lawsuits in Northern New Mexico.* Albuquerque: University of New Mexico Press, 1994.

————. *Spanish and Mexican Land Grants and the Law.* Manhattan, KS: Sunflower University, 1989.

Elder, Jane Lenz, and David J. Weber. *Trading in Santa Fe: John M. Kingsbury's Correspondence with James Josiah Webb, 1853–1861.* Dallas: Southern Methodist University Press, 1996.

Elliott, J. H. *Empires of the Atlantic World: Britain and Spain in America, 1492–1830.* New Haven: Yale University Press, 2006.

Elliott, Melinda. *The School of American Research: A History, The First Eighty Years.* Santa Fe: School of American Research Press, 1987.

Ellis, Bruce T. *Bishop Lamy's Santa Fe Cathedral: With Records of the Old Spanish Church (Parroquia) and Convent Formerly on the Site.* Albuquerque: University of New Mexico Press, 1985.

Ellis, Richard N., ed. *New Mexico, Past and Present: A Historical Reader.* Albuquerque: University of New Mexico Press, 1971.

Encyclopedia of Islam in the United States. Westport, CT: Greenwood, 2007.

England, Tamara. *Josefina's Cookbook: A Peek at Dining in the Past with Meals You Can Cook Today.* Middleton, WI: Pleasant Company, 1998.

Englar, Mary. *The Pueblo: Farmers of the Southwest.* Mankato, MN: Bridgestone Books, 2003.

Epstein, Steven A. *Wage Labor and Guilds in Medieval Europe*. Chapel Hill: University of North Carolina Press, 1991.

Erdoes, Richard, and Alfonso Ortiz. *American Indian Trickster Tales*. New York: Penguin Books, 1998.

Espinosa, Aurelio M. *The Folklore of Spain in the American Southwest*. Norman: University of Oklahoma Press, 1985.

Espinosa, J. Manuel. *Crusaders of the Río Grande: The Story of Don Diego de Vargas and the Reconquest and the Refounding of New Mexico*. Chicago: Institute of Jesuit History, 1942.

———, trans. *First Expedition of Vargas into New Mexico, 1692*. Albuquerque: University of New Mexico Press, 1940.

Esquibel, José Antonio. *The Spanish Recolonization of New Mexico: An Account of the Families Recruited at Mexico City in 1693*. Albuquerque: Hispanic Genealogical Research Center of New Mexico, 1999.

Esquibel, José Antonio, and Charles M. Carrillo. *A Tapestry of Kinship: The Web of Influence among Escultores and Carpinteros in the Parish of Santa Fe, 1790–1860*. Albuquerque: LPD Press, 2004.

Etulain, Richard W. *Contemporary New Mexico*. Albuquerque: University of New Mexico Press, 1994.

———. *New Mexican Lives: Profiles and Historical Stories*. Albuquerque: University of New Mexico Press, 2002.

Ewing, Rex A. *Got Sun? Go Solar: Harness Nature's Free Energy to Heat and Power Your Grid-Tied Home*. Masonville, CO: PixyJack Press, 2009.

Faherty, William Barnaby. *Deep Roots and Golden Wings: 150 Years with the Visitation Sisters in the Archdiocese of Saint Louis*. St. Louis: River City, 1982.

Farago, Claire J., and Donna Pierce. *Transforming Images: New Mexican Santos in-between Worlds*. University Park: Pennsylvania State University Press, 2006.

Fathy, Hassan. *Architecture for the Poor: An Experiment in Rural Egypt*. Chicago: University of Chicago Press, 1973.

Faulk, Odie B., and Laura E. Faulk. *Defenders of the Interior Provinces: Presidial Soldiers on the Northern Frontier of New Spain*. Albuquerque: Albuquerque Museum, 1988.

Fellman, Michael. *Citizen Sherman: A Life of William Tecumseh Sherman*. New York: Random House, 1995.

Fergusson, Erna. *Dancing Gods: Indian Ceremonials of New Mexico and Arizona*. Albuquerque: University of New Mexico Press, 1991. First published 1931.

———. *Mexican Cookbook*. Albuquerque: University of New Mexico Press, 1969. First published 1934.

———. *Murder and Mystery in New Mexico*. Albuquerque: M. Armitage, 1948.

———. *New Mexico: A Pageant of Three Peoples*. Albuquerque: University of New Mexico Press, 1973. First published 1951.

Findley, James S. *The Natural History of New Mexican Mammals*. Albuquerque: University of New Mexico Press, 1987.

Fisher, Nora, ed. *Spanish Textile Tradition of New Mexico and Colorado: Museum of International Folk Art*. Santa Fe: Museum of New Mexico Press, 1979.

Fletcher, Alice C. *Indian Games and Dances with Native Songs: Arranged from American Indian Ceremonials and Sports*. Lincoln: University of Nebraska Press, 1994. First published 1915.

Flores, Camille. *Santa Fe Icons: 50 Symbols of the City Different*. Guilford, CT: Globe Pequot Press, 2010.

Flynn, Kathryn A., comp. and ed. *Treasures on the New Mexico Trails: Discover New Deal Art and Architecture*. Santa Fe: Sunstone Press, 1995.

Flynn, Kathryn A., and Richard Polese. *The New Deal: A 75th Anniversary Celebration*. Layton, UT: Gibbs Smith, 2008.

Foard, Sheila Wood. *Harvey Girl*. Lubbock: Texas Tech University Press, 2006.

Folk Art from the Global Village: The Girard Collection at the Museum of International Folk Art. Santa Fe: Museum of New Mexico Press, 1995.

Folsom, Franklin. *Indian Uprising on the Rio Grande: The Pueblo Revolt of 1680.* With introduction by Alfonso Ortiz. Albuquerque: University of New Mexico Press, 1996. First published 1973.

———. *Red Power on the Rio Grande: The Native American Revolution of 1680.* Albuquerque: University of New Mexico Press, 1989.

Fontana, Bernard L. *Entrada: The Legacy of Spain and Mexico in the United States.* Albuquerque: University of New Mexico Press, 1994.

Foote, Cheryl J. *Women of the New Mexico Frontier, 1846–1912.* Albuquerque: University of New Mexico Press, 2005.

Fox, Margalit. *Talking Hands: What Sign Language Reveals about the Mind.* New York: Simon & Schuster, 2007.

Fradkin, Philip L. *Stagecoach: Wells Fargo and the American West.* New York: Simon & Schuster Source, 2002.

Frank, Lois Ellen. *Foods of the Southwest Indian Nations: Traditional and Contemporary Native American Recipes.* Berkeley: Ten Speed Press, 2002.

Frank, Ross. *From Settler to Citizen: New Mexican Economic Development and the Creation of Vecino Society, 1750–1820.* Berkeley: University of California Press, 2000.

Fun and Games, from the series Ripley's Believe It or Not! Mind Teasers. Mankato, MN: Capstone Press, 1991.

Gallegos, Bernardo P. *Literacy, Education, and Society in New Mexico, 1693–1821.* Albuquerque: University of New Mexico Press, 1992.

Gandert, Miguel, photographer. *Nuevo Mexico Profundo: Rituals of an Indo-Hispano Homeland.* With essays by Ramón Gutiérrez, Enrique Lamadrid, Lucy R. Lippard, Chris Wilson, and Helen R. Lucero. Santa Fe: Museum of New Mexico Press, 2000.

Garate, Donald. *Juan Bautista de Anza: Basque Explorer in the New World.* Reno: University of Nevada Press, 2003.

Gárcez, Antonio R. *Adobe Angels: The Ghosts of Santa Fe.* Santa Fe: Red Rabbit Press, 1992.

García, Nasario, ed. and trans. *¡Chistes! Hispanic Humor of Northern New Mexico and Southern Colorado.* Santa Fe: Museum of New Mexico Press, 2004.

Gardner, Mark L., ed. *Jack Thorp's Songs of the Cowboys.* Illustrations by Ronald Kil. With CD performed by Mark L. Gardner and Rex Rideout. Santa Fe: Museum of New Mexico Press, 2005.

Garmhausen, Winona. *History of Indian Arts Education in Santa Fe: The Institute of American Indian Arts, with Historical Background, 1890 to 1962.* Santa Fe: Sunstone Press, 1988.

Gavin, Robin Farwell. *Traditional Arts of Spanish New Mexico.* Santa Fe: Museum of New Mexico Press, 1994.

Gell-Mann, Murray. *The Quark and the Jaguar: Adventures in the Simple and the Complex.* New York: W. H. Freeman, 1994.

Gibson, Daniel. *Pueblos of the Rio Grande: A Visitor's Guide.* Tucson: Rio Nuevo, 2001.

Gilbert, Fabiola Cabeza de Baca. *Historic Cookery.* Layton, UT: Gibbs Smith, 1997. First published 1931.

Gill, Donald A. *Stories behind the Street Names of Albuquerque, Santa Fe, and Taos.* Chicago: Bonus Books, 1994.

Gilpin, Daniel. *Snails, Shellfish, and Other Mollusks.* Minneapolis: Compass Point Books, 2006.

Gilpin, Laura. *The Enduring Navajo.* Austin: University of Texas Press, 1968.

———. *The Pueblos: A Camera Chronicle.* New York: Hastings, 1942.

———. *The Rio Grande, River of Destiny: An Interpretation of the River, the Land, and the People.* Austin: University of Texas, 1949.

Golden, Gloria. *Remnants of Crypto-Jews among Hispanic Americans.* Mountain View, CA: Floricanto Press, 2005.

Gomez, Laura E. *Manifest Destinies: The Making of the Mexican American Race.* New York: New York University Press, 2007.

Gonzales-Berry, Erlinda, ed. *Pasó por Aquí: Critical Essays on the New Mexican Literary Tradition, 1542–1988.* Albuquerque: University of New Mexico Press, 1989.

González, Deena J. *Refusing the Favor: Spanish-Mexican Women of Santa Fe, 1820–1880.* New York: Oxford University Press, 2000.

Goode's World Atlas. 22nd ed. Skokie, IL: Rand McNally, 2009.

Goodman, Susan, and Carl Dawson. *Mary Austin and the American West.* Berkeley: University of California Press, 2008.

Goodrich, Lloyd, and John I. H. Baur. *American Art of Our Century.* New York: Praeger, 1961.

Gordon, Edward E., and Elaine H. Gordon. *Literacy in America: Historic Journey and Contemporary Solutions.* Westport, CT: Praeger, 2003.

Graham Jr., Frank. *The Audubon Ark: A History of the National Audubon Society.* With Carl Buchheister. New York: Random House, 1990.

Grattan, Virginia L. *Mary Colter: Builder upon the Red Earth.* Rev. ed. Flagstaff, AZ: Grand Canyon Association, 2007.

Gray, Samuel L. *Tonita.* Santa Fe: Avanyu, 1990.

Gray, Virginia, and Alan Macrae. *Mud, Space, and Spirit: Handmade Adobes.* Photographs by Wayne McCall. Santa Barbara, CA: Capra, 1976.

Greathouse, Patricia. *Mariachi.* Layton, UT: Gibbs Smith, 2009.

Green Chile Bible: Award-Winning New Mexico Recipes. Compiled and edited by the Albuquerque Tribune. Santa Fe: Clear Light, 1993.

Greenfield, Amy Butler. *A Perfect Red: Empire, Espionage, and the Quest for the Color of Desire.* New York: HarperCollins, 2006.

Gregg, Andrew K. *New Mexico in the Nineteenth Century: A Pictorial History.* Albuquerque: University of New Mexico Press, 1987.

Gregg, Josiah. *Commerce of the Prairies.* Norman: University of Oklahoma Press, 1954. First published 1844.

Griego y Maestas, José. *Cuentos: Tales from the Hispanic Southwest.* Based on stories originally collected by Juan B. Rael and retold in English by Rudolfo Anaya. Santa Fe: Museum of New Mexico Press, 1980.

Grimes, Ronald L. *Symbol and Conquest: Public Ritual and Drama in Santa Fe.* Albuquerque: University of New Mexico Press, 1992. First published 1976.

Gutiérrez, Ramón A. *When Jesus Came, the Corn Mothers Went Away: Marriage, Sexuality, and Power in New Mexico, 1500–1846.* Stanford, CA: Stanford University Press, 1991.

Hackett, Charles Wilson, ed., and Charmion Clair Shelby, trans. *Revolt of the Pueblo Indians of New Mexico and Otermín's Attempted Reconquest, 1680–1682.* Albuquerque: University of New Mexico Press, 1942.

Hafen, LeRoy R., ed. *The Mountain Men and the Fur Trade of the Far West.* Glendale, CA: A. H. Clark, 1965.

———. *Old Spanish Trail: Santa Fe to Los Angeles.* Reno: University of Nevada Press, 1993.

Haines, Aubrey L. *Yellowstone National Park: Its Exploration and Establishment.* Washington, DC: U.S. National Park Service, 1974.

Hall, Donald. *Ox-Cart Man.* New York: Viking Press, 1979.

Hall, Douglas Kent. *The Thread of New Mexico.* Albuquerque: Albuquerque Museum, 2001.

Hall, E. Boyd. *Portfolio of Spanish Colonial Design in New Mexico.* Albuquerque: LPD, 2001.

Hall, G. Emlen. *Four Leagues of Pecos: A Legal History of the Pecos Grant, 1800–1933.* Albuquerque: University of New Mexico Press, 1984.

Hall, Thomas D. *Social Change in the Southwest, 1350–1880.* Lawrence: University Press of Kansas, 1989.

Hall-Quest, Olga. *Conquistadors and Pueblos: The Story of the American Southwest, 1540–1848.* New York: E. P. Dutton, 1968.

Halladay, Anne M. *Secrets at White Owl.* Austin: Steck-Vaughn, 1967.

Hämäläinen, Pekka. *The Comanche Empire.* New Haven: Yale University Press, 2009.

Hammett, Jerilou, Kingsley Hammett, and Peter Scholz. *The Essence of Santa Fe: From a Way of Life to a Style.* Santa Fe: Ancient City Press, 2006.

Hammett, Kingsley. *Santa Fe: A Walk through Time.* Layton, UT: Gibbs Smith, 2004.

Hammond, George, and Agapito Rey. *Don Juan de Oñate: Colonizer of New Mexico, 1595–1628.* 2 vols. Albuquerque: University of New Mexico Press, 1953.

Hansel, Kathleen, and Audrey Jenkins. *Red Chile Bible: Southwestern Classic and Gourmet Recipes.* Santa Fe: Clear Light, 1997.

Harrelson, Barbara J. *From Every Window: A Glimpse of the Past.* Santa Fe: La Fonda on the Plaza, 2011.

———. *Walks in Literary Santa Fe: A Guide to Landmarks, Legends, and Lore.* Layton, UT: Gibbs Smith, 2007.

Harrington, John Peabody. *29th Annual Report of the Bureau of American Ethnology for the Years 1907–1908.* Washington, DC: Smithsonian, 1916.

———. *Indian Tales from Picuris Pueblo.* Santa Fe: Ancient City Press, 1989.

———. *Old Indian Geographical Names around Santa Fe, New Mexico.* Washington, DC: American Anthropologist, 1920.

Harris, Linda G. *One Book at a Time: The History of the Library of New Mexico.* Albuquerque: New Mexico Library Foundation, 1998.

Harris, Marvin. *Good to Eat: Riddles of Food and Culture.* New York: Simon & Schuster, 1985.

Hart, Stephen Harding, and Archer Butler Hulbert, eds. *The Southwestern Journals of Zebulon Pike, 1806–1807.* Albuquerque: University of New Mexico Press, 2006.

Hathaway, Lynn, ed. *Santa Fe Cares about Kids!* Santa Fe: Santa Fe Children and Youth Commission, 2011.

Havens, Charnell, and Vera Marie Badertscher. *Quincy Tahoma: The Life and Legacy of a Navajo Artist.* Atglen, PA: Schiffer Books, 2011.

Hayes, Joe. *La Llorona = The Weeping Woman: An Hispanic Legend Told in Spanish and English.* Illustrated by Vicki Trego Hill and Mona Pennypacker. Bilingual edition. El Paso: Cinco Puntos Press, 2004.

Hayman, LeRoy. *Aces, Heroes, and Daredevils of the Air.* New York: J. Messner, 1981.

Haywood, John. *New Atlas of World History: Global Events at a Glance.* Princeton, NJ: Princeton University Press, 2011.

Hazen-Hammond, Susan. *A Short History of Santa Fe.* San Francisco: Lexikos, 1988.

———. *Thunder Bear and Ko: The Buffalo Nation and Nambé Pueblo.* New York: Dutton Children's Books, 1999.

Hearne, Vicki. *Animal Happiness: A Moving Exploration of Animals and Their Emotions.* New York: Skyhorse, 1994.

Held, E. B. *A Spy's Guide to Santa Fe and Albuquerque.* Albuquerque: University of New Mexico Press, 2011.

Heller, Lora. *Sign Language for Kids: A Fun and Easy Guide to American Sign Language*. New York: Sterling, 2004.

Hendersen, Helene. *Patriotic Holidays of the United States: An Introduction to the History, Symbols, and Traditions Behind the Major Holidays and Days of Observance*. Detroit: Omnigraphics, 2006.

Hendricks, Rick. *New Mexico in 1801: The Priests' Report*. Los Ranchos de Albuquerque, NM: Rio Grande Books, 2008.

Henri, Robert. *The Art Spirit*. Compiled by Margery Ryerson. 85th anniversary edition. New York: Basic Books, 2007. First published 1923.

Hertz, Cary. *New Mexico's Crypto-Jews: Image and Memory*. Albuquerque: University of New Mexico Press, 2007.

Hertzog, Peter. *La Fonda: The Inn of Santa Fe*. Santa Fe: Press of the Territorian, 1962.

Hewett, Edgar Lee. *Ancient Life in the American Southwest, with an Introduction on the General History of the American Race*. Indianapolis: Bobbs-Merrill Company, 1930.

———. *Campfire and Trail*. Albuquerque: University of New Mexico Press, 1943.

Heyerdahl, Thor. *Kon-Tiki: Across the Pacific by Raft*. Translated by F. H. Lyon. New York: Skyhorse, 2010. First published 1950.

———. *Kon-Tiki Man: An Illustrated Biography of Thor Heyerdahl*. With Christopher Ralling. San Francisco: Chronicle Books, 1990.

Hill, R. Kermit Jr. *A New Mexico Primer: For Students of All Ages*. Santa Fe: Sunstone Press, 2011.

Hill, Rick, Nancy Marie Mitchell, and Lloyd New. *Creativity Is Our Tradition: Three Decades of Contemporary Indian Art at the Institute of America Indian Arts*. Chicago: R. R. Donnelley & Sons, 1992.

Hillerman, Anne. *Children's Guide to Santa Fe*. Santa Fe: Sunstone Press, 2005.

———. *Tony Hillerman's Landscape: On the Road with Chee and Leaphorn*. Photographs by Don Strel. New York: HarperCollins. 2009.

Hillerman, Tony, ed. *The Best of the West: An Anthology of Classic Writing from the American West*. New York: HarperCollins, 1991.

———. *The Blessing Way*. New York: Harper, 2009. First published 1970.

———. *Indian Country: America's Sacred Land*. Photographs by Béla Kalman. Flagstaff, AZ: Northland Press, 1987.

———. *Seldom Disappointed: A Memoir*. New York: HarperCollins, 2001.

———, ed. *The Spell of New Mexico*. Albuquerque: University of New Mexico Press, 1976.

Hillerman, Tony, and Ernie Bulow. *Talking Mysteries: A Conversation with Tony Hillerman*. Albuquerque: University of New Mexico Press, 1991.

Hirliman, Georgelle. *Dear Writer in the Window: The Wit and Wisdom of a Sidewalk Sage*. New York: Penguin Books, 1992.

———. *The Hate Factory: A First-Hand Account of the 1980 Riot at the Penitentiary of New Mexico*. Based on interviews with inmate W. G. Stone. iUniverse, 2005.

Historic Santa Fe Foundation. *Old Santa Fe Today*. 4th ed. Albuquerque: University of New Mexico Press, 1991. First published 1966.

Hoad, Dorothy. *A Guide to Bandelier National Monument*. Los Alamos, NM: Los Alamos Historical Society, 1989.

Hoefer, Jacqueline. *A More Abundant Life: New Deal Artists and Public Art in New Mexico*. Santa Fe: Sunstone Press, 2003.

Hoerig, Karl. *Under the Palace Portal*. Albuquerque: University of New Mexico Press, 2003.

Holling, Holling Clancy. *The Book of Cowboys*. New York: Platt & Munk, 1936.

———. *The Book of Indians*. New York: Platt & Munk, 1935.

————. *Tree in the Trail*. Boston: Houghton Mifflin, 1942.

Holmes, Kenneth L., ed. and comp. *Covered Wagon Women: Diaries and Letters from the Western Trails, 1840–1849*. Lincoln: University of Nebraska Press, 1995.

Holt, Dean W. *American Military Cemeteries: A Comprehensive Illustrated Guide to the Hallowed Grounds of the United States, Including Cemeteries Overseas*. Jefferson, NC: McFarland, 1992.

Hordes, Stanley M. *To the End of the Earth: A History of the Crypto-Jews of New Mexico*. New York: Columbia University Press, 2005.

Hordes, Stanley M., and Carol Joiner. *Historical Markers in New Mexico*. Corrales, NM: Delgado Studios, 1984.

Horgan, Paul. *The Centuries of Santa Fe*. Albuquerque: University of New Mexico Press, 1994. First published 1956.

————. *The Great River: The Rio Grande in North American History*. Hanover, NH: Wesleyan University Press, 1991. First published 1954.

————. *Lamy of Santa Fe: His Life and Times*. Middletown, CT: Wesleyan University Press, 2003. First published 1975.

Horn, Calvin. *New Mexico's Troubled Years: The Story of the Early Territorial Governors*. Albuquerque: Horn & Wallace, 1963.

Horne, Gerald, ed. *Thinking and Rethinking U.S. History*. New York: Council on Interracial Books for Children, 1988.

Horton, Sarah Bronwen. *The Santa Fe Fiesta, Reinvented: Staking Ethno-Nationalist Claims to a Disappearing Homeland*. Santa Fe: School for Advanced Research Press, 2010.

Hotz, Gottfried. *Segesser Hide Paintings: Masterpieces Depicting Spanish Colonial New Mexico*. Santa Fe: Museum of New Mexico Press, 1991. First published 1970.

Hoxie, Frederick E., ed. *Talking Back to Civilization: Indian Voices from the Progressive Era*. New York: Bedford/St. Martin's, 2001.

Hoyt-Goldsmith, Diane. *Las Posadas: An Hispanic Christmas Celebration*. New York: Holiday House, 1999.

Hsi, David, and Janda K. G. Panitz. *From Sundaggers to Space Exploration: Significant Scientific Contributions to Science and Technology in New Mexico*. Santa Fe: New Mexico Academy of Science, 1986.

Huelster, Dick, and Kathryn Huelster. *Dance Ceremonies of the Northern Rio Grande Pueblos*. Santa Fe: High Desert Field Guides, 2005.

Hughes, Dorothy. *Pueblo on the Mesa*. Albuquerque: University of New Mexico Press, 1939.

Hughes, Phyllis, comp. and ed. *Pueblo Indian Cookbook: Recipes from the Pueblos of the American Southwest*. Santa Fe: Museum of New Mexico Press, 1977.

Hulbert, Archer Butler, ed. *Southwest on the Turquoise Trail: The First Diaries on the Road to Santa Fe, Edited, with Bibliographical Resume, 1810–1835*. Colorado Springs: Stewart Commission of Colorado College, 1933.

Hunner, Jon. *J. Robert Oppenheimer, the Cold War, and the Atomic West*. Norman: University of Oklahoma Press, 2009.

Hunner, Jon, Shirley Lail, Pedro Domínguez, Darren Court, and Lucinda Silva. *Santa Fe: A Historical Walking Tour*. Chicago: Arcadia, 2000.

Huntford, Roland. *Two Planks and a Passion: The Dramatic History of Skiing*. New York: Continuum, 2009.

Hurst, James W. *Pancho Villa and Black Jack Pershing: The Punitive Expedition in Mexico*. New York: Praeger, 2008.

Huscher, Philip. *The Santa Fe Opera: An American Pioneer*. Santa Fe: Sunstone Press, 2006.

Huschke, Kai. *50 Hikes in Northern New Mexico: From Chaco Canyon to the High Peaks of the Sangre de Cristos*. Woodstock, VT: Countryman Press, 2007.

Huxley, Aldous. *Brave New World*. New York: Perennial Classics, 1998. First published 1932.

Hyer, Sally. *One House, One Voice, One Heart: Native American Education at the Santa Fe Indian School*. Santa Fe: Museum of New Mexico Press, 1990.

———, ed. *Recording a Vanishing Legacy: The Historic American Buildings Survey in New Mexico, 1933–Today*. Santa Fe: Museum of New Mexico Press, 2001.

Hyslop, Stephen Garrison. *Bound for Santa Fe: The Road to New Mexico and American Conquest, 1806–1848*. Norman: University of Oklahoma Press, 2002.

Ibn Al 'Arabi. *The Bezels of Wisdom*. Translated by R. W. J. Austin. New York: Paulist Press, 1980.

Iowa, Jerome. *Ageless Adobe: History and Preservation in Southwestern Architecture*. Santa Fe: Sunstone Press, 1985.

Jackson, Hal. *Following the Royal Road: A Guide to the Historic Camino Real de Tierra Adentro*. Albuquerque: University of New Mexico Press, 2006.

Jackson, John Brinckerhoff. *Discovering the Vernacular Landscape*. New Haven: Yale University Press, 1984.

Jackson, Steve. *Lucky Lady: The World War II Heroics of the USS* Santa Fe *and* Franklin. New York: Carroll & Graf, 2003.

Jacobs, Frank. *Strange Maps: An Atlas of Cartographic Curiosities*. New York: Viking Studio, 2009.

Jaehn, Tomas. *Germans in the Southwest: 1850–1920*. Albuquerque: University of New Mexico Press, 2005.

———, comp. and ed. *Jewish Pioneers of New Mexico*. Santa Fe: Museum of New Mexico Press, 2003.

James, Will. *Cowboys North and South*. Missoula, MT: Mountain Press, 1995. First published 1924.

———. *Smoky the Cowhorse*. New York: Scribner, 1926.

Janin, Hunt, and Ursula Carlson. *Trails of Historic New Mexico: Routes Used by Indian, Spanish, and American Travelers through 1886*. Jefferson, NC: McFarland, 2010.

Jaramillo, Cleo. *Romance of a Little Village Girl*. San Antonio, TX: Naylor, 1955.

Jenkins, Myra Ellen, and Albert H. Schroeder. *A Brief History of New Mexico*. Albuquerque: University of New Mexico Press, 1974.

John, Elizabeth Ann Harper. *Storms Brewed in Other Men's Worlds: The Confrontation of Indians, Spanish, and French in the Southwest, 1540–1795*. Norman: University of Oklahoma Press, 1996.

Jones, Oakah, Jr. *Los Paisanos: Spanish Settlers on the Northern Frontier of New Spain*. Norman: University of Oklahoma Press, 1979.

Jordan, Louann. *El Rancho de las Golondrinas: Spanish Colonial Life in New Mexico*. Santa Fe: Colonial New Mexico Historical Foundation, 1977.

Jovinelly, Joan, and Jason Netelkos. *The Crafts and Culture of a Medieval Town*. New York: Rosen, 2007.

Julyan, Robert Hixson. *Best Hikes with Children in New Mexico*. Rev. ed. Seattle: Mountaineers Books, 2004.

———. *The Mountains of New Mexico*. Albuquerque: University of New Mexico Press, 2006.

———. *The Place Names of New Mexico*. Rev. ed. Albuquerque: University of New Mexico Press, 1998.

Kabotie, Fred. *Designs from the Ancient Mimbreños, with a Hopi Interpretation*. Flagstaff, AZ: Northland Press, 1982.

Kallen, Stuart A. *A Medieval Merchant*. Detroit: Lucent Books, 2005.

Kanellos, Nicolás, ed. *Noche Buena: Hispanic American Christmas Stories*. New York: Oxford University Press, 2000.

Kane, Charles W. *Medicinal Plants of the American Southwest*. Oracle, AZ: Lincoln Town Press, 2011.

Kaplan, Jim. *The Golden Years of Baseball*. New York: Random House, 1992.

Keegan, Marcia. *Mother Earth, Father Sky: Navajo and Pueblo Indians of the Southwest*. Rev. ed. Santa Fe: Clear Light, 1989.

———. *Pueblo Girls: Growing Up in Two Worlds*. Santa Fe: Clear Light, 1999.

———. *Pueblo People: Ancient Traditions, Modern Living*. Santa Fe: Clear Light, 1999.

———. *Southwest Indian Cookbook: Pueblo and Navajo Images, Quotes, and Recipes*. Santa Fe: Clear Light, 1987.

Keegan, Marcia, and frontier photographers. *Enduring Culture: A Century of Photography of the Southwest Indians*. Santa Fe: Clear Light, 1990.

Keleher, William A. *The Fabulous Frontier, 1846–1912*. Facsimile of 1962 edition. Santa Fe: Sunstone Press, 2008.

———. *Maxwell Land Grant*. Facsimile of 1942 edition. Santa Fe: Sunstone Press, 2008.

———. *Turmoil in New Mexico, 1846–1868*. Facsimile of 1952 edition. Santa Fe: Sunstone Press, 2008.

Kelly, Daniel T. *The Buffalo Head: A Century of Mercantile Pioneering in the Southwest*. With Beatrice Chauvenet. Santa Fe: Vergara, 1972.

Kelly, James C., and Barbara Clark Smith. *Jamestown, Quebec, Santa Fe: Three North American Beginnings*. With contributions by Warren M. Billings, Gilles Proulx, and David J. Weber. Washington, DC: Smithsonian Books, 2007.

Kelly, L. C. *The Assault on Assimilation: John Collier and the Origins of Indian Policy Reform*. Albuquerque: University of New Mexico Press, 1963.

Kelly, Matt. *The Best of* From the Plaza: *Interviews and Opinions from the Plaza of Santa Fe*. Edited by Ardeth and William Baxter. Santa Fe: Lone Butte Press, 1998.

Kennard, Edward A. *Field Mouse Goes to War = Tusan Homichi Tuwvöta*. Hopi text by Albert Yava. Illustrations by Fred Kabotie. Palmer Lake, CO: Filter Press, 1999.

Kessell, John L. *Kiva, Cross, and Crown: The Pecos Indians and New Mexico, 1540–1840*. Washington, DC: National Park Service, 1979.

———. *Pueblos, Spaniards, and the Kingdom of New Mexico*. Norman: University of Oklahoma Press, 2008.

———, ed. *Remote Beyond Compare: Letters of Don Diego de Vargas to His Family from New Spain and New Mexico, 1675–1706*. Albuquerque: University of New Mexico Press, 1989.

———. *Spain in the Southwest: A Narrative History of Colonial New Mexico, Arizona, Texas, and California*. Norman: University of Oklahoma Press, 2002.

Kessell, John L., and Rick Hendricks, eds. *By Force of Arms: The Journals of Don Diego de Vargas, New Mexico, 1691–1693*. Albuquerque: University of New Mexico Press, 1992.

Kessell, John L., Rick Hendricks, and Meredith D. Dodge, eds. *Blood on the Boulders: The Journals of Don Diego de Vargas, New Mexico, 1694–1697*. Albuquerque: University of New Mexico Press, 1998.

———, eds. *Letters from the New World: Selected Correspondence of Don Diego de Vargas to His Family, 1675–1706*. Albuquerque: University of New Mexico Press, 1992.

———, eds. *A Settling of Accounts: The Journals of Don Diego de Vargas, New Mexico, 1700–1704*. Albuquerque: University of New Mexico Press, 2002.

———, eds. *That Disturbances Cease: The Journals of Don Diego de Vargas, New Mexico, 1697–1700*. Albuquerque: University of New Mexico Press, 2000.

———, eds. *To the Royal Crown Restored: The Journals of Don Diego de Vargas, New Mexico, 1692–94*. Albuquerque: University of New Mexico Press, 1995.

Kidder, Alfred Vincent. *An Introduction to the Study of Southwestern Archaeology*. New Haven: Yale University Press, 2000. First published 1924.

King, Bruce. *Cowboy in the Roundhouse: A Political Life*. Santa Fe: Sunstone Press, 1998.

Kitchell, Webster. *God's Dog: Conversation with Coyote*. Santa Fe: Unitarian Universalist Church, 1991.

Knaut, Andrew L. *The Pueblo Revolt of 1680: Conquest and Resistance in Seventeenth-Century New Mexico*. Norman: University of Oklahoma Press, 1995.

Knee, Dana, ed. *Ernest Knee in New Mexico: Photographs, 1930s–1940s*. Santa Fe: Museum of New Mexico Press, 2005.

Knee, Ernest. *Santa Fe, N.M.* New York: Chanticleer Press, 1942.

Kochendoerfer, Violet. *Santa Fe in the Fifties: A Memoir of Change in the City Different*. Santa Fe: Western Edge Press, 1998.

Kraft, James. *Who Is Witter Bynner? A Biography*. Albuquerque: University of New Mexico Press, 1995.

Krahe, Rev. Daniel. *Cristo Rey: A Symphony in Mud*. Lourdes School Press, 1940.

Krause, Martin F., Madeline Carol Yurtseven, and David Acton. *Gustave Baumann: Nearer to Art*. Santa Fe: Museum of New Mexico Press, 1993.

Krenz, Nancy, and Patricia Byrnes. *Southwestern Arts and Crafts Projects, Ages 5–12*. Santa Fe: Sunstone Press, 1979.

Krumgold, Joseph. *And Now Miguel*. New York: Crowell, 1953.

Kubler, George. *The Rebuilding of San Miguel at Santa Fe in 1710*. Colorado Springs: Taylor Museum of the Colorado Fine Arts Center, 1939.

———. *The Religious Architecture of New Mexico in the Colonial Period and since the American Occupation*. Albuquerque: University of New Mexico Press, 1990. First published 1940.

———. *The Shape of Time: Remarks on the History of Things*. New Haven: Yale University Press, 1962.

Kunin, Seth D. *Juggling Identities: Identity and Authenticity among the Crypto-Jews*. New York: Columbia University Press, 2009.

Kusel, Denise. *Only in Santa Fe*. Santa Fe: Sunstone Press, 2005.

Labinsky, Daria, and Stan Hieronymous. *Frank Applegate of Santa Fe: Artist and Preservationist*. Albuquerque: LPD Press, 2001.

Lacy, Ann, and Anne Valley-Fox, comps. and eds. *Frontier Stories: A New Mexico Federal Writers' Project Book*. Santa Fe: Sunstone Press, 2010.

———, comps. and eds. *Lost Treasures and Old Mines: A New Mexico Federal Writers' Project Book*. Santa Fe: Sunstone Press, 2011.

———, comps. and eds. *Outlaws and Desperados: A New Mexico Federal Writers' Project Book*. Santa Fe: Sunstone Press, 2008.

———, comps. and eds. *Stories from Hispano New Mexico: A New Mexico Federal Writers' Project Book*. Santa Fe: Sunstone Press, 2012.

La Farge, John Pen, ed. *Turn Left at the Sleeping Dog: Scripting the Santa Fe Legend, 1920–1955*. Albuquerque: University of New Mexico Press, 2001.

La Farge, Oliver. *Behind the Mountains*. Santa Fe: Sunstone Press, 2008. First published 1956.

———. *The Changing Indian*. Norman: University of Oklahoma Press, 1942.

———. *Laughing Boy*. Boston: Mariner Books, 2004. First published 1929.

———. *The Man with the Calabash Pipe: Some Observations*. Santa Fe: Sunstone Press, 2011. First published 1966.

———. *The Mother Ditch = La Acequia Madre*. Spanish translation by Pedro Ribera Ortega. Santa Fe: Sunstone Press, 1983.

———. *Raw Material: The Autobiographical Examination of an Artist's Journey into Maturity*. Facsimile of 1945 edition. Santa Fe: Sunstone Press, 2009.

La Farge, Oliver, and Arthur N. Morgan. *Santa Fe: The Autobiography of a Southwestern Town*. Norman: University of Oklahoma Press, 1959.

La Pierre, Yvette. *Welcome to Josefina's World, 1824: Growing Up on America's Southwest Frontier.* Middleton, WI: Pleasant Company, 1999.

La Sociedad Folklórica. *Spanish Riddles and Colcha Designs = Adivinanzas Españolas y Diseños de Colcha.* Santa Fe: Sunstone Press, 1994.

Lamadrid, Enrique R., and Jack Loeffler. *Tesoros del Espíritu: A Portrait in Sound of Hispanic New Mexico.* Albuquerque: El Norte/Academic Publications, 1994.

Lamar, Howard Roberts. *The Far Southwest, 1846–1912: A Territorial History.* Albuquerque: University of New Mexico Press, 2000. First published 1966.

———, ed. *The New Encyclopedia of the American West.* New Haven: Yale University Press, 1998.

Lamb, Edgar, and Brian Lamb. *Colorful Cacti of the American Southwest.* New York: Macmillan, 1974.

Lamb, Susan. *Petroglyph National Monument.* Tucson: Southwest Parks and Monuments Association, 1993.

Landau, Elaine. *The Transcontinental Railroad.* New York: Franklin Watts, 2005.

Lange, Charles H., and Carroll L. Riley. *Bandelier: The Life and Adventures of Adolph Bandelier.* Salt Lake City: University of Utah Press, 1996.

Langston, LaMoine "Red." *A History of Masonry in New Mexico, 1877–1977.* Roswell, NM: Hall-Poorbaugh Press, 1977.

Lanner, Ronald M. *The Piñon Pine: A Natural and Cultural History.* Reno: University of Nevada Press, 1981.

Laughlin, Ruth. *Caballeros: The Romance of Santa Fe and the Southwest.* Facsimile of revised 1945 edition. Santa Fe: Sunstone Press, 2007.

———. *The Wind Leaves No Shadow.* Caldwell, ID: Caxton, 1951.

Lavender, David. *Bent's Fort.* Lincoln: University of Nebraska Press, 1954.

———. *The Southwest.* Albuquerque: University of New Mexico Press, 1984.

Lawter, William Clifford Jr. *Smokey Bear 20252: A Biography.* Lindsay Smith, 1994.

Lecompte, Janet. *Rebellion in Rio Arriba, 1837.* Albuquerque: University of New Mexico Press, 1985.

Lee, Russell, John Collier Jr., and Jack Delano. *Threads of Culture: Photography in New Mexico, 1939–1943.* Santa Fe: Museum of New Mexico Press, 1993.

Leeds, Valeria Ann. *Robert Henri in Santa Fe: His Work and Influence.* Santa Fe: Gerald Peters Gallery, 1998.

Lehmberg, Stanford. *Holy Faith of Santa Fe, 1863–2000.* Albuquerque: LPD Press, 2004.

Lenderman, Gary D., ed. *The Santa Fe Republican: New Mexico Territory's First Newspaper, 1847–1849.* Charleston, SC: Gary Lenderman, 2011.

Lenski, Lois. *Cowboy Small.* New York: Random House, 1949.

Levin, Eli. *Santa Fe Bohemia: The Art Colony, 1964–1980.* Santa Fe: Sunstone Press, 2007.

Levine, Frances. *Our Prayers Are in This Place: Pecos Pueblo Identity over the Centuries.* Albuquerque: University of New Mexico Press, 1999.

Levine, Frances, René Harris, and Josef Díaz, eds. *The Threads of Memory: Spain and the United States = El Hilo de la Memoria: Espana y los Estados Unidos.* Bilingual ed. Translated by Enrique Lamadrid and Jerry Gurulé. Published in collaboration with curator Falia González Díaz, Archivo General de Indias, Spain; New Mexico History Museum; El Paso Museum of History; Historic New Orleans Collection; University of New Mexico; and Sociedad Estatal para la Acción Cultural Exterior, Spain. Albuquerque: Fresco Fine Art, 2010.

Lewandowski, Stacia. *Light, Landscape, and the Creative Quest: Early Artists of Santa Fe.* Santa Fe: Salska Arts, 2011.

———. *Walking in the Path of the Artists: A Guide to the Artists' Homes.* Santa Fe: Salski Arts, 2011.

Lewis, Nancy Owen, and Kay Leigh Hagan. *A Peculiar Alchemy: A Centennial History of SAR, 1907–2007*. Santa Fe: School for Advanced Research, 2007.

Leyba, Lucinda Ciddio. *Bruja: The Legend of La Llorona*. Albuquerque: University of New Mexico Press, 2011.

Liberman, Anatoly. *Word Origins and How We Know Them: Etymology for Everyone*. New York: Oxford University Press, 2005.

Lippard, Lucy R. *Down Country: The Tano of the Galisteo Basin, 1250–1782*. Santa Fe: Museum of New Mexico Press, 2011.

Littlefield, Douglas R. *Conflict on the Rio Grande: Water and the Law, 1879—1939*. Norman: University of Oklahoma Press, 2008.

Lockhart, James. *Nahuatl as Written: Lessons in Older Written Nahuatl, with Copious Examples and Texts*. Stanford: Stanford University Press, 2001.

Loeffler, Jack. *La Música de los Viejitos: Hispano Folk Music of the Rio Grande del Norte*. Albuquerque: University of New Mexico Press, 1999.

———, ed. *Survival along the Continental Divide: An Anthology of Interviews*. Albuquerque: University of New Mexico Press, 2008.

Logghe, Joan. *The Singing Bowl*. Albuquerque: University of New Mexico Press, 2011.

Lomelí, Francisco A., and Clark A. Colahan, trans. and eds. *Defying the Inquisition in Colonial New Mexico: Miguel de Quintana's Life and Writings*. Albuquerque: University of New Mexico Press, 2006.

Long, Michael G., ed. *Christian Peace and Nonviolence: A Documentary History*. Maryknoll, NY: Orbis Books, 2011.

Loomis, Noel, and Abraham Nasatir. *Pedro Vial and the Roads to Santa Fe*. Norman: University of Oklahoma Press, 1967.

Lopez, Barry, ed. *Home Ground: Language for an American Landscape*. San Antonio, TX: Trinity University Press, 2006.

Lorence, James J. *The Suppression of* Salt of the Earth*: How Hollywood, Big Labor, and Politicians Blacklisted a Movie*. Albuquerque: University of New Mexico Press, 1999.

Lovato, Andrew Leo. *Elvis Romero and Fiesta de Santa Fe, Featuring Zozobra's Great Escape*. Santa Fe: Museum of New Mexico Press, 2011.

———. *Santa Fe Hispanic Culture: Preserving Identity in a Tourist Town*. Albuquerque: University of New Mexico Press, 2004.

Lowitt, Richard. *Bronson M. Cutting: Progressive Politician*. Albuquerque: University of New Mexico Press, 1992.

Lucero, Donald L. *The Adobe Kingdom: New Mexico 1598–1958, As Experienced by the Families Lucero de Goday y Baca*. Santa Fe: Sunstone Press, 2009.

Lucero, Evelina Zuni. *Night Sky, Morning Star*. Tucson: University of Arizona Press, 2000.

Lummis, Charles Fletcher. *The Land of Poco Tiempo*. Albuquerque: University of New Mexico Press, 1952. First published 1893.

———. *The Man Who Married the Moon, and Other Pueblo Indian Folk-Stories*. New York: Century, 1894.

———. *Mesa, Canyon, and Pueblo: Our Wonderland of the Southwest, Its Marvels of Nature, Its Pageant of the Earth Building, Its Strange Peoples, Its Centuried Romance*. New York: Century, 1925.

———. *The Spanish Pioneers*. Bibliographical Center for Research, 2011. First published 1893.

Lumpkins, William T. *Casa del Sol: Your Guide to Passive Solar House Designs*. Santa Fe: Santa Fe Publishing Company, 1981.

Lux, Annie. *Historic New Mexico Churches*. Photographs by Daniel Nadelbach. Layton, UT: Gibbs Smith, 2007.

Lynch, Cyprian J., ed. *Benavides' Memorial of 1630*. Washington, DC: Academy of American Franciscan History, 1954.

Lynes, Barbara Buhler. *Georgia O'Keeffe and New Mexico: A Sense of Place*. Santa Fe: Georgia O'Keeffe Museum, 2004.

Lynn, Sandra D. *Windows on the Past: Historic Lodgings of New Mexico*. Albuquerque: University of New Mexico Press, 1999.

McCline, John. *Slavery in the Clover Bottoms: John McCline's Narrative of His Life During Slavery and the Civil War*. Edited by Jan Furman. Knoxville: University of Tennessee Press, 1998.

McCord, Richard. *The Chain Gang: One Newspaper Versus the Gannett Empire*. Columbia: University of Missouri Press, 1996.

————. *Santa Fe Living Treasures: Our Elders, Our Hearts*. Santa Fe: Sunstone Press, 2009.

McCracken, Ellen. *The Life and Writing of Fray Angélico Chávez: A New Mexico Renaissance Man*. Albuquerque: University of New Mexico Press, 2009.

McCulloch, Frank. *Revolution and Rebellion: How Taxes Cost a Governor His Life in 1830s New Mexico*. Illustrations by Frank McCulloch Jr. Santa Fe: Sunstone Press, 2001.

McDonough, Patricia M. *Choosing Colleges: How Social Class and Schools Structure Opportunity*. New York: SUNY Press, 1997.

McGeagh, Robert. *Juan de Oñate's Colony in the Wilderness: An Early History of the American Southwest*. Santa Fe: Sunstone Press, 1990.

MacGregor, Greg, and Siegfried Halus. *In Search of Domínguez and Escalante: Photographing the 1776 Spanish Expedition through the Southwest*. Santa Fe: Museum of New Mexico Press, 2011.

McNitt, Frank. *The Indian Traders*. Norman: University of Oklahoma Press, 1962.

Madison, Deborah. *Vegetarian Cooking for Everyone*. New York: Broadway Books, 1997.

Magadi, Athi-Mara. *Santa Fe Originals: Women of Distinction*. Santa Fe: Museum of New Mexico Press, 2003.

Magee, Bryan. *The Story of Philosophy*. New York: Dorling Kindersley, 2001.

Major, Mabel, and T. M. Pearce. *Southwest Heritage: A Literary History with Bibliography*. Rev. ed. Albuquerque: University of New Mexico Press, 1972. First published 1938.

Magoffin, Susan Shelby. *Down the Santa Fe Trail and into Mexico: The Diary of Susan Shelby Magoffin, 1846–1847*. Lincoln: University of Nebraska Press, 1962.

Mails, Thomas E. *The Pueblo Children of the Earth Mother*. New York: Marlowe, 1983.

Mallard, Neil, and U.S. Submarine Force Museum. *Submarine*. New York: DK Publishers, 2003.

Manion, Patricia Jean. *Beyond the Adobe Wall: The Sisters of Loretto in New Mexico, 1852–1894*. Independence, MO: Two Trails, 2001.

Mann, Charles C. *1491: New Revelations of the Americas before Columbus*. 2nd ed. New York: Vintage, 2011.

————. *1493: Uncovering the New World Columbus Created*. New York: Knopf, 2011.

Marley, Greg A. *Chanterelle Dreams, Amanita Nightmares: The Love, Lore, and Mystique of Mushrooms*. White River Junction, VT: Chelsea Green, 2010.

Marrin, Albert. *Empires Lost and Won: The Spanish Heritage in the Southwest*. New York: Simon & Schuster/Atheneum Books for Young Readers, 1997.

Martin, Bill, and John Archambault. *Knots on a Counting Rope*. New York: Henry Holt and Company, 1987.

Martin, Craig. *100 Hikes in New Mexico*. Seattle: Mountaineers Books, 2001.

Martin, Gene, and Mary Martin. *Trail Dust: A Quick Picture History of the Santa Fe Trail*. Denver: Golden Bell Press, 1972.

Martin, Mary L., and Ginny Parfitt. *Santa Fe and Taos: A History in Postcards*. Atglen, PA: Schiffer Publishing, 2007.

Martinez, Eluid Levi. *What Is a New Mexico Santo?* Rev. ed. Santa Fe: Sunstone Press, 1992.

Martinez, Zarela. *Food from My Heart: Cuisines of Mexico Remembered and Reimagined*. New York: Macmillan, 1992.

Mather, Christine. *Santa Fe Christmas*. Santa Fe: Museum of New Mexico Press, 1993.

Mather, Christine, and Sharon Woods. *Santa Fe Style*. New York: Rizzoli International, 1986.

Mathews, Melonie. *Cooking Vegetarian with Melonie Mathews*. Albuquerque: Gathering of Nations Publishing, 2002.

Matson, Tim. *The Book of Non-Electric Lighting: The Classic Guide to the Safe Use of Candles, Fuel Lamps, Lanterns, Gas Lights, and Fire-view Stoves*. 2nd ed. Woodstock, VT: Countryman Press, 2008.

Matthews, Kay. *Cross-Country Skiing in Northern New Mexico: An Introduction and Trail Guide*. Santa Fe: Acequia Madre Press, 1993.

———. *Hiking the Mountain Trails of Santa Fe: A Guide to Trails, People, Places, and Events*. Chamisal, NM: Acequia Madre Press, 1997.

Meinig, D. W. *Southwest: Three Peoples in Geographical Change, 1600–1970*. New York: Oxford University Press, 1971.

Mellick, Jill, and Jeanne Shutes. *The Worlds of P'otsúnú: Geronima Cruz Montoya of San Juan Pueblo*. Albuquerque: University of New Mexico Press, 1996.

Melzer, Richard. *Buried Treasures: Famous and Unusual Gravesites in New Mexico History*. Santa Fe: Sunstone Press, 2007.

———. *Coming of Age in the Great Depression: The Civilian Conservation Corps Experience in New Mexico, 1933–1942*. Las Cruces, NM: Yucca Tree Press, 2000.

———. *Ernie Pyle in the American Southwest*. Santa Fe: Sunstone Press, 1996.

———. *Fred Harvey Houses of the Southwest*. Charleston, SC: Arcadia Publishing, 2008.

———. *New Mexico: Celebrating the Land of Enchantment*. Layton, UT: Gibbs Smith, 2011.

Mercedes Reales: Hispanic Land Grants of the Upper Rio Grande Region. Albuquerque: University of New Mexico Press, 1983.

Merrill, Christopher, and Ellen Bradbury, eds. *From the Faraway Nearby: Georgia O'Keeffe As Icon*. Reading, MA: Addison-Wesley, 1992.

Meyer, Doris. *Speaking for Themselves: Neomexicano Cultural Identity and the Spanish-Language Press, 1880–1920*. Albuquerque: University of New Mexico Press, 1996.

Meyer, Marian. *A Century of Progress: History of the New Mexico School for the Deaf*. Santa Fe: New Mexico School for the Deaf, 1989.

———. *Mary Donoho: New First Lady of the Santa Fe Trail*. Santa Fe: Ancient City Press, 1991.

———. *Santa Fe High School, 1899–1999: Centennial History*. Santa Fe: Marian Meyer, 1999.

Michell, John. *Who Wrote Shakespeare?* New York: Thames & Hudson, 1996.

Midkiff, Ken. *Not a Drop to Drink: America's Water Crisis (and What You Can Do)*. San Francisco: New World Library, 2007.

Milford, Homer E. *Cultural Resource Survey for the Real de los Cerrillos Abandoned Mine Lands Project, Santa Fe County, New Mexico*. Santa Fe: Energy, Minerals, Natural Resources Department, 1996.

———, ed. *Nuevas Leyes de las Minas de España: 1625 Edición de Juan de Oñate*. Santa Fe: Sunstone Press, 1998.

Millay, Edna St. Vincent. *Collected Poems*. New York: Harper Perennial, 1981.

Miller, Michael, ed. *A New Mexico Scrapbook: Memorias de Nuevo Mexico, 23 New Mexicans Remember Growing Up*. Huntsville, AL: Honeysuckle Imprint, 1991.

Mills, Enos Abijah. *Romance of Geology*. Boston: Houghton Mifflin, 1932.

Minogue, Anna Catherine. *Loretto: Annals of the Century*. Kessinger Publishing, 2007. First published 1912.

Mirabel, Robert, Stephen Parks, and Nelson Zink. *Po' Pay Speaks*. Taos, NM: Mirabel et al, Blurb Inc., 2010.

Mirandé, Alfredo, and Evangelina Enríquez. *La Chicana: The Mexican-American Woman*. Chicago: University of Chicago Press, 1981.

Moccasins and Microphones: Modern Native Storytelling through Performance Poetry. CD recorded by Santa Fe Indian School Word Team, with Timothy P. McLaughlin, coach. Santa Fe: Stepbridge Studios, 2010.

Moerman, Daniel E. *Native American Ethnobotany*. Portland, OR: Timber Press, 1998.

Mohawk, John C. *Utopian Legacies: A History of Conquest and Oppression in the Western World*. Santa Fe: Clear Light, 2000.

Momaday, N. Scott. *Circle of Wonder: A Native American Christmas Story*. Albuquerque: University of New Mexico Press, 1994.

———. *House Made of Dawn*. New York: Harper Perennial Modern Classics, 2010. First published 1968.

Montaigne, Michel de. *The Complete Essays*. Translated by M. A. Screech. London: Penguin Classics, 1993. First published 1580.

Montaño, Mary. *Tradiciones Nuevomexicana: Hispano Arts and Culture of New Mexico*. Albuquerque: University of New Mexico Press, 2001.

Montiño, Francisco Martínez. *Arte de Cozina, Pastelería, Vizcochería y Conservería, by Francisco Martínez Montiño, Chef to Philip III, Madrid 1611*, facsimile at Palace of the Governors, New Mexico History Museum, Santa Fe.

Moore, Michael. *Los Remedios: Traditional Herbal Remedies of the Southwest*. Illustrations by Mimi Kamp. Santa Fe: Museum of New Mexico Press, 1990. First published 1977.

———. *Medicinal Plants of the Mountain West*. Rev. ed. Illustrations by Mimi Kamp. Photographs by Mimi Kamp, Henriette Kress, and Elaine Stevens. Santa Fe: Museum of New Mexico Press, 2003.

Moorhead, Max L. *New Mexico's Royal Road: Trade and Travel on the Chihuahua Trail*. Norman: University of Oklahoma Press, 1994. First published 1958.

———. *The Presidio: Bastion of the Spanish Borderlands*. Norman: University of Oklahoma Press, 1975.

Mora, Pat. *A Library for Juana: The World of Sor Juana Inés*. New York: Knopf, 2002.

Mora, Pat, and George Ancona. *Join Hands: The Way We Celebrate Life*. Watertown, MA: Charlesbridge, 2008.

Morand, Sheila. *Santa Fe: Then and Now*. Rev. ed. Santa Fe: Sunstone Press, 2008.

Morgan, Phyllis S. *Marc Simmons of New Mexico: Maverick Historian*. Albuquerque: University of New Mexico Press, 2005.

Morris, Roger. *The Devil's Butcher Shop: The New Mexico Prison Uprising*. Albuquerque: University of New Mexico Press, 1988.

Mosier, John. *Grant*. New York: Palgrave Macmillan, 2006.

Munson, Marlit K., ed. *Kenneth Chapman's Santa Fe: Artists and Archaeologists, 1907–1931: The Memoirs of Kenneth Chapman*. Santa Fe: School for Advanced Research Press, 2007.

Murphy, Barbara Beasley. *Fly Like an Eagle*. New York: Delacorte Press, 1994.

———. *Miguel Lost and Found in the Palace*. Illustrated by George Acona. Santa Fe: Museum of New Mexico Press, 2002.

Murphy, Dan. *New Mexico, the Distant Land: An Illustrated History*. Sun Valley, CA: American Historical Press, 2000.

———. *Santa Fe Trail: Voyage of Discovery*. Las Vegas, NV: KC Publications, 1994.

Myers, Joan. *Along the Santa Fe Trail*. Essay by Marc Simmons. Albuquerque: University of New Mexico Press, 1986.

Myrick, David F. *New Mexico's Railroads: A Historical Survey*. Rev. ed. Albuquerque: University of New Mexico Press, 1990. First published 1970.

Nabhan, Gary Paul. *Gathering the Desert*. Tucson: University of Arizona Press, 1985.

Nabokov, Peter. *Tijerina and the Courthouse Raid*. Albuquerque: University of New Mexico Press, 1969.

Nason, Thelma C. *No Golden Cities*. New York: Crowell-Collier Press, 1971.

———. *Under the Wide Sky: Tales of New Mexico and the Spanish Southwest*. Chicago: Follett, 1965.

National Geographic Atlas of the World. 7th ed. Washington, DC: National Geographic, 1999.

National Geographic Concise History of World Religions: An Illustrated Timeline. Edited by Tim Cooke. Washington, DC: National Geographic, 2011.

Nelson, Mary Carroll. *Michael Naranjo*. Hesperia, CA: Dillon Press, 1975.

Nelson, Melissa K., ed. *Original Instruction: Indigenous Teachings for a Sustainable Future*. Rochester, VT: Bear, 2008.

Nestor, Sarah. *The Native Market of the Spanish New Mexican Craftsman, 1933–1940*. Santa Fe: Sunstone Press, 2009. First published 1978.

New Mexico Atlas and Gazetteer. Freeport, ME: DeLorme Mapping Company, 2011.

New Mexico: A Guide to the Colorful State. Compiled by the Workers of the Writers' Program of the Work Projects Administration in the State of New Mexico. Hastings House, 1953.

New Mexico in Maps. Albuquerque: University of New Mexico Press, 1986.

New Mexico Magazine. *100 Years of Filmmaking in New Mexico*. Santa Fe: New Mexico Magazine, 1998.

New Mexico Office of Cultural Affairs, comp. *Enchanted Lifeways: The History, Museums, Arts, and Festivals of New Mexico*. Santa Fe: New Mexico Magazine, 1995.

Newcomb, Franc Johnson. *Hosteen Klah: Navajo Medicine Man and Sand Painter*. Norman: University of Oklahoma Press, 1964.

Newhall, Beaumont. *The History of Photography: From 1839 to the Present*. 5th ed. New York: Museum of Modern Art, 1982.

Newmann, Dana. *New Mexico Artists at Work*. Santa Fe: Museum of New Mexico Press, 2005.

———. *The Teachers Almanac: A Complete Guide to Every Day of the School Year*. Metuchen, NJ: Center for Applied Research in Education, 1973.

———. *Ready-to-Use Activities and Materials on Desert Indians: A Complete Sourcebook for Teachers K–8*. Metuchen, NJ: Center for Applied Research in Education, 1995.

Nichols, John. *The Milagro Beanfield War*. New York: Owl Books, 2000. First published 1974.

Nickens, Paul, and Kathleen Nickens. *Pueblo Indians of New Mexico: Postcard History Series*. Charleston, SC: Arcadia, 2008.

Niederman, Sharon. *New Mexico's Tasty Traditions: Folksy Stories, Recipes, and Photos*. Santa Fe: New Mexico Magazine, 2010.

———. *A Quilt of Words: Women's Diaries, Letters, and Original Accounts of Life in the Southwest, 1860–1960*. Boulder: Johnson Books, 1988.

Niederman, Sharon, and Miriam Sagan, eds. *New Mexico Poetry Renaissance*. Santa Fe: Red Crane Books, 1994.

Niethammer, Carol. *American Indian Food and Lore.* New York: MacMillan, 1974.

Noble, David Grant. *In the Places of the Spirits.* Santa Fe: School for Advanced Research Press, 2010.

———. *Pueblos, Villages, Forts, and Trails: A Guide to New Mexico's Past.* Albuquerque: University of New Mexico Press, 1994.

———, ed. *Santa Fe: History of an Ancient City.* 2nd ed. Santa Fe: School for Advanced Research Press, 2008.

Nostrand, Richard L. *The Hispano Homeland.* Norman: University of Oklahoma Press, 1992.

Nunn, Tey Marianna, ed. *Our Lady of Controversy: Alma López's Irreverent Apparition.* Austin: University of Texas Press, 2011.

———. *Sin Nombre: Hispana and Hispano Artists of the New Deal Era.* Albuquerque: University of New Mexico Press, 2001.

Nusbaum, Jesse L. *Tierra Dulce: Reminiscences from the Jesse Nusbaum Papers.* Santa Fe: Sunstone Press, 1980.

Nusbaum, Rosemary. *The City Different and the Palace: The Palace of the Governors, Its Role in Santa Fe History, Including Jesse Nusbaum's Restoration Journals.* Santa Fe: Sunstone Press, 1978.

O'Brien, Patrick K. *Atlas of World History.* Oxford: Oxford University Press, 2010.

O'Dell, Scott. *Sing Down the Moon.* New York: Dell, 1970.

Ogden, Scott, and Lauren Springer Ogden. *Plant-Driven Design: Creating Gardens That Honor Plants, Place, and Spirit.* Portland, OR: Timber Press, 2008.

Okrent, Daniel. *Last Call: The Rise and Fall of Prohibition.* New York: Scribner, 2010.

Oliver, Sandra L. *Food in Colonial and Federal America.* Westport, CT: Greenwood Press, 2005.

Ortega, Pedro Ribera. *Cancionero Fiesta.* Santa Fe, 1970.

———. *Christmas in Old Santa Fe.* 2nd ed. Santa Fe: Sunstone Press, 1973.

———. *La Conquistadora: America's Oldest Madonna.* Santa Fe: Sunstone Press, 1975.

———. *La Guadalupana and La Conquistadora in Catholic History of New Mexico.* Santa Fe, 1997.

Ortiz, Alfonso. *American Indian Myths and Legends.* New York: Pantheon Books, 1984.

———. *New Perspectives on the Pueblos.* Albuquerque: University of New Mexico Press, 1972.

———. *The Pueblo.* New York: Chelsea House, 1994.

———. *The Tewa World: Space, Time, Being, and Becoming in a Pueblo Society.* Chicago: University of Chicago Press, 1969.

Ortiz, Simon J. *The People Shall Continue.* San Francisco: Children's Book Press, 1988.

———. *The Good Rainbow Road = Rawa 'Kashtyaa'tsi Hiyaani.* Multilingual ed. Tucson: University of Arizona Press, 2004.

Otero, Miguel Antonio. *My Life on the Frontier, 1864–1882: Incidents and Characters of the Period When Kansas, Colorado, and New Mexico Were Passing through the Last of Their Wild and Romantic Years.* New York: Press of the Pioneers, 1935.

———. *My Nine Years as Governor of the Territory of New Mexico, 1897–1906.* Facsimile of 1940 edition. Santa Fe: Sunstone Press, 2007.

Otero, Rosalie C., A. Gabriel Meléndez, and Enrique R. Lamadrid. *Santa Fe Nativa: A Collection of Nuevomexicano Writing.* Albuquerque: University of New Mexico Press, 2009.

Otero-Warren, Nina. *Old Spain in Our Southwest.* Santa Fe: Sunstone Press, 2006. First published 1936.

Otis, Raymond. *The Santa Fe Volunteer Fire Department: A History of Its Life and Reputation.* Santa Fe: Santa Fe New Mexican Publishing Corporation, 1933.

Pacheco, Allan. *Ghosts-Murder-Mayhem, A Chronicle of Santa Fe: Lies, Legends, Facts, Tall Tales, and Useless Information.* Santa Fe: Sunstone Press, 2004.

Pacheco, Ana. *Saints and Seasons: A Guide to New Mexico's Most Popular Saints.* Santa Fe: Gran Via, 2005.

Padilla, Carmella. *The Chile Chronicles: Tales of a New Mexico Harvest*. Photography by Jack Parsons. Santa Fe: Museum of New Mexico Press, 1997.

———. *El Rancho de las Golondrinas: Living History in New Mexico's La Ciénega Valley*. Santa Fe: Museum of New Mexico Press, 2009.

———. *Eliseo Rodriguez: El Sexto Pintor*. Santa Fe: Museum of New Mexico Press, 2001.

Padilla, Carmella, and Donna Pierce. *Conexiones: Connections in Spanish Colonial Art*. Santa Fe: Museum of New Mexico Press / Spanish Colonial Arts Society, 2002.

Padilla, Genaro M. *The Daring Flight of My Pen: Cultural Politics and Gaspar Pérez de Villagrá's "Historia de la Nueva Mexico, 1610."* Albuquerque: University of New Mexico Press, 2010.

Pagden, Anthony. *Spanish Imperialism and Political Imagination: Studies in European and Spanish-American Social and Political Theory, 1513–1830*. New Haven: Yale University Press, 1990.

Palmer, Gabrielle G., and Donna Pierce. *Cambios: The Spirit of Transformation in Spanish Colonial Art*. Santa Barbara, CA: Santa Barbara Museum of Art, in cooperation with University of New Mexico Press, 1992.

Palmer, Gabrielle G., comp. *El Camino Real de Tierra Adentro*. 2 vols. Santa Fe: Bureau of Land Management, 1909, 1999.

Paponetti, Giovanna. *Kateri, Native American Saint: The Life and Miracles of Kateri Tekakwitha*. Santa Fe: Clear Light, 2010.

Parent, Laurence. *Hiking New Mexico*. Guilford, CT: Globe Pequot Press, 1998.

Parish, William J. *The Charles Ilfeld Company: A Study of the Rise and Decline of Mercantile Capitalism in New Mexico*. Cambridge: Harvard University Press, 1961.

Parks, Carmen. *Farmers Market, Día de Mercado*. Boston: Houghton Mifflin Harcourt, 2010.

Paulson, Gary. *Tucket's Gold*. New York: Delacorte Press, 1999.

Paz, Octavio. *Sor Juana, or, The Traps of Faith*. Translated by Margaret Sayers Peden. Cambridge, MA: Belknap Press, 1989.

Peach, Glen, and Max Evans. *Making a Hand: Growing Up Cowboy in New Mexico*. Santa Fe: Museum of New Mexico Press, 2005.

Pearce, T. M., ed. *New Mexico Place Names: A Geographical Dictionary*. Albuquerque: University of New Mexico Press, 1965.

Perlman, Barbara H. *Allan Houser (Ha-o-zous)*. 2nd ed. Washington, DC: Smithsonian Institution Press, 1992.

Perrigo, Lynn Irwin. *Hispanos: Historic Leaders in New Mexico*. Santa Fe: Sunstone Press, 1985.

Peters, De Witt C. *The Life and Adventures of Kit Carson: The Nestor of the Rocky Mountains, from Facts Narrated by Himself*. New York: W. R. C. Clark & Company, 1858.

Peterson, Jeanne Whitehouse. *I Have a Sister, My Sister Is Deaf*. Illustrations by Deborah Kogan Ray. New York: HarperCollins, 1984.

Phillips, Fred M., G. Emlen Hall, and Mary Black. *Reining in the Rio Grande: People, Land, and Water*. Albuquerque: University of New Mexico Press, 2011.

Phillips, Judith. *New Mexico Gardener's Guide*. Rev. ed. Nashville, TN: Thomas Nelson, 2005.

Pierce, Donna, ed. *¡Vivan las Fiestas!* Santa Fe: Museum of New Mexico Press, 1985.

Pierce, Donna, and Marta Weigle. *Spanish New Mexico*. 2 vols. Santa Fe: Spanish Colonial Arts Society, 1996.

Pierson, Peter. *The History of Spain*. Westport, CT: Greenwood, 1999.

Pike, Zebulon Montgomery. *The Southwestern Journals of Zebulon Pike, 1806–1807*. Albuquerque: University of New Mexico Press, 2006.

Pinkerton, Elaine. *Santa Fe on Foot: Adventures in the City Different*. Santa Fe: Ocean Tree Books, 1994.

Pino, Pedro Baptista. *The Exposition on the Province of New Mexico, 1812.* Translated and edited by Adrian Bustamante and Marc Simmons. Albuquerque: University of New Mexico Press, 1995.

Plants of the Southwest. Pamphlet with commentary by Gail Haggard. Santa Fe: Plants of the Southwest, 2011.

Plato. *The Republic.* Translated with notes and an interpretive essay by Allan Bloom. 2nd ed. New York: Basic Books, 1991.

P'oe T'sa wa. (Estefanita/Esther Martinez). *My Life in San Juan Pueblo: Stories of Esther Martinez.* Edited by Sue-Ellen Jacobs and Josephine Binford. With CD recording by Esther Martinez. Urbana: University of Illinois Press, 2004.

———. *The Naughty Little Rabbit and Old Man Coyote: A Tewa Tale from San Juan Pueblo.* Chicago: Children's Press, 1992.

———. *San Juan Pueblo Tewa Dictionary.* Illustrations by 'P'aá Sen (Peter Povijua). San Juan, NM: San Juan Pueblo Bilingual Program, 1982.

Poling-Kempes, Lesley. *The Harvey Girls: Women Who Opened the West.* New York: Marlowe, 1991.

Post, Stephen S. *7,000 Years on the Piedmont: Excavation of Fourteen Archaeological Sites along the Northwest Santa Fe Relief Route, Santa Fe County, New Mexico.* Santa Fe: Office of Archaeological Studies, 2011.

Powell, Philip Wayne. *Tree of Hate: Propaganda and Prejudices Affecting United States Relations with the Hispanic World.* Albuquerque: University of New Mexico Press, 2008. First published 1971.

Preston, Christine. *The Royal Road: El Camino Real from Mexico City to Santa Fe.* Text by Douglas Preston and José Antonio Esquibel. Albuquerque: University of New Mexico Press, 1998.

Price, L. Greer, ed. *The Geology of Northern New Mexico's Parks, Monuments, and Public Lands.* Socorro: New Mexico Bureau of Geology and Mineral Resources, 2010.

Prince, L. Bradford. *Historical Sketches of New Mexico: From the Earliest Records to the American Occupation.* Facsimile of 1883 edition. Santa Fe: Sunstone Press, 2009.

———. *New Mexico's Struggle for Statehood: Sixty Years of Effort to Obtain Self-Government.* Facsimile of 1910 edition. Santa Fe: Sunstone Press, 2010.

———. *The Student's History of New Mexico.* Facsimile of 1921 second edition. Santa Fe: Sunstone Press, 2008.

Pringle, Henry F. *The Life and Times of William Howard Taft: A Biography.* 2 vols. Newtown, CT: American Political Biography Press, 1998.

Purdy, John L., and James Ruppert. *Nothing But the Truth: An Anthology of Native American Literature.* Upper Saddle River, NJ: Prentice-Hall, 2001.

Pyle, Ernie. *Here Is Your War: Story of G.I. Joe.* New York: Henry Holt, 1945.

Raymer, Dottie. *Molly's Route 66 Adventure.* Middleton, WI: Pleasant Company, 2002.

Read, Benjamin M. *The Illustrated History of New Mexico.* Translated under the direction of the author by Eleuterio Baca. Santa Fe: New Mexican Printing Company, 1912.

Readicker-Henderson, ed. *A Short History of the Honey Bee: Humans, Flowers, and Bees in the Eternal Chase for Honey.* Portland, OR: Timber Press, 2009.

Redding, Mary Anne, ed. *Through the Lens: Creating Santa Fe.* Photographs edited by Krista Elrick and Mary Anne Redding. Santa Fe: Museum of New Mexico Press, 2008.

Reeve, Agnesa. *The Small Adobe.* Layton, UT: Gibbs Smith, 2001.

Reeve, Frank Driver. *History of New Mexico.* New York: Lewis Historical Publishing Company, 1961.

Regnier, Linda Black, and Katie Regnier. *Best Easy Day Hikes: Santa Fe.* Guilford, CT: Morris, 2006.

Remini, Robert Vincent. *Daniel Webster: The Man and His Time.* New York: W. W. Norton, 2009.

Reséndez, Andrés. *Changing National Identities at the Frontier: Texas and New Mexico, 1800–1850.* Cambridge, UK: Cambridge University Press, 2004.

Rhodes, Eugene Manlove. *Pasó por Aquí*. Norman: University of Oklahoma Press, 1973. First published 1926.

Riddle, Kenyon, John K. Riddle, and Nancy Riddle Madden, eds. *Records and Maps of the Old Santa Fe Trail*. Rev. ed. West Palm Beach, FL: John K. Riddle, 1963.

Rijmes, Joanne. *Living Treasures: Celebration of the Human Spirit, A Legacy of New Mexico*. Text by Karen Nilsson Brandt and Sharon Niederman. Santa Fe: Western Edge Press, 1997.

Riley, Carroll L. *Becoming Aztlan: Mesoamerican Influence in the Greater Southwest, AD 1200–1500*. Salt Lake City: University of Utah Press, 2005.

———. *The Kachina and the Cross: Indians and Spaniards in the Early Southwest*. Salt Lake City: University of Utah Press, 1999.

———. *Rio del Norte: People of the Upper Rio Grande from the Earliest Times to the Pueblo Revolt*. Salt Lake City: University of Utah Press, 1995.

Riskin, Marci L., ed. *New Mexico's Historic Places: The Guide to National and State Register Sites*. Santa Fe: Ocean Tree Books, 2000.

———. *The Train Stops Here: New Mexico's Railway Legacy*. Albuquerque: University of New Mexico Press, 2005.

Ritch, William C. *Biographical Sketch of Donaciano Vigil*. Santa Fe: New Mexico State Records Center and Archives, Donaciano Vigil Papers.

Rittenhouse, Jack DeVere. *The Man Who Owned Too Much: Maxwell's Land Grant, Together with an 1895 Newspaper Account of the Life of Lucien Maxwell*. [Houston]: Stagecoach Press, 1958.

———. *The Santa Fe Trail: A Historical Bibliography*. Albuquerque: University of New Mexico Press, 1971.

Rivera, José A. *Acequia Culture: Water, Land, and Community in the Southwest*. Albuquerque: University of New Mexico Press, 1998.

———. *La Sociedad: Guardians of Hispanic Culture along the Rio Grande*. Albuquerque: University of New Mexico Press, 2011.

Robb, John Donald. *Hispanic Folk Music of New Mexico and the Southwest: A Self-Portrait of a People*. Norman: University of Oklahoma Press, 1980.

Robert, Calvin A., and Susan A. Roberts. *A History of New Mexico*. Rev. ed. Albuquerque: University of New Mexico Press, 1991.

Roberts, David. *The Pueblo Revolt: The Secret Rebellion That Drove the Spaniards Out of the Southwest*. New York: Simon & Schuster, 2005.

Roberts, John B., and Elizabeth A. Roberts. *Freeing Tibet: 50 Years of Struggle, Resilience, and Hope*. New York: AMACOM, 2009.

Robertson, Edna. *Los Cinco Pintores*. Santa Fe: Museum of New Mexico Press, 1975.

Robertson, Edna, and Sarah Nestor. *Artists of the Canyons and Caminos: Santa Fe, Early Twentieth Century*. Salt Lake City: Ancient City Press, 2006. First published 1976.

Robinson, Gary. *Native American Night Before Christmas*. Santa Fe: Clear Light, 2010.

———. *Native American Twelve Days of Christmas*. Santa Fe: Clear Light, 2011.

Robinson, Jennifer Meta, and J. A. Hartenfeld. *The Farmers' Market Book: Growing Food, Cultivating Community*. Bloomington: Indiana University Press, 2007.

Rochlin, Harriet, and Fred Rochlin. *Pioneer Jews: A New Life in the Far West*. Boston: Houghton Mifflin Harcourt, 2000.

Rodriguez, Román Álvarez. *Abelgas: Paisajes, Evocationes y Remembranzas*. Salamanca, Spain: Ediciones Almar, 2003.

Rodriguez, Rosina Ransom. *My Name Is Santa Fe and They Call Me the City Different*. Santa Fe: Vaya Con Dios-Artes, 1991.

Rodriguez, Sylvia. *Acequia: Water-Sharing, Sanctity, and Place*. Santa Fe: School for Advanced Research Press, 2006.

———. *The Matachines Dance: A Ritual Dance of the Indian Pueblos and Mexican/Hispano Communities*. Santa Fe: Sunstone Press, 2009.

Rogers, Everett M., and Nancy R. Bartlit. *Silent Voices of World War II: When Sons of the Land of Enchantment Met Sons of the Land of the Rising Sun*. Santa Fe: Sunstone Press, 2005.

Romero, Orlando, and David Larkin. *Adobe: Building and Living with Earth*. New York: Houghton Mifflin, 1994.

Rossi, Ann. *Cultures Collide: Native Americans and Europeans, 1492–1700*. Washington, DC: National Geographic Children's Books, 2004.

Rothschild, David de. *Plastiki: Across the Pacific on Plastic, An Adventure to Save Our Oceans*. San Francisco: Chronicle Books, 2011.

Roybal, David. *Taking on Giants: Fabián Chavez, Jr. and New Mexican Politics*. Albuquerque: University of New Mexico Press, 2008.

Rubin, Susan Goldman. *Wideness and Wonder: The Life and Art of Georgia O'Keeffe*. San Francisco: Chronicle Books, 2010.

Rudisill, Richard. *Photographers of the New Mexico Territory, 1854–1912*. Santa Fe: Museum of New Mexico Press, 1973.

Rudofsky, Bernard. *Architecture without Architects: A Short Introduction to Non-Pedigreed Architecture*. Albuquerque: University of New Mexico Press, 1987. First published 1964.

Ruiz, Joseph J. *The Little Ghost Who Wouldn't Go Away: A Children's Story in Spanish and English*. Santa Fe: Sunstone Press, 2000.

Rushing, W. Jackson III. *Allan Houser: An American Master (Chiricahua Apache, 1914–1994)*. New York: Abrams, 2004.

Russell, Marian. *Land of Enchantment: Memoirs of Marian Russell along the Santa Fe Trail*. Albuquerque: University of New Mexico Press, 1985.

Russell, Marion. *Along the Santa Fe Trail: Marion Russell's Own Story*. Adapted by Ginger Wadsworth. Illustrated by James Watling. Morton Grove, IL: Albert Whitman, 1993.

Sabin, Edwin L. *Kit Carson Days, 1809–1868: Adventures in the Path of Empire*. Lincoln: University of Nebraska Press, 1995.

Sachsen-Altenburg, Hans von, and Laura Gabiger. *Winning the West: General Stephen Watts Kearny's Letter Book, 1846–1847*. Booneville, MO: Pekitancui, 1998.

Sacre, Antonio. *La Noche Buena: A Christmas Story*. New York: Abrams Books for Young Readers, 2010.

Sagel, Jim. *Always the Heart = Siempre el Corazón*. Santa Fe: Red Crane Books, 1998.

———. *Garden of Stories = Jardín de Cuentos*. Santa Fe: Red Crane Books, 1996.

Saint Michael's College. *75 Years of Service, 1859–1934: An Historical Sketch of Saint Michael's College*. Santa Fe: Saint Michael's College, 1934.

Salazar, J. Richard. *The Military Career of Donaciano Vigil*. Guadalupita, NM: Center for Land Grant Studies, 1994.

Saldívar, Ramón. *The Borderlands of Culture: Américo Paredes and the Transnational Imaginary*. Durham: Duke University Press, 2006.

Sánchez, Joseph P. *Between Two Rivers: The Atrisco Land Grant in Albuquerque History, 1692–1968*. Norman: University of Oklahoma Press, 2008.

———. *Explorers, Traders, and Slavers: Forging the Old Spanish Trail, 1678–1850*. Salt Lake City: University of Utah Press, 1997.

———. *The Río Abajo Frontier, 1540–1692: A History of Early Colonial New Mexico*. Albuquerque: Albuquerque Museum, 1987.

Sánchez, Joseph P., and Bruce A. Erickson, comps. and eds. *From Mexico City to Santa Fe: A Historical Guide to El Camino Real de Tierra Adentro.* Los Ranchos de Albuquerque, NM: Rio Grande Books, 2011.

Sanchez, Richard F., ed. *White Shell Water Place: An Anthology of Native American Reflections on the 400th Anniversary of the Founding of Santa Fe.* Santa Fe: Sunstone Press, 2010.

Sanders, Don, and Susan Sanders. *The American Drive-In Movie Theater.* Osceola, WI: Motorbooks International, 2003.

Sando, Joe S. *The Pueblo Indians.* San Francisco: Indian Historian Press, 1976.

———. *Pueblo Nations: Eight Centuries of Pueblo Indian History.* Santa Fe: Clear Light, 1992.

———. *Pueblo Profiles: Cultural Identity through Centuries of Change.* Santa Fe: Clear Light, 1998.

Sando, Joe S., and Herman Agoyo, eds. *Po'pay: Leader of the First American Revolution.* Santa Fe: Clear Light, 2005.

Sandweiss, Martha A. *Laura Gilpin: An Enduring Grace.* Fort Worth, TX: Amon Carter Museum, 1986.

Sanford, William R. *The Santa Fe Trail in American History.* Berkeley Heights, NJ: Enslow, 2000.

Santayana, George. *The Birth of Reason and Other Essays.* New York: Columbia University Press, 1968.

Sasaki, Chris. *Constellations: The Stars and Stories.* New York: Sterling, 2003.

Sayers, Dorothy L. *The Nine Tailors: Changes Rung on an Old Theme, in Two Short Touches and Two Full Peals.* New York: Harcourt Brace Jovanovich, 1989. First published 1934.

Schaafsma, Polly. *Rock Art in New Mexico.* Santa Fe: Museum of New Mexico Press, 1992.

Schaefer, Jack. *Collected Stories.* New York: Arbor House, 1985. First published 1966.

———. *Monte Walsh.* Lincoln, NE: Bison Books, 2003. First published 1963.

———. *Old Ramon.* Illustrations by Harold West. New York: Walker, 1963.

———. *Shane.* Critical edition edited by James C. Work. Lincoln: University of Nebraska Press, 1984. First published 1949.

———. *Stubby Pringle's Christmas.* Illustrations by Lorence Bjorklund. Boston: Houghton Mifflin, 1964.

Scharff, Virginia. *Twenty Thousand Roads: Women, Movement, and the West.* Los Angeles: University of California Press, 2002.

Scharff, Virgina, and Carolyn Brucken. *Home Lands: How Women Made the West.* Los Angeles: Autry National Center of the American West / University of California Press, 2010.

Scheinbaum, David. *Beaumont's Kitchen: Lessons on Food, Life, and Photography with Beaumont Newhall.* Santa Fe: Radius Books, 2009.

Schneider, Jill. *Route 66 across New Mexico: A Wanderer's Guide.* Photographs by D. Nakii. Albuquerque: University of New Mexico Press, 1991.

Scholes, France V. *Church and State in New Mexico.* Albuquerque: University of New Mexico Press, 1937.

———. *Troublous Times in New Mexico, 1659–1670.* Albuquerque: University of New Mexico Press, 1942.

Scholes, France V., Marc Simmons, and José Antonio Equibel, eds. *Juan Domínguez de Mendoza: Solider and Frontiersman of the Spanish Southwest, 1627–1693.* Translated by Eleanor B. Adams. Albuquerque: University of New Mexico Press, 2012.

Schroeder, Susan, and Stafford Poole, eds. *Religion in New Spain.* Albuquerque: University of New Mexico Press, 2007.

Schmauss, Anne, Mary Schmauss, and Geni Krolick. *For the Birds: A Month-by-Month Guide for Attracting Birds to Your Backyard.* New York: Stewart, Tabor & Chang, 2008.

Schmickle, William E. *The Politics of Historic Districts: A Primer for Grassroots Preservation.* Lanham, MD: Altamira Press, 2006.

Scott, Eleanor. *The First Twenty Years of the Santa Fe Opera*. Santa Fe: Sunstone Press, 1976.

Seasons of Santa Fe: A Cookbook. Santa Fe: Kitchen Angels, 2000.

Segale, Sister Blandina. *At the End of the Santa Fe Trail*. Bruce Publishing Company, 1948.

Seligman, Arthur. *First Annual Report of the Mayor of Santa Fe, April 1st, 1910 to March 31st, 1911*. Santa Fe: New Mexican Printing Company, 1911.

Seth, Laurel, and Ree Mobley, eds. *Folk Art Journey: Florence D. Bartlett and the Museum of International Folk Art*. Santa Fe: Museum of New Mexico Press, 2003.

Seth, Sandra, and Laurel Seth. *Adobe! Homes and Interiors of Taos, Santa Fe, and the Southwest*. Stamford, CT: Architectural Book Publishing Company, 1988.

Shapiro, Jason. *Before Santa Fe: Archaeology of the City Different*. Santa Fe: Museum of New Mexico Press, 2008.

Sheldrake, Rupert. *Dogs That Know When Their Owners Are Coming Home, and Other Unexplained Powers of Animals*. New York: Three Rivers Press, 2011.

Shepard, Tori Warner. *Now Silence: A Novel of World War II*. Santa Fe: Sunstone Press, 2008.

Sheppard, Carl D. *The Archbishop's Cathedral*. Santa Fe: Cimarron Press, 1994.

———. *Creator of the Santa Fe Style: Isaac Hamilton Rapp, Architect*, Albuquerque: University of New Mexico Press, 1988.

———. *The Saint Francis Murals of Santa Fe: The Commission and the Artists*. Santa Fe: Sunstone Press, 1989.

Sherman, John. *Santa Fe: A Pictorial History*. 2nd ed. Virginia Beach, VA: Donning, 1996.

Shoulders, Debbie, and Michael Shoulders. *D Is for Drum: A Native American Alphabet*. Chelsea, MI: Sleeping Bear Press, 2006.

Sides, Hampton. *Blood and Thunder: An Epic of the American West*. New York: Doubleday, 2006.

———. *Ghost Soldiers: The Forgotten Epic Account of World War II's Most Dramatic Mission*. New York: Doubleday, 2001.

Silverberg, Robert. *The Pueblo Revolt*. Lincoln: University of Nebraska Press, 1994.

Silverman, Buffy. *Recycling: Reducing Waste*. Chicago: Heinemann Library, 2008.

Simmons, Marc. *Along the Santa Fe Trail*. Photographs by Joan Myers. Albuquerque: University of New Mexico Press, 1986.

———. *Charles F. Lummis: Author and Adventurer, A Gathering*. Santa Fe: Sunstone Press, 2008.

———. *Coronado's Land: Essays on Daily Life in Colonial New Mexico*. Albuquerque: University of New Mexico Press, 1991.

———. *José's Buffalo Hunt: A Story from History*. Albuquerque: University of New Mexico Press, 2003.

———. *The Last Conquistador: Juan de Oñate and the Settling of the Far Southwest*. Norman: University of Oklahoma Press, 1991.

———. *Little Lion of the Southwest: A Life of Manuel Antonio Chaves*. Chicago: Sage Books, 1973.

———. *New Mexico: An Interpretive History*. Albuquerque: University of New Mexico Press, 1988.

———. *New Mexico Mavericks: Stories from a Fabled Past*. Santa Fe: Sunstone Press, 2005.

———. *The Old Trail to Santa Fe: Collected Essays*. Albuquerque: University of New Mexico Press, 1996.

———, ed. *On the Santa Fe Trail*. Lawrence: University Press of Kansas, 1986.

———. *The Sena Family: Blacksmiths of Santa Fe*. Illustrated by Kirk Hughey. Santa Fe: Press of the Palace of the Governors, 1981.

———. *Spanish Government in New Mexico*. Albuquerque: University of New Mexico Press, 1990.

———. *Spanish Pathways: Readings in the History of Hispanic New Mexico*. Albuquerque: University of New Mexico Press, 2001.

———. *Two Southwesterners: Charles Lummis and Amado Chaves*. Cerrillos, NM: San Marcos Press, 1968.

————. *Witchcraft in the Southwest: Spanish and Indian Supernaturalism on the Rio Grande.* Lincoln: University of Nebraska Press, 1980.

————. *Yesterday in Santa Fe: Episodes in a Turbulent History.* Santa Fe: Sunstone Press, 1989. First published 1969.

Simmons, Marc, and Hal Jackson. *Following the Santa Fe Trail: A Guide for Modern Travelers.* Rev. ed. Santa Fe: Ancient City Press, 2001.

Simmons, Marc, and Frank Turley. *Southwestern Colonial Ironwork: The Spanish Blacksmithing Tradition.* Santa Fe: Sunstone Press, 2007. First published 1980.

Sinclair, Upton. *The Jungle.* New York: Barnes & Noble Classics, 2003. First published 1906.

Siringo, Charles Angelo. *Riata and Spurs: The Story of a Lifetime Spent in the Saddle as Cowboy and Detective.* Santa Fe: Sunstone Press, 2007. First published 1927.

Slifer, Dennis. *Rock Art Images of Northern New Mexico.* Santa Fe: High Desert Field Guides, 2005.

————. *Signs of Life: Rock Art of the Upper Rio Grande.* Santa Fe: Ancient City Press, 1998.

Smith, David J. *If the World Were a Village: A Book about the World's People.* Toronto, ON: Kids Can Press, 2011.

————. *Mapping the World by Heart.* Illustrated by Peter H. Reynolds. Edited by Julia A. Young. Dedham, MA: FableVision Learning, 2010.

————. *This Child, Every Child: A Picture Book about the Rights of Children.* Toronto, ON: Kids Can Press, 2011.

Smith, Marcus J. *The Hospital at the End of the Santa Fe Trail.* Santa Fe: Rydall Press, 1977.

Smith, Pamela. *Passions in Print: Private Press Artistry in New Mexico, 1834–Present.* With Richard Polese. Santa Fe: Museum of New Mexico Press, 2006.

Smithsonian Institution. *29th Annual Report of the Bureau of American Ethnology.* Washington, DC: Smithsonian Institution, 1907–08.

Snow, David H. *New Mexico's First Colonists: The 1597–1600 Enlistments for New Mexico, Under Juan de Oñate, Adelantado, and Gobernador.* Albuquerque: Hispanic Genealogical Research Center of New Mexico, 1998.

————. *The Santa Fe Acequia Systems: Summary Report on Their History and Present Status, with Recommendations for Use and Protection.* Santa Fe: City of Santa Fe Planning Department, 1988.

Solomon, Steven. *Water: The Epic Struggle for Wealth, Power, and Civilization.* New York: Harper, 2010.

Spears, Beverly. *American Adobes: Rural Houses of Northern New Mexico.* Albuquerque: University of New Mexico Press, 1986.

————. *Sand River in Bloom: Arroyo de los Chamisos, Santa Fe, New Mexico.* Santa Fe: Beverly Spears, 2010.

Sperry, Armstrong. *Wagons Westward: The Old Trail to Santa Fe.* Boston: David R. Godine, 2001. First published 1936.

Spicer, Edward H. *Cycles of Conquest: The Impact of Spain, Mexico, and the United States on the Indians of the Southwest, 1544–1960.* Tucson: University of Arizona Press, 1970.

Spinden, Herbert Joseph, trans. *Songs of the Tewa.* New York: Exposition of Indian Tribal Arts, 1933.

Spivey, Richard L. *The Legacy of Maria Poveka Martinez.* Santa Fe: Museum of New Mexico Press, 2003.

Spoto, Donald. *Reluctant Saint: The Life of Francis of Assisi.* New York: Viking Compass, 2002.

Spragg-Braude, Stacia. *To Walk in Beauty: A Navajo Family's Journey Home.* Santa Fe: Museum of New Mexico Press, 2009.

Stanley, F. *The Civil War in New Mexico.* Santa Fe: Sunstone Press, 2011. First published 1960.

————. *The Cuidad de Santa Fe, 1846–1912.* Pampa, TX: Pampa Print Shop, 1965.

Stark, Gregor, and E. Catherine Rayne. *El Delirio: The Santa Fe World of Elizabeth White.* Santa Fe: School of American Research Press, 1998.

Stedman, Myrtle, and Wilfred Stedman. *Adobe Architecture*. Santa Fe: Sunstone Press, 1987.

Steele, Thomas J., ed. and trans. *Archbishop Lamy: In His Own Words*. Albuquerque: LPD Press, 2000.

⸻. *Santos and Saints*. Rev. ed. Santa Fe: Ancient City Press, 1994.

Steele, Thomas J., Paul Rhetts, and Barbe Awalt, eds. *Seeds of Struggle / Harvest of Faith: The Papers of the Archdiocese of Santa Fe Catholic Cuarto Centennial Conference on the History of the Catholic Church in New Mexico*. Albuquerque: LPD Press, 1998.

Stein, R. Conrad. *The Story of Mexico: The Mexican War of Independence*. Greensboro, NC: Morgan Reynolds, 2008.

Stevens, T. Rorie. *The Death of a Governor: The Massacre of Charles Bent, First American Civil Governor of the Territory of New Mexico*. Jacksonville, TX: Jayroe Graphic Arts, 1971.

Stowe, Harriet Beecher. *Uncle Tom's Cabin*. New York: Barnes & Noble Classics, 2003. First published 1852.

Stratton, Eugene Aubry. *Plymouth Colony: Its History and People, 1620–1691*. Salt Lake City: Ancestry, 1986.

Strauss, Rochelle. *One Well: The Story of Water on Earth*. Toronto, ON: Kids Can Press, 2007.

Street Maps: Santa Fe County, Los Alamos, Española, Taos. Santa Fe: Horton Family Maps, 2011.

Stuart, David E. *The Magic of Bandelier*. Santa Fe: Ancient City Press, 1989.

⸻. *Pueblo Peoples on the Pajarito Plateau: Archaeology and Efficiency*. Albuquerque: University of New Mexico Press, 2010.

Stubbs, Stanley A. *Bird's Eye View of the Pueblos*. Norman: University of Oklahoma Press, 1950.

Sutter, L. M. *New Mexico Baseball: Miners, Outlaws, Indians, and Isotopes, 1880 to the Present*. Jefferson, NC: McFarland, 2010.

Swentzell, Rina. *Children of Clay: A Family of Pueblo Potters*. Minneapolis: Lerner, 1992.

Szaaz, Margaret Connell, ed. *Between Indian and White Worlds: The Cultural Broker*. Norman: University of Oklahoma Press, 1994.

Szarkowski, John. *Ansel Adams at 100*. Boston: Little, Brown, 2001.

Szasz, Ferenc M., and Richard W. Etulain, eds. *Religion in Modern New Mexico*. Albuquerque: University of New Mexico Press, 1997.

Sze, Corinne P. *El Zaguan: The James L. Johnson House, 545 Canyon Road; A Social History*. Santa Fe: Historic Santa Fe Foundation, 1997.

⸻. *Fairview Cemetery, Santa Fe, NM*. Santa Fe: Fairview Cemetery Association, 2004.

⸻, ed. *Within Adobe Walls: A Santa Fe Journal; Selections from the Charlotte White Journals*. Santa Fe: Historic Santa Fe Foundation, 2001.

Tabor, Nancy Maria Grande. *El Gusto del Mercado Mexicano = A Taste of the Mexican Market*. Watertown, MA: Charlesbridge, 1996.

Talbert, Mark. *Holding the Reins: A Ride through Cowgirl Life*. New York: Harper Collins, 2003.

Tashel, Carole. *Gardening the Southwest: How to Care for Your Land While Growing Food, Beauty and Medicine*. Santa Fe: Healing Earth Publications, 1999.

Taylor, Anne. *Southwestern Ornamentation and Design: The Architecture of John Gaw Meem*. Santa Fe: Sunstone Press, 1989.

Taylor, Nick. *American-Made: The Enduring Legacy of the WPA; When FDR Put the Nation to Work*. New York: Bantam Books, 2008.

Taylor, Quintard. *In Search of the Racial Frontier: African Americans in the American West, 1528–1990*. New York: W. W. Norton, 1999.

Temkin, Samuel. *Luis de Carvajal: A Biography*. Santa Fe: Sunstone Press, 2011.

Terrell, John Upton. *Pueblos, Gods, and Spaniards*. New York: Dial Press, 1973.

Thomas, Alfred Barnaby, ed. and trans. *Forgotten Frontiers: A Study of the Spanish Indian Policy of Don Juan Bautista de Anza, Governor of New Mexico, 1777–1787, From the Original Documents in the Archives of Spain, Mexico, and New Mexico*. Norman: University of Oklahoma Press, 1932.

Thomas, D. H. *The Southwestern Indian Detours: The Story of the Fred Harvey/Santa Fe Railway Experiment in Detourism*. Phoenix: Hunter, 1978.

Thompson, Alice Anne. *American Caravan*. Independence, MO: Two Trails Press, 2007.

Thompson, Mark. *American Character: The Curious Life of Charles Fletcher Lummis and the Rediscovery of the Southwest*. New York: Arcade, 2001.

Thornton, Elizabeth. *The Best of Santa Fe and Beyond*. Santa Fe: Adobe, 1999.

Thorp, Nathan Howard "Jack." *Tales of the Chuckwagon*. Whitefish, MT: Kessinger, 2010. First published 1926.

Tierney, Gail. *Roadside Plants of Northern New Mexico*. Santa Fe: Lightning Tree, 1983.

Tobias, Henry J. *A History of the Jews in New Mexico*. Albuquerque: University of New Mexico Press, 1992.

Tobias, Henry J., and Charles E. Woodhouse. *Santa Fe: A Modern History, 1880–1990*. Albuquerque: University of New Mexico Press, 2001.

Tocqueville, Alexis de. *Democracy in America*. New York: Bantam Books, 2000. First published 1835.

Tórrez, Robert J. *Myth of the Hanging Tree: Stories of Crime and Punishment in Territorial New Mexico*. Albuquerque: University of New Mexico Press, 2008.

———. *New Mexico's Spanish and Mexican Archives: A History*. Guadalupita, NM: Center for Land Grant Studies, 1994.

Tórrez, Robert J., and Robert Trapp, comps. and eds. *Rio Arriba: A New Mexico County*. Los Ranchos de Albuquerque, NM: Rio Grande Books, 2010.

Traugott, Joseph. *The Art of New Mexico: How the West Is One*. Santa Fe: Museum of New Mexico Press, 2007.

Trefousse, Hans L. *Rutherford B. Hayes*. New York: Times Books, 2002.

Tripp, Valerie. *Meet Josefina: An American Girl*. Middleton, WI: Pleasant Company, 1997.

Tryk, Sheila. *Santa Fe Indian Market: Showcase of Native American Art*. Photographs by Mark Nohl. Santa Fe: Tierra, 1993.

Turkle, Brinton. *Do Not Open*. New York: E. P. Dutton, 1985.

———. *Thy Friend Obadiah*. New York: Viking, 1969.

Turner, David G. *Artists of 20th-Century New Mexico: The Museum of Fine Arts Collection*. Santa Fe: Museum of New Mexico Press, 1992.

Turner, Don. *The Massacre of Governor Bent*. Amarillo, TX: Humbug Gulch Press, 1969.

Turner, Frederick W. *Beyond Geography: The Western Spirit against the Wilderness*. Rev. ed. New Brunswick, NJ: Rutgers University Press, 1992.

Twitchell, Ralph Emerson. *The Leading Facts of New Mexico History*. Facsimile of 1911 edition. Santa Fe: Sunstone Press, 2007.

———. *The Military Occupation of the Territory of New Mexico from 1846 to 1851*. Facsimile of 1909 edition. Santa Fe: Sunstone Press, 2007.

———. *Old Santa Fe: The Story of New Mexico's Ancient Capital*. Facsimile of 1925 edition. Santa Fe: Sunstone Press, 2007.

———. *The Spanish Archives of New Mexico*. 2 vols. Facsimile of 1914 edition. Santa Fe: Sunstone Press, 2008.

Udall, Sharyn Rohlfsen. *Modernist Painting in New Mexico, 1913–1935*. Albuquerque: University of New Mexico Press, 1984.

———. *Spud Johnson and Laughing Horse*. Santa Fe: Sunstone Press, 2008.

Udall, Stewart L. *The Forgotten Founders: Rethinking the History of the Old West*. Washington, DC: Shearwater Books, 2002.

———. *To the Inland Empire: Coronado and Spanish Legacy*. Photographs by Jerry Jacka. Garden City, NY: Doubleday, 1987.

Udry, Janice May. *A Tree Is Nice*. Illustrations by Marc Simont. New York: Harper, 1956.

Underhill, Ruth. *Life in the Pueblos*. Santa Fe: Ancient City Press, 1946.

Ungnade, Herbert E. *Guide to the New Mexico Mountains*. Albuquerque: University of New Mexico Press, 1972.

Uschan, Michael V. *The 1940s*. San Diego: Lucent Books, 1999.

Usner, Don J. *New Mexico Route 66 on Tour: Legendary Architecture from Glenrio to Gallup*. Santa Fe: Museum of New Mexico Press, in collaboration with New Mexico Historic Preservation Division, 2001.

Valley-Fox, Anne. *How Shadows Are Bundled*. Albuquerque: University of New Mexico Press, 2009.

Van Dresser, Peter. *A Landscape for Humans: A Case Study of the Potentials for Ecologically Guided Development in an Uplands Region*. Albuquerque: Biotechnic Press, 1972.

———. *Passive Solar House Basics*. Santa Fe: Ancient City Press, 1995.

Van Ness, John R. *Hispanos in Northern New Mexico*. New York: AMS Press, 1991.

Velarde, Pablita. *Old Father Story Teller*. Santa Fe: Clear Light, 1989.

Velázquez de la Cadena, Mariano, comp. *A New Pronouncing Dictionary of the Spanish and English Languages*. With Edward Gray and Juan L. Iribas. Rev. ed. Englewood Cliffs, NJ: Prentice-Hall, 1973. First published 1852.

Verzuh, Valerie, and Antonio Chavarria. *Painting the Native World: Life, Land, and Animals*. Santa Fe: Museum of Indian Arts and Culture, 2009.

Vestal, Stanley. *The Mountain Men*. Boston: Riverside Press, 1937.

———. *The Old Santa Fe Trail*. Boston: Houghton Mifflin, 1939.

Vigil, Arnold, ed. *Enduring Cowboys: Life in the New Mexico Saddle*. Albuquerque: New Mexico Magazine, 1999.

Vigil, Maurillo E. *Los Patrones: Profiles of Hispanic Political Leaders in New Mexico History*. Lanham, MD: University Press of America, 1980.

Villagrá, Gaspar Pérez de. *Historia de la Nueva México, 1610*. Translated and edited by Miguel Encinias, Alfred Rodriguez, and Joseph P. Sánchez. Albuquerque: University of New Mexico Press, 1992.

WPA Guide to 1930s New Mexico, Compiled by the Workers of the Writers' Program of the Work Projects Administration in the State of New Mexico. Tucson: University of Arizona Press, 1989.

Walker, Randi Jones. *Protestantism in the Sangre de Cristos, 1850–1920*. Albuquerque: University of New Mexico Press, 1991.

Wallace, Lew. *Ben Hur: A Tale of the Christ*. New York: Modern Library, 2002. First published 1880.

Wallace, Susan E. *The Land of the Pueblos*. Santa Fe: Sunstone Press, 2006.

Walsh, Michael. *Roman Catholicism: The Basics*. New York: Routledge, 2005.

Warner, Louis H. *Archbishop Lamy: An Epoch Maker*. Santa Fe: Santa Fe New Mexican Publishing Company, 1936.

Warren, Nancy Hunter. *New Mexico Style: A Sourcebook of Traditional Architectural Details*. Santa Fe: Museum of New Mexico Press, 1995.

Waters, Frank. *The Man Who Killed the Deer*. Chicago: Sage Books, 1970. First published 1942.

———. *The Woman at Otowi Crossing: A Novel*. Athens, OH: Sage Books, 1987. First published 1966.

Weatherford, Jack. *Indian Givers: How Native Americans Transformed the World*. New York: Three Rivers Press, 2010.

Webber, Christopher. *The Zarzuela Companion*. Lanham, MD: Scarecrow Press, 2002.

Weber, David J., ed. and trans. *The Extranjeros: Selected Documents from the Mexican Side of the Santa Fe Trail, 1825–1828*. Santa Fe: Stagecoach Press, 1967.

———. *Foreigners in Their Native Land: Historical Roots of the Mexican Americans*. Rev. ed. Albuquerque: University of New Mexico Press, 2003. First published 1973.

———. *The Mexican Frontier, 1821–1846: The American Southwest Under Mexico*. Albuquerque: University of New Mexico Press, 1982.

———. *Myth and the History of the Spanish Southwest*. Albuquerque: University of New Mexico Press, 1990.

———. *On the Edge of Empire: The Taos Hacienda of los Martínez*. Albuquerque: University of New Mexico Press, 1996.

———. *The Spanish Frontier in North America*. New Haven: Yale University Press, 1992.

———, ed. *What Caused the Pueblo Revolt of 1680?* Boston: Bedford/St. Martin's, 1999.

Weber, Susan Topp. *Christmas in Santa Fe*. Layton, UT: Gibbs Smith, 2010.

Weckmann, Luis. *The Medieval Heritage of Mexico*. New York: Fordham University Press, 1992.

Weigle, Marta. *Alluring New Mexico: Engineered Enchantment, 1821–2001*. Santa Fe: Museum of New Mexico Press, 2010.

———. *Brothers of Light, Brothers of Blood: The Penitentes of the Southwest*. Santa Fe: Sunstone Press, 2007.

———. *New Mexicans in Cameo and Camera*. Albuquerque: University of New Mexico Press, 1985.

———, ed. *Telling New Mexico: A New History*. With Frances Levine and Louise Stiver. Santa Fe: Museum of New Mexico Press, 2009.

Weigle, Marta, and Kyle Fiore. *Santa Fe and Taos: The Writer's Era, 1916–1941*. Rev. ed. Santa Fe: Sunstone Press, 2008.

Weigle, Marta, and Peter White. *The Lore of New Mexico*. Albuquerque: University of New Mexico Press, 2003.

Weigle, Richard D. *The Colonization of a College: The Beginnings and Early History of St. John's College in Santa Fe*. Santa Fe: St. John's College Print Shop, 1985.

Westphall, Victor. *Mercedes Reales: Hispanic Land Grants of the Upper Rio Grande Region*. Albuquerque: University of New Mexico Press, 1983.

Whaley, Charlotte. *Nina Otero-Warren of Santa Fe*. Santa Fe: Sunstone Press, 2007.

When Cultures Meet: Remembering San Gabriel del Yunge Oweenge: Papers from the October 20, 1984 Conference Held at San Juan Pueblo, New Mexico. Santa Fe: Sunstone Press, 1987.

Wiggins, Walt. *William Lumpkins: Pioneer Abstract Expressionist*. Ruidoso Downs, NM: Pintores Press, 1990.

Williams, Jerry L. *New Mexico in Maps*. Albuquerque: University of New Mexico Press, 1986.

Williams, Robin P. *Sweet Swan of Avon: Did a Woman Write Shakespeare?* 2nd ed. Berkeley: Wilton Circle Press, 2011.

Wills, W. H. *Early Prehistoric Agriculture in the American Southwest*. Santa Fe: School of American Research Press, 1988.

Wilson, Chris. *Facing Southwest: The Life and Houses of John Gaw Meem*. New York: W. W. Norton, 2001.

———. *The Myth of Santa Fe: Creating a Modern Regional Tradition*. Albuquerque: University of New Mexico Press, 1997.

Wilson, Chris, and Stefanos Polyzoides, eds. *The Plazas of New Mexico*. San Antonio, TX: Trinity University Press, 2011.

Winegarten, Debra. *Katherine Stinson: The Flying Schoolgirl*. Austin: Eakin Press, 2000.

Winslow, Kate, and Julia Ward. *Fun with the Family: Hundreds of Ideas for Day Trips with the Kids.* Guilford, CT: Globe Pequot Press, 2005.

Wislizenus, A. *Memoir of a Tour to Northern Mexico, Connected with Colonel Doniphan's Expedition in 1846 and 1847: An Early Account of Travel Over the Old Santa Fe Trail.* Albuquerque: Calvin Horn Publisher, 1969. First published 1848.

Witt, David L. *Ernest Thompson Seton: The Life and Legacy of an Artist and Conservationist.* Layton, UT: Gibbs Smith, 2010.

Witynski, Karen, and Joe E. Carr. *Hacienda Style.* Layton, UT: Gibbs Smith, 2008.

———. *The New Hacienda.* Layton, UT: Gibbs Smith, 2003.

Wolf, Robert, ed. *Ayer y Ahora = Yesterday and Today: Stories of Santa Fe and Northern New Mexico.* Lansing, IA: Free River Press, 2006.

Wood, Margaret. *A Painter's Kitchen: Recipes from the Kitchen of Georgia O'Keeffe.* Santa Fe: Museum of New Mexico Press, 2009.

Wood, Nancy, ed. *The Serpent's Tongue: Prose, Poetry, and Art of the New Mexican Pueblos.* Boston: E. P. Dutton, 1997.

Wright, Sandi. *The Adventures of Santa Fe Sam.* Santa Fe: Art Academy de los Niños, 2010.

Wroth, William, and Robin Farwell Gavin, eds. *Converging Streams: Art of the Hispanic and Native American Southwest.* Santa Fe: Museum of Spanish Colonial Art, 2010.

Wurzburger, Rebecca, Tom Aageson, Alex Pattakos, and Sabrina Pratt, eds. *Creative Tourism: A Global Conversation; How to Provide Unique Creative Experiences for Travelers Worldwide.* Santa Fe: Sunstone Press, 2009.

Wyman, Leland Clifton. *The Sacred Mountains of the Navajo in Four Paintings by Harrison Begay.* Flagstaff: Northern Arizona Society of Science & Art, 1967.

Yoder, Walter D. *The American Pueblo Indian Activity Book.* Santa Fe: Sunstone Press, 1994.

———. *The Big American Southwest Activity Book.* Santa Fe: Sunstone Press, 1997.

———. *The Big Spanish Heritage Activity Book.* Santa Fe: Sunstone Press, 1997.

———. *The Camino Real (The King's Road) Activity Book: Spanish Settlers in the Southwest.* Santa Fe: Sunstone Press, 1994.

———. *The Santa Fe Trail Activity Book: Pioneer Settlers in the Southwest.* Santa Fe: Sunstone Press, 1994.

Zeleny, Carolyn. *Relations between the Spanish Americans and the Anglo Americans in New Mexico.* New York: Arno, 1974.

Zieselman, Ellen. *The Hand-Carved Marionettes of Gustave Baumann: Share Their World.* With an essay by Elizabeth Cunningham. Photographs by Blair Clark. Santa Fe: Museum of New Mexico Press, 2000.

Zinn, Howard. *A People's History of the United States: 1492–Present.* Rev. ed. New York: Harper Perennial Modern Classics, 2005.

Zollinger, Norman. *Riders to Cibola: A Novel.* Santa Fe: Museum of New Mexico Press, 1977.

Index

CPSIA information can be obtained at www.ICGtesting.com
Printed in the USA
BVOW051210020413

317079BV00001B/1/P